# Culture and power in
# educational organizations

# Culture and power in educational organizations

A READER EDITED BY
**Adam Westoby**
at the Open University

OPEN UNIVERSITY PRESS
MILTON KEYNES · PHILADELPHIA

Open University Press
Open University Educational Enterprises Limited
12 Cofferidge Close
Stony Stratford
Milton Keynes MK11 1BY, England

*and*
242 Cherry Street
Philadelphia, PA 19106, USA

321370

First published 1988

**British Library Cataloguing in Publication Data**

Culture and power in educational organizations:
a reader. – (E814).
Vol. 2
1. School management and organization
2. Universities and colleges – Administration
3. Organizational behavior
I. Westoby, Adam
371        LB2806

ISBN 0-335-10297-2
ISBN 0-335-15548-0 Pbk

**Library of Congress Cataloging in Publication Data**

Culture and power in educational organizations.
   Contents: – vol. 2. E814.
   1. School management and organization.
2. Organizational behavior.   3. Educational sociology.
4. Bureaucracy.   5. Power (Social sciences)
LB2805.C838       1988       371.2       87-24738
ISBN 0-335-10297-2
ISBN 0-335-15548-0 (pbk.)

Typeset by Rowland Phototypesetting Limited
Bury St Edmunds, Suffolk
Printed in Great Britain
by Biddles Limited, Guildford and King's Lynn.

# Contents

# Acknowledgements

All possible care has been taken to trace ownership of the material included in this volume, and Open University Press would like to make grateful acknowledgement for permission to reproduce it here.

1. L. A. Bell (1980). 'The school as an organization: a reappraisal', *British Journal of Sociology of Education*, I(2):183–192.
2. W. B. Tyler (1985). 'The organizational structure of the school', *Annual Review of Sociology*, 11: 1985, by Annual Reviews Inc., 49–73.
3. P. J. Miller (1973). 'Factories, monitorial schools and Jeremy Bentham: the origins of the "management syndrome" in popular education', *Journal of Educational Administration and History*, 5:10–20.
4. K. E. Weick (1976). 'Education organizations as loosely coupled education', *Administrative Science Quarterly*, 21:1–19.
5. T. Packwood (1977). 'The school as a hierarchy', *Educational Administration*, 5(2):1–6.
   C. Turner (1977). 'Organizing educational institutions as anarchies', *Educational Administration*, 5(2):6–12.
   plus reciprocal comments by T. Packwood and C. Turner, *Educational Administration*, 5(2):12–14.
6. John W. Meyer and Brian Rowan, 'The structure of educational organizations', *Environments and Organizations*, ed. Marshall W. Meyer and Associates, San Francisco, Jossey Bass. Copyright 1978 by Jossey-Bass Inc.
7. T. B. Greenfield (1978). 'The decline and fall of science in educational administration', *Interchange*, 17(2):57–80.
8. H. L. Gray (1982). 'A perspective on organization theory', *The Management of Educational Issues*, ed. H. L. Gray, Lewes, Falmer Press.

9. P. M. Ribbins, C. B. Jarvis, R. E. Best and D. M. Oddy (1981).'Meanings and contexts: the problem of interpretation in the study of a school', in P. Ribbins and H. Thomas (eds), *Research in Educational Management and Administration*, British Education Management and Administration Society, Coombe Lodge, pp. 160–172.
10. D. Reynolds and K. Reid (1985). 'The second stage: towards a reconceptualisation of theory and methodology in school effectiveness research', *Studying School Effectiveness*, ed. D. Reynolds, Lewes, Falmer Press.
11. I. Goodson (1984). 'Beyond the subject monolith: subject traditions and sub-cultures', *New Directions in Educational Leadership*, ed. P. Harling (1984), Lewes, Falmer Press.
12. T. E. Deal (1985). 'The symbolism of effective schools', *Elementary School Journal*, 85(5):601–620.
13. W. G. Ouchi and A. L. Wilkins (1985). 'Organizational culture', *Annual Review of Sociology*, 11: 1985, by Annual Reviews Inc., 457–483.
14. E. Hoyle (1982). 'Micropolitics of educational organizations', *Educational Management and Administration*, 10(2):87–89.
15. K. E. Shaw (1983). 'Rationality, experience and theory', *Educational Management and Administration*, 11(3):167–172.
16. S. B. Bacharach (1983) 'Notes on a political theory of educational organizations', *Consensus and Power in School Organizations. Final Report*, S. B. Bacharach et al. (1983), Cornell University, Ithaca, NY.
17. P. C. Gronn (1983). 'Talk as the work: the accomplishment of school administration', *Administrative Science Quarterly*, 28(March): 1–21.
18. T. Becher (1984). 'Principles and politics: an interpretive framework for university management', *International Journal of Institutional Management in Higher Education*, 8(3):191–199.
19. F. W. Lutz (1986). 'Witches and witchfinding in educational organizations', *Educational Administration Quarterly*, 221(1):49–67. Copyright© 1986 reprinted by permission of Sage Publications Inc.
20. C. Hardy, A. Langley, H. Mintzberg and J. Rose (1984). 'Strategy formation in the university setting', *College and University Organization*, ed. J. L. Bess, New York, New York University Press.

# Introduction

**Adam Westoby**

This reader, like its companion volume (Ozga 1987), has been prepared in conjunction with a course on Educational Organizations and Professionals (E814) within the Open University's taught MA in education programme, and is a set book for students on that course.[1] But the articles within it merit a wider readership. This Introduction sets out some of the reasons for their choice, within a thumbnail-sketch of the field from which they are drawn, and mentions some of the most interesting questions which they pose or imply – delineating, thus, the intention and character of the volume.

The study of educational organizations overlaps with, and much of it is coloured by, the literature of educational management.[2] (The same is true, *mutatis mutandis*, of the study of organizations more generally.) This selection, however, has not been assembled for its utility to professional educational managers (though they too will find it useful), but rather for all those who find themselves involved in or with educational organizations and who wish to think systematically about them, to penetrate their opacities and to understand their functioning and eccentricities better. If it has a guiding prejudice, it is the democratic one that it would be better if the realities, as well as the formalities, of organizational life were more visible to more of those who live it or are affected by it.

The study of organizations, more than most other areas of the social sciences, is one of cheerful admixture. Theorists mingle with observers and experimenters, managers and practitioners rub shoulders with consultants and critics, and journalists and evangelists proliferate. Between these categories there is a high degree of interchange, both intellectual and human. Thus one of the most vivid (and to my mind heartening) items included here, Deal's 'The Symbolism of Effective Schools', is by a senior scholar of educational organizations but is at the same time a piece of unashamed exhortation. Deal marshalls episodes from a variety of organizational cultures, all of which he directs at empowering those who run American schools to transform them into happier, better places of learning – and in so doing to esteem themselves more. And many of the other articles speak to the concerns of those working in educational organizations just as much as they extend the debates among those studying them. Methodologically speaking, too, the study of organizations reflects its practical roots. It is an eclectic zone of theoretical pluralism and 'triangulation' from diverse types of evidence, in which it is accepted that explanations are partial, temporary, and often *ad hoc*. Methodological and doctrinal differences do arise, of course (and passages from some exchanges are included here), but they seem less prone to harden into settled 'wars of perspective' than in other areas of social science.

The principal foci of this collection – the questions of organizational culture and of power – derive from the significant peculiarities of *educational* organizations. Characteristics which are present in many other types of organization, but appear there only as secondary features or aberrations are, in educational organizations, quite central. Educational goals, for example, generally prove difficult or impossible to define; the main direct and indirect 'technologies' used (teaching and the education of teachers) are of considerable antiquity but still only vaguely understood; and (a corollary of these features) the core of the labour force consists of autonomously working craft-professionals. Education's goals are vague because they include the all-round social and intellectual development of young people, and the institution's ethos or culture therefore enters directly into the fundamental characteristics of its 'output' (not just the *manner* of its production) in a way that in, say, a solicitor's firm or a jam factory it does not. (Unlike solicitors or jam companies, teachers or education authorities are not liable to actions for educational negligence – still less under the Trades Descriptions Act.) And within the educational institution, social power, an irreducible part of the 'glue' that holds any complex organization together, moves in flux around unclear and shifting purposes.

In educational organizations, therefore, aspects which are present in almost all organizations are enlarged so as to form a distinct type. We may cast these – and particularly their problematic goals – into relief if we make a contrast (necessarily over-simple, but still useful) with one of the 'images' which has been central to organization theory – that of the machine (which, as Miller's essay will remind us, has long been influential in the history of education). Like machinery (and unlike whole societies and many social institutions), formal organizations are human artefacts. Both are built to a deliberate design for consciously entertained purposes, and are often re-designed and reconstructed in the course of their working lives. Both have structures which are intelligible only in terms of their purposes, which may be complex but can (if only in principle and approximately) be described. Both are to some degree unpredictable, and will fulfil their intended purposes only fallibly and approximately.

This raises an interesting side-question: why should theoretical questions of the structure and functioning of organizations come to be separated out at all from practical problems of their design and operation? Engineers, for example, do not thus distinguish a meta-topic of machinery-as-such from their particular studies of materials, design, failure, maintenance and so on. Nor do they puzzle overmuch about the purposes of machinery which already exists. An important part of the reasons for the difference lies in the different components of which the artefacts are formed. Collectivities of human beings cooperating in formal organizations *do* have some resemblances to machines. But, in contrast to other constructed systems, formal organizations have an additional, interior, cause of imperfection (and richness), in that the purposes in pursuit of which they operate are not only those externally given to them, but also include those which arise from the habits, wills and interests of their human components. They are, so to speak, riddled with intention, through, with and against which they must operate. This mediates the relation between design and functioning, and grounds the existence of organization studies as a separate field.

Education simply heightens this condition to a qualitative degree. When – as in organizations for learning and teaching – external goals can be defined only in general terms, and must be pursued through individualistic workers using techniques which cannot be controlled in any detail, purposes interior to the organization take on a collective life of their own, shaping both what sort of habitat the organization is and what it accomplishes. It is then essential that our conceptual tools be ones capable of examining the social habitat – the culture – in ways that take account of what is informal, ephemeral and covert as well what is visible and official. And when formal authority is only slackly connected with control over outcomes it is important to be able to refocus our attention away from the gross, formal instruments of management onto the actual, molecular, sources and mechanisms of power.

Yet any organization, in order to be such, must in some sense order the activities of its members. Machine-like metaphors and systems models therefore persist as central points of reference in organization studies, and an important part of its modern history is concerned either with elaborating them or with developing views which implicitly or explicitly qualify or dispute them. Within this, educational organizations have frequently been catalysts, since the resistance of educational processes to external definition and control makes educational organizations an acid test of neatness in theory and a stimulus to the development of more multi-layered conceptions. This dialectic between education and organization theory has generated many of the items in this volume. It can, of course, make no claim whatsoever to comprehensiveness, but I have tried to include some examples where the 'hard case' of education has stretched and extended our understanding of organizations.

★

Section I consists of two overview articles. Bell's emphasizes the ill-defined and contested character of educational goals and decisions, a topic pursued in later parts. Tyler's review essay explores the poor fit between the study of school organization and prevailing paradigms in the sociology of education. Section II, on problems of structure, starts with Miller's study of projects in the early nineteenth century which sought to organize schools with factory or military precision. Set against today's professionalization of teachers and complexities of curriculum and pedagogy, Jeremy Bentham or Andrew Bell's proposals for systems to achieve lists of learning goals with minimum time and cost, and using teachers with the least training feasible, can seem merely an historical curiosity. But it should be recalled that it was only at about this time that the modern conception of class teaching, with pupils mutually reinforcing each others' learning in feedback with the teacher, was taking shape in the minds of advanced educationalists (Hamilton 1987).

The departures prompted by Weick's article underline how deep-going were assumptions that educational organizations could or should be treated as closely regulable systems. In taking up the idea of 'loose coupling'[3] Weick referred to the attachments between elements and events in educational organizations being 'circumscribed, infrequent, weak . . . , unimportant, and/or slow to respond' and to the 'impermanence, dissolvability and tacitness' of the 'glue' holding the organization together. He sought to begin developing a vocabulary for use in analysing how ' "soft" structures develop, persist, and impose crude orderliness among their elements'. His article, rich in conceptual suggestions, caused the idea of loose coupling rapidly to make its way in the study of organizations in general, and also generated a wave of empirical research aimed at detecting, defining, measuring and comparing the phenomenon, especially among American schools; this is well reviewed in Firestone (1985), who shows that loose coupling is more pronounced in secondary schools, where professional specialization between teachers is more developed, than in elementary schools.

Meyer and Rowan's article represents a line of thought which both qualifies and amplifies the idea of 'loose coupling'. It is true, they argue, that some aspects of educational organizations – what teachers do, the actual content and results of instruction, criteria for entry to upper grades – are only loosely, if at all, controlled. But other aspects – teachers' credentials, timetabling and the consequent distribution of the curriculum (but not necessarily the interdependencies within it) – are rather exactly specified. Moreover, certain commonly encountered forms of *structure* of educational organizations are consistent with a wide variety in the activities within them. Why this combination of loose internal control over the substance of education with detailed insistence on some of its visible (if formal) manifestations? Because, argue Meyer and Rowan, educational organizations are in the business of satisfying socially institutionalized expectations expressed through public bureaucracies, and their structures and public rituals are geared to this. Conversely, teaching may adapt to teachers' or parents' informal pressures, producing big differences in what actually transpires in classrooms with but little alteration in public or formal aspects.

A further line of attack on views of education as rationally organized around its public goals comes from the study of processes of choice. In the early 1970s Cohen, March and Olsen (1972) proposed an alternative to the by then conventional expectation that organizational decision-taking should move through rational sequences of identifying and defining problems, rehearsing alternative solutions, then choosing among them. This picture is, they argued, improbable (and inappropriate) in an important class of organizations (of which educational organizations are a conspicuous subset) which they defined as *organized anarchies* – that is, those with problematic and/or disputed goals, poorly understood technologies (e.g. teaching), and fluid participation by members in the organization and its decision processes. Choices will then be significantly decoupled from both goals and problems and will be made (or not) as a product of the ways in which problems, solutions and people wander into and adhere to each other in 'garbage can' choice situations. Cohen and March (1974) first applied the 'organized anarchy' model to American universities in one of the major reports to the Carnegie Commission, set up after the campus troubles of the 1960s, and it was subsequently explored in a number of other settings. The exchange between Turner and Packwood reprinted here turns on its applicability and desirability in English schools.

If the organization constrains the individuals within it only feebly, perhaps *they* should be considered its primary constituents? Section III starts with a recent item from the crossfire between T. B. Greenfield and his critics – launched by Greenfield's (1974/5) paper proposing a phenomenological understanding of organizations, in particular educational ones. It was false, he urged, to see an organization as real over and above the subjectivities of its members, their perceptions of it and the values and meanings they instil into it. Reifying organizations serves to project as general goals the purposes and views of those who control them – which are in reality as subjective as anyone else's. His main critics responded with positivist defences of objective social science and organizational studies, and the occasional hint that Greenfield's outlook was subversive of good order.[4] The debate resonated loudest within educational administration journals, and Greenfield's article represents his summing up for the prosecution against educational administration's claims to science.

Some of Greenfield's views (like his suggestion that teachers may helpfully be compared to concentration camp guards: Greenfield 1979) seem to arise from the safety of too much distance. But some empirical spin-offs of the debate among students of English education are equally interesting. Gray's essay develops (in the form of commentaries on twelve 'propositions') a workaday 'therapeutic' insight into 'organizations as subjectivities' in British education. The short essay by Ribbins *et al.*, 'Meanings and Contexts', is less pragmatic, but more concrete. It is an early published output of their in-depth study of organization and attitudes in pastoral care in a large comprehensive school, 'Rivendell' (their main published account is in Best *et al*. 1983).

When visible structures and formal means of control are soft or loose, habits and attitudes assume greater importance. Section IV offers a small sampling among the very diverse efforts that have been made to bring concepts of organizational 'climate', 'ethos' and 'culture' to bear on education. One source of such ideas is research on 'school effectiveness'. Studies aimed at accounting for differences of educational achievement find that the largest fractions of the variance in it are explained by individual pupils' background characteristics, such as social class, parents' educational level etc. But inclusion of the individual school and its characteristics as independent variables can often substantially increase the proportion of variance explained. In the United States in the 1970s a considerable body of research attempted to apply various multi-dimensional measures of 'climate' to explain differences in schools' effectiveness.[5] There was less quantitative research in Britain, though one major concern of Rutter *et al*.'s (1979) study of inner London secondary schools was the effects of differences of school 'ethos' on achievement. The essay by Reynolds and Reid included here resumes British research into school characteristics and effectiveness, making their case for integrating data from different sources and gathered with different methodologies.

Deal's article takes pragmatism a stage further, gathering from organizational life a rich tool-kit of anecdotes and suggestions for improving schools. Its roots lie in the crusade to understand and improve organizations with the aid of concepts of 'culture' – a notion richer but less measurable than that of 'climate'. This movement has been led from the United States, but a United States whose corporations have been goaded by Japanese rivals, and intrigued by the quite different organizational mores of their competitors. Ouchi and Wilkins's 'Organizational Culture' reviews both its literary aspect and some practical facets, in which managers have laid hands upon the subtleties of anthropology's most variegated construct. Some have recognized with a start that what they have been doing all along is enacting organizational culture, and, taking the taken-for-granted by the horns, have set about doing it better, or in some cases have attempted to rebuild organizational culture *de novo*. In the United States the movement has reached well into the education system. Academic social scientists have been drawn in, their fears about bruising their nice theoretical distinctions often submerged in their enthusiasm for making a difference. Ouchi and Wilkins's more measured treatment, and Deal's more involved essay, illustrate different degrees of immersion.

The prime advantage of the concept of organizational culture over those of climate, ethos and so on is that it captures its active nature better. A school or college's culture lives, and lives on, through the comings and goings of individuals. Rituals of departure, for example, often have the socialization of newer entrants as one of their main functions. And since organizational culture exists only if internalized by individuals, it must also be active in selecting those individuals it can incorporate – for example, in the recruitment and conditioning, the retention or exgurgitation, of teachers.

Yet the culture of an educational organization is no simple unity. Included within it are elements from a number of external or background cultures or systems of norms (those which preponderate in the families of students, and the professional cultures of teachers, for example). At the same time it is internally highly differentiated, combining these and other elements quite distinctively in different areas. The individual teacher, for example, experiences each working situation as a point of imbrication of various and conflicting cultures and subcultures. The essay by Goodson examines just one plane of this – the development of subject subcultures among English teachers. It sketches both the mutual competition of subject cultures as repositories of sectional interests among teachers, and their part in education's reproduction of social differences.

Each of these two processes works through at all levels of the education system, from the classroom upwards. At the same time each is an example of how organizational cultures within education serve as both vehicles and sites for conflicting interests and the resulting contests of power. Sections V and VI are concerned with power in education, though keeping their focus within the individual institution. The *micropolitics* of education are lived within infrastructures whose informality and complexity bespeak their almost absolute autonomy of the macropolitical system. The short papers by Hoyle and Shaw offer a readable entry to some of the conceptual and practical issues posed by opening up political processes within British schools for examination. (Hoyle's (1986) short book provides an expanded outline of his views; this may be compared with Ball's (1987) more radical and inclusive book-length treatment of the micropolitics of schools.) Bacharach's paper enters the same arena through a more extended review of theoretical problems in sociological conceptualizations of educational organizations. A blind-spot hitherto, he argues, may have been inattention to intra-institutional politics – so that what ideas of 'loose coupling', for example, mainly testify to is that many relevant outcomes are determined by political processes which are poorly reflected in formal structures and lines of authority. This view has been reinforced by empirical studies (e.g. Barnett 1984) of the power which subordinate teachers wield over their formal superiors. By their control over access to resources – people, materials and information – they build and exploit dependencies on the part of those who stand above them in the organizational hierarchy, thus attenuating, complicating, even reversing, formal mechanisms of control.

Factors underlying the distribution of power are one thing; the active cultural competencies which allow one to put one's power resources into motion – whether legitimated by the organization or not – are another. The early study of management proceeded in relative ignorance of what managers

actually *do* when they manage. As the question came to be put to the empirical
test it turned out that what they do most (i.e. two-thirds or more) of the time
is talk (Mintzberg 1973). Gronn's case study applies itself to the question of
how, through talking, a head and his teaching staff mutually manage each
other, showing how much can be gleaned from micro-analysis of the
discourse through which an issue is borne through corridors to committee.

One reason for the number of perceptive works on universities as
organizations (and perhaps for a number of the uncritical ones) is that many
organizational theorists work in them. In Section VI we turn to their distinctive cultures and their more involved patterns of power. All educational
organizations are to some degree 'bottom heavy' – in the phrase by which
Burton Clark (1983) characterized universities. In the most general sense this
is because their core members – teachers – are specialized professionals
working in an autonomous and relatively isolated way, and subject to
hierarchical controls which are often more formal than real. But in most
higher education institutions the sheer weight of the base is reinforced by its
internal structuring into a more or less complex system of committees.
Committee systems representative of teaching staff are an expression, and a
crucial form of organization, of teachers' claims to professionalism and their
concomitant autonomy within bureaucratized organizations. They exist in
very many types of educational institution, but it is in universities, with their
stress on academic freedom and their theoretical subordination of decisions
and policy to the academic collectivity, that they are most elaborately
developed. With the ramification of committees and subcommittees comes
greater blurring of the basis, timing and even location of actual decisions, and
what Noble and Pym (1970) defined as the 'receding locus of power' in
universities.

The articles in Section VI examine such interpenetrations of academic
interests and values with administrative bureaucracies. Becher and Lutz each
make a virtue of familiarity, and approximate the intimacy of case studies.
Becher distils a narrative of the internal political moves in a 'typical' British
university faced with its cut in the real value of government grant. A 'backstage' coalition of the most powerful units convenes round an initial budget,
punitive of those it excludes. But such maximum demands are whittled
down in the 'front stage' of the public committee system, the main cuts being
shifted away from the academic units, which are the portions of the organization mainly represented there. Lutz draws on the anthropological study of
witch-finding and witch-persecuting practices to illuminate the trials of a
new dean in a US university's School of Education. Put in by the central
administration to reorganize the School, he comes to be defined as a
maleficent outsider, is subjected to the guerrilla warfare of a recalcitrant
faculty, and is finally abandoned by his central administration and driven to
resign.

Finally, Hardy *et al.* use the example of universities in a reworking and
broadening of concepts of *organizational strategy* – something which is not

necessarily deliberately aimed at or defined by specific goals or means, but which none the less emerges as broad consistencies across a wide range of activities. What can appear to be 'garbage-can' decisions in 'organized anarchies' are in fact the unpredictable outcomes of numerous local and temporary contests of power. The many sources, fluid characteristics and shifting balances of power mean that outcomes are only loosely linked to intentions, and sometimes decoupled from them entirely. Organizational strategy, in an institution like a university, arises not from the working of any central administrative intelligence, but rather from its general organizational culture, formed by the habits, values and assumptions which pervade it.

The selection of pieces included here is inevitably partial and uneven. But I hope it will provide some indication of the range and fertility of the organizational concepts that can help us understand how education works – and some examples of what the study of education can contribute to understanding organizations.

## Notes

1. The other set books for the course are J. Ozga (ed.), *Schoolwork* (Milton Keynes: Open University Press, 1987), S. J. Ball, *The Micro-Politics of the School* (London: Methuen, 1987), S. J. Ball and I. Goodsons (eds), *Teachers' Lives and Careers* (Lewes: Falmer Press, 1985), M. Lawn and G. Grace (eds) *Teachers: the Culture and Politics of Work* (Lewes: Falmer Press, 1987) and G. Morgan, *Images of Organization* (London: Sage, 1986).
2. Recent introductions are Handy and Aitken (1986) and Bush (1986).
3. Some of the core ideas, and the phrase, were already in circulation: see, for example, Bidwell (1965) and Glassman (1973).
4. See, for example, Hills (1980) and Willower (1979, 1980 and 1985).
5. American research is reviewed in Anderson (1982). Reflections on the rather different uses made of the term in Britain are in Strivens (1985).

## References

Anderson, Carolyn S. (1982). 'The search for school climate: a review of the research', *Review of Educational Research* 52(3):368–420.

Ball, S. J. (1987). *The Micro-Politics of the School*, London, Methuen.

Barnett Bruce G. (1984). 'Subordinate teacher power in school organizations', *Sociology of Education* 57(1):43–55.

Best, R., Ribbins, P. and Jarvis, C. with Oddy, D. (1983). *Education and Care: the study of a school and its pastoral organization*, London, Heinemann.

Bidwell, C. (1965). 'The school as a formal organization', in March, J. (ed.) *Handbook of Organizations*, Chicago, Rand McNally.

Bush, A. (1986). *Theories of Educational Management*, London, Harper & Row.

Clark, Burton R. (1983). *The Higher Education System*, Berkeley, University of California Press.

Cohen, M. D., and March, J. D. (1974). *Leadership and Ambiguity: the American College President*, New York, McGraw-Hill.

Cohen M. D., March J. G., and Olsen J. P. (1972). 'A garbage can model of organizational choice', *Administrative Science Quarterly* 17(1):1–25.

Firestone, William A. (1985). 'The study of loose coupling: problems, progress and prospects', *Research in Sociology of Education and Socialization* 5:3–30.

Glassman, R. B. (1973). 'Persistence and loose coupling in living systems', *Behavioural Science* 18:83–98.

Greenfield, T. B. (1979). 'Organization theory as ideology', *Curriculum Inquiry* 9(2):97–112.

Greenfield, T. B. (1974/5). 'Theory in the study of organizations and administrative structures: a new perspective', paper delivered to the third International Intervisitation Programme on Educational Administration, London, 1974. An expanded version was published as 'Theory about organizations: a new perspective and its implication for schools', in Hughes M. (ed.) *Administering Education: International Challenge*, Athlone, London, 1975.

Hamilton, D. (forthcoming) *Towards a theory of Schooling*.

Hills, R. Jean (1980). 'A critique of Greenfield's "New Perspective"', *Educational Administration Quarterly* 16(1) Winter: 20–44.

Handy, C., and Aitken, R. (1986). *Understanding Schools as Organizations*, Harmondsworth, Penguin.

Hoyle, E. (1986). *The Politics of School Management*, London, Hodder & Stoughton.

Mintzberg, H. (1973). *The Nature of Managerial Work*, New York, Harper & Row.

Noble, T., and Pym, B. (1970). 'Collegial authority and the receding locus of power', *British Journal of Sociology* 21:431–45.

Rutter, M., Maughan, B., Mortimore, P. and Ouston, J., with Smith, A. (1979). *Fifteen Thousand Hours: secondary schools and their effects on children*, London, Open Books.

Strivens, J. (1985). 'School climate: a review of a problematic concept', in Reynolds, D. (ed.) *Studying School Effectiveness*, Lewes, Falmer Press.

Willower, D. J. (1979). 'Ideology and science in organization theory', *Educational Administration Quarterly* 14:20–42.

Willower, D. J. (1980). 'Contemporary issues in theory in educational administration', *Educational Administration Quarterly* 15:20–42.

Willower, D. J. (1985). 'Philosophy and the study of educational administration', *Journal of Educational Administration* 23(1):7–22.

**Section I**

# Overviews

# 1

# The school as an organization: a reappraisal

**L. A. Bell**

In 1970 Brian Davies argued that, 'We lack anything like an adequate sociology of the school and that one aspect of that lack is in terms of our knowledge of schools as organisations' (Davies, 1970, p. 250).

He suggests that theoretical and conceptual weaknesses pervade the organizational analysis. The literature in this field reveals a bewildering plethora of approaches to the sociology of organizations, many of which appear to have unreconciled differences between them. It also indicates that the analytical emphasis focused upon the development of inter-organizational comparisons and, as a result, the development of specific organizations and their particular nature has tended to be neglected. Yet, in spite of these difficulties Davies argues that it would be better to explore the relevance of existing organizational theory for the sociology of education rather than to deny its existence. Only by so doing might the analysis of schools as organizations be advanced.

Hoyle, making a similar point, also notes the neglect of the study on schools as organizations within British sociology of education (Hoyle, 1965). He too identifies a series of inadequacies and suggests that when organiz-ational theory is applied to schools the result might be at best a partial analysis. For example pupils might be much more amenable than teachers and thus the emphasis of research might be more upon the selection and differentiation of pupils and on their subculture rather than on the authority structure or the decision-making processes within the school. Hoyle himself pointed out subsequently that the most significant organizational studies, such as Hargreaves (1967), King (1969) and Lacey (1970) have been more concerned with the pupil world than the staff world and therefore they tell us little about how schools operate and how decisions are made in any direct sense (Hoyle, 1973).

The development of the study of schools as organizations thus appears to have been inhibited by the selective nature of the application of organizational analysis to schools and by a failure to take account of the major conceptual difficulties which exist within much of the literature on organizational theory. This has led to the development, albeit embryonic, of a view of schools as organizations which may be, at best, inappropriate and, at worst, misleading. Unfortunately, the espousal of the very theory to which sociologists of education in Britain appear to have been directed by both Hoyle and Davies has tended to exacerbate this situation. A brief consideration of some of the major strands in the organizational analysis of the school will illustrate this point and might enable some tentative suggestions for an alternative, or at least a complementary, perspective to be offered.

## Schools as organizations

Where the organizational aspects of the school have been considered they have had attributed to them features such as clear goals, identifiable personnel, a relevant and explicit technology and relationships based on positional rather than personal factors. These structure features are thought to produce consistency, predictability and stability. Taken together the extent to which a school's organization is thought to exhibit these characteristics indicates something about the nature of its authority and control structures. If an organization is found to be unpredictable or thought to be irrational in its decision-making then those who are subjected to this unpredictability or irrationality are aggrieved because such events are unexpected in the context of a formal organization. Similarly when some sections of an organization fail to respond to the demands of other sections in the expected way a degree of tension is created between the sections and perhaps between the members of those sections. This is as true of schools as it is of any other form of organization. The expectations and the assumptions on which they are based may, however, rest on an unrealistic notion of the nature of schools as organizations, although this tends not to be reflected in the relevant sociological literature.

## The organizational goals of schools

Banks (1976) begins her discussion of schools as organizations wth Etzioni's definition which identifies the central feature of any organization as being a structure designed to pursue specific goals (Etzioni, 1964). She reinforces the Parsonian position that it is the primacy of goal orientation that provides the main feature for distinguishing organization from other social structures (Parson, 1964). Thus basic to the idea of any organzation whether it is a school, a prison or a large corporation, is the idea of a means–end relationship

of the formal social arrangements to the goals of the organizations. Organizations themselves are assumed to have a relatively high level of predictability,
stability and consistency. This is thought to be as true of schools as of other
organizations.

This view is echoed by Musgrave (1968) and Shipman (1975). The
latter, pointing out that schools are established to achieve definite ends,
argues that four fundamental organizational goals can be identified for
schools, although he does indicate that there may be a difference in emphasis
between different types of educational institutions. The former states firmly
that, 'Schools can be viewed as organisations in some ways akin to factories'
(Musgrave, 1968, p. 67). The goals of education, it is argued, penetrate down
to the classroom and influence the work of the teacher. This suggests that
such factors as the division of labour, power and communication in the
school are deliberately planned to facilitate the achievement of the school's
goals. Lambert, Bullock and Millham (1970), in similar vein, have developed
a practical manual for the study of schools as organizations. They place their
emphasis on instrumental, expressive and maintenance goals and produce an
analysis which presupposes that such goals attract a degree of consensus, can
be identified and related to structures intended to achieve them.

Lambert *et al.* (1970) do recognize, however, that such an analysis of
abstract goals may appear unreal and theoretical, a point which appears to
have been conveniently overlooked in much of the literature. Davies (1970)
suggests that the major problem in discussing organizational goals is that of
identifying how goals are set and whose goals count as the goals of the
organization. This focus on goals tends to suggest that schools are highly
effective goal-seeking organizations. Yet schools certainly can be regarded as
operating adequately when official goals are not reflected in the real state of
the school. Frequently, attempts to identify the organizational goals of
schools produce an analysis which is at such a high level of abstraction as to
defy specification (e.g. Shipman, 1975). This, in turn, may be the result of
wide variations of goals between schools, the differences between schools
themselves, and the difficulty in obtaining any real consensus of what the
goals of schools are and ought to be, let alone how such goals might be
achieved. Perhaps, therefore, the analysis of schools as organizations should
reflect this situation and recognize the essentially problematic nature of goals
in the organizational structure of the school.

## Schools as bureaucracies

If the identification of goals is regarded as one essential factor in understanding the organizational characteristics of schools then the nature of the
structures designed to achieve those goals is equally important. The classical
approach to an analysis of these structures has involved the application of the
Weberian concept of bureaucracy which can be seen as an organizational

response to an increase in the size and complexity of units of administration. Musgrove argues that, 'Schools today have most of the salient characteristics of bureaucracies as described by Max Weber' (Musgrove, 1973, p. 163). The complex nature of the activities carried out by schools demands, it is argued, both the efficiency and rationality initially claimed by Weber for this form of organization. Musgrove (1973) has suggested that in order to achieve its goals, the school's activities must be regulated by an impartially applied, consistent system of abstract rules and that the duties of members of staff must be officially prescribed, a division of labour maintained, and a hierarchy of authority, resulting in a clear delineation of status and function between the various positions in the hierarchy, established.

This view of bureaucracy has been somewhat modified by subsequent research (see Mouzelis, 1967), and a number of writers have emphasized the problems arising from trying to make use of Weber's approach to bureaucracy (e.g. Clignet, 1974; Albrow, 1970). Nevertheless, a number of studies have treated the school as a bureaucracy (see Anderson, 1968; Bidwell, 1965; Corwin, 1970). King (1973), argues that everyday experience of schools confirms that they do exhibit many of the characteristics contained in the original Weberian formulation whilst Reid (1978), after a discussion of this particular approach to bureaucracy, suggests that many schools do, in fact, approximate to it.

In so arguing, such writers have tended somewhat to be uncritical in their application of organization theory to schools. They attempt to analyse what goes on in schools as though both the activity and its institutional setting existed independently of the larger society, insulated from it and uninfluenced by it. They tend to ignore the findings of case studies on the structure and culture of schools which support the view that schools create, through their own organizational framework, many of the problems of disorder and non-involvement which they experience (Hargreaves, 1967; Lacey, 1970). The tensions which might be produced within a school by emphasis on an impersonal application of rules are, as Bobbitt et al. (1974) suggest, serious enough to merit more detailed consideration than they often receive in this type of analysis. The same may be claimed for the conflict of values which can sometimes be observed between the administrator and the teacher who sees his position as a professional being challenged by the bureaucrat (Corwin, 1970). Under the influence of this relatively uncritical analysis, schools have tended to be regarded as stable, predictable institutions within which office holders apply agreed rules and procedures in a consistent, impartial manner. By implication, it is thought that the membership of the school can easily be identified or, as the systems approach might have it, the boundaries clearly defined (Sugerman, 1975). This, in turn, indicates that the relationship between members is clear, specific and based on a thoroughly understood technology for achieving desired goals. Relationships with the external environment tend to be stable and predictable, or, where this is not the case, can be coped with by the application of the relevant rules and procedures, although perhaps contingency theory suggests a more complex process than this is sometimes at work (see Tyler, 1973). On the evidence derived from this type of analysis an observer might expect, for example, that decisions formulated in schools would be the results of a logical and rational process in which those eligible to participate did so, and that the importance of the decision to be taken would be the fundamental determinant of the priority attributed to it by the potential decision-makers. In some ways this could be a less than accurate analysis of what may be happening. It may also be positively misleading since it is predicated on the assumption that schools have more control over such factors as the environment within which they operate than perhaps is the case.

## The turbulent environment

The view of organizations which attributes to them orderliness and rationality may be extremely attractive, especially to those working in schools. It promises consistency, predictability and a stable and secure framework within which to work. There is, however, increasing evidence that at least some organizations are not always like this. Cyert and March (1963), suggested that the overall rational pattern of behaviour in organizations based on a set of commonly held goals was frequently modified by a large number of departmental, rather than organizational, interests. Experience in schools leads to the belief that this is equally true of departments and groups in schools. This position is frequently reinforced by appeals to the notion of professional autonomy. A recent study of the introduction of mixed ability teaching in a comprehensive school illustrates several ways in which semi-autonomous departmental activity not only lead to a modification of the overall goal, but, in certain circumstances, to an almost complete reversal of policy (Bell, Pennington and Burridge, 1979). As a result of this and similar factors, individuals often discover that they work in schools which are, organizationally, more complex, less stable and less understandable than they have previously assumed and than the sociology of education literature might suggest. Perhaps it needs to be recognized more explicitly that organizations, including schools, sometimes operate in a complex and unstable environment over which they exert only modest control and which is capable of producing effects which penetrate the strongest and most selective of boundaries. Although most schools are not directly subject to the free range of market forces which create severe problems for some industrial organizations, many schools are now unable to disregard pressures emanating from their wider environment. They are no longer able to respond to the uncertainty which such pressures often bring by attempting to buffer themselves against the unforeseen or by gaining control over the source of the uncertainty and thus restoring stability. The external pressures are, in many cases, too strong for that. It has not proved possible, for example, for most schools to use either of these techniques to counteract the effect of restrictions in public expenditure on them. They have been subjected to pressures on their spending as LEAs have attempted to meet the demands from national and local politicians that all expenditure should be restricted in order to limit the increase in rates and conform to government cash limits. At the same time the costs of necessary books and material have drastically increased. Similarly, schools have not always been able to respond effectively to the recent external criticism of content, method and objectives of education which has come from parents, politicians and industrialists. This criticism has found expression in, and among other things the establishment of, the Assessment of Performance Unit at the DES and the recommendations of the Taylor Report. These and other similar pressures have created a situation in which the internal organization of the school has begun to resemble what has been called an anarchic organization (Cohen, March and Olsen, 1972). Yet such characteristics as those displayed by an anarchic organization rarely, if ever, feature in the sociological literature on schools.

## The school as an anarchic organization

The anarchic organization is not, as its name might imply, a formless or unpredictable collection of individuals. Rather it is an organization with a structure of its own which is partly determined by external pressures and partly a product of the nature of the organization itself. It is anarchic in the sense that the relationship between goals, members and technology is not as clearly functional as conventional organization theory indicates that it will be. Cohen et al. (1972) suggest that much organizational activity can best be understood as being characterized by unclear goals, unclear technology and fluid membership since such characteristics, it is argued, may be instrumental in creating a set of internal responses to perceive ambiguities. Cohen and March (1974) argued that many of the forty-two college principals which they studied for their report to the Carnegie Commission on Higher Education were frequently required to take decisions in situations in which considerable ambiguity surrounded goals, technology and participants. This work was followed by a series of case studies on such disparate areas of educational decision-making as the selection of a dean for an American university, desegregation decisions in San Francisco, the reorganization of the University of Oslo and a study of a Danish Technical University (March and Olson, 1976). Such work has, I believe, begun to provide a theoretical framework within which it might be possible to re-examine the organization of schools within the British education system, although, as yet, this re-examination is at a purely exploratory level.

The external demands which are made on schools from a wide variety of sources often conflict with each other, especially at a time of limited and even declining resources. This, taken with the different views about the nature and content of education which already exists within the teaching profession, has led in many schools to a situation in which it is not very clear what the goals of the school are. Different members of the school may perceive different goals or attribute different priorities to the same goals or even be unable to define goals which have any operational meaning. Thus whilst it is commonly expected that those who work in schools should have some overall purpose it is likely that the organizational context of many schools actually renders this either impossible or very difficult. Hence schools face an ambiguity of purpose, the result of which is that the achievement of goals which are educational in any real sense has ceased to be central to the functioning of the school. Thus husbanding scarce resources tends to have priority over the facilitation of learning, uncertainty generated by falling pupil numbers overshadows much of the work done with existing pupils and a common sense of direction is frequently not evident in the teaching which does take place. Furthermore, it has often been found difficult to specify a constant set of educational goals. They have tended to change over time and may even vary between different parts of the school organiza-tion. They are frequently stated in terms which are notoriously difficult to translate into action and, whilst goals may be imputed to schools by observing the behaviour of a range of people within them, this imputation itself tends to be as ambiguous as the goals since it is extremely difficult to obtain general agreement on it.

Given, then, that the education goals are ambiguous and may well not occupy a focal position in school life, the way in which schools attempt to fulfil these goals is equally unclear. Even when the goals are expressed in the most general of terms related to the facilitating of learning, different edu-cational and political ideologies may lead teachers to approach their tasks in a number of ways. More fundamentally, however, teachers are often unsure about what it is they want their pupils to learn, about what it is the pupils have learned about and how, if at all, learning has actually taken place. The learning process is inadequately understood and therefore pupils may not always be learning effectively whilst the basic technology available in schools is often not understood because its purposes are only vaguely recognized. In such a situation new teachers do not so much acquire the skills of teaching as learn how to conform to the normative and formal structures in order to reduce the demands made upon then by the organization to acceptable proportions. Since the related technology is so unclear the processes of teaching and learning are clouded in ambiguity. This produces a range of situations between teachers, and between teachers and pupils, within which rules and procedures cannot be operated with bureaucratic consistency, impartiality and predictability because the various parties involved do not perceive with any degree of clarity what is expected of them and what may justifiably be expected of others.

Thus, although the schools manage to exist as entities their processes are not really understood by members. They operate on the basis of procedures such as trial and error, learning from the accidents of past experience and pragmatic inventions of necessity. This situation, itself, may be unidentified, with the result that some schools manage to operate *as if* the technology were clear. The participants share notions about cause-and-effect relationships in educational activity which are used to make judgements about those activities and to take decisions about the nature and direction of changes. When situations arise which are not easily accounted for within this framework such situations are regarded as abnormal. This can lead to the creation or reinforcement of boundaries between schools and the wider community as teachers fall back to a defensive position from which they perhaps use their claim to professional autonomy to fight off demands for accountability. Thus, because those within schools do not fully understand their own technology and so do not appreciate its weakness, they may be in danger of attempting to turn schools into increasingly closed institutions which try to shut out parents and other interested parties. This is equally true of relationships inside schools between departments as Bell *et al.* (1979) have shown. Some departments felt that the changes were either too difficult to implement or were not producing the expected improvements in pupil performances. They reacted by attempting to operate as semi-autonomous units within the larger school in an effort to shut out other teachers who, they felt, might be unduly critical of their 'failures'. This happened in spite of the fact that it was pointed out that the goal of improving the overall standard of pupil performance and the technology used, the implementation of mixed ability teaching, were not directly connected in a causal relationship. This general failure to understand the technology on which schools are based results, therefore, not only in an inability to make the most of it but also in the attribution of expectations to the technology which it is too diffuse and weak to fulfil. This situation, when not appreciated, may produce unfortunate consequences for the schools' internal and external relationships.

This situation is exacerbated by the conflict which may be produced by the attempts to limit access to the school at a time when the actual membership of the school appears to be in a fluid state. This is true in two senses. First, the school consists of groups of pupils and teachers all of whom make a wide range of demands on the organization. By their very nature schools gain and lose large numbers of pupils each year and, until recently, they also experienced a high turnover in teaching staff. The interests of this changing group, and their ensuing demands, are not pre-determined and therefore the best ways to meet these demands are not always predictable. Schools are thus open to a wide variety of possible demands and influences which may effect their activities. The recent developments in community education have resulted in another form of fluidity in the membership of some schools. Membership is no longer limited to teachers and pupils. It might include local pensioners, youth groups, sports clubs and a whole variety of other members of the public at large. At any one time it may prove extremely difficult to say who belongs to the school and who does not. Membership of the school is also fluid in the sense that the extent to which individuals are willing and able to participate in its activities. Their degree of commitment may change over time and according to the nature of the activity itself. In this way schools are peopled by participants who wander in and out. The notion of membership is thus ambiguous and therefore it becomes extremely difficult to attribute responsibility to a particular member of the school for some areas of the schools activities whilst, over other areas, there exist considerable conflicts of interests.

Thus it can be argued that when these characteristics are found in any organization, including schools, then the predominant ethos within that organization is unpredictability (Turner, 1977). The more traditional forms of organizational analysis will, therefore, tend to confuse rather than clarify and conceal more than they reveal. It may, for example, not be apparent from such an analysis that once the school is regarded as an unpredictable organization existing within a turbulent environment then certain skills are required by those working in the school. An individual must be highly adaptive, creative and flexible in order to react to constantly changing situations which cannot be predicted. He will need to have full discretion and full delegated powers from his superiors in order to cope with such situations. It is likely that the decisions made by such an individual will be short term and made in an attempt to respond to immediate demands and, as such, may be subject to rapid modification. For such responses to be understood the traditional notion of the school as an hierarchical decision-making structure with a horizontal division into departments and a vertical division into authority levels needs to be abandoned. Such a conceptualization is unsuitable for the analysis of an anarchic organization. The fundamental importance of unclear technology, fluid membership and the problematic nature and position of educational goals has to be accorded due recognition in any sociology of the school.

## Anarchic schools and organizational choice

It has been suggested above that the more traditional approaches to the sociology of the school provide a particular set of expectations about two schools' functions and, in particular, about how decisions are taken in a situation of an unclear technology, fluid membership and problematic goals, the taking of decisions and the solution of the problems cannot be based on some notion of common goals to be implemented by the application of a known and understood set of techniques. Such problems are more likely to consist of linking together problems, solutions, participants and choices in conditions of ambiguity such that there are no criteria for making the connections. Hence the ideal solution and its related problem may not be linked. If, for example, the problem with which the school is concerned is to raise standards there may be a whole range of possible solutions to that problem. The one adopted may depend more on the amount of time and energy devoted to its solution or on some partially understood notion of the relationship between learning and teaching, than on any concept of the 'ideal' solution. The area of unpredictability refers mainly to the way in which these factors are combined rather than to their long- or short-term feasibility. Once the possibility is recognized of seeing patterns in the apparently unpredictable and disordered processes of making choices when goals are unclear, technology is uncertain and the cast of participants changes over time, then it becomes clear that not only has this anarchy an identifiable structure of its own but that this should be the focus of concern for the study of the school as an organization. In any organization in which it is not always possible to base decision-making on some perception of common goals, decisions will be taken in some other way (Cohen and March, 1974). The ideal solution and the problem may be happily united but this is not likely to be the most common procedure. Neither will a series of such decisions necessarily be consistent with each other since there is no common point of reference. Decisions are more likely to be made by 'flight' or by 'oversight' (Cohen et al., 1972).

In a school which is concerned, for example, with attempting to raise standards there may exist a vast array of other problems, some of which will be related to the question of standards and some of which will not. The staff may be unwilling to teach in particular ways, use particular materials or group children according to certain criteria. Timetabling may present a serious difficulty because of shortage of staff in specialist areas or because of the conflicting demands being made by different departments. Raising standards will, therefore, be but one of a number of problems confronting a similar set of people at the same time. As a result solutions may be chosen and attached to problems unsuccessfully, remaining there until some more attractive choice comes along (flight). So the solution to raising standards may be thought to be the introduction of mixed ability teaching (Bell et al., 1979). Perhaps with experience it is seen that this is not the hoped-for solution and that it has exacerbated some other problems. However the failed solution is likely to remain in operation much longer than might be supposed if the criteria of rational planning were to apply because the mixed ability teaching and the problem which it was meant to solve, that of improving standards, have become linked in the ambiguous environment of the organized anarchy and will remain so until sufficient people have sufficient time to examine other possible solutions to that problem. Similarly, the choice of mixed ability teaching as a solution to the problem of how to raise standards, whether it is successful or not, may have been made without concern for other problems which exist at the same time (decision by oversight). This would mean that those problems would be ignored in any attempt to solve one other problem. This might result in a whole range of other problems, such as those already outlined, attaching themselves to the introduction of mixed-ability teaching as a solution, although the choice of solution was made without reference to these other problems.

## Ground rules for anarchic schools

Once the implication of decision-making processes such as flight and over-sight are recognized, then the whole approach to the analysis of such processes needs to be re-examined. It is clear that ambiguity of this type does have an identifiable pattern. It is also clear that sometimes the attempt to solve a particular problem serves purposes other than seeking answers to immediate problems. Having thus identified the nature of these methods of making choices, it is possible to develop a sociology of the school which not only embraces the recognition of such anarchic tendencies but which does not place undue emphasis on order, stability, practicability and rationality and which can provide practical guidelines for those working in schools. For example it might enable schools to discover ways of coping with some of the more ambiguous social problems, problems for which there are no clear solutions, to which schools are increasingly being asked to provide responses. It might also help those involved in decision-making, or those wishing to be involved, to minimize the impact of flight and oversight since an analysis of decision-making in organized anarchies which would provide the basis for such a sociology of the school indicates that those people who take part in decision-making not only bring with them potential solutions to problems but also bring problems seeking solutions.

## References

Albrow, M. (1970). *Bureaucracy*, London Macmillan.
Anderson, J. (1968). *Bureaucracy in Education*, Baltimore, Johns Hopkins Press.
Banks, O. (1976). *The Sociology of Education*, London, Batsford.
Bell., L. A., Pennington, R. C. and Burridge, J. B. (1979) Going mixed ability: some observations on one school's experience, *Forum* 21 (3).
Bidwell, C. E. (1965). The school as a formal organisation, in March, J. G. (ed.) (1965) *Handbook of Organisations*, London, Rand-McNally.
Bobbitt, H. R. *et al.* (1974). *Organisational Behaviour: Understanding and Prediction*, London, Prentice Hall.
Clignet, R. (1974). *Liberty and Equality in the Education Process*, London, Wiley.
Cohen, M. D. & March, J. G. (1974). *Leadership and Ambiguity: The American College President*, New York, McGraw-Hill.
Cohen, M. D., March, J. G. and Olsen, J. P. (1972). A garbage can model of organisational choice, *Administrative Science Quarterly* 17, pp. 1–25.
Corwin, R. G. (1970). *Militant Professionalism: A Study of Organisational Conflict in High Schools*, London, Appleton-Century-Crofts.
Cyert, R. M. and March, J. G. (1963). *A Behavioural Theory of the Firm*, Englewood Cliffs, Prentice Hall.
Davies, W. B. (1970). Organisational analysis of educational institutions, in Brown, R. (ed.) (1973). *Knowledge, Education and Cultural Change*, London, Tavistock.
Etzioni, A. (1964). *Modern Organisations*, Englewood Cliffs, Prentice Hall.

Hargreaves, D. H. (1967). *Social Relationships in Secondary Schools*, London, Routledge & Kegan Paul.

Hoyle, E. (1965). Organisational analysis in the field of education, *Educational Research* 7(2).

Hoyle, E. (1973). The study of schools as organisations, in Butcher, H. J. and Pont, A. B. (eds) (1973) *Educational Research in Britain*, 3, London, University of London Press.

King, R. (1969). *Values and Involvement in a Grammar School*, London, Routledge & Kegan Paul.

King, R. (1973). *School Organisation and Pupil Performance* London, Routledge & Kegan Paul.

Lacey, C. (1970). *Hightown Crammer*, Manchester, Manchester University Press.

Lambert, R., Bullock, R. and Millham, S. (1970). *A Manual to the Sociology of the School*, London, Weidenfeld & Nicolson.

March, J. G. and Olsen, J. P. (1976). *Ambiguity and Choice in Organisations*, Bergen Universitetslaget.

Mouzelis, N. (1967). *Organisation and Bureaucracy*, London, Routledge & Kegan Paul.

Musgrave, P. W. (1968). *The School as an Organisation*, London, MacMillan.

Musgrove, F. (1973). *Research on the sociology of the school*, in Taylor, W. (ed.) (1973) *Research Perspectives in Education*, London, Routledge & Kegan Paul.

Parson, T. (1964). *Structure and Process in Modern Societies*, London, Prentice Hall.

Shipman, M.D. (1968). *Sociology of the School*, London, Longmans.

Sugarman, B. (1975). The school as a social system in Houghton, V., McHugh, R. and Morgan, C. (eds) (1975). *Management in Education*, London, Ward Lock.

Turner, C. M. (1977). Organising educational institutions as anarchies, *Education Administration* 5, pp. 6–12.

Tyler, W. (1973). The organisational structure of the secondary school, *Educational Review* 25, pp. 223–36.

# 2
# The organizational structure of the school

**William B. Tyler**

*Abstract*

The sociology of school organization is today fragmented by a bewildering variety of theoretical perspectives – interactionist, neo-Durkheimian, phenomenological, to name a few. Central to the development in this field over the past decade has been the rejection of the ideal-type of bureaucratic organization as formulated by Weber and the attempt to locate formal structures of the school within the strategies and motives of teachers, pupils and administrators. The result has been, however, a certain loss of theoretical focus and a failure to think through the contradictions of particular perspectives and to formulate their partial insights into more rigorous and embracing conclusions. The ascendant model of school structure is now that of the loosely coupled system, in which technologies are uncertain, goals unclear, and the formal structures of which tend towards anarchy. This model contrasts markedly with other dominant perspectives, notably those in the structuralist tradition (e.g. Bernstein, Foucault) that describe school organization in terms of a close theoretical relationship between pedagogy, ideology, and the apparatus of control and surveillance. This review explicates these tensions and contradictions in contemporary accounts of school structure and suggests ways in which they may be reconciled.

## Introduction

Despite the number of authoritative reviews of the school as a formal organization (Bidwell 1965; Dreeben 1973; Davies 1973, 1981; Boyd and Crowson 1981), the sociological study of the school as an institution has proven to be lacking in both depth and specificity (Corwin 1974; Bell 1980; Allison 1983). Although the school was organizationally mature and culturally ubiquitous before schooling assumed its age-specific, bureaucratic and obligatory features in the late nineteenth century (Reimer 1971), it has somehow managed to remain at the margins of sociological interest. This is not to say that the structural features of school *systems* have lacked extensive theoretical or sociohistorical analysis (Durkheim 1977; Hopper 1971; Archer 1979), but rather that the formal properties of the school – the localized administrative entity concerned with the face-to-face instruction of the young – have tended to be ignored within the mainstream sociological enterprise. Apart from the lively interest shown by administrative theorists in school organization, social-scientific focus has been on the whole polarized – whether towards such macrosociological questions as the correspondence between school and work organization (Bowles and Gintis 1976) or towards the micro or interactional aspects of control in classrooms (Woods 1983). The aim of this review therefore is to identify and to expose the rich though often hidden veins of sociological enquiry that treat the school as an institution in its own right.

This apparent neglect may result from the schools' lack of a technology that links inputs to a rationally-deducible index of performance – or even of a clear and unambiguous set of procedures by which such a criterion could be defined. Indeed, the school has most often been conceptualized in the past decade as a 'loosely coupled' set of events and personnel and functions (Weick 1976), analogous to a football game played on a sloped field with numerous goals and a rather anarchic system of scoring (J. March, personal communication quoted by Weick 1976:1). Though schools may possess many of the formal properties of the Weberian ideal-type of bureaucracy (such as a hierarchy of offices, a fixed and official division of labor, formalized procedures, and promotion by expertise – Weber 1946:196–244), it is the indeterminacy of their decision-making processes that appears to characterize their organizational structures – a feature they share with other educational institutions such as colleges (March and Olsen *et al.* 1976). Some theorists have gone so far as to claim that school organization is shaped more by the logic of public confidence surrounding the myths and ceremonies of certification than by any internal relationship between their official goals and their instructional practices (Meyer and Rowan 1983).

Inherent within these post-Weberian models of school organization are some unresolved theoretical problems. If schools are loosely coupled or anarchic organizations, what can one give as the reasons for this, within a more general and comparative perspective? Is it possible to produce a theoretical scheme which might generate an entirely different set of empirical forms, which are nevertheless recognizable as schools? Secondly, if the formal requirements of system-oriented theory of school structure could be met, what might be the implications of this for the interactive order of this institution – that is to say, the realm of face-to-face communication and experience so central to our definition of the school? How tight are the links between the formal and interactional spheres of schooling and how might one draw lines of causation between them? According to Goffman (1983:11) this relationship is, typically for modern societies, another example of loose coupling, which he defines precisely as 'a nonexclusive linkage between interactional practices and social structures.' He suggests that this linkage may be compared to 'a set of transformation rules, or a membrane selecting how various relevant social distinctions will be managed within the interaction,' Do these insights however merely compound the special difficulties of constructing a theoretical model of the school that implies at least some degree of unity, integration, and consensus?

The rejection of a holistic approach to school organization implied by loose coupling (Willower 1982:93) may be a less adequate response than first appears. Although schools are ostensibly autonomous from the pressures of the market (and consequently perhaps further enjoy a degree of subunit independence), the loose coupling metaphor has only heuristic value unless it is embedded more precisely within a general perspective that constitutes the sociohistorical context of the apparently autonomous actor within a specific theoretical tradition or paradigm (Morgan 1980). Two diverse fields associated with school organization may serve to illustrate the need for some kind of theoretical synthesis, despite the apparently high levels of indeterminacy, discontinuity, and autarchy typical of organizational analysis of schools at the empirical level. The first of these is seen in the renaissance in recent years of the school effectiveness debate (Reynolds 1982) in which certain aspects of internal organization are taken as causal influences on a school's behavioral and academic performance. The second problem area is defined by the role played by the ostensibly meritocratic and rationalized forms of schooling within theories of social reproduction, Marxist and non-Marxist (Bourdieu and Passeron 1977; Bernstein 1977; Sharp 1980), as well as by those who follow the archeological method of institutional analysis of Foucault (Jones and Williamson 1979). In neither of these two opposed fields of enquiry – the one prescriptive and unashamedly empiricist, the other intensely theoretical – is the apparent looseness of school organization anything more than a starting point.

Within the school effectiveness research, for example, there are increasing applications of econometric methods that employ latent variables (the linear combination of the manifest or observed variables) which are assigned weights according to a prespecified model, in order to better estimate the contribution that school and home make to individual levels of performance (Noonan and Wold 1977). Such methods are considerably more sophisticated than earlier approaches that attribute causal significance by the increment in variance explained (Coleman 1966; Peaker 1975). They are, in addition, more theoretically justifiable than the rather inductive derivation of a composite process or climate variable from a host of indices of the school's internal state (e.g. Rutter *et al.* 1979 and critiques by Goldstein 1981; Cuttance 1981).

Whatever the methodological orientation of this tradition of research, however, its apparent aim is to identify the processes and structures that reduce the unexplained variations in outcomes, to construct much tighter models of the school as a social system than those of contemporary sociological theories of school organization. Indeed, the search for the effective school appears to reinforce in practice the unidimensionality of such constructions, notably in the recommendations of the Rutter group for the tight ship approach to school management (1979:186–94).

The search for less-apparent sources of structuring beneath the surface of empirical data also characterizes the theorists of models of social reproduction. Here the attention is guided, not by some predictive model that links theoretically opaque but quantifiable processes to a desired effect, not by any hypothesized interdependence among such variables as organizational goals, instructional methods and administrative arrangements, but rather it is guided by the invisible positioning effects of ideology which systematically maintains a particular construction of the teaching and learning process (Bernstein 1982). In this instance any apparent looseness of the system, whether in pockets of autonomy at the lower level of the hierarchy, or in the absence of causal interdependence among abstracted indices of context, structure and outcomes, may eventually be interpreted as a covert form of class domination rather than as a functionally significant strategy.

The ritual classifications that seem to allow for the decoupling of activities and outcomes from formal controls (Meyer and Rowan 1983) could, for example, contain within them ideological messages that may facilitate the reproduction of class power in indirect and subtle ways.

Any review of the literature on school organization therefore will need to explain why both the prescriptive and critical approaches to school structure depend on rather tighter explanatory models than do conventional organizational theories. In order to clarify the paradoxes and difficulties associated with metaphors of loose coupling and organized anarchy, an attempt will therefore be made to provide the grounds for discovering theoretical affinities within what have been rather disparate and often contending approaches to the school as an organization. First of all, the organizational and administrative literature offers a rich source of empirical inquiry into schools and it will be used to trace the changing interpretations of the Weberian approach up to the point of its rejection. Secondly, an attempt will be made to underscore the inadequacies of the post-Weberian model by pointing to the contributions that have been made to an understanding of school structures by the *verstehende* and interactionist stream of Weberian sociology. Finally, the review will return to consider the points of contact between these two so-called normative and interpretive approaches (Karabel and Halsey 1977) and from there, the possible grounds for their synthesis in some of the recent structuralist and neo-Durkheimian treatments of the school as an institution.

## The school as a complex organization

Much of the organizational literature on the school appears to aim to demonstrate the negative case. Although it is granted that the coordination and administration apparatus of schools has many features of the bureaucratic ideal-type, it is agreed by most analysts that the more interesting aspects of the social structure of schools elude such a construct. Public or state schools appear moreover to be relieved from many of the more routine functions and activities by virtue of their being administered by larger units that are in the main responsible for the negotiation of salary levels, the certification and recruitment of staff, the maintenance of plant and the procurement of resources. These are usually a far remove from the instructional activity of the school and so appear not to be of great day to day interest to teachers (Lortie 1969:35–6; Hanson 1976, 1977:31). The attractiveness of explanations of school structure that begin with the task of instruction (as characterized by the contingency model reviewed below) rather than with administrative systems and public accountability is therefore understandable. However, even this model has been rejected by many sociological and administrative theorists recently because of its poor predictive and explanatory power. The tendency to debunk any hyper-rational model of organization (Wise 1979) has led to some exciting but not yet fully realized insights into the unique features of school structure.

### The bureaucratic model

Most of the empirical study of organization that has employed the Weberian ideal-type as an instrument of comparative analysis has indicated that bureaucracy should be conceived as a number of independently varying dimensions rather than as a unitary construct. Schools appear to be no exception to this pattern, despite the relative paucity of empirical study. Although Bidwell could claim in fact as late as 1965 that there was 'no existing study of the prevalence or incidence either of bureaucratic structures or processes in school systems' (p. 992) there have been a number of studies that are of interest. These inquiries owe a good deal to the theoretical and empirical contributions of Corwin (1968, 1970, 1975, 1981), who has done much to synthesize the administrative and the sociological perspective in the study of the school as a bureaucracy. The dominant theme of Corwin's – and of other researchers' – inquiries into bureaucratic/professional conflict at the school level has been to explore some of the insights of the Parsonian theory of organization which locates a central tension in the Weberian model between the normative demands of hierarchy and of expertise (Parsons 1947, 1956).

There are two fairly distinct methodological traditions in the study of bureaucracy and these are well represented in the research on schools. The first is the perceptual approach associated with Hall's Organizational Inventory (Hall 1963). The second is the Aston approach, which uses more descriptive, less subjective data (Pugh *et al.* 1968). Despite their differences, each provides data to challenge the earlier postwar research that assumed bureaucracy is a unitary type, either present or absent (Gouldner 1954). Each of these methodologies attempts to capture a similar set of bureaucratic characteristics (centralization of decision-making, functional specialization, procedural specification). The Hall approach relies on the responses of subordinates (teachers) to a range of perceptual items scored as a Likert-type scale (e.g. the division of labor item is: 'One thing people like around here is the variety of work'). The Aston strategy on the other hand is to obtain detailed descriptive data from a lengthy interview with the chief executive (usually the principal or headteacher). Here each aspect or dimension is measured by the presence or absence within the organization of various types of functions, documentary controls and standardized procedures and by an indication of the location in the hierarchy where a set of decisions are taken.

Empirical research supports the claim that there are two axial principles of school organization, irrespective of the methodology employed or of the tension between them. The first adaptations of the Hall Organizational Inventory to schools were carried out in Canada (MacKay 1964a, 1964b; Robinson 1966; McKague 1969). These showed that the dimensions of bureaucratic control (hierarchy of authority, presence of rules and procedural specification, and impersonality) tended to be positively intercorrelated among themselves but correlated negatively with measures of complexity (technical expertise and division of labor). Punch (1969), also using the Hall methodology, isolated two distinct factors (authority and expertise) in a sample of Canadian schools. In the United States, Hage and Aiken (1970) employed the Hall inventory as part of a wider comparative inquiry into the hypothesized effect of bureaucratic control on rates of change in several types of organization, while J. G. Anderson (1966, 1968) also carried out extensive research into innovation at the school level. Later B. D. Anderson (1973) used a modification of MacKay's scale in a sample of Canadian high schools as part of an investigation into the effects of bureaucracy on student alienation, although the factorial pattern he discerned was somewhat different from that obtained in the earlier studies.

Using a version of the Aston schedule, Kelsey (1973) undertook a comparative study of secondary schools in England and in Canada but was apparently limited in his analysis by the narrow definition of specialization in the original schedule. Heward (1975) also used a version of the Aston schedule in an inquiry into the organizational background to innovation in sample English primary and secondary schools. She found – in common with many of the replications of the original Aston study (Pugh and Hinings 1976) – that centralization was negatively related to nearly all of the main measures of bureaucratic structure. Sousa and Hoy (1981) used both methodologies in a study of fifty-two secondary schools in the United States. Their findings indicate a high degree of correlation between the two sets of measures, although the low relationship between hierarchy of authority (Hall inventory) and centralization (Aston schedule) indicates that they 'clearly were not measuring the same thing' (1981:34). These researches then carried out a principal-components analysis which yielded four factors whose interpretation was relatively straightforward: organizational control, rational specialization (accounting together for about a half of the total variance in the two sets of measures), system centralization, and formalization of routine.

The multidimensionality of measures of organizational structure in schools appears therefore to provide some support for the theoretical tradition that has attempted to modify the Weberian ideal-type in the direction suggested by Parsons, whether for professional organizations in general (e.g. Litwak 1961) or for schools in particular (Katz 1964; Bidwell 1965; Corwin 1974; Lortie 1969, 1975). Hanson (1975, 1976–77) has reformulated the bureaucratic model to take account of some of these complexities embodied in what he calls 'Lortie's tangle' – the 'several strands of hierarchical control, collegial control and autonomy' (Lortie, 1969:1). Hanson sets out a conceptual framework (the Interacting Spheres Model), which delineates two zones of influence, authority and power that interact in a fragile and delicate balance. Because of this separation, the bureaucratic model taken by itself is held to 'range from weak to inadequate as a conceptual tool in the affairs of management and analysis' (1976–1977:37). One may perhaps extend this distinction upwards as is suggested by Sousa and Hoy's factorial separation of the control apparatus within the school from the overall degree of centralization in the surrounding system. In their analysis it appeared that the loci of power 'can be high within the school building or high within the educational system or high or low within both' (1981:36).

There seems to be some disagreement, however, within these analyses as to the source of the principle of separation between the two spheres of influence – power or authority. Does it lie in the collegiate norms and values of the teaching profession, in the physical separation of the teacher's workspace, or in the internal elaboration of the school system as it grows? The first of these explanations is stressed by Hanson. Limited as their sphere of influence may be, teachers do have a 'degree of autonomy surrounding the conduct of affairs in the classroom, as well as the discretion to make curricular decisions within well-defined limits' (1976:37). This is one of the main sources of the tendency towards debureaucratization attributed to schools by Bidwell (1965:1012) – a normative strain between the nurturant ideology of teachers and universalistic demands of the administrative system, in addition to the more familiar source of conflict noted by Parsons (1947). In contrast with this, one could advance the contingency explanations of school organization that would follow Lortie (1964:274) in treating the physical separation of the teacher's workspace (sometimes referred to as the egg-crate model of the school) as one of the most important determinants of intraschool variation.

One cannot however rule out a third possibility, based on research into school systems, that suggests a more cautious, evolutionary explanation of the emergence of a loosely coupled professional subsystem. A study of educational innovations in school systems by Daft and Becker (1978: 144) indicates that organizational complexity, the seedbed of later professional activity, is itself a 'consequence not a cause' of innovations originating in the administrative system. These researchers propose a dual core model of innovation that would indicate that the association found among professional activity, high complexity, and low centralization in many of the studies of bureaucratic structure reviewed above may be spurious and limited only to an emergent technical core that is loosely coupled both internally and externally to the administrative system. Conversely, structural innovation is most successful 'when the technical core is tightly coupled to the administrative core and when authority is centralized with administrators' (Daft 1978:208). Such a conclusion would indicate that the reported multidimensionality of organizational structure could be an artefact of the level of analysis chosen (i.e. schools instead of their parent systems) and of the research design (cross-sectional rather than longitudinal). Certainly, this developmental model would give another perspective on the rather disparate and often curvilinear relationships between bureaucratization and other variables such as teacher satisfaction (Moeller and Charters 1966; Musgrove 1970:104; Allison 1983:25) and level of innovation (Corwin 1975:25).

### The contingency model of school organization

Of the three possible explanations of the bifurcated nature of authority in schools, the one which lends itself most readily to a rigorous testing by survey methods is the contingency model, which posits a close interdependence between the task environment and patterns of administration and governance. This model has implications for the other two as well. If, in the first instance, collegiality is nothing more than a collective response to the fairly routine demands of a craft technology, then it would appear to be a rather shaky basis for claims towards professional autonomy. In the second place, the high importance that contingency theorists place on the structural imperatives arising from the task may enable the analyst to specify rather more precisely where the motor of organizational change resides; it could thereby provide an empirically testable set of causal propositions as to organizational growth and differentiation.

The contingency model, which has its origins within a technical-functionalist theory of the firm, has enjoyed a wide and continuing following in the comparative study of organizations (Lawrence and Lorsch 1967:185–210; Perrow 1972:50–91; 1973:145–76) and can be seen as a concurrent development to the multidimensional interpretation of the Weberian ideal-type. It proposes that organizational features are best explained as functional responses to the uncertainty, variability and interconnectedness of the task environment, which is often constituted as a function of organizational size.

When this environment is stable and predictable, something like the classical bureaucratic type is most appropriate (particularly for a large concern); but when the raw material that people work with is poorly understood and variable, then a more effective strategy is to delegate authority to specialists and to coordinate activities through flatter and more participatory administrative systems.

In the secondary school field the contingency approach has been used both as a theoretical foundation for programs of organizational development and innovation (Fullan 1982; Moon 1983) and as an analytical model for explaining administrative adaptation (Derr and Gabarro 1972; Tyler 1973, Hanson and Brown 1977). Researchers and commentators have consistently stressed the advantages of participatory collaborative structures, particularly in the technical core, as a response to the increased diversity of intake and the rapidity of curricular change. At the higher levels of school management, however, the case for implementing such strategies is less categorical, and the patterns of organizational change appear to be more indirect and gradual. Richardson's (1973) detailed case study of a large English comprehensive school over a period of several years, inspired by a sociotechnical systems model (which shares many features of the contingency approach but is somewhat less deterministic), provides a rich source of evidence for this more complex view of administrative response to school-wide changes in the technical core. The headteacher in this school appeared able to incorporate a participatory and consultative form of management within a strictly differentiated and hierarchical structure. This strategy indirectly reinforced the lines of command yet at the same time rendered them more responsive and supple. Such an account resonates with Perrow's hypothetical example (1972:73–4) of the process by which a traditional bureaucratic public school accepted a major innovation in the form of a new instructional unit, thereby preserving its overall stability and continuity.

If applications of the contingency model to the secondary school have tended to be partial, fragmentary and ambiguous, the same does not hold for the research in the primary or elementary school, where applications have been rigorous, sustained, and theoretically aware. This is so not only at the classroom level (Bossert 1979; Cohen *et al.* 1979a) but also by extension at the organizational level, largely as a result of the introduction of more informal, integrated, and pedagogically sophisticated methods associated with team teaching and the open-space classroom. The most important research in this area was carried out during the 1970s by US federal educational research and development centers at Stanford University (Meyer *et al.* 1971; Bredo 1975, 1977; Cohen *et al.* 1979b, 1981) and at the University of Oregon (Pellegrin 1970; Packard *et al.* 1978; Charters and Packard 1979). These research groups both explored and tested some of the fundamental propositions of the contingency model in large samples of elementary schools over a number of years. The research design enabled these groups to determine the extent to which changes in instructional technology (teaming and open space) affected patterns of task structure (interdependence and collaboration) as well as the more general features of school administration (the degree of collegial influence, principal's style of supervision).

Although it is not possible to do justice here to the large volume of materials produced by these interrelated projects, it may be fair to say that the contingency model has met here with only patchy and qualified support. The studies each fall into two parts: the first cross-sectional surveys, which indicated that many of the hypothesized effects did take place following teaming; and the second, more painstaking and cautious longitudinal follow-up studies which showed just how fragile and impermanent instructional innovation in school can be and how indeterminate its measurable effects. Not only did it appear that 'instructional interdependence tends to be transitory, emerging and disappearing in the course of school year' (Cohen 1981:172), but the content of team decisions did not accord with the high uncertainty/problem-solving orientation of the model; decisions were concerned largely with routine and mechanistic functions such as cross-grouping (Bredo 1975). Regression analyses of structural ('work and governance') variables on the more technological ones, showed rather low levels of prediction, with explained variance ranging between twenty and fifty per cent (Charters and Packard 1979:43, Table 2). It would appear from these and associated studies that consistent and predictable changes in the organizational structure of elementary schools do not occur unless there is a high degree of teacher interdependence over a number of different task areas – an effect which appears to be reinforced by the increased visibility afforded by open space architecture

### The school as a loosely coupled system

In the light of these findings it is perhaps no surprise that many researchers who were associated with contingency and Weberian models should in the 1970s have been attracted to alternative perspectives on school organization, particularly to those that provide a less determinate and rationalized picture of the school as a social system. Reviving some of Bidwell's insights into the endemic looseness of coordinative processes in school, several theorists have attempted to reconceptualize educational organization in terms more in keeping with ambiguity of goals and uncertainty of technology than with models borrowed from the study of commercial and business enterprises. There have been several varieties of this post-Weberian approach, all deceptively similar and cross-fertilizing, but in many respects epistemologically and theoretically diverse.

The first alternative to Weberian approaches to be proposed was the so-called garbage can/organized anarchy model of Cohen *et al.* (1972), developed for colleges and universities but considered by many to be applicable to schools (Bell 1980:187; Allison 1983: 17–18). In fact the term 'loose coupling' was used in this context and later extended by Weick in the seminal paper cited above as a general metaphor for research into all forms of educational organizations (1976). In this paper the concepts of rational planning and hierarchical control were rejected in favour of a model that stressed the loose connections between stable subassemblies, which Weick considers to be 'the crucial elements in any organization or system' but which maintain their own identity at all times (1976:3). Meyer and Rowan (1983) have made a further contribution by using the term 'decoupling' to imply not merely the empirical responsiveness of these subassemblies to one another, but the disconnections in the theoretically-constituted elements of goals, technology, and organization – 'Loose coupling implies a disconnection of bureaucratic structure from technical activity and of this activity from its effects' (Meyer and Rowan 1983:71). The forces of cohesion in educational systems in this approach are not internal but external, deriving from their collective effort to manage the 'societally agreed-on rites defined in societal myths (or institutional rules) of education' (p. 76). Tight coupling exists only at the level of control over the ritual classifications, which are so important for legitimation processes in the schooled corporate society.

This rather rapid transition from contingency and functionalist theories of the school to revisionist or conflict interpretations thus exposes by implication many of the problems of the model of the school as a loosely coupled system. Although there have been some studies inspired directly or indirectly by this model (Abramowitz and Tenenbaum 1978; Hannaway and Sproull 1979; Bell 1979, 1980; Rowan 1982), it seems to have generated a good deal of confusion and is perhaps responsible to a large extent for the amorphous state of theorizing in this area. The central theoretical problem is the status of the events, units, or subassemblies that are loosely coupled. If Weick wishes to 'convey the image that each loosely coupled event preserves its own identity and some evidence of its physical and logical separateness' (1976:3), then it must be asked, according to what criteria (e.g. power, authority or expertise) is any identity to be constituted? Does the physical separateness of the buildings of a split-site school always provide a given basis for some kind of dual identity, or is it a mere administrative detail? Is the 'logical' basis of separation between subject departments to be found in the formal structure of the official statements or in the 'logic of confidence' invested in academic disciplines by public attitudes and beliefs (Meyer and Rowan, 1983:90–2).

So many difficulties arise in applying this model that it appears to be both vacuous and confusing. Neverthless, it is instructive to unravel some of the problems it raises in order to see a way ahead. Three main sources of ambiguity can be discerned in the loose-coupling literature. It will be argued that these can only be understood in terms of the functionalist theories of the school and the unresolved problems rooted in the legacy from the contingency model.

1. What kinds of environments promote loose coupling? Although the

review of the innovation literature suggests that loose coupling occurs most often in the professionalized technical core of this school and would therefore be typical of the rapidly changing, even turbulent environment, Weick in a more recent paper (1980) has argued that this view is mistaken and that it is a strategy more characteristic of environments with low variability and high homogeneity. This would contrast loose coupling, as Willower (1982:94) has pointed out, with the type of environmental contexts for which the organized–anarchy model was developed, characterized by their extreme fluidity and intractability. In the terms of the sociotechnical typology of Emery and Trist (1965) in which environments are classified by their 'causal textures', one might ask whether loose coupling is promoted by the placid, randomized environment or by the more unpredictable disturbed–reactive type. This confusion permeates the literature. While some theorists of school organization have pointed out the advantages of loose coupling as a strategy for turbulent conditions (Turner 1977; Bell 1980), others such as Meyer and Rowan have stressed its advantages for maintaining stable and institutional-ized relations in the sociopolitical environment. This ambiguity is probably more acute because loose coupling theorists tend to ignore or dismiss the sociotechnical and functionalist framework.

2.  Does a decentralist strategy imply loose or tight coupling? Just as the question of environmental strategy brings with it difficulties, so does the classification of the internal interdependencies of the school system by the loosely coupled model. Weick's recent paper is consistent in that it considers discretion and decentralization as more typical of a tightly coupled system – as a more sophisticated organizational response demanded by greater uncertainty – but there are still problems in identifying the incidence of such tightness in the internal life of schools. If one were to follow the low-variability/low discretion/loose-coupling causal sequence, then it would appear that the authoritarian, formalized regimes typical of the one-room schools of yesteryear are in fact more loosely coupled than the open space, informal elementary schools of today. This may be so in terms of a more general model of regulation, but it is a difficult argument to sustain within a perspective that is attempting to revise if not demolish conceptions of rationality and efficiency associated with the classical bureau-cratic model.

3.  What role do values play in a loosely coupled system? When one replaces a technical-rational model of school organization with one some-what more amorphous, there is a strong possibility, following the four-function paradigm of Parsons, that societal values will become a more salient feature of subsequent functionalist explanations. Despite the full elaboration of this paradigm by Hills for public schools (1976), there still remains the difficulty within the Parsonian theory of organization of constructing a model that asserts the primacy of values (in the societal sense) over the more precisely defined, externally referenced functions that pertain to the mana-gerial, the technical, and the institutional spheres. This difficulty fails to arise

not because, as Willower (1982:93) claims, loose coupling (which refers to internal and not external relations) is a logical consequence of such functional differentiation, but rather because societal values seem to have very tenuous causal links with empirical variations in school structure. It is perhaps more useful, therefore, as Dreeben (1976:871) argues, to begin with the organiza-tional activities scheme rather than with the values-goals-functions scheme (though both are to be found in Parsons' writings on organizations); it is within these areas that most of the problematics of the distribution of authority reside. However, when the role of societal values is downgraded into the maintenance of consensually derived norms of performance and mechanisms of public accountability, it has the paradoxical consequence of producing an explanation of school structure very similar to that found in revisionist literature. From a Parsonian perspective, Dreeben sees the mechanisms of administrative control in schools in much the same terms as Meyer and Rowan. He argues that control is exercised through quasi-feudal administrative structures whose zones of authority and interest are defined in terms of administrative task, rather than by the normative elements that one might infer from a societal function such as pattern maintenance.

The rather bizarre uses by conflict theorists of the symbolic apparatus of mechanical solidarity (ritual, ceremony, myth) may therefore be explained to some extent by the normative vacuum created when functionalist theorists failed to bridge the gap between societal values on the one hand and the primitive segmentations of task and interest on the other. The Durkheimian affinity between the quasi-feudal units of school structure and the ritual classifications of certification and performance implies a pre- rather than a post-bureaucratic model of the school. Such a marriage of structure and symbol seems nevertheless to have little to do either with the models of the innovative organization that found such currency in the 1960s, with the classical statements of the school as an agent of moral regulation (Durkheim 1977), or as a central institution in a society dominated by legal-rational modes of authority (Weber 1946:240–4). Since this stream of organizational literature has led to what seems to be a theoretical impasse, it may be well to view the school not as a set of causally related functions, but rather as an emergent property of the interests, interpretations, and face-to-face interactions of its members.

### The interactive order and school organization

The conception of the school as a site where individuals and groups interact rather than as an externally defined system of functions and activities does not necessarily detract from a sociological interest in its organizational forms. The ideographic, interactionist, and phenomenological accounts of school organization have been given forceful support in recent organizational literature (Greenfield 1975, 1980). These approaches attempt to demonstrate that, far from being a collection of segmented functions, schools are problematic and tension-ridden formations whose structural variations are best explained through the meanings, negotiations and strategies of individual actors. The school, in other words, can be conceived not as a given structure but as a product of the collective and often implicit accommodations among teachers, students and administrators (as well as of parents, supervisory personnel, and ancillary staff). This structure is far from being rock-solid. Indeed, it is a rather precarious arrangement where negotiated rules and not collective rituals are the stuff of everyday social encounter and where the relationship between actions and their effects is only infrequently ambiguous or unclear from the perspective of students or teachers themselves.

It is possible in this approach to recapture the interpretative traditions so important to the Weberian perspective on organizations (King 1980). In so doing one can discover a normative system that has proven not only to be remarkably resilient but to have itself undergone some profound transformations in its patterns of involvement, communication, and control. Many of these more fundamental changes often elude the more episodic and situational type of analysis offered by an interactionist perspective and are enriched by some of the attempts at synthesis with the macro concerns of classical sociology (as discussed in the following section). The central question here however is to review recent research into the nature of the interdependence of the everyday experience of students and teachers on the one hand and the formal structures in which they find themselves on the other. Are these links, as Goffman suggests, also loosely coupled, or can one detect some greater degree of determinacy here than in the case of organizational components themselves? What is the nature of the relationship between the formal structure of the school and the motives, strategies and actions of everyday life for teachers and students?

The dominant feature of interactionist approaches to school organization appears to be the discovery of the conflict between teachers and students; thereby they trace the roots of institutional power to the competing interests of these two groups. In Waller's important and original contribution to the sociology of school organization, mutual hostility and perpetual conflict characterize the relations between students and staff. Even the most orderly school is 'a despotism in a state of perilous equilibrium' (1932:10). Bidwell claims that the matrix of forces acting on the administrative system is such as to reinforce the repressive character of the classroom and to push the social system of the school in the direction of what Gouldner (1954) calls a punishment-centered (rather than a representative) bureaucracy (1965:980). Bidwell locates Gordon's participant observation of a high school (1957) in this tradition, particularly for his evidence of classroom conflict deriving from the incompatibilities between the teacher's academic demands and those of the student culture. One way out of this dilemma for Gordon's teachers (which Bidwell sees as having the ultimate effect of debureaucratizing the authority structure of the school) was to allocate grades in order to disrupt the social structure of the student group and then to step in with affective support when students began to conform. The bureaucratic struc-ture of the school seems therefore to be often no more than a shell in which a variety of ploys and stratagems for getting by are enacted.

Substantively, very little seems to have changed in schools since these early studies. The research of Woods (1979) within an interactionist perspec-tive is of particular interest since it explores, in an English secondary modern school in the early 1970s, a model of student adaptation developed by Wakeford (1969) which incorporates elements both from Merton's (1957) functionalist theory of deviance and from Goffman's typology of inmate strategies in *Asylums* (1961). Student subcultures are seen by Woods to be neither pro nor anti school in the simple terms suggested by a good deal of this literature (e.g. Hargreaves, 1967) but rather in terms of their strategic adaptations to the educational bureaucracy, Woods (1979:18–19) identifies two primary paths to conformity – 'instrumental compliance' and 'ritualism'; there is another which he characterizes as a form of 'secondary adjustment' typical of the nonacademic student. This is colonization, a term indirectly taken from Goffman's work on total institutions, which means 'working the system' and 'getting by'. Here there is a parallel with the Waller–Gordon tradition; in order for control to be exercised at all, many of the bureaucratic strictures have to be removed or negotiated into an operable form. The same capacity to devise strategies of coping also characterizes the teacher perspec-tive in Woods' study. Following Becker's study of the Chicago schoolteacher in the early 1950s (1976), Woods sets out a range of possible survival strategies, only one of which comes anywhere near an officially approved definition of the teacher's role (1979:146–69).

Are school routines and procedures to be understood as instruments of collective control and domination (cf. Waller 1932:312), or do they have some consensual basis? According to Cusick, who carried out with his associates a number of remarkable participant-observer investigations into the student perspective in high schools in the United States (Cusick 1973; Cusick *et al.* 1976), the formal structure of the school merely provides a loose structure for the containment and minimal instruction of a student body divided along the lines of race, class and gender. Confronted with what is essentially a holding operation, administrators divide and rule. In the school studied by Cusick, a very repressive structure denied students any real power by absorbing much time in routine activities and waiting about in groups. From this perspective, conflict is managed not so much through direct hierarchical control and punishment or through collective rituals (as in Waller's schools) but rather by administrative strategies of suppression and fragmentation. The complexities, intentional or not, of these global methods of control provide some context for understanding the debureaucratizing strategies of teachers and the colonization of the system by disaffected groups of pupils.

Against the organizational model which stresses the softness of the schools' technology, its imprecision of goals and looseness of administrative mechanisms, one could in the light of this conflict-interactionist approach discern a quite determinate model, where the room for structural variation is strictly constrained by the 'perilous equilibrium' of control. Such a model does not need to be a coercive despotism, however, but can be maintained by a variety of implicit and calculative forms that have considerably greater refinement and flexibility. One such mechanism is explored by King and Ripton (1970) in a study of what they call 'collective reciprocity'. True to the interactionist tradition, these researchers questioned the consensual view of school organization and suggested instead a dynamic model of control based on a kind of contract emerging out of 'the near congruency between teachers' career needs and the students' conception of education as an instrumental process' (p. 46). The dynamic of collective reciprocity in this study of Canadian high schools in the late 1960s bears a remarkable similarity to the 'primary mode' of adaptation identified by Woods; it could be usefully complemented by the latter's expansion of the interactionist model to the lower-ability groups. Another mechanism for the containment of conflict has been identified by Reynolds (1976) in the idea of 'the truce' between teachers and pupils. This implies that if teachers will not try to interfere in the expressive domain (e.g. by enforcing rules about smoking, uniforms and chewing gum) then pupils are likely to be more cooperative in the classroom, with apparently desirable effects on the school overall rates of delinquency, truancy, academic failure and behavior.

It is, however, difficult to put forward a model of conflict and the strategies for its containment and dispersal in schools without taking into account the rich or even dense network of rules through which this is mediated. The systemic or even consensual aspects of the modalities of control are perhaps as important as its substantive realization in any one school. One of the consensual aspects appears to be the acute awareness of students of principles of fair play and of rule violation that do not apparently arise out of specific negotiations or contexts. Werthman's 1963 study of delinquent boys shows that even among a deviant group, evaluation procedures are rigorously scrutinized and that any signs of bias were met with disruptive behavior. However much Woods' students appeared to dislike schools, they appeared to operate according to their own core of institutional norms, which were constant across classrooms (1979:111). A study of 'trouble' in an English comprehensive school by Marsh *et al.* (1978) identified a number of teacher offences deserving of retribution; the most unforgivable was when a 'soft' teacher unsuccessfully tried to assert authority (1978:38). The phenomenological study of deviance in classrooms carried out by Hargreaves *et al.* (1975) called into question the centrality of 'role' in the interactionist and conflict framework by showing the fundamental importance of the rule system by which teachers and pupils establish order through the construction of normal behavior. At this deeper level, notwithstanding the individual and collective strategies of accommodation and of conflict resolution, one could argue that the interactive sphere is not entirely at odds with the universalistic norms of the formal bureaucratic framework, but rather it shares the same stock of taken-for-granted knowledge.

It is noteworthy that the problem of classroom order should re-emerge from a tradition that initially was obsessed with strategies of control. That the functionalist concern with boundary, order and normative consensus should emerge from the study of the minute details of rule-maintenance may not, however, be so surprising. When an action theorist takes an interest in rules-in-use, it almost inevitably leads to consideration of the consensual basis of commonsense knowledge in institutions, and it may even suggest that teachers and pupils experience these rules as social facts in the Durkheimian sense. Indeed, Hargreaves (1979) argues that many of Durkheim's ideas on order in schools have been misunderstood by the labelling theorists who have taken a naive and superficial antifunctionalist interpretation of the notion of social pathology. In his view, egoism and anomie, if applied strictly in the Durkheimian sense, 'prove to be rather unconvincing explanations of school counter-cultures or teacher-designated deviants, but are more persuasive in relation to "indifferent" or "instrumentalist" pupil types'. In other words, the 'typical' or 'primary' forms of adaptation are those most pathological or unhealthy, while the counter-school groups such as Willis' 'lads' (1977) are by no means the true deviants. Hargreaves' applications of a Durkheimian perspective resonate with Testanière's (1968, 1972) distinction between 'traditional' and 'anomic' forms of misbehavior in French secondary schools. It would seem that sociological explanations of particular instances of disruption must sooner or later come to terms with such transformations of the moral order in schools and the dislocations that these generate in the apparatus of control.

The re-emergence of interest in frameworks of internal cohesion more general than those created and sustained in particular encounters does not of course resolve the very vague question as to how loosely coupled the formal and the interactive orders of the school may be. However, it does suggest that the strength of any link may itself be indicative of a particular stage of institutional evolution and may be inaccessible by purely interpretative methodologies. This leads us then to consider the final and most ambitious theoretical project in the sociology of school organization – the attempt to provide a framework which synthesizes the organizational and the interactionist perspectives on the school. Although the problem of synthesis is a general one, the most notable attempt to resolve it in the sociology of the school has been that of Bernstein. In recent years also, some of the followers of Foucault's theory of discourses have attempted a very similar task – to locate the hidden regulative principles of institutional transformation in terms which embrace both objectivity and subjectivity, power as well as knowledge. It will be of some interest therefore to review these two projects briefly and to suggest points of contact between them.

## Towards synthesis: Bernstein and Foucault

One of the underlying themes of this review has been that partial insights generated by organizational models and by interactionist approaches have each proven unsatisfactory as general sociological explanations of school structure. In the first instance, the recent emphasis of the first tradition on the role of ritualized and prebureaucratic elements of formal control is inadequate to deal with the dense and sophisticated, rule-based systems of regulation found in the internal life of the school. In the second place, the interactionist perspective has proven to lack a sociohistorical dimension that might explain the normative transformations of school life and the cultural shifts that affect the methodologies of investigation themselves; neither of these are directly available to the consciousness of individual actors. How can these two traditions be combined to provide an understanding in greater depth of the formal patterns of control and authority in educational institutions?

Bernstein's attempt to synthesize these two levels of analysis is based on a theory of communication that ultimately stems from the Durkheimian opposition between mechanical and organic solidarity (1977). This opposition has been developed over the past two decades in the form of several polarities of school types (stratified/differentiated; open/closed) or of the dominant principles of moral regulation (collection code/integrated code). As a normative or moral response (and not a primarily adaptive one, as a Parsonian theorist might claim) to changes in the division of labor, there has been a significant shift in the modalities of control that characterize the socialization process in late capitalist societies – away from visible and hierarchical forms towards invisible, indirect and personalized forms. However, because they represent a form of privilege associated with access to the institutions of cultural innovation and reproduction that tend to flourish in mature and late capitalist societies, these more ostensibly open and less coercive modalities are just as likely to be the instrument of class repetition and of cultural domination as were the older individualized forms of rationality that gave a cultural advantage to the propertied classes in earlier phases of capitalism.

It is not the intention here to give a detailed critique of this complex and evolving framework (see Cherkaoui 1977; Gibson 1977), which owes as much to Weber as it does to Durkheim, but rather to evaluate its uses as an instrument of institutional analysis. The main advantage of Bernstein's theory of school structure is that it liberates the Durkheimian framework from a fixation with function, consensus and solidarity and focuses instead on the formal features or modalities through which power and control (roughly 'classification' and 'framing' respectively) are realized. It is therefore entirely compatible with a conflictual and interactionist perspective (indeed, the Meadian framework is embodied in the differentiation of role options available in the more evolved structures) and leads to a critical awareness of the regulative properties of communication in which research traditions themselves are located.

Although the potential of this synthetic theory is enormous for providing unique insights into the deritualization of the culture of the schools and
into the bonds between the formal and the interactive order, its empirical
validation has been fraught with some difficulty. King carried out a number
of empirical tests (1976, 1981) of Bernstein's framework in a sample of
secondary schools in the southwest of England and concluded that his results
gave 'only limited support for some of the propositions of Bernstein's
sociology of the school' (1976:439). More recently, Tyler (1983) has argued
that King's conclusions are premature, because the methodology employed
(versions of the Aston schedule) was probably affected by the way the
probabilistic features of the principle of coding necessarily intrude into the
empirically observable patterns of association among scale items and dimensions of organizational structure. He recommends a canonical (or latent
variable) approach to the analysis of the association between indices of
classification and of framing. He demonstrates the power of this method to
reveal strong and significant indices of correlation in comparative samples of
work organizations. One might conclude therefore that a fair and adequate
test of Bernstein's theory on school organizations has yet to be carried out.

Foucault's concern has been with the nexus between power and knowledge in the form of what he calls 'the discourse' as it is worked out in the
changing technologies of practice in various institutional and disciplinary
domains including the school (Foucault 1977; see Sheridan 1980 for a review
of Foucault's work). A central feature of his method is to uncover the
regulative principles whereby behavior is defined and normalized through
microtechnologies of physical control. In the realm of school organization,
this method leads not to the role of pedagogy as a vehicle of class reproduction but to the techniques of surveillance and punishment that enable
institutional power to be made both diffuse and invisible. One of these
methods is embodied in the architectural arrangement, devised by the
English utilitarian philosopher Bentham, known as the Panopticon; it did not
find wide use in its original form yet embodied an important aspect of design
in prisons, schools, asylums, and factories. This building, consisting of a
number of insulated chambers around a central observation tower, had the
effect of inducing in the inmate 'a state of conscious and permanent visibility
that assures the permanent functioning of power' (Foucault 1977:201). The
theory of discourse that gives rise to such practices is at the same time both
specific and synthetic (in the terms of the orientations to school structure
presented in the earlier sections). Popular schooling in its discursive sense is
not simply an instrument of socialization nor an agent of class domination but
rather a set of practices which only in certain historical instances takes on
these meanings and functions. Although some authors (Musgrove 1970:
55–57; Wallace 1980:137) have commented on the panopticist features of
the open-space classroom, the fullest treatment of popular schooling
using Foucault's 'archeological' method to discover its discursive and non-
discursive properties and transformations is that of Jones and Williamson

(1979). From an analysis of early nineteenth-century English schooling, these authors argue that schooling existed as means of securing public morality and of preventing crime – a practical embodiment in its architecture and structure of the two disciplines of bodily discipline and of the regulation of population science that emerged at this time.

Atkinson (1981) draws some lines of intellectual lineage between Foucault's work and that of Bernstein by placing both in the tradition of French structuralism. This is an important insight elaborated by Diaz (1984) as part of a larger project on the nature of pedagogic discourse. This author concludes that Bernstein's work can be situated in a structuralist perspective because of his attempt to isolate the fundamental patterning (or 'grammar') of the power and control by which cultural reproduction is realized; it is however more difficult to place Foucault, whose analysis is less systematic in this sense. Power in Foucault's writings is not derived from macroforces such as state and class but is its own basis and can only be approached through microsituations (Diaz 1984:11).

One important point of comparison resides in the parallels one might draw between Foucault's claim that there has been an institutional shift from traditional forms of the exercise of power from visibility towards invisibility (as say in the Panopticon), and the transition from mechanical to organic solidarity where the institutional authority is itself invisible but the objects of power (e.g. the teachers and students in the open-space classrooms, researched in the team teaching studies reviewed above) are highly visible and continually supervised (Diaz 1984:17). There is a twist to this analogy that has not been adequately treated either by Diaz or by other commentators such as Musgrove, who in fact sees the open-space classroom as a threat to the power of assistant teachers. On the contrary, however, Bernstein's invisible pedagogy or integrated code (typical of the highly evolved form of organic solidarity) depends not on the hierarchical control of a principal or head-teacher but on the internalization of abstract principles of orientation and action by teachers and students themselves. The arrangement of the various elements of these two theoretical approaches – knowledge, power, control and subject – in such a discursive transformation has yet to be explicated.

### Conclusion

This review of attempts at theoretical synthesis would indicate an image of the school as a more tightly coupled system than organizational and administrative approaches now suggest. The way ahead for the sociological study of the school organization therefore appears to be through a cross-fertilization of the various approaches and perspectives discussed, rather than the dismissal or rejection of any one either because of its apparent abstruseness or its lack of theoretical sophistication.

Three major themes have now appeared that have to be common to all three sections on the sociology of school organization – (*a*) the competition, not always clearcut, between spheres of professional activity and bureaucratic authority; (*b*) the dialectic between externally produced societal constraints and internal processes of differentiation and sociotechnical change; and (*c*) the transformation of the regulative basis of order and control away from the condensed symbolic forms such as the ceremonies and visible hierarchies familiar to Waller (1932) into more indirect and invisible modalities of control and surveillance represented by such devices as the complex timetable, the unit for disruptive students, and the permissive course option scheme. Implicit in this review therefore is an agenda for future research into the school as a social system that could direct lines of inquiry along one or more of these axes of theoretical tension. Such a redirection might serve both to reverse the polarization of research perspectives that characterizes contemporary literature on the school and to enliven and revive the central concerns of the classical sociological tradition in the organization of social reproduction.

## References

Abramowitz, S., Tennenbaum, E. 1978. *High School '77*. Washington, DC: National Institute of Education.

Allison, D. J. 1983. Towards an improved understanding of the organizational nature of schools. *Educ. Admin. Q.* 19:7–34.

Anderson, B. D. 1973. School bureaucratization and alienation from high school. *Sociol. Educ.* 46:315–34.

Anderson, J. G. 1966. Bureaucratic rules: bearers of bureaucratic authority. *Educ. Admin. Q.* 2:7–34.

Anderson, J. G. 1968. *Bureaucracy in Education*. Baltimore: Johns Hopkins Univ. Press.

Archer, M. 1979. *Social Origins of Educational Systems*. London: Sage.

Atkinson, P. 1981. Bernstein's·structuralism. *Educ. Anal.* 3:85–95.

Becker, H. 1976. The career of the Chicago public schoolteacher. See Hammersley and Woods, 1976, pp. 68–74.

Bell, L. A. 1979. The planning of educational change in a comprehensive school. ·*Durham Newcastle Res. Rev.* 42:1–8.

Bell, L. A. 1980. The school as an organization: A reappraisal. *Brit. J. Sociol. Educ.* 1:183–9.

Bernstein, B. 1977. *Class, Codes and Control*, Vol. 3. *Towards a Theory of Educational Transmissions*. London: Routledge & Kegan Paul. 2nd edn.

Bernstein, B. 1982. Codes, modalities and the process of cultural reproduction: a model. In *Cultural and Economic Reproduction in Education: Essays on Class, Ideology and the State*, pp. 304–55. London: Routledge & Kegan Paul.

Bidwell, C. E. 1965. The school as a formal organization. In *Handbook of Organizations*, ed. J. G. March, pp. 972–1022. Chicago: Rand-McNally.

Bossert, S. T. 1979. *Tasks and Social Relationships in Classrooms*. Cambridge: Cambridge Univ. Press.

Bourdieu, P., Passeron, J. C. 1977. *Reproduction in Education, Society and Culture.* Transl. R. Nice. London: Sage (From French).

Bowles, S., Gintis, H. 1976. *Schooling in Capitalist America: Educational Reform and the Contradictions of Economic Life.* London: Routledge & Kegan Paul.

Boyd, W. L., Crowson, R. L. 1981. The changing conception and practice of public school administration. In *Review of Research in Education,* ed. C. Berliner, 9:311–73. Washington, DC: Am. Educ. Res. Assoc.

Bredo, E. 1975. Collaborative relationships on teaching problems: implications for collegial influence, team morale and instructional practices. *Stanford University, Calif. Technical Report No. 45.*

Bredo, E. 1977. Collaborative relationships among elementary school teachers. *Sociol. Educ.* 50:300–9.

Charters, W. W. Jr., Packard, J. S. 1979. *Task Interdependence, Collegial Governance and Teacher Attitudes in the Multiunit Elementary School.* Eugene, OR.: Center for Educational Policy and Management.

Cherkaoui, M. 1977. Bernstein and Durkheim: two theories of change in educational systems. *Harv. Educ. Rev.* 47:556–64.

Cohen, E. G., Intili, J. K., Robbins, S. H. 1979a. Tasks and authority: a sociological view of classroom management. In *Classroom Management: Seventy-eighth Yearbook of the National Society for the Study of Education,* ed. D. L. Duke, 2:116–43. Chicago: Univ. Chicago Press.

Cohen, E. G., Deal, T. E., Meyer, J. W., Scott, W. R. 1979b. Technology and teaming in the elementary school. *Sociology of Education* 52:20–33.

Cohen, E. G. 1981. Sociology looks at team teaching. See Kerckhoff and Corwin, 1981, pp. 116–43.

Cohen, M. D., March, J. G. and Olsen, J. P. 1972. A garbage can model of organizational choice. *Admin. Sci. Q.* 17:1–25.

Coleman, J. S. 1966. *Equality of Educational Opportunity.* Washington, DC: US Dept. HEW.

Corwin, R. G. 1968. Education and the sociology of complex organization. In *On Education – Sociological Perspectives,* ed. D. A. Hansen, J. E. Gerstl, pp. 156–223. New York: Wiley.

Corwin, R. G. 1970. *Militant Professionalism: a Study of Organizational Conflict in High Schools.* New York: Appleton-Century-Crofts.

Corwin, R. G. 1974. Models of educational organization. In *Review of Research in Education,* ed. F. N. Kerlinger, J. B. Carroll, 2:274–95. Itasca, Ill.: Peacock.

Corwin, R. G. 1975. Innovation in organizations: the case of schools. *Sociol. Educ.* 48:1–37.

Corwin, R. G. 1981. Patterns of control and teacher militancy: theoretical continuities in the idea of 'loose coupling'. See Kerckhoff and Corwin, 1981, pp. 261–91.

Cusick, P. A. 1973. *Inside High School.* New York: Holt.

Cusick, P. A., Martin, W., Palonsky, S. 1976. Organizational structure and student behavior in secondary school. *J. Curr. Stud.* 8:3–14.

Cuttance, P. F. 1981. Post hoc rides again: a methodological critique of 'Fifteen Thousand Hours: Secondary Schools and their Effects on Children'. *Qual. and Quant.* 15:315–34.

Daft, R., Becker, S. W. 1978, *The Innovative Organization: Innovation Adoption in School Organization.* New York: Elsevier.

Daft, R. 1978. A dual-core model of organizational innovation. *Acad. Mgmt. J.* 21:193–210.

Davies, B. 1973. Organizational analysis of eductional institutions. In *Knowledge, Education and Cultural Change*, ed. R. Brown, pp. 249–95. London: Tavistock.

Davies, B. 1981. Schools as organizations and the organization of schooling. *Educ. Anal.* 3:47–67.

Derr, C. B., Gabarro, J. J. 1972. An organizational contingency theory for education. *Educ. Admin. Quart.* 8:26–43.

Diaz, M. 1984. On pedagogical discourse: Bernstein and Foucault. Unpublished manuscript, Univ. of London Inst. of Educ.

Dreeben, R. 1973. The school as a workplace. In *Second Handbook of Research Teaching*, ed. R. Travers, pp. 450–73. Chicago: Rand-McNally.

Dreeben, R. 1976. The organizational structure of schools and school systems. See Loubser *et al.*, 1976, 2:857–73.

Durkheim, E. 1977. *The Evolution of Educational Thought*. Transl. P. Collins, London: Routledge & Kegan Paul (from French).

Emery, F. E., Trist, E. L. 1965. The causal texture of organizational environments. *Human Relations*. 18:21–32.

Foucault, M. 1977. *Discipline and Punish: the Birth of the Prison*. Transl. A. Sheridan. Middlesex, Eng.: Penguin (from French).

Fullan, M. 1982. *The Meaning of Educational Change*. New York: Teachers College Press.

Gibson, R. 1977. Bernstein's classification and framing: a critique. *Higher Educ. Rev.* 9:23–46.

Goffman, E. 1961. *Asylums*. Garden City, NY: Doubleday.

Goffman, E. 1983. The interaction order. *Am. Sociol. Rev.* 48:1–17.

Goldstein, H. 1981. The statistical procedures. In *Fifteen Thousand Hours a Discussion*, ed. B. Tizard *et al.*, pp. 21–5. Univ. of London Inst. of Education.

Gordon, C. W. 1957. *The Social System of the High School*. Glencoe, Ill.: Free Press.

Gouldner, A. 1954. *Patterns of Industrial Bureaucracy*. New York: Free Press.

Greenfield, T. B. 1975. Theory about organization: a new perspective and its implications for schools. In *Administering Education: International Challenge*, ed. M. Hughes, pp. 71–9. London: Athlone.

Greenfield, T. B. 1980. The man who comes back through the door in the wall: discovering truth, discovering self, discovering organizations. *Educ. Admin. Q.* 16:41–2.

Hage, J., Aiken, M. 1970. *Social Change in Complex Organizations*. New York: Random House.

Hall, R. 1963. The concept of bureaucracy: an empirical assessment. *Am. J. Sociol.* 69:32–40.

Hammersley, M., Woods, P., eds 1976. *The Process of Schooling*. London: Routledge & Kegan Paul.

Hannaway, J., Sproull, L. S. 1979. Who's running the show: coordination and control in educational organizations. *Admin. Notebook* 27.

Hanson, M. 1975. The modern bureaucracy and the process of change. *Educ. Admin. Q.* 11:21–36.

Hanson, M. 1976–7. Beyond the bureaucratic model: a study of power and autonomy in educational decision-making. *Interchange* 7:27–38.

Hanson, M., Brown, M. E. 1977. A contingency view of problem solving in schools: a case analysis. *Educ. Admin. Q.* 13:71–91.

Hargreaves, D. 1967. *Social Relations in a Secondary School.* London: Routledge & Kegan Paul.

Hargreaves, D., Hestor, S. K., Mellor, F. 1975. *Deviance in Classrooms.* Routledge & Kegan Paul.

Hargreaves, D. 1979. Durkheim, deviance and education. In *Schools, Pupils and Deviance,* ed. L. Barton and R. Meighan, pp. 17–31. Driffield, Eng.: Nafferton.

Heward, C. M. 1975. *Bureaucracy and Innovation in Schools.* PhD thesis. Univ. of Birmingham, Eng.

Hills, R. J. 1976. The public school as a type of organization. See Loubser *et al.,* 1976, 2:829–856.

Hopper, E. ed., 1971. *Readings in the Theory of Education Systems.* London: Hutchinson.

Jones, K., Williamson, K. 1979. The birth of the schoolroom. *Ideol. and Consciousness* 1:58–110.

Karabel, J., Halsey, A. H., eds 1977. Educational research: a review and an interpretation. Editors' introduction to *Power and Ideology in Education,* pp. 1–85. New York: Oxford Univ. Press.

Katz, F. E. 1964. The school as a complex social organization. *Harv. Ed. Rev.* 34:428–55.

Kelsey, J. G. 1973. *Conceptualization and Instrumentation for the Comparative Study of School Operation.* PhD thesis. Univ. Alberta, Edmonton.

Kerckhoff, A., Corwin, R. G. eds 1981. *Research in Sociology and Socialization: Research on Educational Organizations, Vol. 2.* Greenwich, Conn.: Jai.

King, A. C., Ripton, R. A. 1970. Teachers and students: a preliminary analysis in collective reciprocity. *Can. Rev. Sociol. & Anthropol.* 7:35–48.

King, R. A. 1976. Bernstein's sociology of the school: some propositions tested. *Brit. J. Sociol.* 27:430–43.

King, R. A. 1980. Weberian perspectives on the sociology of the school. *Brit. J. Sociol. Educ.* 1:7–23.

King, R. A. 1981. Bernstein's sociology of the school – a further testing. *Brit. J. Sociol.* 32:259–65.

Lawrence, P. R., Lorsch, J. W. 1967. *Organization and Environment: Managing Differentiation and Integration.* Boston: Harvard Univ. Press.

Litwak, E. 1961. Models of organization which permit conflict. *Am. J. Sociol.* 67:177–84.

Lortie, D. C. 1964. The teacher and team teaching: Suggestions for long-range research. In *Team Teaching,* ed. J. T. Shapin and H. F. Olds., Jr., pp. 270–305. NY: Harper & Row.

Lortie, D. C. 1969. The balance of control and autonomy in elementary school teaching. In *The Semi-Professions and their Organization,* ed. A. Etzioni, pp. 1–53. New York: Free Press.

Lortie, D. C. 1975. *The Schoolteacher: a Sociological Study.* Chicago: Univ. of Chicago Press.

Loubser, J. J., Baum, R. C., Effrat, A., Lidz, V. M., eds 1976. *Explorations in General Theory in Social Science: Essays in Honor of Talcott Parsons, 2 Vols.* New York: Free Press.

McKague, T. R. 1969. *A Study of the Relationship between School Organization and the*

*Variables of Bureaucratization and Leader Attitudes.* PhD thesis. Univ. of Alberta, Edmonton.

MacKay, D. A. 1964a. *An Empirical Study of Bureaucratic Dimensions and their Relationships to Other Characteristics of School Organization.* PhD thesis. Univ. of Alberta, Edmonton.

MacKay, D. A. 1964b. Should schools be bureaucratic? *Can. Admin.* 4:5–8.

March, J. G., Olsen, J. P. et al. 1976. *Ambiguity and Choice in Organizations.* Oslo: Universitetsforlaget.

Marsh, P., Rosser, E., Harre, R. 1978. *The Rules of Disorder.* London: Routledge & Kegan Paul.

Merton, R. 1957. *Social Theory and Social Structure.* Chicago: Free Press.

Meyer, J., Cohen, E. G., Brunetti, F., Molnar, S., Lueders-Salmon, E. 1971. The impact of the open space school upon teacher influence and autonomy. *Technical Report No. 21* Center for Res. and Dev. in Teaching, Stanford Univ., Calif.

Meyer, W., Rowan, B. 1983. The structure of educational organizations. In *Organizational Environments: Ritual and Rationality*, ed. J. W. Meyer, W. R. Scott, pp. 71–98. London: Sage.

Moeller, G. H., Charters, W. W. Jr 1966. Relation of bureaucratization to sense of power among teachers. *Admin. Sci. Q.* 10:444–55.

Moon, B. ed. 1983. *Comprehensive Schools: Challenge and Change.* Windsor, Eng.: NFER-Nelson.

Morgan, G. 1980. Paradigms, metaphors and puzzle-solving in organizational theory. *Admin. Sci. Q.* 25:605–22.

Musgrove, F. 1970. *Patterns of Power and Authority in English Education.* London: Methuen.

Noonan, R., Wold, H. 1977. NIPALS path modelling with latent variables. *Scand. J. Educ. Res.* 21:33–61.

Packard, J. S., Charters, W. W. Jr., Duckworth, K., Jovick, T. G. 1978. *Management Implications of Team Teaching: Final Report.* Eugene, OR. Univ. of Oregon.

Parsons, T. 1947. Introduction. In M. Weber, *The Theory of Social and Economic Organization*, pp. 3–86. Transl. A. M. Henderson, T. Parsons. New York: Free Press (from German).

Parsons, T. 1956. Suggestions for a sociological approach to the theory of organization. I. *Admin. Sci. Q.* 1:63–85.

Peaker, G. F. 1975. *An Empirical Study of Education in Twenty-Two Countries.* Stockholm: Almqvist & Wiksell.

Pellegrin, R. J. 1970. Professional satisfaction and decision making in the multiunit schools. *Technical Report No. 7.* Center for the Advanced Study of Educ. Admin., Eugene, OR. Univ. of Oregon.

Perrow, C. 1972. *Organizational Analysis: a Sociological View.* London: Tavistock.

Perrow, C. 1973. *Complex Organizations: a Critical Essay.* Glenview, Ill.: Scott, Foresman.

Pugh, D. S., Hickson, D. J., Hinings, C. R., Turner, C. 1968. Dimensions of organization structure. *Admin. Sci. Q.* 13:65–106.

Pugh, D. S., Hinings, C. R. eds 1976. *Organizational Structure: Extensions and Replications – the Aston Programme II.* Farnborough, Eng.: Saxon House.

Punch, K. F. 1969. Bureaucratic structure in schools: towards a redefinition and measurement. *Educ. Admin. Q.* 5:43–57.

Reimer, E. 1971. *School is Dead.* Harmondsworth, Eng.: Penguin.

Reynolds, D. 1976. The delinquent school. See Hammersley and Woods, 1976, pp. 217–29.

Reynolds, D. 1982. The search for effective schools. *School Organization* 2:215–37.

Richardson, E. 1973. *The Teacher, the School and the Task of Management.* London: Heinemann.

Robinson, N. 1966. *A Study of the Professional Role Orientation of Teachers and their Relationship to Bureaucratic Characteristics of School Organizations.* PhD. thesis. Univ. of Alberta, Edmonton.

Rowan, B. 1982. Organizational structure and the institutional environment: The case of the public schools. *Admin. Sci. Q.* 27:259–79.

Rutter, M., Maugham, B., Mortimore, P., Ouston, J., Smith, A. 1979. *Fifteen Thousand Hours: Secondary Schools and their Effects on Children.* London: Open Books.

Sharp, R. 1980. *Knowledge, Ideology and the Politics of Schooling: Towards a Marxist Analysis of Education.* London: Routledge & Kegan Paul.

Sheridan, A. 1980. *Michel Foucault: the Will to Truth.* London: Tavistock.

Sousa, D. A., Hoy, W. K. 1981. Bureaucratic structure in schools: a refinement and synthesis in measurement. *Educ. Admin. Q.* 17:21–39.

Testanière, J. 1968. Le Chahut traditionnel et le chahut anomique. *Rev. Franc. Sociol.* 8:17–33 (Suppl.)

Testanière, J. 1972. Crise scolaire et revolte lyceenne. *Rev. Franc. Sociol.* 13:3–34.

Turner, C. M. 1977. Organizing educational institutions as anarchies. *Educ. Admin.* 5:6–12.

Tyler, W. 1973. The organizational structure of the secondary school. *Educ. Rev.* 25:223–36.

Tyler, W. 1983. *Organizations, Factors and Codes: a Methodological Enquiry into Bernstein's Theory of Educational Transmissions.* PhD thesis. Univ. of Kent at Canterbury, Eng.

Wakeford, J. 1969. *The Cloistered Elite: a Sociological Analysis of the English Boarding School.* London: Macmillan.

Wallace, G. 1980. The constraints of architecture on aims and organization in five middle schools. In *Middle Schools: Origins, Ideology and Practice,* ed. A. Hargreaves, L. Tickle, pp. 125–140. London: Harper & Row.

Waller, W. 1932. *The Sociology of Teaching.* NY: Wiley.

Weber, M. 1946. *From Max Weber: Essays in Sociology.* Transl. H. H. Gerth, C. W. Mills. New York: Oxford Univ. Press (from German).

Weick, K. 1976. Educational organizations as loosely coupled systems. *Admin. Sci. Q.* 21:1–19.

Weick, K. 1980. Loosely coupled systems: relaxed meanings and thick interpretations. Unpublished manuscript, Cornell University, Ithaca, NY.

Werthman, C. 1963. Delinquents in school: a test for the legitimacy of authority. *Berkeley J. Sociol.* 8:39–60.

Willis, P. 1977. *Learning to Labour.* Farnborough: Saxon House.

Willower, D. J. 1982. School organizations: perspectives in juxtaposition. *Educ. Admin. Q.* 18:89–110.

Wise, A. 1979. Why educational policies often fail; the hyper-rationalization hypothesis. *J. Curr. Stud.* 9:43–5.

Woods, P. 1979. *The Divided School.* London: Routledge & Kegan Paul.

Woods, P. 1983. *Sociology and the School: an Interactionist Viewpoint.* London: Routledge & Kegan Paul.

**Section II**

# On problems of structure

# 3

# Factories, monitorial schools and Jeremy Bentham: the origins of the 'management syndrome' in popular education

**P. J. Miller**

It is frequently asserted that contemporary public school administration is conditioned by what may be termed 'a business management syndrome'. Usually the assertion is made with some distaste, the educational administrator's use of industrial management techniques being treated as a kind of cancerous growth in a previously healthy body of school administration. Callahan, for example, in his assiduously investigated study of the influence of business ideas upon schooling in the United States, found that their conscious and deliberate adoption began about 1900.[1] The increasing extent of their influence disturbed him. For after all, he points out, 'Education is not a business. The school is not a factory'.[2]

Such puzzlement about the pervasiveness of 'business ideas' in public education is in large part due to a failure to penetrate to the source of such an outlook. For in fact the 'business management syndrome' in popular education is not a recent importation: it has been there from the beginning, a kind of innate characteristic or psychological trait which has helped form not only the procedures of the public school but, perhaps more importantly, a characteristic approach to the problems of public school administration. The origins of this particular attitude of mind are varied and complex. Principally, however, they lie in two distinct yet not unrelated developments of the early nineteenth century; the widely hailed success and consequent prestige of the early factory system, the principles of which seemed equally applicable to the operation of schools, and the growing acceptance in the English-speaking world of utilitarian ethical theory as it related to the solution of social and institutional problems.

An illustration, and to some extent an explanation, of the early and close affinity perceived between the worlds of industry and education is provided by an examination of the basic similarities between the problems faced by managers of factories and monitorial schools, and of the approaches used in their solution. The way in which utilitarian ethical theory introduced a 'business-like' element into the perception and treatment of educational problems is most clearly evident in the analysis mode of the principles of monitorial school management by that archetypical analytic and administrative mind, Jeremy Bentham. Indeed, in his *Chrestomathia* (1816)[3] are to be found an outlook on and psychology of school administration that were early and deeply imbedded in English popular education.

The similarity of outlook bred in the managers of factories and schools arose not so much as a result of any deliberate or slavish imitation but rather because of the affinity of the problems facing them. For example, the initial difficulty faced by any would-be capitalist or manufacturing entrepreneur in the early days of the industrial revolution was the raising of capital. Similarly, particularly in the days before any deep state involvement in popular education, this was the most serious problem facing those public minded citizens who sought to provide proper moral, religious and intellectual training for the lower orders of society.

By the middle of the eighteenth century, the use of the joint-stock company principle had begun to effect important changes in the world of commerce and industry. It was to affect education just as profoundly. 'Power, it was found, could be multiplied indefinitely at any one point, if a number of persons put together their small sums of money and handed the management over to a chosen few.'[4] The establishment and successful operation of subscription charity schools, Sunday schools and monitorial schools depended at bottom upon the application of this commercial idea to education.

School managers, like factory managers, were made well aware that they were dealing with the allocation of limited resources, and consequently that it was essential to effect economies in time, labour and expense. Indeed it was this concern which led directly to the discovery of and enthusiastic reception accorded to the monitorial system of instruction. As Andrew Bell, one of its 'inventors', complained, 'Machinery has been contrived for spinning twenty skeins of silk, and twenty hanks of cotton, where one was spun before; but no contrivance has been sought for, or devised, that twenty children may be educated in moral and religious principles with the same facility and expense, as one was taught before.'[5] The great strength of the monitorial system was that it seemed to do just this.

Indeed, so powerful and persuasive were the metaphors of 'mechanisms' and 'industry' that even Samuel Taylor Coleridge could not resist its appeal. For him, as for everyone, the monitorial system was 'an incomparable machine', a 'vast moral steam engine'.[6] Cheap, apparently efficient, and above all mechanical, the system effected considerable economies in time and labour. Thus, Joseph Lancaster, the other 'inventor' of monitorial instruction, proclaimed of his system, that it was a 'new plan', 'by means of which, one master alone can educate one thousand boys, in Reading, Writing, and Arithmetic, as effectually, and with as little Trouble, as Twenty or Thirty have ever been instructed by the usual modes of Tuition.'[7] Perhaps the most widely representative view of the system was that of Thomas Bernard who glowingly reported, 'The grand principle of Dr. Bell's system is the division of labour applied to intellectual purposes. . . It is the division of labour in his schools that leaves the master the easy task of directing the movements of the whole machine, instead of toiling intellectually at a single part. The principle in manufactories, and in schools is the same.'[8]

Bernard was not engaging in fantasy. The division of labour, or to use the terminology of current educational discourse, differentiated staffing, was an innovation both of factories and monitorial schools. Breaking down the productive (or instructional) process into its constituent elements and allocating to individuals those tasks which they could perform easily and competently not only speeded up the process; it made possible differentiated pay scales and effected economies in wages. Such various and esoteric functions and occupations in a wool factory as sorters, pickers, winnowers, scribblers, scourers and glossers had their counterparts in the monitorial schools. Lancaster, for example differentiated clearly between the tasks and payments of himself as master and such various monitors as the monitor of ruling books, the monitor of absentees, inspecting monitors, teaching monitors, monitors of slates, and the monitor general.

Central to the idea of the joint-stock company, and indeed to any efficient business, is the concept of accountability. In much the same way that managers of factories were responsible to owners or investors for the outcomes of their industrial or commercial operations, so too were the executives of various societies for the education of the poor accountable to their subscribers.

The acceptance of the principle of accountability and the consequent need to justify expenditures required, of course, that outputs be measured and, in some sense, quantified and standardized. That such was the case with the monitorial schools is again well illustrated by Joseph Lancaster, who in 1803 reported to his patrons that, due to his reorganization of the system and the introduction of new methods of tuition in spelling and arithmetic, 'proficiency' in these areas had been 'more than doubled' with 'individual scholars spelling 20,000 words and working 2,000 sums . . . per annum; whereas, the same space of time, in the common modes of tuition, would have been . . . irretrievably lost in idleness'.[9]

By far the most intimate connection between industrial and school management concerned the vital question of personnel supervision and control. Both schools and factories housed inmates who, in one way or another, felt obliged to attend. And while in the beginning the complexity of the problem was to some extent due to the 'newness' of industrialism and popular education, it was also inherent in the nature of the institutions of factories and schools.[10]

> Men used to working at home were generally not inclined to go to the factory. In the early days factory labour consisted of the most ill-assorted elements. . . . All these unskilled men, unused to collective work, had to be taught, trained, and above all disciplined by the manufacturer. He had so to speak to turn them into a human machine, as regular in its working, as accurate in its movements, and as exactly combined for a single purpose as the mechanism of wood and metal to which they become accessory.[10]

To devise ways of ensuring regular attendance at prescribed hours, to get all individuals to work steadily – to do exactly what they were told, no more and no less – and above all to impose order and discipline, these were to be the most persistent and intractable problems faced by the managers of factories and schools. Jedediah Strutt, for example, in his detailed analysis of the 'offences' committed in his factory between 1805 and 1813, lists such typical school misdemeanours as going home without leave, absence without leave, idleness, looking through the windows, riotous behaviour, riding on each other's back, dancing, fighting, playing tricks, swearing, insolence, telling lies, teasing animals, and refusal to carry out orders.[11] For such offences, forfeits or fines were deducted from worker's wages, and although corporal punishment was forbidden in Strutt's mill, it was often brutally used by lesser overseers in other factories to 'discipline' women and children. Registers recording attendance, absenteeism and tardiness, 'black books' noting various delinquencies, records detailing the allocation of rewards, prizes and punishments, coloured blocks which placed beside a workman or student denoted his worth at that particular time, all were freely used in the schools and factories of the period. So important was the problem of control that Andrew Ure, in his famous panegyric on the factory system, written in 1835, recognized the major contribution of Arkwright to industry to be not his inventions but the devising and administering of 'a successful code of factory discipline, suited to the necessities of factory diligence'.[12]

Not surprisingly, in an age beginning to be dominated by utilitarian ethical theory, the system of control and discipline employed in factories and schools was heavily dependent upon rewards and punishments. Joseph Lancaster, for example, in his Borough Road Free School established in 1798, had 250 students and a total budget in 1801 of £118 10s, of which £84 15 s went on his salary and a surprising £18 13s, or 16 per cent, on prizes and rewards. Three years later the school had over 500 students and a total budget of £223 7s, of which £49 8s, or 22 per cent, was expended on prizes and rewards.[13]

That the dispensing or withholding of rewards and punishments was seen as the most effective means of control and discipline in factories and schools meant, of course, that the notion of extrinsic motivation was relied upon completely to effect the purposes of both institutions. And while there may be some point to the criticisms of 'humanists' that it was primarily this reliance which effected the alienation of worker from his work, student from his learning, the fact remains that the concept itself was early entrenched in the psychology of factory and school management.

Both Lancaster and Bell were well aware of, and indeed took great pride in, the obvious similarities between the operations of their monitorial schools and those of industry. But while they were as conscious of the overriding importance of organizational and administrative matters as any industrialist, neither was possessed of a sufficiently analytic mind (or, of course, sufficient leisure) to tackle the task of explicitly formulating the managerial principles upon which their schools were conducted. This assignment, however, was willingly undertaken and most capably executed by Jeremy Bentham, perhaps the most highly analytic mind of the early nineteenth century.

Jeremy Bentham's personal involvement with the monitorial system began in 1815. For some time, he and his friends had been impressed by the practical, mechanical and efficient nature of the system. There seemed to be no reason why it should be confined to the instruction of the lower orders of society in reading, writing and arithmetic.[14] Why not, they argued, apply it to all branches of useful knowledge? Why not make a comprehensive analysis of such knowledge and prepare it for systematic presentation to the middle and higher ranks of society? Why not, in fact, establish an experimental and profitable private school designed specifically for such a purpose?

Support for the project was readily forthcoming: contributions were pledged while Bentham offered his garden as the site for the school and volunteered to take a major part in its management. The scheme under way, he was free to begin work on the fascinating tasks of drawing up plans for the school; constructing an 'encyclopedical table' of all those arts and sciences which were 'conducive to well being'; translating these 'arts and sciences' into a school curriculum; analysing the principles of learning and teaching; devising a six-year school programme covering all branches of useful knowledge; and, finally, formulating the principles of the school's management.

Although the inevitable controversy over whether religious instruction should be given in the school eventually resulted in the scheme being abandoned, Bentham completed these various tasks and in 1816 *Chrestomathia*, his only major work on education, appeared. Despite the fact that it was little read by the general public, *Chrestomathia* must rank as one of the more important educational works of the nineteenth century. For as J. S. Mill remarked of Bentham (and Coleridge), although they 'have never been read by the multitude . . . , they have been the teachers of teachers'.[15] While *Chrestomathia* may not have greatly influenced public opinion, there can be little doubt that it affected powerfully the thinking of philosophical radicals like Brougham, Romilly, Chadwick and Lowe who were to dominate so many commissions of enquiry, royal commissions and government departments. Moreover, and equally important to the historian of education, in

*Chrestomathia* one is confronted by attitudes to childhood, curricula and instruction that were typical of a large and increasingly important segment of the English middle classes. Certainly, many of the principles of school management enunciated by Bentham were to exercise a lasting influence upon English popular education.

There are discussed in *Chrestomathia* no less than thirty-eight principles of school management which are applicable to all branches of intellectual instruction.[16] Fortunately, for purposes of generalization, they are arranged in five categories, concerning respectively; the most effective placement and utilization of teaching personnel; 'the preservation of discipline' or 'the exclusion of disorder'; securing 'the forthcomingness of evidence . . . in the most correct, complete, durable and easily accessible shape' on all matters to do with the purposes of the school; 'securing perfection . . . in the perform-ance of every exercise . . . in the instance of every scholar'; and, finally, the achievement of 'the union of the maximum of despatch with the maximum of uniformity'.[17]

Category I contains six principles, each concerning 'the quality and functions of the Persons, by whom the performance of the several exercises is to be directed'. Central to them all is the first, the 'Scholar-Teacher employ-ment maximizing principle', which consists 'in employing, as teachers to the rest, some of the most advanced . . . among the scholars themselves . . .'[18] To an essentially practical mind such as Bentham, the advantages of the principle were obvious. As he succinctly and bluntly put it:

> Advantages gained, I. *Saving in money.* Every professional teacher would need to be paid; no such Scholar-Teacher needs to be paid; or is paid. II. *Saving in time.* Under the inspection of one professional General Master, the whole number of Scholars may be cast into as many classes as there are different branches of instruction, and different degrees of proficiency in each: each such class under the direction of its Scholar-Teacher; the instruction of all these classes going on at the same time.[19]

The next four principles follow from the first, and deal with the efficient placement of monitors and the precise definition of their and the master's responsibilities. They are designed, in effect, to make possible a 'rational' division of labour. The concept of accountability is provided for in the sixth principle which not only allows but encourages regular visitation and superintendency of the institution by all those individuals contributing to its support. For Bentham, this was an advantage unique to schools instituted and supported by private contributions.

Under Category II are discussed a further six principles, all concerning the preservation of discipline, or 'the effectual and universal performance of the several prescribed Exercises, and the exclusion of disorder'. Once again, the psychological affinity between Bentham's concept of school adminis-tration and the management of factories is obvious, both in the reliance upon the extrinsic motivation provided by rewards and punishments, and in the concern to effect economies in the former. It is important to add, however, that the principles themselves derive not so much from any conscious attempt to utilize in education the proven methods and techniques of industry as from a rigid application to the operation of a school of utilitarian ethical theory. When dealing with the control of behaviour through the dispensing of rewards and punishments, the author of *The Principles of Morals and Legislation* was, so to speak, on home-ground.

Thus, the first two principles concern the minimizing both of rewards and punishments. The 'punishment minimizing, and corporal punishment excluding principle' needed no justification, and required that the suffering produced by any act of punishment be but slightly greater 'to the person under temptation . . . than the enjoyment expected from the offence'.[20] The 'reward economizing principle', however, is justified, not only on grounds of its effecting a reduction of expenditures, but also because rewards cannot be poured 'into one bosom, but at the expense of suffering . . . inflicted upon others'.[21] The reward, therefore, must be the least sufficient to impel the individual to do what is required of him.

The guarantee of economy in dispensing rewards and punishments is contained in the 'constant and universal inspection promising principle', or the 'Panopticon principle', which for Bentham was to be the cornerstone of the whole edifice of order and discipline, both in schools and in society. Significantly, the Panopticon was originally invented by Bentham's brother, Samuel, who was interested in the problem of prison design. It was, in fact, a prison in which

> one inspector, or at most a very small number of inspectors, is in a position to supervise all the cells which are arranged concentrically around a central pavilion: . . . the fundamental advantage of the Panopticon is so evident that one is in danger of obscuring it in the desire to prove it. To be incessantly under the eyes of the inspector is to lose in effect the power to do evil and almost the thought of wanting to do it.[22]

The principle, Bentham believed, could be extended to factories, mad-houses, hospitals, poor-houses and schools, all of which housed inmates who required constant inspection. What was required to keep children away from unprofitable play and mischief was simply the awareness that they were under the eye of a master every moment.[23]

It might be argued, admitted Bentham elsewhere, that such a system was nothing less than spying. But, he went on, there was no secrecy involved; indeed, 'the object of the inspection principle is . . . to make them not only suspect, but be assured that whatever they do is known, even though that should not be the case'.[24] Vice was thus prevented, rather than disco-vered and then punished. It might also be charged that the awareness of being under constant inspection would produce a generation of timid men, totally lacking in initiative. But surely, he went on, what mattered was 'would *happiness* be most likely to be increased or diminished by this discipline? Call them soldiers, call them monks, call them machines: so they be but happy ones, I should not care'.[25]

The introduction of this principle required that the school be constructed in such a way that the master could see everything and everyone, while remaining himself, when he desired, unseen. By this single innovation in school design, Bentham confidently expected to do more than just prevent the occurrence of any overt misbehaviour by students and monitors. As he himself put it, 'Morals reformed, health preserved, industry invigorated instruction diffused, public burthens lightened, . . . all by a simple idea in architecture'.[26]

Of course, if the purposes of the school were to be realized, it was necessary that students should do more than passively behave themselves. They must work – hard and consistently. And to 'encourage' them to do so, an appropriate and inexpensive system of rewards and punishments was required. In his 'place-capturing, or extempore degradation and promotion principle', Bentham elaborated such a system. Each class in the school was to be arranged in a row representing a gradation of honour and merit. Attendant upon the 'saying of lessons', a continual process of promotion and degradation was to take place, formal instruction being converted, in this way, into a highly competitive game. Thus punishment would be attached 'instantaneously upon demerit, and . . . reward upon merit . . . without further trouble or expense in any shape'.[27]

Finally, in a system of discipline so heavily dependent upon rewards and punishment, justice must not only be done, but be seen to be done. To guarantee this, Bentham enunciated two further principles, the 'appeal providing principle', whereby a scholar could appeal the decision of a monitor to the master himself, and the 'scholar-jury principle', which would preserve the master from the reproach of tyranny, train students in 'the exercise of the functions of the judicature', and add the force of social pressure to the maintenance of order in the school.

In Category III are enunciated four principles which have to do with securing factual information about the progress of every student in the school.[28] No one recognized more clearly than Bentham and the Philosophical Radicals that for sound decisions to be made in any field, be it politics, economics, health or education, accurate information must be instantly available. Moreover record-keeping was a necessary condition for true accountability.

In the proposed Chrestomathic school, Bentham provided for extensive records to be kept, detailing the age of scholars and monitors, their attendance, the dates of their entering and leaving each class in the school, the number and types of their delinquencies, and the rewards and punishments dispensed to them. A history of the progress of every scholar and monitor would thus be available, not only to the master but to any contributor or parent who wished to see what he was getting for his money. One of the more important responsibilities of the master was this book-keeping function.[29]

In Category IV Bentham included no less than fourteen principles which have for their object the achievement of complete mastery of the prescribed instructional content by every student, his mastery to be demonstrated by the student's obtaining a maximum score on a series of standardized tests. In a very real sense, Bentham perceived the various relationships between the school, the subscribers, the student's and their parents to be contractual ones.[30] For a specified sum of money, paid by subscribers or parents, the school contracted to perform a certain set of operations, and, more importantly, to achieve agreed upon objectives. The fulfilment of the contract by the school could only be demonstrated by each student 'proving' that he had, indeed, totally 'mastered' the instructional content. Anything less would mean that the school had failed to live up to the terms of the contract; anything more would mean that the school was exceeding the terms of the contract and presumably misallocating funds.

All the principles under this category are therefore designed to ensure nothing less and certainly nothing more than the fulfilment of the terms of a contract, that is effectively to instruct each student in 'the several prescribed exercises'. Among the more significant principles are the following: that no student admitted to the school be presumed incapable of 'imbibing the instruction'; that the instructional content and objectives be so precisely formulated that every student and monitor immediately apprehend what was required of him; that no student be allowed to move out of a class until he had achieved a 'perfect performance', in effect, 'continuing to be taught, until he has learnt'; that material already 'mastered' be regularly recapitulated to ensure its retention and logical connection with new information; that charts and schematic representations of material cover all areas of the school visible to students so that they would 'learn' during the few moments in the day when they were not being instructed; and that all outside distraction be eliminated by an appropriate placement of windows.[31]

For Bentham, it was not enough that contractual obligations be undertaken and met; they must be discharged as efficiently as possible. Thus, in Category V, he discussed his final eight principles of school management, all of which have 'for their special object, the union of the maximum of despatch with the maximum of uniformity; thereby proportionably shortening the time, employed in the acquisition of the proposed body of instruction, and increasing the number of pupils made to acquire it, by the same Teachers, at the same time.'[32] The aim of producing a standardized product, in as short a time as possible, in as large a quantity as possible, with as little expenditure as possible, was as much an ideal of Bentham for education as it was of any industrialist for his business.

The principles themselves are largely self-explanatory, and require little or no comment. To the twentieth-century reader many of them may perhaps seem somewhat trivial. What is important, however, is not so much the specific principles themselves as the intention behind them, and thus their impact. To save time, to save money, to increase the output of a uniform product while holding expenses steady – these were objectives which were to condition the approach to and outlook on popular or elementary education from its very inception. It is a mark of Bentham's genius that, at the very outset of popular education, he was able to penetrate to and uncover the bedrock of administrative principles upon which not only the monitorial school but subsequent institutions of public education were to be constructed and conducted.

Lacking an effective system of central and local government, possessed of a chaotic legal system, confronted with war abroad and discontent at home, experiencing the pangs of rapid population growth, increasing urbanization and emerging industrialism, English society in the late eighteenth and early nineteenth centuries faced social problems which defied traditional solutions and traditional modes of thought. The approach of the nineteenth century to the resolving of these difficulties was to be created by a fusion of evangelical religion and Benthamite utilitarianism. Thus, while the awareness of social problems was heightened and the direction of the new society greatly affected by the puritanical and humanitarian spirit of evangelicalism, the actual method of tackling social issues was largely determined by the critical and practical outlook of Benthamism. Certainly, the tendency to treat social problems as essentially business problems can be traced to Benthamism, and this to some extent explains the emergence and continuing strength of a 'management syndrome' in English popular education.

But even if the influence of Bentham is ignored, when one considers the close affinities between the problems of factory and school management – raising funds, allocating limited resources, the crucial question of accountability and the difficulties of imposing order and discipline – 'It is hardly surprising that the solutions proposed, accepted and put into practice were in so many respects similar. And while the replacement of monitors by pupil-teachers, the evolution of a teaching profession, the expansion of curricula, the introduction of more enlightened pedagogy and the gradual increase of government aid may all be looked upon as educational advances, there are no grounds for maintaining that any of them represented or was accompanied by a deliberate rejection of an already well-established business management syndrome. For in the final analysis, the close relationship between business management and school administration was and perhaps still is due not so much to any imitation one of the other but rather to the essential similarity of those two recent and yet founding institutions of modern society, the factory and the school.

# APPENDIX
## PRINCIPLES OF SCHOOL MANAGEMENT:
applicable to INTELLECTUAL INSTRUCTION, to all branches
without distinction

Adopted from J. Bentham's *Chrestomathia, Instruction Table II*

I. Principles, relative to the *Official Establishment*: i.e. to the *quality* and *functions* of the Persons, by whom the performance of the several *Exercises* is to be directed.
1. *Scholar-Teacher employment maximizing* principle.
2. *Contiguously proficient Teacher preferring* principle.
3. *Scholar-Tutor employment maximizing*, or *Lesson-getting Assistant employing*, principle.
4. *Scholar-Monitor employment maximizing*, or *Scholar Order-preserver employment maximizing*, principle.
5. *Master's time economizing*, or *Nil per se quod per suos*, principle.
6. *Regular Visitation*, or *Constant Superintendency providing*, principle.

II. Principles, having, for their special object, the preservation of *Discipline*: i.e. the effectual and universal performance of the several prescribed *Exercises*, and the exclusion of *disorder*; i.e. of all practices *obstructive* of such performance, or productive of *mischief* in any *other* shape; and, to that end, the correct and complete observance of all *arrangements* and *regulations*, established for either of those purposes.
1. *Punishment minimizing*, and *Corporal Punishment excluding* principle.
2. *Reward economizing* principle.
3. *Constant and universal Inspection promising* and *securing* principle.
   Note: To this belongs the *Panopticon Architecture employing principle*.
4. *Place-capturing*, or *Extempore degradation and promotion* principle.
5. *Appeal* (from Scholar-master) *providing* principle.
6. *Juvenile Penal Jury*, or *Scholar Jurymen employing* principle.

III. Principles, having, for their special object, the securing the *forthcomingness* of *Evidence*: namely, in the most correct, complete, durable and easily accessible shape: and thereby the most constant and universal *notoriety* of all *past* matters of *fact*, the knowledge of which can be necessary, or conducive, to the propriety of all *subsquent* proceedings; whether for securing the due performance of *Exercises*, as per Col. I or for the exclusion of *disorder*, as per Col. II.
1. *Aggregate Progress Registration*, or *Register employing*, principle.
2. *Individual* and *comparative proficiency registration*, or *Place – competition – result Registration employing*, principle.
3. *Delinquency registration*, or *Black-Book employing*, principle.
4. *Universal Delation* principle, or *Non-Connivance tolerating*, principle.

IV. Principles, having for their special object, the securing *perfection*: namely in the performance of *every Exercise*, and that in the instance of *every Scholar*, without exception.
1. *Universal proficiency promising* principle.
2. *Non-conception*, or *Non-intellection, presuming*, principle.
3. *Constantly* and *universally perfect performance exacting*, or *No-imperfect tolerating*, principle.
4. *Gradual progression securing*, or *Gradually progressive Exercises employing*, principle.

5. *Frequent and adequate recapitulation exacting* principle.
6. Place-capturing probative exercise employment *maximizing* principle.
7. Fixt verbal standard employment, and Verbal conformity exaction, *maximizing* principle.
8. Organic Intellection-Test employment *maximizing* principle.
9. Note-taking-Intellection-Test employment *maximizing* principle.
10. *Self service exaction maximizing* principle.
11. *Task-descriptive enunciation and promulgation exacting* principle.
12. Constant all-comprehensive and illustrative Tabular Exhibition *maximizing* principle.
13. *Distraction preventing*, or *Exterior object excluding* principle.
14. *Constantly and universally apposite Scholar-classification securing*, principle.
V. Principles, having, for their special object, the union of the maximum of *despatch* with the maximum of *uniformity*: thereby proportionably *shortening* the *time*, employed in the acquisition of the proposed body of instruction, and *increasing* the *number* of Pupils, made to acquire it, by the *same Teachers*, at the *same time*.
1. *Simplification maximizing*, or *Short lesson employing*, principle.
2. *Universal-simultaneous-action promising* and *effecting* principle.
3. *Constantly-uninterrupted-action promising* and *effecting* principle.
4. *Word of command employing*, or *Audible-direction abbreviating* principle.
5. *Universally visible signal*, or *pattern employing*, or *Universally* and *simultaneously visible direction employing*, principle.
6. *Needless repetition* and *commoration excluding* principle.
7. *Remembrance assisting* Metre-employment maximizing principle.
8. *Employment varying*, or *Task-alternating* principle.

## Notes and references

1. R. E. Callahan, *Education and the Cult of Efficiency* (Chicago, 1968), p. vii.
2. *Ibid.*
3. Jeremy Bentham, *Chrestomathia* (1816). *Works of Jeremy Bentham* (ed. J. Bowring), (New York, 1962), Vol. 8, pp. 1–191.
4. H. Wodehouse, *A Survey of the History of Education* (1930), p. 141.
5. Andrew Bell, *Extract of a Sermon on the Education of the Poor* (1807), p. 17.
6. W. H. G. Armytage, *Four Hundred Years of English Education* (1964), p. 90.
7. Joseph Lancaster, *Improvements in Education* (1806), p. 23.
8. Society for the Bettering of the Condition of the Poor, (ed. Thomas Bernard), *Of the Education of the Poor* (1809), pp. 34, 36.
9. Lancaster, *op. cit.*, pp. 17–18.
10. Paul Mantoux, *The Industrial Revolution in the Eighteenth Century* (1962), p. 375.
11. R. S. Fitton and A. P. Wadsworth, *The Strutts and the Arkwrights, 1758–1830*, pp. 234–7.
12. Andrew Ure, *The Philosophy of Manufactures* (1835), (1967 edn.), p. 15.
13. Lancaster, *op. cit.*, pp. 13–19. In this connection, it is interesting to speculate what degree of student motivation could be generated by a modern school system which allocated over 20 per cent of its budget to 'prizes and rewards'.
14. In fact, Bentham was aware that the system was in use both at the High School, Edinburgh, and at Charterhouse School. See Bentham, *op. cit.*, pp. ii, 59.

15. J. S. Mill, *On Bentham and Coleridge* (1838), (1962 edn.), p. 39.
16. See Appendix.
17. Bentham, *op. cit.*, pp. 46–53.
18. *Ibid.*, p. 46.
19. *Ibid.*
20. *Ibid.*, p. 48.
21. *Ibid.*
22. E. Halevy, *The Growth of Philosophic Radicalism* (1955), p. 83.
23. Jeremy Bentham, *Panopticon* (1787), Works, Vol. iv, p. 62.
24. *Ibid.*, p. 66.
25. *Ibid.*, p. 44.
26. *Ibid.*, p. 39.
27. Bentham, *Chrestomathia, op. cit.*, p. 48. A principle, incidentally, employed by Lancaster in his school.
28. *Ibid.*, p. 49.
29. At the ninteenth century wore on and the machinery for allocating government grants to schools become more complex, this function was to become increasingly important. By the middle of the century, the school register was as ubiquitous and as sacred as it is today in many parts of the world.
30. The similarities between Bentham's views here and those underlying one of the most recent innovations in public education, performance contracting, are obvious.
31. Bentham, *Chrestomathia, op. cit.*, pp. 49–52.
32. See Appendix.

4

# Educational organizations as loosely coupled systems

**Karl E. Weick**

In contrast to the prevailing image that elements in organizations are coupled through dense, tight linkages, it is proposed that elements are often tied together frequently and loosely. Using educational organizations as a case in point, it is argued that the concept of loose coupling incorporates a surprising number of disparate observations about organizations, suggests novel functions, creates stubborn problems for methodologists, and generates intriguing questions for scholars. Sample studies of loose coupling are suggested and research priorities are posed to foster cumulative work with this concept.[1]

Imagine that you're either the referee, coach, player or spectator at an unconventional soccer match: the field for the game is round; there are several goals scattered haphazardly around the circular field; people can enter and leave the game whenever they want to; they can throw balls in whenever they want; they can say 'that's my goal' whenever they want to, as many times as they want to, and for as many goals as they want to; the entire game takes place on a sloped field; and the game is played as if it makes sense (March, personal communication).

If you now substitute in that example principals for referees, teachers for coaches, students for players, parents for spectators and schooling for soccer, you have an equally unconventional depiction of school organizations. The beauty of this depiction is that it captures a different set of realities within educational organizations than are caught when these same organizations are viewed through the tenets of bureaucratic theory.

Consider the contrast in images. For some time people who manage organizations and people who study this managing have asked, 'How does an organization go about doing what it does and with what consequences for its people, processes, products, and persistence?' And for some time they've heard the same answers. In paraphrase the answers say essentially that an organization does what it does because of plans, intentional selection of means that get the organization to agree upon goals,' and all of this is accomplished by such rationalized procedures as cost-benefit analyses, division of labor, specified areas of discretion, authority invested in the office, job descriptions, and a consistent evaluation and reward system. The only problem with that portrait is that it is rare in nature. People in organizations, including educational organizations, find themselves hard pressed either to find actual instances of those rational practices or to find rationalized practices whose outcomes have been as beneficent as predicted, or to feel that those rational occasions explain much of what goes on within the organization. Parts of some organizations are heavily rationalized but many parts also made some provocative suggestions about newer, more unconventional ideas about organizations that should be given serious thought. A good example of this is the following observation by John M. Stephens (1967:9–11):

[There is a] remarkable constancy of educational results in the face of widely differing deliberate approaches. Every so often we adopt new approaches or new methodologies and place our reliance on new panaceas. At the very least we seem to chorus new slogans. Yet the academic growth within the classroom continues at about the same rate, stubbornly refusing to cooperate with the bright new dicta emanating from the conference room. . . . [These observations suggest that] we would be making a great mistake in regarding the management of schools as similar to the process of constructing a building or operating a factory. In these latter processes deliberate decisions play a crucial part, and the enterprise advances or stands still in proportion to the amount of deliberate effort exerted. If we must use a metaphor or model in seeking to understand the process of schooling, we should look to agriculture rather than to the factory. In agriculture we do not start from scratch, and we do not direct our efforts to inert and passive materials. We start, on the contrary, with a complex and ancient process, and we organize our efforts around what seeds, plants, and insects are likely to do anyway. . . . The crop, once planted, may undergo some development even while the farmer sleeps or loafs. No matter what he does, *some* aspects of the outcome will remain constant. When teachers and pupils foregather, some education may proceed even while the Superintendent disports himself in Atlantic City.

It is crucial to highlight what is important in the examples of soccer and schooling viewed as agriculture. To view these examples negatively and dismiss them by observing that 'the referee should tighten up those rules,' 'superintendents don't do that,' 'schools are more sensible than that,' or 'these are terribly sloppy organizations' is to miss the point. The point is although researchers don't know what these kinds of structures are like, researchers do know they exist and that each of the negative judgments expressed above makes sense only if the observer assumes that organizations are constructed and managed according to rational assumptions and therefore are scrutable only when rational analyses are applied to them. This paper attempts to expand and enrich the set of ideas available to people when they try to make sense out of their organizational life. From this standpoint, it is unproductive to observe that fluid participation in schools and soccer is absurd. But it can be more interesting and productive to ask, how can it be that even though the activities in both situations are only modestly connected, the situations are still recognizable and nameable? The goals, player movements, and trajectory of the ball are still recognizable and can be labeled 'soccer.' And despite variations in class size, format, locations, and architecture, the results are still recognized and can be labeled 'schools.' How can such loose assemblages retain sufficient similarity and permanence across time that they can be recognized, labeled, and dealt with? The prevailing ideas in organization theory do not shed much light on how such 'soft' structures develop, persist, and impose crude orderliness among their elements.

The basic premise here is that concepts such as loose coupling serve as sensitizing devices. They sensitize the observer to notice and question things that had previously been taken for granted. It is the intent of the program described here to develop a language for use in analyzing complex organizations, a language that may highlight features that have previously gone unnoticed. The guiding principle is a reversal of the common assertion, 'I'll believe it when I see it' and presumes an epistemology that asserts, 'I'll see it when I believe it.' Organizations as loosely coupled systems may not have been seen before because nobody believed in them or could afford to believe in them. It is conceivable that preoccupation with rationalized, tidy, efficient, coordinated structures has blinded many practitioners as well as researchers to some of the attractive and unexpected properties of less rationalized and less tightly related clusters of events. This paper intends to eliminate such blindspots.

## The concept of coupling

The phrase 'loose coupling' has appeared in the literature (Glassman, 1973; March and Olsen, 1975) and it is important to highlight the connotation that is captured by this phrase and by no other. It might seem that the word coupling is synonymous with words like connection, link, or interdependence, yet each of these latter terms misses a crucial nuance.

By loose coupling, the author intends to convey the image that coupled events are responsive, *but* that each event also preserves its own identity and some evidence of its physical or logical separateness. Thus, in the case of an educational organization, it may be the case that the counselor's office is loosely coupled to the principal's office. The image is that the principal and the counselor are somehow attached, but that each retains some identity and separateness and that their attachment may be circumscribed, infrequent, weak in its mutual affects, unimportant, and/or slow to respond. Each of those connotations would be conveyed if the qualifier loosely were attached to the word coupled. Loose coupling also carries connotations of impermanence, dissolvability, and tacitness all of which are potentially crucial properties of the 'glue' that holds organizations together.

Glassman (1973) categorizes the degree of coupling between two systems on the basis of the activity of the variables which the two systems share. To the extent that two systems either have few variables in common or share weak variables, they are independent of each other. Applied to the educational situation, if the principal-vice-principal-superintendent is regarded as one system and the teacher-classroom-pupil-parent-curriculum as another system, then by Glassman's argument if we did not find many variables in the teacher's world to be shared in the world of a principal and/or if the variables held in common were unimportant relative to the other variables, then the principal can be regarded as being loosely coupled with the teacher.

A final advantage of coupling imagery is that it suggests the idea of building blocks that can be grafted onto an organization or severed with relatively little disturbance to either the blocks or the organization. Simon (1969) has argued for the attractiveness of this feature in that most complex systems can be decomposed into stable subassemblies and that these are the crucial elements in any organization or system. Thus, the coupling imagery gives researchers access to one of the more powerful ways of talking about complexity now available.

But if the concept of loose coupling highlights novel images heretofore unseen in organizational theory, what is it about these images that is worth seeing?

## Coupled elements

There is no shortage of potential coupling elements, but neither is the population infinite.

At the outset the two most commonly discussed coupling mechanisms are the technical core of the organization and the authority of office. The relevance of those two mechanisms for the issue of identifying elements is that in the case of technical couplings, each element is some kind of technology, task, subtask, role, territory, and person, and the couplings are task-induced. In the case of authority as the coupling mechanism, the elements include positions, offices, responsibilities, opportunities, rewards, and sanctions and it is the couplings among these elements that presumably hold the organization together. A compelling argument can be made that *neither* of these coupling mechanisms is prominent in educational organizations found in the United States. This leaves one with the question what *does* hold an educational organization together?

A short list of potential elements in educational organizations will provide background for subsequent propositions. March and Olsen (1975) utilize the elements of intention and action. There is a developing position in psychology which argues that intentions are a poor guide for action, intentions often follow rather than precede action, and that intentions and action are loosely coupled. Unfortunately, organizations continue to think that planning is a good thing, they spend much time on planning, and actions are assessed in terms of their fit with plans. Given a potential loose coupling between the intentions and actions of organizational members, it should come as no surprise that administrators are baffled and angered when things never happen the way they were supposed to.

Additional elements may consist of events like yesterday and tomorrow (what happened yesterday may be tightly or loosely coupled with what happens tomorrow) or hierarchial positions, like, top and bottom, line and staff, or administrators and teachers. An interesting set of elements that lends itself to the loose coupling imagery is means and ends. Frequently, several different means lead to the same outcome. When this happens, it can be argued that any one means is loosely coupled to the end in the sense that there are alternative pathways to achieve that same end. Other elements that might be found in loosely coupled educational systems are teachers–materials, voters–schoolboard, administrators–classroom, process–outcome, teacher –teacher, parent–teacher, and teacher–pupil.

While all of these elements are obvious, it is not a trivial matter to specify which elements are coupled. As the concept of coupling is crucial because of its ability to highlight the identity and separateness of elements that are momentarily attached, that conceptual asset puts pressure on the investigator to specify clearly the identity, separateness, and boundaries of the elements coupled. While there is some danger of reification when that kind of pressure is exerted, there is the even greater danger of portraying organizations in inappropriate terms which suggest an excess of unity, integration, coordination, and consensus. If one is nonspecific about boundaries in defining elements then it is easy – and careless – to assemble these ill-defined elements and talk about integrated organizations. It is not a trivial issue explaining how elements persevere over time. Weick, for example, has argued (1974:363–4) that elements may appear or disappear and may merge or become separated in response to need-deprivations within the individual, group, and/or organization. This means that specification of elements is not a one-shot activity. Given the context of most organizations, elements both appear and disappear over time. For this reason a theory of how elements become loosely or tightly coupled may also have to take account of the fact that the nature and intensity of the coupling may itself serve to create or dissolve elements.

The question of what is available for coupling and decoupling within an organization is an eminently practical question for anyone wishing to have some leverage on a system.

## Strength of coupling

Obviously there is no shortage of meanings for the phrase loose coupling. Researchers need to be clear in their own thinking about whether the phenomenon they are studying is described by two words or three. A researcher can study 'loose coupling' in educational organizations or 'loosely coupled systems.' The shorter phrase, 'loose coupling,' simply connotes things, 'anythings,' that may be tied together either weakly or infrequently or slowly or with minimal interdependence. Whether those things that are loosely coupled exist in a system is of minor importance. Most discussions in this paper concern loosely coupled systems rather than loose coupling since it wishes to clarify the concepts involved in the perseverance of sets of elements across time.

The idea of loose coupling is evoked when people have a variety of situations in mind. For example, when people describe loosely coupled systems they are often referring to (1) slack times – times when there is an excessive amount of resources relative to demands; (2) occasions when any one of several means will produce the same end; (3) richly connected networks in which influence is slow to spread and/or is weak while spreading; (4) a relative lack of coordination, slow coordination or coordination that is dampened as it moves through a system; (5) a relative absence of regulations; (6) planned unresponsiveness; (7) actual causal independence; (8) poor observational capabilities on the part of a viewer; (9) infrequent inspection of activities within the system; (10) decentralization; (11) delegation of discretion; (12) the absence of linkages that should be present based on some theory – for example, in educational organizations the expected feedback linkage from outcome back to inputs is often nonexistent; (13) the observation that an organization's structure is not coterminous with its activity; (14) those occasions when no matter what you do things always come out the same – for instance, despite all kinds of changes in curriculum, materials, groupings, and so forth the outcomes in an educational situation remain the same; and (15) curricula or courses in educational organizations for which there are few prerequistes – the longer the string of prerequistes, the tighter the coupling.

## Potential functions and dysfunctions of loose coupling

It is important to note that the concept of loose coupling need not be used normatively. People who are steeped in the conventional literature of organizations may regard loose coupling as a sin or something to be apologized for. This paper takes a neutral, if not mildly affectionate, stance toward the concept. Apart from whatever affect one might feel toward the idea of loose coupling, it does appear *a priori* that certain functions can be served by having a system in which the elements are loosely coupled. Below are listed seven potential functions that could be associated with loose coupling plus additional reasons why each advantage might also be a liability. The dialectic generated by each of these oppositions begins to suggest dependent variables that should be sensitive to variations in the tightness of coupling.

The basic argument of Glassman (1973) is that loose coupling allows some portions of an organization to persist. Loose coupling lowers the probability that the organization will have to – or be able to – respond to each little change in the environment that occurs. The mechanism of voting, for example, allows elected officials to remain in office for a full term even though their constituency at any moment may disapprove of particular actions. Some identity and separateness of the element 'elected official' is preserved relative to a second element, 'constituency,' by the fact of loosely coupled accountability which is measured in two, four, or six year terms. While loose coupling may foster perseverance, it is not selective in what is perpetuated. Thus archaic traditions as well as innovative improvisations may be perpetuated.

A second advantage of loose coupling is that it may provide a sensitive sensing mechanism. This possibility is suggested by Fritz Heider's perceptual theory of things and medium. Heider (1959) argues that perception is most accurate when a medium senses a thing and the medium contains many independent elements that can be externally constrained. When elements in a medium become either fewer in number and/or more internally constrained and/or more interdependent, their ability to represent some remote thing is decreased. Thus sand is a better medium to display wind currents than are rocks, the reason being that sand has more elements, more independence among the elements, and the elements are subject to a greater amount of external constraint than is the case for rocks. Using Heider's formulation metaphorically, it could be argued that loosely coupled systems preserve many independent sensing elements and therefore 'know' their environments better than is true for more tightly coupled systems which have fewer externally constrained, independent elements. Balanced against this improvement in sensing is the possibility that the system would become increasingly vulnerable to producing faddish responses and interpretations. If the environment is known better, then this could induce more frequent changes in activities done in response to this 'superior intelligence.'

A third function is that a loosely coupled system may be a good system for localized adaptation. If all of the elements in a large system are loosely coupled to one another, then any one element can adjust to and modify a local unique contingency without affecting the whole system. These local adaptations can be swift, relatively economical, and substantial. By definition, the antithesis of localized adaptation is standardization and to the extent that standardization can be shown to be desirable, a loosely coupled system might exhibit fewer of these presumed benefits. For example, the localized adaptation characteristic of loosely coupled systems may result in a lessening of educational democracy.

Fourth, in loosely coupled systems where the identity, uniqueness, and separateness of elements is preserved, the system potentially can retain a greater number of mutations and novel solutions than would be the case with a tightly coupled system. A loosely coupled system could preserve more 'cultural insurance' to be drawn upon in times of radical change than in the case for more tightly coupled systems. Loosely coupled systems may be elegant solutions to the problem that adaptation can preclude adaptability. When a specific system fits into an ecological niche and does so with great success, this adaptation can be costly. It can be costly because resources which are useless in a current environment might deteriorate or disappear even though they could be crucial in a modified environment. It is conceivable that loosely coupled systems preserve more diversity in responding than do tightly coupled systems, and therefore can adapt to a considerably wider range of changes in the environment than would be true for tightly coupled systems. To appreciate the possible problems associated with this abundance of mutations, reconsider the dynamic outlined in the preceding discussion of localized adaptation. If a local set of elements can adapt to local idiosyncrasies without involving the whole system, then this same loose coupling could also forestall the spread of advantageous mutations that exist somewhere in the system. While the system may contain novel solutions for new problems of adaptation, the very structure that allows these mutations to flourish may prevent their diffusion.

Fifth, if there is a breakdown in one portion of a loosely coupled system, then this breakdown is sealed off and does not affect other portions of the organization. Previously we had noted that loosely coupled systems are an exquisite mechanism to adapt swiftly to local novelties and unique problems. Now we are carrying the analysis one step further, and arguing that when any element misfires or decays or deteriorates, the spread of this deterioration is checked in a loosely coupled system. While this point is reminiscent of earlier functions, the emphasis here is on the localization of trouble rather than the localization of adaptation. But even this potential benefit may be problematic. A loosely coupled system can isolate its trouble spots and prevent the trouble from spreading, but it should be difficult for the loosely coupled system to repair the defective element. If weak influences pass from the defective portions to the functioning portions, then the influence back from these functioning portions will also be weak and probably too little, too late.

Sixth, since some of the most important elements in educational organizations are teachers, classrooms, principals, and so forth, it may be consequential that in a loosely coupled system there is more room available for self-determination by the actors. If it is argued that a sense of efficacy is crucial for human beings, then a sense of efficacy might be greater in a loosely coupled system with autonomous units than it would be in a tightly coupled system where discretion is limited. A further comment can be made about self-determination to provide an example of the kind of imagery that is invoked by the concept of loose coupling.

It is possible that much of the teacher's sense of – and actual – control comes from the fact that diverse interested parties expect the teacher to link their intentions with teaching actions. Such linking of diverse intentions with actual work probably involves considerable negotiation. A parent complains about a teacher's action and the teacher merely points out to the parent how the actions are really correspondent with the parent's desires for the education of his or her children. Since most actions have ambiguous consequences, it should always be possible to justify the action as fitting the intentions of those who complain. Salancik (1975) goes even farther and suggests the intriguing possibility that when the consequences of an action are ambiguous, the stated *intentions* of the action serve as surrogates for the consequences. Since it is not known whether reading a certain book is good or bad for a child, the fact that it is intended to be good for the child itself becomes justification for having the child read it. The potential trade-off implicit in this function of loose coupling is fascinating. There is an increase in autonomy in the sense that resistance is heightened, but this heightened resistance occurs at the price of shortening the chain of consequences that will flow from each autonomous actor's efforts. Each teacher will have to negotiate separately with the same complaining parent.

Seventh, a loosely coupled system should be relatively inexpensive to run because it takes time and money to coordinate people. As much of what happens and should happen inside educational organizations seems to be defined and validated outside the organization, schools are in the business of building and maintaining categories, a business that requires coordination only on a few specific issues – for instance, assignment of teachers. This reduction in the necessity for coordination results in fewer conflicts, fewer inconsistencies among activities, fewer discrepancies between categories and activity. Thus, loosely coupled systems seem to hold the costs of co-ordination to a minimum. Despite this being an inexpensive system, loose coupling is also a nonrational system of fund allocation and therefore, unspecifiable, unmodifiable, and incapable of being used as means of change.

When these several sets of functions and dysfunctions are examined, they begin to throw several research issues into relief. For example, oppositions proposed in each of the preceding seven points suggest the importance of contextual theories. A predicted outcome or its opposite should emerge depending on how and in what the loosely coupled system is embedded. The preceding oppositions also suggest a fairly self-contained research program. Suppose a researcher starts with the first point made, as loose coupling increases the system should contain a greater number of anachronistic practices. Loosely coupled systems should be conspicuous for their cultural lags. Initially, one would like to know whether that is plausible or not. But then one would want to examine in more fine-grained detail whether those anachronistic practices that are retained hinder the system or impose structure and absorb uncertainty thereby producing certain economies in responding. Similar embellishment and elaboration is possible for each function with the result that rich networks of propositions become visible. What is especially attractive about these networks is that there is little precedent for them in the organizational literature. Despite this, these propositions contain a great deal of face validity when they are used as filters to look at educational organizations. When compared, for example, with the bureaucratic template mentioned in the introduction, the template associated with loosely coupled systems seems to take the observer into more interesting territory and prods him or her to ask more interesting questions.

## Methodology and loose coupling

An initial warning to researchers: the empirical observation of unpredictability is insufficient evidence for concluding that the elements in a system are loosely coupled. Buried in that caveat are a host of methodological intricacies. While there is ample reason to believe that loosely coupled systems can be seen and examined, it is also possible that the appearance of loose coupling will be nothing more than a testimonial to bad methodology. In psychology, for example, it has been argued that the chronic failure to predict behavior from attitudes is due to measurement error and not to the unrelatedness of these two events. Attitudes are said to be loosely coupled with behavior, but it may be that this conclusion is an artifact produced because attitudes assessed by time-independent and context-independent measures are being used to predict behaviors that are time and context dependent. If both attitudes and behaviors were assessed with equivalent measures, then tight coupling might be the rule.

Any research agenda must be concerned with fleshing out the imagery of loose coupling – a task requiring a considerable amount of conceptual work to solve a few specific and rather tricky methodological problems before one can investigate loose compling.

By definition, if one goes into an organization and watches which parts affect which other parts, he or she will see the tightly coupled parts and the parts that vary the most. Those parts which vary slightly, infrequently, and aperiodically will be less visible. Notice, for example, that interaction data – who speaks to whom about what – are unlikely to reveal loose couplings. These are the most visible and obvious couplings and by the arguments developed in this paper perhaps some of the least crucial to understand what is going on in the organization.

An implied theme in this paper is that people tend to overrationalize their activities and to attribute greater meaning, predictability, and coupling among them than in fact they have. If members tend to overrationalize their activity then their descriptions will not suggest which portions of that activity are loosely and tightly coupled. One might, in fact, even use the presence of apparent overrationalization as a potential clue that myth making, uncertainty, and loose coupling have been spotted.

J. G. March has argued that loose coupling can be spotted and examined only if one uses methodology that highlights and preserves rich detail about context. The necessity for a contextual methodology seems to arise, interestingly enough, from inside organization theory. The implied model involves cognitive limits on rationality and man as a single channel information processor. The basic methodological point is that if one wishes to observe loose coupling, then one has to see both what is and is not being done. The general idea is that time spent on one activity is time spent away from a second activity. A contextually sensitive methodology would record both the fact that some people are in one place generating events and the fact that these same people are thereby absent from some other place. The rule of thumb would be that a tight coupling in one part of the system can occur only if there is loose coupling in another part of the system. The problem that finite attention creates for a researcher is that if some outcome is observed for the organization, then it will not be obvious whether the outcome is due to activity in the tightly coupled sector or to inactivity in the loosely coupled sector. That is a provocative problem of interpretation. But the researcher should be forewarned that there are probably a finite number of tight couplings that can occur at any moment, that tight couplings in one place imply loose couplings elsewhere, and that it may be the *pattern* of couplings that produces the observed outcomes. Untangling such intricate issues may well require that new tools be developed for contextual understanding and that investigators be willing to substitute nonteleological thinking for teleological thinking (Steinbeck, 1941: ch. 14).

Another contextually sensitive method is the use of comparative studies. It is the presumption of this methodology that taken-for-granted understandings – one possible 'invisible' source of coupling in an otherwise loosely coupled system – are embedded in and contribute to a context. Thus, to see the effects of variations in these understandings one compares contexts that differ in conspicuous and meaningful ways.

Another methodological trap may await the person who tries to study loose coupling. Suppose one provides evidence that a particular goal is loosely coupled to a particular action. He or she says in effect, the person wanted to do this but in fact actually did that, thus, the action and the intention are loosely coupled. Now the problem for the researcher is that he or she may simply have focused on the wrong goal. There may be other goals which fit that particular action better. Perhaps if the researcher were aware of them, then the action and intention would appear to be tightly coupled. Any kind of intention–action, plan–behavior, or means–end depiction of loose coupling may be vulnerable to this sort of problem and an exhaustive listing of goals rather than parsimony should be the rule.

Two other methodological points should be noted. First, there are no good descriptions of the kinds of couplings that can occur among the several elements in educational organizations. Thus, a major initial research question is simply, what does a map of the couplings and elements within an educational organization look like? Second, there appear to be some fairly rich probes that might be used to uncover the nature of coupling within educational organizations. Conceivably, crucial couplings within schools involve the handling of disciplinary issues and social control, the question of how a teacher gets a book for the classroom, and the question of what kinds of innovations need to get clearance by whom. These relatively innocuous questions may be powerful means to learn which portions of a system are tightly and loosely coupled. Obviously these probes would be sampled if there was a full description of possible elements that can be coupled and possible kinds and strengths of couplings. These specific probes suggest, however, in addition that what holds an educational organization together may be a small number of tight couplings in out-of-the-way places.

### Illustrative questions for a research agenda

*Patterns of loose and tight coupling: certification versus inspection*

Suppose one assumes that education is an intrinsically uninspected and unevaluated activity. If education is intrinsically uninspected and unevaluated, then how can one establish that it is occurring? One answer is to define clearly who can and who cannot do it and to whom. In an educational organization this is the activity of certification. It is around the issues of certification and of specifying who the pupils are that tight coupling would be predicted to occur when technology and outcome are unclear.

If one argues that 'certification' is the question 'who does the work' and 'inspection' is the question 'how well is the work done,' then there can be either loose or tight control over either certification or inspection. Notice that setting the problem up this way suggests the importance of discovering the distribution of tight and loosely coupled systems within any organization. Up to now the phrase loosely coupled systems has been used to capture the fact that events in an organization seem to be temporally related rather than logically related (Cohen and March, 1974). Now that view is being enriched by arguing that any organization must deal with issues of certification (who does the work) and inspection (how well is the work done). It is further being suggested that in the case of educational organizations there is loose control on the work – the work is intrinsically uninspected and unevaluated or if it is evaluated it is done so infrequently and in a perfunctory manner – but that under these conditions it becomes crucial for the organization to have tight control over who does the work and on whom. This immediately suggests the importance of comparative research in which the other three combinations are examined, the question being, how do these alternative forms grow, adapt, manage their rhetoric, and handle their clientele. Thus it would be important to find organizations in which the controls over certification and inspection are both loose, organizations where there is loose control over certification but tight control over inspection, and organizations in which there is tight control both over inspection and over certification. Such comparative research might be conducted among different kinds of educational organizations within a single country (military, private, religious schooling in the United States), between educational and noneducational organizations within the same country (for example, schools versus hospitals versus military versus business organizations) or between countries looking at solutions to the problem of education given different degrees of centralization. As suggested earlier, it may not be the existence or nonexistence of loose coupling that is a crucial determinant of organizational functioning over time but rather the patterning of loose and tight couplings. Comparative studies should answer the question of distribution.

If, as noted earlier, members within an organization (and researchers) will see and talk clearly about only those regions that are tightly coupled, then this suggests that members of educational organizations should be most explicit and certain when they are discussing issues related to certification for definition and regulation of teachers, pupils, topics, space, and resources. These are presumed to be the crucial issues that are tightly controlled. Increasing vagueness of description should occur when issues of substantive instruction – inspection – are discussed. Thus those people who primarily manage the instructional business will be most vague in describing what they do, those people who primarily manage the certification rituals will be most explicit. This pattern is predicted *not* on the basis of the activities themselves – certification is easier to describe than inspection – but rather on the basis of the expectation that tightly coupled subsystems are more crucial to the survival of the system and therefore have received more linguistic work in the past and more agreement than is true for loosely coupled elements.

### Core technology and organizational form

A common tactic to understand complex organizations is to explore the possibility that the nature of the task being performed determines the shape of the organizational structure. This straightforward tactic raises some interesting puzzles about educational organizations. There are suggestions in the literature that education is a diffuse task, the technology is uncertain.

This first question suggests two alternatives: if the task is diffuse then would not any organizational form whatsoever be equally appropriate *or* should this directly compel a diffuse form of organizational structure? These two alternatives are not identical. The first suggests that if the task is diffuse then any one of a variety of quite specific organizational forms could be imposed on the organization and no differences would be observed. The thrust of the second argument is that there is one and only one organizational form that would fit well when there is a diffuse task, namely, a diffuse organizational form (for instance, an organized anarchy).

The second question asks if the task in an educational organization is diffuse, then why do all educational organizations look the way they do, and why do they all look the same? If there is no clear task around which the shape of the organization can be formed then why is it that most educational organizations do have a form and why is it that most of these forms look indentical? One possible answer is that the tasks of educational organizations do not constrain the form of the organization but rather this constraint is imposed by the ritual of certification and/or the agreements that are made in and by the environment. If any of these nontask possibilities are genuine alternative explanations, then the general literature on organizations has been insensitive to them.

One is therefore forced to ask the question, is it the case within educational organizations that the technology is unclear? So far it has been argued that loose coupling in educational organizations is partly the result of uncertain technology. If uncertain technology does not generate loose coupling then researchers must look elsewhere for the origin of these bonds.

### *Making sense in/of loosely coupled worlds*

What kinds of information do loosely coupled systems provide members around which they can organize meanings, that is, what can one use in order to make sense of such fleeting structures? (By definition loosely coupled events are modestly predictable at best.) There is a rather barren structure that can be observed, reported on, and retrospected in order to make any sense. Given the ambiguity of loosely coupled structures, this suggests that there may be increased pressure on members to construct or negotiate some kind of social reality they can live with. Therefore, under conditions of loose coupling one should see considerable effort devoted to constructing social reality, a great amount of face work and linguistic work, numerous myths (Mitroff and Kilmann, 1975) and in general one should find a considerable amount of effort being devoted to punctuating this loosely coupled world and connecting it in some way in which it can be made sensible. Loosely coupled worlds do not look as if they would provide an individual many resources for sense making – with such little assistance in this task, a predominant activity should involve constructing social realities. Tightly coupled portions of a system should not exhibit nearly this preoccupation with linguistic work and the social construction of reality.

## Conclusion: a statement of priorities

More time should be spent examining the possibility that educational organizations are most usefully viewed as loosely coupled systems. The concept of organizations as loosely coupled systems can have a substantial effect on existing perspectives about organizations. To probe further into the plausibility of that assertion, it is suggested that the following research priorities constitute a reasonable approach to the examination of loosely coupled systems.

### 1. Develop conceptual tools capable of preserving loosely coupled systems

It is clear that more conceptual work has to be done before other lines of inquiry on this topic are launched. Much of the blandness in organizational theory these days can be traced to investigators applying impoverished images to organizational settings. If researchers immediately start stalking the elusive loosely coupled system with imperfect language and concepts, they will perpetuate the blandness of organizational theory. To see the importance of and necessity for this conceptual activity the reader should re-examine the fifteen different connotations of the phrase 'loose coupling' that are uncovered in this paper. They provide fifteen alternative explanations for any researcher who claims that some outcome is due to loose coupling.

### 2. Explicate what elements are available in educational organizations for coupling

This activity has high priority because it is essential to know the practical domain within which the coupling phenomena occur. Since there is the further complication that elements may appear or disappear as a function of context and time, this type of inventory is essential at an early stage of inquiry. An indirect benefit of making this a high priority activity is that it will stem the counterproductive suspicion that 'the number of elements in educational organizations is infinite.' The reasonable reply to that comment is that if one is precise in defining and drawing boundaries around elements, then the number of elements will be less than imagined. Furthermore, the researcher can reduce the number of relevant elements if he has some theoretical ideas in mind. These theoretical ideas should be one of the outcomes of initial activity devoted to language and concept development (Priority 1).

### 3. Develop contextual methodology

Given favorable outcomes from the preceding two steps, researchers should then be eager to look at complex issues such as patterns of tight and loose coupling keeping in mind that loose coupling creates major problems for the researcher because he is trained and equipped to decipher predictable, tightly coupled worlds. To 'see' loosely coupled worlds unconventional methodologies need to be developed and conventional methodologies that are underexploited need to be given more attention. Among the existing tools that should be refined to study loose coupling are comparative studies and longitudinal studies. Among the new tools that should be 'invented' because of their potential relevance to loosely coupled systems are nonteleological thinking (Steinbeck, 1941), concurrence methodology (Bateson, 1972:180–201), and Hegelian, Kantian, and Singerian inquiring systems (Mitroff, 1974). While these latter methodologies are unconventional within social science, so too is it unconventional to urge that we treat unpredictability (loose coupling) as our topic of interest rather than a nuisance.

*4. Promote the collection of thorough, concrete descriptions of the coupling patterns in actual educational organizations*

No descriptive studies have been available to show what couplings in what patterns and with what strengths existed in current educational organizations. This oversight should be remedied as soon as possible.

Adequate descriptions should be of great interest to the practitioner who wants to know how his influence attempts will spread and with what intensity. Adequate description should also show practitioners how their organizations may be more sensible and adaptive than they suspect. Thorough descriptions of coupling should show checks and balances, localized controls, stabilizing mechanisms, and subtle feedback loops that keep the organization stable and that would promote its decay if they were tampered with.

The benefits for the researcher of full descriptions are that they would suggest which locations and which questions about loose coupling are most likely to explain sizeable portions of the variance in organizational outcomes. For example, on the basis of good descriptive work, it might be found that both tightly and loosely coupled systems 'know' their environments with equal accuracy in which case, the earlier line of theorizing about 'thing and medium' would be given a lower priority.

*5. Specify the nature of core technology in educational organizations*

A surprisingly large number of the ideas presented in this paper assume that the typical coupling mechanisms of authority of office and logic of the task do not operate in educational organizations. Inquiry into loosely coupled systems was triggered partly by efforts to discover what *does* accomplish the coupling in school systems. Before the investigation of loose coupling goes too far, it should be established that authority and task are not prominent coupling mechanisms in schools. The assertions that they are not prominent seem to issue from a combination of informal observation, implausibility, wishful thinking, looking at the wrong things, and rather vague definitions of core technology and reward structures within education. If these two coupling mechanisms were defined clearly, studied carefully, and found to be weak and/or nonexistent in schools, *then* there would be a powerful justification for proceeding vigorously to study loosely coupled systems. Given the absence of work that definitively discounts these coupling mechanisms in education and given the fact that these two mechanisms have accounted for much of the observed couplings in other kinds of organizations, it seems crucial to look for them in educational organizations in the interest of parsimony.

It should be emphasized that if it *is* found that substantial coupling within educational organizations is due to authority of office and logic of the task, this does not negate the agenda that is sketched out in this paper. Instead, such discoveries would (1) make it even more crucial to look for patterns of coupling to explain outcomes, (2) focus attention on tight and loose couplings within task and authority induced couplings, (3) alert researchers to keep close watch for any coupling mechanisms other than these two, and (4) would direct comparative research toward settings in which these two coupling mechanisms vary in strength and form.

### 6. Probe empirically the ratio of functions to dysfunctions associated with loose coupling

Although the word 'function' has had a checkered history, it is used here without apology – and without the surplus meanings and ideology that have become attached to it. Earlier several potential benefits of loose coupling were described and these descriptions were balanced by additional suggestions of potential liabilities. If one adopts an evolutionary epistemology, then over time one expects that entities develop a more exquisite fit with their ecological niches. Given that assumption, one then argues that if loosely coupled systems exist and if they have existed for sometime, then they bestow some net advantage to their inhabitants and/or their constituencies. It is not obvious, however, what these advantages are. A set of studies showing how schools benefit and suffer given their structure as loosely coupled systems should do much to improve the quality of thinking devoted to organizational analysis.

### 7. Discover how inhabitants make sense out of loosely coupled worlds

Scientists are going to have some big problems when their topic of inquiry becomes low probability couplings, but just as scientists have special problems comprehending loosely coupled worlds so too must the inhabitants of these worlds. It would seem that quite early in a research program on loose coupling, examination of this question should be started since it has direct relevance to those practitioners who must thread their way through such 'invisible' worlds and must concern their sense-making and stories in such a way that they don't bump into each other while doing so.

## Notes

1. This paper is the result of a conference held at La Jolla, California, 2–4 February 1975 with support from the National Institute of Education (NIE). Participants in the conference were, in addition to the author, W. W. Charters, Center for Educational Policy and Management, University of Oregon; Craig Lundberg, School of Business, Oregon State University; John Meyer, Dept. of Sociology, Stanford University; Miles Meyers, Dept. of English, Oakland (Calif.) High School; Karlene Roberts, School of Business, University of California, Berkeley; Gerald Salancik, Dept. of Business Administration, University of Illinois; and Robert Wentz, Superintendent of Schools, Pomona (Calif.) United School District. James G. March, School of Education, Stanford University, a member of the National Council on Educational Research, and members of the NIE staff were present as observers. This conference was one of several on organizations.

## References

Bateson, Mary Catherine (1972). *Our Own Metaphor*. New York: Knopf.
Cohen, Michael D., and James G. March (1974) *Leadership and Ambiguity*. New York: McGraw-Hill.
Glassman, R. B. (1973). 'Persistence and loose coupling in living systems.' *Behavioral Science* 18:83–98.
Heider, Fritz (1959). 'Thing and medium.' *Psychological Issues* 1(3):1–34.
March, J. G., and J. P. Olsen (1975). 'Choice Situations in Loosely Coupled Worlds.' Unpublished manuscript, Stanford University.
Meyer, John W. (1975). 'Notes on the Structure of Educational Organizations.' Unpublished manuscript, Stanford University.
Mitroff, Ian I. (1974). *The Subjective Side of Science*. New York: Elsevier.
Mitroff, Ian I., and Ralph H. Kilmann (1975). 'On Organizational Stories: An Approach to the Design and Analysis of Organizations Through Myths and Stories.' Unpublished manuscript, University of Pittsburgh.
Salancik, Gerald R. (1975). 'Notes on Loose Coupling: Linking Intentions to Actions.' Unpublished manuscript, University of Illinois, Urbana-Champaign.
Simon, H. A. (1969). 'The architecture of complexity.' *Proceedings of the American Philosophical Society* 106:467–82.
Steinbeck, John (1941). *The Log from the Sea of Cortez*. New York: Viking.
Stephens, John M. (1967). *The Process of Schooling*. New York: Holt, Rinehart, and Winston.
Weick, Karl E. (1974). 'Middle range theories of social systems.' *Behavioral Science* 19:357–67.

# 5
# Hierarchy, anarchy and accountability: contrasting perspectives. An exchange

**Tim Packwood and Colin Turner**

### (i) The school as a hierarchy (by Tim Packwood)

Criticism of the hierarchy has become *passé*. Authoritarian, anti-individual, anti-professional, inflexible, ineffective and outdated are just some of the epithets that are levelled. Yet work on the Homes, Schools and Social Services Project undertaken by the Educational Studies Unit of Brunel University[1] demonstrated both the hierarchy's ubiquity and its complexity as an organizational form in the schools. This paper, then, attempts to present a fuller picture of the hierarchy in the school situation, describing its components and arguing that the epithets mentioned above are not necessarily deserved.

As is well known, the hierarchy is a time-honoured form of organization for getting work done. While partnerships serve for small-scale operations and collegiates for some highly specialized individual services, the hierarchy is the general structure in all developed cultures for achieving work objectives that are beyond the control of the single individual. Through a series of manager–subordinate relationships it explicitly locates accountability for work.[2] The manager in the hierarchy is accountable not only for his, or her, performance, but also for the work of subordinates. And managers can only carry this accountability if they are given corresponding authority to sanction the work of subordinates – to have a voice in their selection, to assess their work and to be able to initiate their removal from role.

Articles of management and rules of government made under Section 17 of the 1944 Education Act clearly place managerial accountability for the work of a school on the headteacher. He, or she, is answerable for what goes on to the LEA and the governing body.[3] Proponents of the autonomous, self-regulating collegiate should note that this clear locus of accountability would be sacrificed. LEA's and/or governors would be potentially required to have a direct relationship with all qualified teaching staff. This would inevitably make management complicated and time-consuming and would hardly satisfy those who argue for clearer, more accessible and responsive systems of accountability in our public institutions.

In the larger schools there will be additional levels of management in the sense defined above, but it is impossible to generalize regarding their location.[4] The Burnham system identifies salary gradings which, although reflecting judgements on competence and work, are not the same as managerial positions. So much depends on the individual institution; upon its history, geography, size, staff and the preferences of its policy makers. In so far as it is possible to speculate, it would appear that secondary schools approach two levels of management, a headteacher with a head of department on the academic side and with a head of house or year for pastoral work. But there are many exceptions. Some teachers feel that only the headteacher can occupy a managerial position while in other situations deputy heads and/or heads of buildings or component subschools may well occupy intervening levels of management.

The presence of the managerial relationship does not necessarily imply authoritarianism. First, the formalization of authority in a working relationship says nothing about the style through which the authority is exercised. The presence of authority is a prerequisite for authoritarianism but it must be remembered that manager and subordinate, headteacher and teacher, are mutually interdependent. The success of the former depends on the latter and *vice versa*. Any manager, therefore, who consistently ignores or tramples on the feelings of his, or her, subordinates is most unwise. Secondly, there are limits to the application of authority. No manager can so define a subordinate's role that there is no room for the exercise of discretion and judgement. And if this were to be attempted the manager would in effect be doing the subordinate's job and thus neglecting other aspects of his, or her, own work. It is a strength of the hierarchy that managers can adjust the room for discretion in their subordinate's work to match emerging capacities and capabilities. As a general rule, newcomers to the institution have their work prescribed, and are watched, fairly closely. They are then given more scope when they have proved themselves.[5] In the teachers' case this discretion, inherent in work, is strengthened by that accruing from their professional status. As professionals it is expected that teachers are competent to decide how to meet the educational needs of the children with whom they work. Clearly this freedom is limited. There are regulations to be followed, syllabi and timetables will be laid down and various resource constraints must be observed, but the art of actually teaching or providing pastoral care is a matter for the individual teacher alone. In England this professional area is not well defined. There is no one body to set and monitor binding standards, rather these emerge from the work of teaching institutions, from Her Majesty's Inspectors and Local Authority Advisors, from the exhortations of advisory committees, and, perhaps most important, from the norms of local institutional practice. As Hughes has argued,[6] the headteacher can have an important role as leading professional as well as chief executive.[7]

Clearer enunciation of professional standards would certainly help define the teachers' freedom. Indeed, all the signs suggest that if teachers do not take this on, others will do it for them. Freedom would also be strengthened if there were a clearer recognition that all members of an institution, managers and subordinates alike, have an interest in the way that policy is developing. Jaques suggests[8] that institutions require a formalized procedure through which the most senior manager can negotiate the policy to be adopted with all the staff involved or their representatives. As has been implied earlier, without staff acceptance policy implementation is not going to be of the best.[9] Clearly there would be an important role for the teacher unions in this process. So far the argument has attempted to show some of the potential strengths within the managerial relationship and to rebut some of the criticisms so often made. Yet the hierarchy is far more than a system of manager–subordinate relationships, including a wide and complex structure of lateral relationships. Understanding of these is vital to any consideration of how total school services impact on the child. Here we can identify:[10]

1 Managerial assistant relationships, the assistant being accountable for helping a manager perform some aspect of his, or her, work without taking on full accountability for the work of other subordinates or the authority to sanction their work. Two classes have been identified:

  • staff officer, concerned with particular specialized aspects of work, for example, programming or personnel;
  • supervisory staff, potentially concerned with the whole range of the manager's work.[11]

2 Coordinating relationships, where someone is made accountable for integrating a particular aspect of the work of others, but without taking full accountability for their work and on the basis of negotiation rather than directive authority.

3 Monitoring relationships, where someone is made accountable for reviewing particular activities carried out by others, again without taking accountability for their work and on the basis of negotiating, rather than directing, any changes.

4 Collateral relationships between organizational equals, that depend upon mutual agreement or reference of problems to a manager.

5 Service-giving relationships, where service-seekers have authority to expect work that has been sanctioned by policy from others, without directing their work.

This potential richness in the hierarchy is seldom recognized by critics, or indeed by those who draw up organization charts, but the variations in accountability and authority are very real for those involved and make a great deal of difference to life at work. It would seem advantageous to recognize the differences and to be clear as to what is required. Deputy heads and senior masters or mistresses frequently occupy staff officer or supervisory, rather than managerial, relationships to other members of staff, yet this distinction is rarely made explicit. Similarly, if a head of building or subschool is expected to monitor the quality of subject teaching his age range of pupils receive or the discipline in the classrooms, why not say what this involves? It may mean that the headteacher and his senior staff will have to get down to thinking about what constitutes satisfactory teaching and discipline, but that is no bad thing.

Secondary schools do present a particular complexity, not found to the same extent in other public and private sector organizations, through their role diffusion. This occurs widely, particularly where the school hierarchy is divided into separate pastoral and academic structures. Heads of subject departments may be tutors, and heads of house will be members of subject departments. While this duality of work is economic and indeed serves to link the two functions together, it inevitably fragments accountabilities. It is generally the case that there is no one in a management position over both the sub-hierarchies below the level of headteacher. There is no one, then, other than the headteacher who is able to cast authoritative judgement over the teacher's work as a whole. Inevitably this concern must pull the headteacher's attention down into the internal organization, leaving less time for that considerable part of the work concerned with negotiations across the school boundary.[12]

It would seem probable that as, and if, teaching becomes more professionalized, and as demands for staff participation[13] grow, there will be an increase in the use of coordinating[14] rather than managerial relationships within hierarchies. The vertical stereotype will thus give way to a broader, looser configuration, thereby emphasizing the freedom from direction that some see as part of the road to professionalism.[15] The last thirty years has also brought an increased use of meetings in the schools, which emphasize equality and bring together the various parts of the hierarchy to respond rapidly to emerging needs.[16]

The suggestion, then, is that the hierarchy is not outdated in our schools. Rather, it provides for the work of many to be integrated and for accountability to be identified and maintained. It can accommodate professionals and professional freedom and it is capable of recognizing, nurturing and responding to its members' needs in ways that are beyond other forms of organization. There are many possible forms of working relationship within the hierarchy and this potential needs to be recognized in structuring. The need for looking at structure is continuous. Schools are made up of people. Changes in personal capacities and interactions with a changing environment require recognition and channelling in working arrangements. To neglect this is to encourage obsolescence and/or free licence.

This being so, it is dysfunctional that organization is so neglected in our training institutions and in so many of our schools. So much of a person's life effort goes into work and so much of his, or her, being is drawn from it that organization should be more than an area of knowledge that is 'picked up' or seen as of secondary importance. Many educationalists are proposing that future training should be more in-service orientated[17] and since discussion of organization is probably most meaningful within the particular local context, need and opportunity could be usefully matched.

### Notes and references

1. The Educational Studies Unit was set up with DES Finance in 1974 under the direction of Professor Maurice Kogan. Work is currently being undertaken in two outer London Boroughs. Researchers are working with staff from secondary schools, social service departments, the Education Welfare Service, the School Psychological Service, the Careers Service, the Child Guidance Service and the Juvenile Bureau to identify and clarify the gamut of issues surrounding re-lationships between the schools, homes and other welfare agencies. Work is also being undertaken with pupils and parents.
2. Definitions of the managerial relationship, and other forms that are mentioned later in the paper, have emerged from work carried out by Jaques and other members of the Brunel Institute of Organisation and Social Studies in a wide variety of private and public sector organizations. See E. Jaques, *A General Theory of Bureaucracy*, Heinemann, 1976.
3. The immediate locus of accountability above the school is ambiguous, although hopefully the situation will be clarified through the efforts of the Taylor Commit-tee. See R. Glatter, 'Reforming School Managements: Some Structural Issues', *Educational Administration*, Vol. 5, No. 1. Also, T. Packwood, 'Permuting the Relating Game of Governors and Governed', *Education*, 29 August 1975.
4. Managerial levels, in the sense of manager–subordinate relationships, should reflect the work that has to be done. The presence of a managerial position thus reflects a qualitative shift in activities. Rowbottom and Billis suggest that discrete qualitative categories of work can be identified in institutions 'across the board', and that ideally the various levels of work should be matched by levels of management. See R. Rowbottom and D. Billis 'The Stratification of Work and Organisation Design', *Human Relations*, 1976, 29(11).
5. The process of initial assessment may be formalized in a probationary period, although a similar experience of close managerial attention is likely whenever a new activity is taken on.
6. M. G. Hughes, 'The Professional as Administrator: The Case of the Secondary School Head', in *Management in Education I*, V. Houghton, R. McHugh and C. Morgan (eds), Ward Lock Educational in association with The Open University Press, 1975.
7. Position in a managerial hierarchy clearly rules out individual autonomy for the teachers but it does not prohibit what Hill calls group autonomy, an assertion by professionals that they can only be managed by one of their own. It is un-likely that posts of headteacher could be widely opened to any but qualified

teachers. See M. Hill, *The State, Administration and the Individual*, Fontana, 1976.

8. E. Jaques, *A General Theory of Bureaucracy, op. cit.*

9. Following the wider implications of this proposal there would be a need for Directors of Education, and perhaps Chief Executives, to negotiate the future local authority policy framework for education with headteachers.

10. It is quite possible that other relationships remain to be identified. The particular conditions of educational institutions may indeed throw up particular forms that are not duplicated elsewhere, but this is a matter for further investigation.

11. Many deputy roles prove to be built around the supervisory relationship.

12. E. Richardson, *The School, the Teacher and the Task of Management*, Heinemann, 1973.

13. Participation, like management, serves too general a descriptive use. It embraces a spectrum of interactions ranging from sharing in decision making with managers, through consultation, to being 'kept in the picture'.

14. So-called matrix structures make use of coordinated teams in the sense defined in this paper.

15. W. Taylor, 'The Head as Manager: Some Criticisms', in *The Role of the Head*, R. S. Peters (ed.), Routledge & Kegan Paul, 1976.

16. Despite their peculiar character meetings maintain the differentiation of working relationships. Whatever the style adopted meetings with a manager have different properties from those with a coordinator or between collaterals. Strictly, the former are consultative since the manager cannot abdicate his, or her, own accountability to a majority vote.

17. See, for example, 'Back to Base' by R. Aitken, Director of Education for Coventry, in *The Times Educational Supplement*, 8 October 1976.

## (ii) Organizing educational institutions as anarchies
## (by Colin Turner)

Most people work on the assumption that the organizations of which they are a part work best when they have a high level of predictability, stability and constancy and a low level of risk-taking and mutability. A generally desirable characteristic of organizations, so it would seem, is that they should have a pattern of behaviour that is fairly predictable and on the basis of this members are able to establish procedural and operational routines, and engage in rational planning.[1]

March and Olsen[2] state that anarchic organizations are distinguished from predictable organizations by three characteristics: problematic preferences, fluid membership and unclear technology. If we look at the college of further education or polytechnic, it is possible to see all three characteristics represented strongly. Problematic preferences imply that the organization is never very clear what its goals are, what it is really trying to do, and it is a matter of common observation that schools and colleges are very unsure about this. Different members of the organization see different goals or give different priorities to the same goals, or are unable to define their goals to the point where they have any operational meaning. So, given any particular programme of action towards a particular goal, one can never know which of the staff, if any, will see this preferentially.

Colleges have fluid membership to the degree that they relax controls on formal membership. The recent acceleration of community-based college programmes and activities implies a flow in and out of the organization of various sectors of the general public on deliberately non-controlled lines. Once the college library is opened to the general public, the coffee area to any old-age pensioners who want to drop in, the halls and sports facilities to any local clubs who want to use them, then the membership is fluid. No one can say, at any time, exactly who belongs to the college and who does not.

All teaching institutions work with an unclear technology. Teachers are hard put to know what it is their students have learnt, at the end of the day, and certainly do not know how the learning has actually happened. The whole learning process is still more or less a mystery, only at the fringes partially illuminated by the work of educational theorists. Teachers base their professional skill on hunches that may or may not be correct, and use techniques which may or may not help the student to learn effectively. While the state of the science of teaching is at such an early primitive level, we have to accept that schools and colleges work in a technology they hardly understand.

If we see schools and colleges as organizational anarchies, we must also see them as operating within turbulent environments, for it must follow that if they possess the three characteristics of anarchies, they cannot try to define a stable bit of the environment out of the pervasive turbulence in order to reinforce a constancy in the organization that does not exist.

Once it is accepted that the school or college is an unpredictable organization in a turbulent field, then much current thinking and activity which has been built upon the pretence that this was not the case can be rejected. We would not give emphasis to MBO or PPBS, to standardized rules and procedures, to well defined powers of decision-making and authority within a hierarchy, to accountability for ones' subordinates to ones' superiors. All those activities concerned with keeping the boundaries strong and with rejecting all except the acceptable parts of the environment, become irrelevant. The organization lowers its defences so that it can respond to the turbulence outside. A much greater degree of uncontrolled interpenetration of the environment and the school or college takes place. In such an organization, individuals need to be highly adaptive as they meet and handle constantly changing situations. Not only must they be capable of flexibility and creative response, but also must be able to avoid the temptation of trying to stamp order and routine on the turbulence in which they operate, for even those who can be flexible may well prefer routinized activities.

It follows that most decisions the individual makes will be short run: they will be made on the assumption that they answer an immediate need in existing conditions, but may be modified or contradicted very soon, and certainly will have no permanent use. Furthermore, adaptive short-run decision-making can only be handled by the man on the spot. He needs full discretion, full delegated powers, and full trust from his superiors in his capacity to handle the situations he is asked to meet. In particular, this means that the on-the-spot decision maker must be allowed to take risk-decisions – indeed not only allowed but encouraged and supported. These decision makers, who may well be operating on the fringe of the boundaries at the intermeshing of the organization and its environment, are likely more often than not to be comparatively junior staff members. This has clear implications for the structuring of the organization. The traditional hierarchic decision-making structure, with the organization divided horizontally into specialized departments and vertically into authority levels, has some advantage in a stable organization when decisions can move up and down the chain of command and be made or approved by the appropriate superior as a part of the total organizational plan. It is, however, entirely unsuitable for the anarchic organization where adaptive short-run decisions are made at the front line.[3] Hierarchies discourage risk-taking, trust and innovation. This is a particular problem for colleges of further education which have built up strong hierarchic structures; less so for schools where only the larger have hierarchies of any significance; least so perhaps for colleges of education and universities.

Another management style that has grown particularly in colleges over the last five years is that of collegial, participative or committee management. This is equally unsuitable to the anarchic organization. Committees aim at political solutions which reach nearest to complete consensus, they take a long time to reach decisions, and they tend to avoid risk-taking ones. They generally try to increase rather than decrease predictability by developing more procedures, more rules, more routines.

Ideally the structure should encourage member's autonomy and discourage dependency, be flexible enough to operate on constantly changing environments and shifting boundaries.

To encourage staff in autonomous decision-making, it is not enough to dismantle the bureaucratic machinery of the organization. Selection procedures and job socialization are most powerful reinforcers of the status quo. The stronger the boundaries that separate the organization from the outside environment, the more powerful these reinforcers. This is particularly true of those organizations Carlson calls 'domestic'.[4] The 'domestic' organizations, such as hospitals, schools, national and local government departments, have a more or less guaranteed existence whatever their performance, unlike the 'wild' organizations, the entrepreneurial shops and factories, which have to survive against tough competition from rivals and where no survival is guaranteed. So if a positive policy of dissolving most of the boundaries is instituted group cohesion and group pressures within the organization will be reduced. Staff members will have many more sources of information that will help define their jobs, much from outside the walls competing with safe sources from within.

Educational institutions can therefore choose to follow a path of boundary dissolution, free exchange with the environment, debureaucratization, selecting staff for autonomy and investing in them full decision-making powers. The hardest part for many managers in colleges to accept is the uselessness of the current concept of accountability. In the anarchic organization it is nonsensical for one professional to be held accountable for the activities of those professionals who are named as subordinate to him. Every professional must be answerable for what he does, but only to the ultimate authority he serves – in most cases the Local Education Committee representing the public. Anything else starts to reimpose that artificial order, the arena of safety, and the suppression of innovation and risk, that one is trying to avoid.

The free-ranging autonomous decision makers that we envisage will not be happy if left in isolation. Decision-making, particularly in uncertain conditions involving risk, creates high levels of stress in individuals. There must be ways in the institution whereby the individual can reduce this stress. Most commonly this is done among professions, as Pelz[5] has shown, by communication with other colleagues, either in inconsequential gossip or talking through problems. This can be formalized by the device of paired consultancy, in which two colleagues agree to report to each other what they have been doing, discussing and analysing in a helping and supporting relationship. Such a system would be more appropriate to the anarchic institution than the pervasive procedure of formal delegation and reporting back.

Ultimately one would hope that changes in teacher training would reinforce the efforts of those colleagues which accept a high degree of unpredictability and try to organize appropriately.

Of course, there are always parts of the anarchic organization which need a higher level of order and predictability. The argument is not that there should be no planning or ordering at all. The college has to be financed, stock has to be controlled, buildings planned and erected, staff and students routed to the parts of the building in which they need to be. For these kinds of purposes an efficient management team is required, but its activities should not set the style, as it generally does now, for the climate of the college or the remaining activities of the staff. Management teams are primarily responsible for establishing the state of readiness of the system to respond to legitimate demands. Areas of order and routine are comparatively small, and even within them the assumption that their plans have any great predictive value is generally fictional. As we know, it is seldom that the forecasts of size and demand on which staff are recruited, stock obtained and buildings erected turn out to have much accuracy.

## Summary

The argument of this article is that organizations can aim to be highly predictable or accept a high degree of unpredictability. The significant variable is in the openness of relations with the environment and the strength of the organizational boundary. It is suggested that some schools and colleges are beginning to increase the variety of interaction with the environment and decrease the impermeability of their boundaries.

It is argued that some organizations, such as the college or school, are by the nature of their enterprise, anarchic, and where this is so, attempts to retain predictability by strong boundary maintenance are irrelevant, since unpredictability is built into the organization.

If the college and school are, or should be seen to be, unpredictable, anarchic organizations with no clear boundaries and a turbulent environment, it is argued that this has consequences for the style of running such institutions. In particular, we have stressed the value of the development of an autonomous staff and the devolution of decision-making, the danger of hierarchic or committee systems of management, and the irrelevance of much of the current thinking in the area of MBO.

## References

1. T. Kynaston Reeves and B. A. Turner, 'A theory of organisation and behaviour in batch production factories', *Administrative Science Quarterly*, March 1972, Vol. 17, No. 1, pp. 81–98.
2. M. D. Cohen, J. G. March and J. P. Olsen, 'A garbage can model of organisational choice', *Administrative Science Quarterly*, March 1972, Vol. 17, No. 1, pp. 1–25.
3. See M. G. Abbott, 'Hierarchical impediments to innovation in educational organisations', and V. A. Thompson, 'Hierarchy, specialisation and organisational conflict', in F. D. Carver and T. J. Sergiovanni (eds) *Organisations and Human Behaviour: Focus on Schools*, McGraw-Hill, 1969.
4. R. O. Carlson, 'Environmental constraints and organisational consequences', in D. E. Griffiths (ed.), *Behavioural Science and Educational Administration*, National Society for the Study of Education, 1964.
5. D. C. Pelz, 'Some social factors related to performance in a research organisation', *Administrative Science Quarterly*, 1956, Vol. 1, pp. 310–25.

## (iii) Comment on Colin Turner's paper (Tim Packwood)

The idea of anarchy probably frequently appeals to those of us whose time is spent in grappling with the vagaries of complex institutions. At root, however, Colin Turner's paper is not about anarchy but is concerned with the serious business of making educational organizations operate effectively in situations of uncertainty while providing satisfying and meaningful work for their employees.

Over much of the argument for his ideal model, I suspect there is no very great divergence in our two viewpoints. I cannot, however, see the hierarchy solely in terms of the classical pyramid. It is too simple to equate the hierarchy with long chains of management. As I have attempted to argue in my own paper, it can draw upon a variety of working relationships. It is based upon vertical managerial relationships but also utilizes a whole range of horizontal relationships with very different properties of accountability and authority. The small primary school does not have tiers of senior positions, it is, nevertheless, hierarchical with the headteacher carrying managerial accountability and authority in respect of what is done.

It is, then, meaningless to talk of *the* hierarchy. The ideal is always related to particular situations, pressures and personalities and can never be immutable. The environmental factors Colin Turner mentions, together with a growing professional awareness would seem to call for flatter hierarchies with a greater emphasis on coordination. And I would certainly accept that they call for a more open *style* of organization.

It is on the question of the abolition of accountability that we really part company. Accountability does not vanish in conditions of environmental turbulence. Indeed, if the careers of employees in 'the wilder organizations' are examined, say, for example, football team managers, the presence, and application, of accountability is readily apparent. I cannot see, either, that accountability is necessarily inimical to discretion, delegation and trust. If these are not given, the hierarchy loses all point.

The alternative, as I think Colin Turner recognizes, is autonomy. And here the result might well be anarchy. The case for autonomy is strongest where a particular service is mediated through one named professional, as is the case in the health service. The education of any child is, however, an integrated process involving many teachers. If teachers were autonomous, the risk of fragmentation would be too great, particularly as the process only operated on the basis of short-run decisions. Direct control by the public representatives provides no safeguard. In practice, this would be most unlikely to work but the attempt would mark a contradiction in the members' role and if successful would surely put an end to autonomy.

The hierarchy, through its properties of accountability and authority, is a rational attempt to combine the activities of many in securing desired ends. Without accountability the organization runs as 'catch as catch can' and any outcome depends upon the power of the individuals concerned. Education is too important for that and it cannot solely depend upon short-term decisions. The result would be unhappy, uneducated children and unhappy, frustrated staff.

The educational environment is undoubtedly turbulent and increasingly unpredictable. The hierarchy must adapt, which means a greater flexibility in structure and a readiness by staff to consider change. Certain management techniques may well prove to be inappropriate and should be discarded. The style of management, too, must move with the times. I differ from Colin Turner in believing that the substance of the hierarchical system is desirable and, further, in my optimism that it can be applied to meet the needs of the future.

### (iv) Comment on Tim Packwood's paper (Colin Turner)

I have long been a *passé* critic of hierarchic systems of organization, but I have never denied their strengths and Tim Packwood describes these admirably. I accept fully his analysis of the variety of hierarchic workings. For some kinds of organizations in some kinds of settings and at the right time of development, I have no doubt that hierarchic systems have much to commend them. My belief is that these criteria do not apply to colleges or schools. Hierarchies have worked reasonably well for predictable operations producing relatively standard products or administering rule-bound services, but even here there are disadvantages to which Packwood does not give much weight. These costs have been well-researched though there is an inclination for those at the top of hierarchies not to believe they exist.

We know well enough that hierarchies, however flexibly organized, inhibit innovation and adaptation to the environment, distort communication flows, and create hostility and alienation at the base of the organization. The larger the institution, the more these effects tend to be mutually reinforcing. For example, the distortion of communication flows in a large comprehensive school or college means that information tends to be guarded in certain areas where it becomes a source of power. Those with poor connections into these information modules feel alienated from sources of power, and since they are most likely to be those at the base of the hierarchy, this reinforces existing alienation. Such teachers are also likely to experience most frustration in innovating, and be most aware of the failure of feedback communication up the system.

All these are well-known disadvantages of hierarchic systems, to set against the advantages Packwood describes. What concerns me rather more about his article is his analysis of accountability, because I suspect that this is at the centre of our differences. I endorse Max Abbott's comment that the doctrine of accountability is largely nonsensical in educational institutions. It is of course a useful tool to enhance the power of the head or principal, though it does very little to help him organize educational activity in his institution any better. It is a useful principle to work to if one wants to run a tight organization following predictable ways within strongly defended boundaries against outside intrusion. If the head is accountable for everything, then he is not likely to allow activities to happen that he is not fully aware of or which he cannot control. Hence much of a head's concern is in protecting his boundaries, controlling transactions across it and disputing uncertain areas of control, such as, for example, responsibility for evening classes in his school building.

I see such attitudes as becoming out of touch with the situation as it is developing, in which there will be a free-flowing interaction with a transient environment, high levels of unpredictability, and with power and control as negotiated commodities between various groups of people inside and outside the institution. In such situations, each member of staff becomes accountable to the public he serves and to colleagues with whom he directly works. The headmaster or principal would still, of course, be responsible for making sure resources are made available for agreed programmes.

I found Packwood's discussion of hierarchy and professionalism valuable. It is ironic, however, that under hierarchic systems of accountability, the professional teacher has been able to create a private area of concern which is not available for scrutiny by the headmaster or the public. If teaching operations in the classroom are seen as private areas, then hierarchic control tends to be exercised on all activities other than those of teaching by rules and regulations, monitoring and checking, and this often becomes a major irritant to teachers. In the kind of organization I am advocating, with autonomy given to the teacher or the task team, the learning process becomes much more open to public scrutiny and debate. The headmaster or principal is not interposed between the teacher or team on the one hand and the legitimate concern of the public on the other, with an effective screen of hierarchic accountability.

I will accept rather more readily the advantages of hierarchic accountability, when it is apparent to me that this involves proper appraisal of the teaching activities of the professional staff. Accountability without appraisal really gets the worst of both our worlds.

# 6
# The structure of educational organizations

**John W. Meyer and Brian Rowan**

Large-scale educational organizations have become dominant forms in almost all countries (Coombs, 1968). That is, not only has *formal* education become dominant, but this education is organized in large bureaucracies managed by political systems; no longer is it simply a matter of exchange between families and local educational organizations.

This circumstance is not surprising. Many other social activities have come under political and bureaucratic control in modern societies. It is customary to suppose that, as the scale of these activities expands, higher levels of coordination and control are required, and that bureaucratic controls emerge to structure these activities efficiently. This view does not fit educational organization, however. There is a great deal of evidence that educational organizations (at least in the United States) *lack* close internal coordination, especially of the content and methods of what is presumably their main activity – instruction. Instruction tends to be removed from the control of the organizational structure, in both its bureaucratic and its collegial aspects. This property of educational organizations, among others, has led March and Olsen (1976) and Weick (1976) to apply the term 'loosely coupled' to educational organizations. By this they mean that *structure is disconnected from technical (work) activity, and activity is disconnected from its effects*.

In this chapter we offer an explanation of the rise of large-scale educational bureaucracies that consistently leave instructional activities and outcomes uncontrolled and uninspected. We argue that educational bureaucracies emerge as personnel-certifying agencies in modern societies. They use standard types of curricular topics and teachers to produce standardized types of graduates, who are then allocated to places in the economic and stratification system on the basis of their certified educational background. In such matters as controlling who belongs in a particular *ritual classification* – for example, who is a certified mathematics teacher, a fifth-grader, an English major – educational organizations are very tightly, not loosely, organized. As large-scale educational organizations develop, they take on a great deal of control over the ritual classifications of their curriculum students, and teachers. The reason for this is that the standardized categories of teachers, students, and curricular topics give meaning and definition to the internal activities of the school. These elements are *institutionalized* in the legal and normative rules of the wider society. In fact, the ritual classifications are the basic components of the theory (or ideology) of education used by modern societies, and schools gain enormous resources by conforming to them, incorporating them, and controlling them (Meyer and Rowan, 1977).

Schools less often control their instructional activities or outputs, despite periodic shifts toward 'accountability.' They avoid this kind of control for two reasons. First, close supervision of instructional activity and outputs can uncover inconsistencies and inefficiencies and can create more uncertainty than mere abstract and unenforced demands for conformity to bureaucratic rules. Second, in the United States centralized governmental and professional controls are weak. Schools depend heavily on local funding and support. Maintaining only nominal central control over instructional outputs and activities also maintains societal consensus about the abstract ritual classifications by making local variations in the content and effectiveness of instructional practices invisible. This also allows instructional practices, although prescribed by rules institutionalized at highly generalized levels, to become adapted to unique local circumstances.

In the American situation, attempts to tightly link the prescriptions of the central theory of education to the activities of instruction would create conflict and inconsistency and discredit and devalue the meaning of ritual classifications in society. Educators (and their social environments) therefore decouple their ritual structure from instructional activities and outcomes and resort to a 'logic of confidence': higher levels of the system organize on the assumption that what is going on at lower levels makes sense and conforms to rules, but they avoid inspecting it to discover or assume responsibility for inconsistencies and ineffectiveness. In this fashion, educational organizations work more smoothly than is commonly supposed, obtain high levels of external support from divergent community and state sources, and maximize the meaning and prestige of the ritual categories people use, employ, and produce.

Our argument hinges on the assertion that education is highly institutionalized in modern society. Its categories of students and graduates, as well as its ritual classification of production procedures – types of teachers, topics, and schools – are all derived from highly institutionalized rules and beliefs. Educational organizations derive power and resources when such rules are institutionalized in society, and they are thus inclined to incorporate and remain in close conformity with such categorical rules.

In this chapter we (1) describe the prevailing pattern of control in educational oranizations, (2) consider the inadequacies of conventional explanations of this pattern, (3) formulate an alternative interpretation, and (4) consider some research implications and issues in organization theory that arise from the discussion.

## Patterns of control in educational organizations

The literature on educational organizations manifests a peculiar contradiction. On the one hand, there are depictions of the educational system as highly coordinated and controlled – to the point of restricting local innovation (for instance, Holt, 1964; Rogers, 1968). On the other hand, conventional sociological discussions hold that actual educational work – instruction – occurs in the isolation of the self-contained classroom, removed from organizational coordination and control. In this view, local innovations fail, not because the system is rigid but because the system lacks internal linkages (Lortie, 1973; Deal, Meyer, and Scott, 1975). Both of these views contain an element of truth. Instructional activities – the *work* of the organization – are coordinated quite casually in most American educational institutions; but the ritual classifications and categories that organize and give meaning to education are tightly controlled. Our first concern is to describe this situation in more detail.

### Loose coupling of structure and activities

Consider some of the ways in which educational organizations lack coordination and control over the technical activity within them – a situation called 'loose coupling' by March and Olsen (1976) and Weick (1976).

### Evaluation

Educational work takes place in the isolation of the classroom, removed from organizational controls of a substantive kind (see, for instance, Bidwell, 1965; Dreeben, 1973; Lortie, 1973). Neither teaching nor its output in student socialization is subject to serious organizational evaluation and inspection (Dornbusch and Scott, 1975). The weak formal inspection of instruction is evident from a 1972 survey of San Francisco Bay area elementary schools conducted by the Environment for Teaching Program (Cohen *et al.*, 1976). Survey data were obtained from thirty-four district superintendents, 188 principals of schools within these districts, and 231 teachers in sixteen of the schools. The schools were selected by stratified random sampling from the population of elementary schools in the eight counties adjoining San Francisco Bay. The data show that the inspection of instructional activity is delegated to the local school and takes place infrequently. For example, only one of the thirty-four superintendents interviewed reported that the district office evaluates teachers directly. Nor does it appear that principals and peers have the opportunity to inspect and discuss teachers' work: Of the principals surveyed, 85 per cent reported that they and their teachers do not work together on a daily basis. Further, there is little evidence of interaction among teachers: A majority of the principals report that there are no day-to-day working relations among teachers within the same grade level, and 83 per cent report no daily work relations among teachers of different grades. Teachers reaffirm this view of segmented teaching. Two-thirds report that their teaching is observed by other teachers infrequently (once a month or less), and half report a similar infrequency of observation by their principals.

Direct inspection of the teaching task is, of course, only one means of organizational control. Organizations can also exert control by inspecting outputs (Ouchi and Maguire, 1975). Schools, for example, could determine which teachers have students that score well on standardized tests. But a striking fact about American education at all levels is that student achievement data are rarely used to evaluate the performance of teachers or schools. For example, in 1972, only one of thirty-four superintendents in the Environment for Teaching survey reported using standardized achievement data to evaluate district schools. Many reasons have been given for this failure to employ output controls – among them, the unavailability and low reliability of the measures. These reasons are made less plausible by the fact that such measures are routinely used to assess and determine the life chances of students.

### Curriculum and technology

Another critical ingredient of organizational control – a teaching technology or even a detailed instructional program of socially agreed-on efficacy – is largely missing in schools. Routine technologies with high consensual standards of efficiency are thought, in organization theory, to create great pressures for effective control (Perrow, 1970). In schools, however, there are few detailed standards of instructional content or procedure. For example, 93 per cent of the principals interviewed in the Environment for Teaching survey report having only general or informal curriculum guidelines, as opposed to detailed policies. Such diffuse standards are even more the case with teaching methods. Only 4 percent of the principals report that they are extremely influential in determining the instructional methods used by teachers.

There is a similar lack of coordination and control over technical interdependencies. Schools appear to minimize problems of coordination that might arise from instructional practices. For example, it may seem necessary for sixth-graders to have mastered fifth-grade work, but in fact students are often processed from grade to grade with little regard for how much they have learned. In this way schools minimize sequential interdependencies inherent in their instructional core, and teachers adapt informally to student variability. Schools also minimize the interdependence among instructional programs. Webster (1976) reports that specialized program administrators seldom interact or discuss the activities of other programs.

*Authority*

It also seems that educational administrators have little direct authority over instructional work. While administrators have a generalized responsibility to plan and coordinate the content and methods of instruction, their authority to carry out these activities is in fact evanescent. As an illustration, only 12 per cent of the San Francisco Bay area principals say they have real decision power over the methods teachers use. On issues other than instruction, however, principals assume real decision rights: of those surveyed, 82 per cent claim to decide about scheduling, 75 per cent about pupil assignment; and 88 per cent claim to decide (alone or with district consultation) about hiring.

These data and examples suggest that educational organizations only marginally control their central instructional functions – especially when it is remembered that the data concern elementary schools, which are the types of schools ordinarily thought to have the highest levels of control, as organiz- ations, over the content and methods of instruction. An important caveat is needed, however: This discussion is limited to American schooling. In contrast, schools observed in Britain show much more internal coordination. Evaluation and control are exerted under the authority of the headmaster, whose role in the school and in British society is substantial and is rooted in established tradition. Similarly, some continental educational systems also vest substantive power and authority in central ministries. Our description of the loose control of instruction, as well as our subsequent explanation, will therefore need to take into account particular features of American society and education.

*The tight control of ritual classifications*

The description just given has highlighted the structural looseness (Bidwell, 1965) of educational organizations. But, although the evidence seems to show loose controls in the area of instruction, there is some evidence of tight organizational controls in such areas as the credentialing and hiring of teachers, the assignment of students to classes and teachers, and scheduling. This suggests that within schools certain areas of organizational structure are more tightly controlled than others. In contrast to instructional activities, there seem to be centralized and enforced agreements about exactly what teachers, students, and topics of instruction constitute a particular school. Also, in the allocation of space, funds, and materials schools exercise considerable control. Teachers in different, isolated classrooms seem to teach similar topics, and students learn many of the same things. One of the main emphases in our discussion will be to explain how educational organizations, with few controls over their central activities, achieve adequate coordination, and how they persist so stably.

The tight control that educational organizations maintain over the ritual or formal classification systems is central to our understanding of edu- cation as an institution. To a considerable extent educational organizations function to maintain the *societally agreed-on rites defined in societal myths (or institutional rules) of education.* Education rests on and obtains enormous resources from central institutional rules about what valid education is. These rules define the ritual categories of teacher, student, curricular topic, and type of school. When these categories are properly assembled, education is understood to occur; but for the rites to occur in a legitimate way some general exigencies of the physical and social world require practical management. All participants assembled for their ritual performances must be properly qualified and categorized. Consider the procedures for controlling the properties of ritually defined actors, for assembling the legitimate curricular topics, and for assembling these into an accredited school.

### Teacher classifications

There are elaborate rules for classifying teachers. There are elementary school teachers, high school teachers, and college teachers – each type with its own specifications, credentials, and categories of specialists. Each type has a legitimate domain outside of which instruction would be deemed inappropriate; for example, elementary teachers do not teach college physics. Each type also possesses appropriate credentials, which are defined and controlled in an elaborate way (see Woellner, 1972, for specific descriptions). Educational organizations, then, have detailed, definitive specifications delineating which individuals may teach in which types of classes and schools.

Further, particular educational organizations maintain lists of teachers, with their formal assignments to topics, space, students, and funds. These teachers are defined by name, recorded background and training, and types of credentials. Schools are very tightly coupled organizations in defining who their teachers are and what properties these teachers have. Yet there is almost no formal control exercised to ensure that each teacher enacts the substance of the typological category in daily activity. That is, documents of what teachers *do* are either nonexistent or vacuous, while documents that *define persons as teachers* are elaborately controlled.

### Student classifications

Similarly, elaborate sets of formal rules define types of students. Students are sharply distinguished by level or grade, by programs or units completed, by subject area specialization, and even by special abilities (for instance, educationally handicapped). Student classifications are tightly controlled, and schools can define exactly which students are fifth-graders, chemistry majors, or enrollees. Adding a new type of student (for instance, economics majors or emotionally handicapped students) is an explicit and important organizational decision. But, while the documents and rules relevant to the classification of students are explicit and carefully maintained, little formal organization ensures that students are being treated (or acting in a manner) appropriate to their type (for instance, see Hobbs, 1975). It is very clear whether a given school has an economics major or not, but there may be no one in the organization who keeps track of exactly what economics majors study or learn.

Further, there are rules governing the students' entrance into and movement through the system. Residence, age, previous education, or ethnic background often govern entrance into a particular school, grade, or program. Changes from any ritual category – for instance, to sixth-grader or to college student – require close coordination ensuring the propriety of the ritual transition. However, although there is a great clarity in formal assignment or transition, few formal organizational mechanisms ensure that these assignments are enacted substantively – for instance, that twelfth-graders are actually doing twelfth-grade work or that third-graders who are being promoted have actually met some standards.

### Topic classifications

Definitive sets of topics are organized in schools and assigned to teachers, students, space, and funds. Each school has a formalized set of curricular topics. An elementary school, for instance, may cover the standard elementary curriculum from kindergarten through the sixth grade. A high school may offer instruction in history and business but not in Latin. There is a definitive agreement, built into the school's formal structure, about the topics in which the school is and is not offering instruction at any given time. These topics are carefully documented, as are the particular teachers who manage them and the particular students who receive (or have received) instruction in them; but there is extraordinarily little formal control to define exactly what any given topic means or to ensure that specific topics are taught in the same way. Business courses, for example, can vary greatly from teacher to teacher. Similarly, what actually constitutes sixth-grade mathematics can show remarkable variation from classroom to classroom. Yet, despite the vacuity in specified content, elaborate rules make sure that each elementary school has something called a sixth-grade, and that this sixth-grade contains instruction in something called sixth-grade mathematics.

### School classifications

Finally, students, teachers, and topics are assembled into formal units by an elaborate and precise set of rules. Such units are then assigned to funds, space, and materials. The expected location of each teacher and student is recorded in detail, as are the topics they will cover, and missing teachers or students are promptly recorded.

The assembly of teachers, students, and topics into classrooms creates the larger institutional classification called 'school,' and although little attention may be focused on what actually goes on in these units, detailed records are kept by districts, local and state boards of education, and accrediting agencies that certify their existence as valid schools of a particular class (for instance, elementary schools or colleges). So, for example, elaborate lists of state high schools are kept, even though one may stress college-level work while another provides only very rudimentary instruction.

The internal and external emphasis on the formal categorical status of schools and their elements may seem at first to be a misdirected obsession; but in many ways the meaning of schooling in modern society seems to be captured by these definitions and categories. Without such general understandings, the educational system would not receive the massive social support that it does. Without such social classifications and understandings, parents and the state would not legitimately extend broad powers over children to random adult strangers. What sensible person would devote years and money to disorganized (and not demonstrably useful) study without the understanding that this is 'college' or 'economics'? These shared ideas of teacher, student, topic, and school – and some implicit assumptions about what will or will not go on – give schooling its social plausibility.

## Conventional explanations of the organization of schools

Educational organizations are formed to instruct and socialize. Their specific activity in these two areas, however, seems to be diffusely controlled, in good part outside formal organizational controls. On the other hand, the ritual classifications of schools are precisely specified, closely inspected, and tightly controlled. Our purpose here is to discuss explanations that are often used to account for this pattern of control in educational organizations. The conventional dynamic in these accounts begins with the question of what is wrong with schools and then goes on to a consideration of how it can be changed. Our problem, however, is to account for this situation, not to decry it. By way of clarification, we consider the following conventional accounts.

### *The reform perspective*

Reformers abound in the world of education. They paint a picture of schools as archaic, as organizations not yet rationalized by proper output measures, evaluation systems and control structures, and therefore as systems that rely mainly on traditional types of authority among students, teachers, and school administrators. Reformers imagine that rationalized control and accounting measures can drive out less 'modern' mechanisms of control once a few recalcitrant and reactionary groups are eliminated.

The difficulty with the reform view is its faith in the inevitable progression toward rationalization. This idea is not new. In many ways it characterizes Horace Mann's ideas, and it certainly describes the perspective of the educational reformers of the late nineteenth century (for example, see Cubberly, 1916). The 'new' organizational forms advocated at that time were to bring measurement, evaluation, and organizational control to instruction (Tyack, 1974). The guiding image was that of the factory, with its emphasis on organizationally controlled design and production. But a good case can be made that there is now less organizational control and evaluation of instruction than there was in the nineteenth century, before all of the reforms (Tyack, 1974).

One cannot keep on asserting that the educational system is archaic, a passive anachronism itching for reform, when it seems to systematically eliminate innovations that bring inspection, evaluation, coordination, and control over instructional activities (Callahan, 1962). In any event, the view that education is weakly controlled because it lacks output measures is misdirected. Schools use elaborate tests to evaluate pupils and to shape the course of their present and future lives; but the same data are almost never aggregated and used to evaluate the performance of teachers, schools, or school systems. (Some data of this kind are made available for school and district evaluation in California, but only under the pressure of the state legislature, not the local school system.)

One other feature of the reform perspective deserves special note. Reformers tend to view American education as fragile, inept, disorganized, and on the edge of chaos and dissolution. Schools are seen to be in a poor state of organizational 'health' (Miles, 1975). This is an astonishing description of a network of organizations that has grown rapidly for many decades, that obtains huge economic resources in a stable way year after year, that is protected from failure by laws that make its use compulsory, that is constantly shown by surveys to have the confidence and support of its constituency (Acland, 1975), and that is known to have high levels of job satisfaction among its participants (Meyer *et al.*, 1971). Reformers may wish educational organizations were on their last legs, but all the 'crises' that reformers have declared have subsided quickly, and the system has remained stable.

### The decentralist stance

Another view has it that educational organizations are oligarchic structures, headed by educational administrators and the elites that control them. In this view, educators are entrenched bureaucrats, resisting local community control and evaluation and building up their status rights and immunities in the system. This system resists accountability, the argument goes, and should be decentralized to the local level, where the lay public can be involved in educational decision making (for example, see Fantini and Gittell, 1973; Rogers, 1968).

This view does not easily come into accord with the following facts. First, the American educational system has enormous popular support. This is inconsistent with the view that the system is controlled by a resistant and entrenched bureaucracy, unless one argues that the entire populace is afflicted with false consciousness in the matter. Second, even if the bureaucrats who presumably control the educational system were uninterested in effective education and were only seeking self-aggrandizement, why would they not inspect and control teachers more carefully to make sure that they conform to elite or bureaucratic interests?

In fact, the main difficulty with the decentralist's position is that it ignores the fact that local control of education in America is not in conflict with the organizational structures we have described. We will later argue that the local community obtains important benefits from the present dearth of systematic inspection and evaluation and that accountability could arise only from more, not less, centralization of educational power.

### The professionalization of teaching

It is possible to argue that educational instruction is not controlled by central administrators but rather by the teaching profession. In this view, schools are loosely coupled simply because they provide a setting in which professional teachers, thoroughly socialized to use the expert techniques of their discipline, ply their trade. Educational administrators merely form a sort of holding company to provide and maintain the facilities in which teachers work, in much the same way as hospital administrators service doctors.

This view is not seriously maintained in most quarters. Teachers themselves turn out not to believe this myth of professionalism. Dornbusch and Scott (1975) show that teachers report that their training has little to do with their ability to perform effectively (in sharp contrast to nurses, for example). In the San Francisco Bay area survey reported earlier (Cohen *et al.*, 1976), of the elementary teachers interviewed, 77 per cent agreed that the personality characteristics of the teacher were more important for success in teaching than any particular knowledge or professional skills a teacher might possess.

Moreover, the school is not organized to delegate all the responsibilities for instruction to teachers. Thus a school is unlike a hospital, where doctors, not administrators, control task activities. In schools there is a more generalized locus of responsibility for planning and coordinating instructional matters. Centralized policies about what teachers should teach, how they should teach, and what materials they should use to teach are often developed jointly by teachers, administrators, and sometimes parents.

Teachers, then, *appear* to be professionals because they have much discretion within a loosely coupled system. The myth of teacher professionalism is an interesting and important feature of the American educational system. It does not, however, provide an explanation for the structure of educational organizations.

### Organization theory

The most conventional idea in organizations research that could be used to explain the lack of central control over instructional activities is the idea of 'goal displacement': the notion that organizations shift their control systems to focus on those outputs for which they are most accountable – in this case, the ritual classifications – and not on those which they were originally intended to maximize. This idea is, in large measure, true, but it does not go far enough. First, while both the school and the environment have evolved an elaborate scheme to control ritual classifications, the idea of goal displacement does not explain why a tacit agreement not to create an accounting scheme based on the 'actual effectiveness' of these classifications evolved.

Second, in one sense goals may not be far displaced after all. We should not lose sight of the fact that a very high proportion of the resources schools receive *is* devoted to instructional activity. Teachers' salaries are a major expenditure item, as are instructional materials. Administrators and other district staff make up a very small proportion of the total employees of most school districts. The resources, in other words, continue to be focused on the instructional aspects of the system, even though achievement of instructional goals is not measured.

This fact suggests that educational organizations direct resources to their main goals but do not carefully control or evaluate the consequences of these allocations. It is as if society allocates large sums of money and large numbers of children to the schools, and the schools in turn allocate these funds and children to a relatively uncontrolled and uninspected classroom. All of this seems to be done in a great act of ritual faith.

As we will see, this depiction is not inappropriate. Further, the parties involved may not be as foolish as they seem in conventional depictions of education. It is unfortunately true that most depictions of the educational system see its organizational administrators as somehow misdirected. The reformers see backwardness everywhere the magic of rationalization does not reach; the decentralists see self-aggrandizement; the myth of professionalism depicts administrators as factotums who submit to professional authority; and organization theorists see administrators who have lost sight of their original purposes. It may make sense, however, to consider another view of educational organization – one in which the participants are sensible people running a highly successful enterprise.

## The organization of schooling: another interpretation

The explanation developed here begins with the context in which educational organizations are presently found. Modern education today takes place in large-scale, public bureaucracies. The rise of this kind of educational system is closely related to the worldwide trend of national development. The first step in our argument, therefore, is to relate national development to the organization of education.

### The growth of corporate schooling

From the preceding characterizations, we know that bureaucratic schooling has not arisen from a need to coordinate and standardize instruction, for this is precisely what modern American educational organizations do not do. Nor do these bureaucratic organizations merely fund and administer an exchange between educational professionals and families needing educational services. Educational bureaucracies present themselves not as units servicing education but as organizations that embody educational purposes in their collective structure. A theory of their emergence and dominance should explain why these bureaucracies assume jurisdiction over educational instruction.

The most plausible explanation is that modern schools produce education for *society*, not for individuals or families. In the nineteenth and twentieth centuries national societies everywhere took over the function of defining and managing the socialization of their citizen personnel (Coombs, 1968; Meyer and Rubinson, 1975; Ramirez, 1974). In national societies, education is both a right and duty of citizenship (Bendix, 1964). It also becomes an important way of gaining status and respect (for example, see Blau and Duncan, 1967). For reasons that do not require elaborate discussion here, education becomes the central agency defining personnel – both citizen and elite – for the modern state and economy.

Since the Second World War the trend toward corporate control of education has intensified. As nation-states have consolidated their control over a growing number of elements of social life, they have established educational systems to incorporate citizens into the political, economic, and status order of society. This incorporation is managed by a large public bureaucracy that uniformly extends its standardization and authority through all localities. Thus, educational organizations have come to be increasingly structured by centers of political authority (Meyer and Rubinson, 1975).

Bailyn (1960), Field (1972), Katz (1968), and Tyack (1974) describe the steps of this process in pre-twentieth-century American history. First local, and later national, élites became concerned with the social control of peripheral citizen groups – who need control precisely because they *are* citizens. At first, the rural New Englanders who escaped from the control of clergy and town community (Bailyn, 1960), then the Irish immigrants (Field, 1972; Katz, 1968), and finally the great waves of nineteenth-century immigration (Tyack, 1974) created the pressures to control, standardize, and coordinate the educational system. As these steps progressed, the impetus to organize schooling on a large scale – to certify and classify pupils, to certify teachers, to accredit schools, and to control formal curriculum – gained force.

The growth of corporate control of education has major implications for educational organizations. As citizen personnel are increasingly sorted and allocated to positions in the social structure on the basis of classified or certified educational properties, the ritual classifications of education – type of student, topic, teacher, or school – come to have substantial value in what might be called the societal identity 'market.' A workable identity market presupposes a standardized, trustworthy currency of social typifications that is free from local anomalies. Uniform categories of instruction are therefore developed, and there is a detailed elaboration of the standardized and certified properties comprising an educational identity.

The result of this social expansion of education is a basic change in social structure. Education comes to consist, not of a series of private arrangements between teachers and students, but rather of a set of standardized public credentials used to incorporate citizen personnel into society. Society and its stratification system come to be composed of a series of typifications having educational meaning; ordinary citizens are presumed to have basic literacy. Strata above ordinary citizens are composed of high school and college graduates. The upper levels contain credentialed professionals, such as doctors and lawyers.

Thus, as societies and nation-states use education to define their basic categories of personnel, a large-scale educational bureaucracy emerges to standardize and manage the production of these categories. The credentials that give individuals status and membership in the wider collectivity must come under collective control. Such collective control would not be necessary if instruction were conceived of as merely a private matter between individuals and teachers. But, as educational organizations emerge as the credentialing agency of modern society and as modern citizens see their educational and corporate identities linked – that is, as education becomes the theory of personnel in modern society – it is consequently standardized and controlled.

Society thus becomes 'schooled' (Illich, 1971). Education comes to be understood by corporate actors according to the *schooling rule*: education is a certified teacher teaching a standardized curricular topic to a registered student in an accredited school. The nature of schooling is thus socially defined by reference to a set of standardized categories, the legitimacy of which is publicly shared. As the categories and credentials of schooling gain importance in allocation and membership processes, the public comes to expect that they will be controlled and standardized. The large-scale public bureaucracy created to achieve this standardization is now normatively constrained by the expectations of the schooling rule. To a large degree, then, education is coordinated by shared social understandings that define the roles, topics, and contents of educational organizations.

### The organizational management of standardized classifications

The political consolidation of society and the importance of education for the allocation of people to positions in the economic and stratification system explain the rise of large-scale educational bureaucracies. These processes also explain why educational organizations focus so tightly on the ritual classifications of education. Educational organizations are created to produce schooling for corporate society. They create standard types of graduates from standard categories of pupils using standard types of teachers and topics. As their purposes and structures are defined and institutionalized in the rules, norms, and ideologies of the wider society, the legitimacy of schools and their ability to mobilize resources depend on maintaining congruence between their structure and these socially shared categorical understandings of education (Dowling and Pfeffer, 1975; Meyer and Rowan, 1977; Parsons, 1956).

Consider this matter from the viewpoint of any rational college president or school superintendent. The whole school will dissolve in conflict and illegitimacy if the internal and external understanding of its accredited status is in doubt: if it has too few PhDs or properly credentialed teachers on its faculty, it may face reputational, accreditational, or even legal problems. If it has one too many 'economics' courses and one too few 'history' courses (leave aside their actual content), similar disasters may occur as the school falls short of externally imposed accrediting standards. No matter what they have learned, graduates may have difficulty finding jobs. No matter what the school teaches, it may not be capable of recruiting funds or teachers. Thus, the creation of institutionalized rules defining and standardizing education creates a system in which schools come to be somewhat at the mercy of the ritual classifications. Failure to incorporate certified personnel or to organize instruction around the topics outlined in accreditation rules can bring conflict and illegitimacy.

At the same time, the creation of institutionalized rules provides educational organizations with enormous resources. First, the credentials, classifications, and categories of schooling constitute a language that facilitates exchange between school and society. Social agencies often provide local schools with 'categorical funding' to support the instruction of culturally disadvantaged or educationally handicapped students or to support programs in bilingual or vocational education. Second, schools can exploit the system of credentials and classifications in order to gain prestige. They can carefully attend to the social evaluations of worth given to particular ritual classifications and can maximize their honorific worth by hiring prestigious faculty, by incorporating programs that are publicly defined as 'innovative,' or by upgrading their status from junior college to four-year college. Finally, the school relies on the ritual classifications to provide order. Social actors derive their identities from the socially defined categories of education and become committed to upholding these identities within the context of their school activities. To the degree that actors take on the obligation to be 'alive to the system, to be properly oriented and aligned in it' (Goffman, 1967), the whole educational system retains its plausibility.

In modern society, then, educational organizations have good reason to tightly control properties defined by the wider social order. By incorporating externally defined types of instruction, teachers, and students into their formal structure, schools avoid illegitimacy and discreditation. At the same time, they gain important benefits. In schools using socially agreed-on classifications, participants become committed to the organization. This is especially true when these classifications have high prestige (McCall and Simmons, 1966). Also, by labelling students or instructional programs so that they conform to institutionally supported programs, schools obtain financial resources. In short, the rewards for attending to external understandings are an increased ability to mobilize societal resources for organizational purposes.

*The avoidance of evaluation and inspection*

We have explained why schools attend to ritual classifications, but we have not explained why they do not attend (as organizations) to instruction. There are two ways that instructional activities can be controlled in modern education bureaucracies. First, many of the properties of educational identities may be certified in terms of examinations. Second, many of the ritual classifications involve a reorganization of educational activity, and some school systems organize an inspection system to make sure these implications are carried through. Thus, two basic kinds of instructional controls are available to educational organizations – the certification of status by testing, and/or the inspection of instructional activity to ensure conformity to rules.

Our explanation of the loose control of instruction in US school systems must in part focus on specific features of US society, since most other societies have educational bureaucracies that employ one or both forms of instructional control. In many other nations, for example, assignment to a classification such as student, graduate, or teacher is determined by various tests, most often controlled by national ministries of education. Also, national inspectors are often employed to attempt to make sure that teachers and schools conform to national standards of practice, regardless of the educational outcome. Thus, in most societies the state, through a ministry of education, controls systems of inspection or examination that manage the ritual categories of education by controlling either output or instructional procedure (Ramirez, 1974; Rubinson, 1974).

In American society, tests are used in profusion. However, most of these tests are neither national nor organizational but, rather, are devices of the individual teacher. The results seldom leave the classroom and are rarely used to measure instructional output. In the United States, the most common national tests that attempt to standardize local output differences – the Scholastic Aptitude Test (SAT) and the Graduate Record Examination (GRE) – are creatures of private organization. Further, only the New York State Board of Regents examination approximates (and at that in a pale way) an attempt to standardize curriculum throughout a political unit by using an examination system.

The apparent explanation for this lack of central control of instruction in American education is the decentralization of the system. Schools are in large part locally controlled and locally funded. While higher levels of authority in state and federal bureaucracies have made many attempts to impose evaluative standards on the educational system, the pressures of continued localism defeat them; category systems that delegate certification or evaluation rights to the schools themselves are retained. The reason for this is clear: A national evaluation system would define almost all the children in some communities as successes and almost all those in others as failures. This could work in a nationally controlled system, but it is much too dangerous in a system that depends on legitimating itself in and obtaining resources from

102 John W. Meyer and Brian Rowan

local populations. Why, for instance, should the state of Mississippi join in a national credentialing system that might define a great proportion of its schools and graduates as failures? It is safer to adapt the substantive standards of what constitutes, say, a high school graduate to local circumstances and to specify in state laws only categories at some remove from substantive competence.

There is yet another way in which the institutional pattern of localism reduces organizational controls over instruction. In the United States the legitimacy of local control in some measure deprofessionalizes school administrators at all levels (in contrast to European models). They do not carry with them the authority of the central, national, professional, and bureaucratic structures and the elaborate ideological backing such authority brings with it. American administrators must compromise and must further lose purely professional authority by acknowledging their compromised role. They do not have tenure, and their survival is dependent on laypersons in the community, not professionals. Their educational authority of office is, therefore, lower than that of their European counterparts, especially in areas dealing with central educational matters such as instruction and curriculum. This situation is precisely analogous to the 'red' versus 'expert' conflict found in many organizations in communist societies, where organizational managers must often act contrary to their expert opinion in order to follow the party line. The profusion of local pressures in American society turns school administrators into 'reds,' as it were.

### The organizational response: decoupling and the logic of confidence

*Decoupling*

American educational organizations are in business to maintain a 'schooling rule' institutionalized in society. This rule specifies a series of ritual categories – teachers, students, topics and schools – that define education. Elaborate organizational controls ensure that these categories have been incorporated into the organization; but the ritual categories themselves and the system of inspection and control are formulated to avoid inspecting the actual instructional activities and outcomes of schooling. That is, a school's formal structure (its ritual classifications) is 'decoupled' from technical activities and outcomes.

External features of American education, especially the local and pluralistic basis of control, help to account for this pattern, but there are more elaborate internal processes involved as well. From the viewpoint of an administrator, maintaining the credibility of his or her school and the validity of its ritual classifications is crucial to the school's success. With the confidence of the state bureaucracy, the federal government, the community, the profession, the pupils and their families, and the teachers themselves, the legitimacy of the school as a social reality can be maintained. However, if these groups decide that a school's ritual classifications are a 'fraud,' every-thing comes apart.

There are several ways in which the decoupling of structures from activities and outcomes maintains the legitimacy of educational organiz-ations. Consider some reasons why an American administrator would avoid closely inspecting the internal processes of the school.

First, the avoidance of close inspection, especially when accompanied by elaborate displays of confidence and trust, can increase the commitments of internal participants. The agreement of teachers to participate actively in the organized social reality of the ritual classifications of education is crucial, and an administrator can trade off the matter of conformity to the details of instruction and achievement in order to obtain teachers' complicity and satisfaction. By agreeing that teachers have instructional competence and by visibly not inspecting instructional activities, an administrator shifts maxi-mal social responsibility for upholding the rituals of instruction to the teachers. The myth of teacher professionalism and the autonomy associated with it, for example, function to increase the commitments of teachers.

A second reason for avoiding close inspection and evaluation arises from the fact that a good deal of the value of education has little to do with the efficiency of instructional activities. If education is viewed as a ceremonial enactment of the rituals of schooling, the quality of schooling can be seen to lie in its *costs*: spectacular buildings, expensive teachers in excessive number (a low student–teacher ratio), and elaborate and expensive topics (French for first-graders, or nuclear physics). To the state, the accrediting agencies, the community, and the participants themselves, costs of these kinds index the quality and meaning of a school. It therefore makes little sense to view a school as if it were producing instructional outcomes in an economic marketplace, since an economizing perspective would treat many of the critical features of a school as costly waste, as liabilities rather than assets. It is enormously damaging for a school to view the categories that validate it, as well as the cost of their upkeep and prestige, as liabilities. The ritual of schooling is evaluated according to a logic in which quality and costs are equivocal. Expenditures per student or the number of books in the library are among common indices of educational quality, even though maximizing these indices may require a studied inattention to an economizing logic. The wise administrator will call attention to the elaborate and expensive structure of ritual classification his school has, not to the amount of learning achieved per dollar.

Third, decoupling protects the ritual classification scheme from uncer-tainties arising in the technical core. In education it is quite common that rules of practice institutionalized at state and federal levels create technical uncer-tainty at the local level. State-mandated curricula may be too advanced for the students at hand, and innovative state and federal programs often need to be adapted to the specific circumstances unique to the local school. Measuring what pupils actually learn in these programs or what teachers are actually teaching introduces unnecessary uncertainty, increases coordinative costs and creates doubts about the effectiveness of the status structure of the school and the categorical rules that define appropriate education.

Fourth, decoupling allows schools to adapt to inconsistent and con-flicting institutionalized rules. Schools, of necessity, are plural organizations adapted to plural environments (Udy, 1970). This is especially true of American schools, with their welter of external pressure. One way to manage the uncertainty, conflict, and inconsistency created by this pluralistic situ-ation is to buffer units from each other. Udy, in fact, sees this as a major ex-planation for the differentiation of modern organizations into specialized com-ponents. When differentiation is accompanied by isolation and autonomy of subunits rather than by interdependence and coordination, jurisdictional disputes among categories of professionals or incompatibilities among incon-sistent programs are avoided. For example, in schools, the work of a large number of specialists–vocational educators, speech therapists, reading special-ists – is organized separately and buffered from the usual classroom work.

Our point is this: By decoupling formal structure from activities, uncertainty about the effectiveness of the ritual categories is reduced. When the behavior of teachers and students is uninspected or located in isolated classrooms, the state, the community, and administrators are presented with little evidence of ineffectiveness, conflict, or inconsistency. Also, the teacher and student are free to work out the practicalities of their own unique relationship little disturbed by the larger social interpretation of which activity is appropriate to a given category. Further, in a pluralistic setting the number of ritual classifications institutionalized in the environment is large, and there are frequent additions and subtractions. By decoupling ritual subunits from one another, the school is able to incorporate potentially inconsistent ritual elements and to recruit support from a larger and more diverse set of constituencies.

By minimizing the resources devoted to coordination and control, the school furthers its ability to increase the ceremonial worth of its ritual categories. This strategy also cuts down the costs involved in implementing new categories and maximizes their chance of success. New programs or specialists need not be integrated into the structure; they merely need to be segmentally added to the organization. Further, new categories need not even imply a substantial reorganization of activity, as the activities of particular ritual actors and programs remain uninspected. The decoupling of the internal structure of education is therefore a successful strategy for maintaining support in a pluralistic environment.

### The logic of confidence

The classifications of education, however, are not rules to be cynically manipulated. They are the sacred rituals that give meaning to the whole enterprise, both internally and externally. These categories are understood everywhere to *index* education. They are not understood to *be* education, but they are also not understood simply to be alienating bureaucratic constraints. So the decoupling that is characteristic of school systems must be carried out by all participants in the utmost good faith.

Interaction in school systems, therefore, is characterized both by the assumption of good faith and the actualities of decoupling. This is *the logic of confidence*: Parties bring to each other the taken-for-granted, good-faith assumption that the other is, in fact, carrying out his or her defined activity. The community and the board have confidence in the superintendent, who has confidence in the principal, who has confidence in the teachers. None of these people can say what the other does or produces, but the plausibility of their activity requires that they have confidence in each other.

The logic of confidence is what Goffman (1967) calls 'face work' – the process of maintaining the other's face or identity and thus of maintaining the plausibility and legitimacy of the organization itself. Face work avoids embarrassing incidents and preserves the organization from the disruption of an implausible performance by any actor. Goffman (1967: 12–18) discusses three dimensions of this face-saving procedure: avoidance, discretion, and overlooking. Decoupling promotes each of these dimensions. Avoidance is maximized when the various clusters of identities are buffered from each other, when the organization is segmentalized, and when interaction across units is minimized (as by the self-contained classroom). Discretion is maximized when inspection and control are minimized or when participants are cloaked with 'professional' authority. Finally, participants often resort to overlooking embarrassing incidents or to labelling them as deviant, as characteristic of particular individuals, and therefore as nonthreatening to the integrity of the ritual classification scheme.

It must be stressed that face work and the logic of confidence are not merely personal orientations but are also institutional in character. For instance, a state creates a rule that something called 'history' must be taught in high schools. This demand is not inspected or examined by organizational procedures but is controlled through confidence in teachers. Each teacher of history has been credentialed. There is an incredible sequence of confidences here, with faces being maintained up and down the line: the state has confidence in the district, the district in the school, and the school in the teacher. The teacher is deserving of confidence because an accrediting agency accredited the teacher's college. The accrediting agency did not, of course, inspect the instruction at the college but relied on the certification of its teachers, having confidence in the universities the teachers attended. The accrediting agency also has confidence in the organization of the college – its administrators and departments. These people, in turn, had confidence in their teachers, which enabled them to label certain courses as 'history' without inspecting them. The chain goes on and on. Nowhere (except in the concealed relation between teacher and pupil) is there any inspection. Each link is a matter of multiple exchanges of confidence.

The most visible aspect of the logic of confidence in the educational system is the myth of teacher professionalism. Even in higher education – where teachers typically have no professional training for teaching – the myth is maintained. It serves to legitimate the confidence the system places in its teachers and to provide an explanation of why this confidence is justified. This explains one of the most puzzling features of educational professionalism – why the professional status of teachers rises dramatically with the creation of an educational bureaucracy. It is conventional to assume that professionalism and bureaucracy are at odds, although the evidence rarely supports this view (Corwin, 1970). In fact, even though the ideology supporting the creation of large American educational bureaucracies argued for close control, evaluation, and inspection of teachers, it seems clear that these bureaucracies greatly lowered the amount of such control (Tyack, 1974). Prebureaucratic teachers were often under direct inspection and control of the community that hired them. The bureaucracy, justified on the grounds that it would assume responsibility for inspection and control of instruction, however, almost immediately began to inspect and control only the superficial and categorical aspects of teachers. To account for this lack of specific inspection and control of instruction, the myth of professionalism arose very early, despite the original intentions of the founders. Our argument – that professionalism serves the requirements of confidence and good faith – explains this growth: the myth of teacher professionalism helps to justify the confidence placed in teachers and to legitimate the buffering of uncertainty in the performance of pupils and teachers in educational organizations.

*Overview of the argument*

With the growth of corporate society, especially the growth of nation-states, education comes into exchange with society. Schooling – the bureaucratic standardization of ritual classifications – emerges and becomes the dominant form of educational organization. Schools become organized in relation to these ritual categories in order to gain support and legitimacy. In America the local and pluralistic control of schools causes these classifications to have little impact on the actual instructional activities of local schools. Thus the official classifications of education, although enforced in public respects, are decoupled from actual activity and can contain a good deal of internal inconsistency without harm. As a result, American schools in practice contain multiple realities, each organized with respect to different internal or exogenous pressures. These multiple realities conflict so little because they are buffered from each other by the logic of confidence that runs through the system.

In this fashion, educational organizations have enjoyed enormous success and have managed to satisfy an extraordinary range of external and internal constituents. The standardized categories of American society and its stratification system are maintained, while the practical desires of local community constituents and the wishes of teachers, who are highly satisfied with their jobs, are also catered to. As new constituents rise up and make new demands, these pressures can be accommodated within certain parts of the system with minimal impact on other parts. A great deal of adaptation and change can occur without disrupting actual activity; and, conversely, the activities of teachers and pupils can change a good deal, even though the abstract categories have remained constant.

## Implications for research and theory

The arguments we have discussed have many implications for research on educational organizations. We see schools (and other organizations) as vitally – and in complex way – affected by their institutional environments. Much more research is needed, carefully examining such institutional variations – among societies or among institutions within societies – and their organizational impact.

*Propositions comparing societies*
First, the formal structure of educational organizations tends to come into correspondence with environmental categories. These ritual categories, further, tend to be linked to the nation-state, implying that formal education structure ought to vary more between societies than within them. Second, educational content and instruction is organizationally most loosely coupled in societies with pluralistic systems of control, such as the United States, and is more tightly controlled in countries with centralized systems. Further, ambiguities and vacuities in the educational languages specifying the meaning and implications of the ritual elements of educational organization should be found to be greatest in pluralistic systems. Third, the more education is a national institution of central importance, the more loosely coupled is its internal structure and the more control rests on the logics of confidence and of professionalization.

*Propositions comparing education and other institutions*
First, instructional work in institutionalized educational systems is less closely inspected or coordinated than similar work in other institutions such as businesses or armies. Second, educational structures are more responsive to even inconsistent environmental pressures than are organizations in other institutional settings. In part, this is because they are buffered from their own internal technical work activity. This situation permits more internal and external constituent groups to perceive that they have power in education organizations than is true in other organizations.

*Propositions comparing educational organizations*
First, the formal structure of educational organizations responds to environmental (or societal) categories. It varies less in response to variations in the

actual characteristics of clienteles or of problems of instruction. Similarly, changes in environmental rules defining education produce more rapid formal structural changes than do changes in the content or methods of instruction. Second, educational organizations are internally coordinated and legitimated by their environmental categories, not primarily by their own technical activity or instructional output. Variations in their success at maintaining correspondence with environmental rules predict the success, survival, and stability of educational organizations more than do variations in their instructional effectiveness. Third, loosely coupled educational organizations structurally respond more effectively to environmental pressures and changes than do tightly coupled organizations. Instruction adapts more quickly, in such organizations, to the informal pressures of teachers and parents, while structures respond more quickly to environmental institutional categories.

### Propositions comparing internal components of organization

First, in educational organizations, feedback concerning the work and output of teachers and schools tends to be eliminated, even if it happens to exist. Participants employ logic of confidence, and overlook observations of actual work and outcomes. Feedback on the categorical status of teachers, schools, students, and programs tends to be retained.

Second, educational organizations respond to external institutional pressures with programmatic or categorical change, minimizing the impact on instruction. They respond to variations in teacher or parent preference with activity change, but not necessarily with categorical change. Each part or level of the system responds relatively independently to its environment. Thus the greatest part of organizationally planned innovation in instruction is never implemented, and the greatest part of instructional innovation is not organizationally planned.

Third, the loose coupling of instructional activity in educational organizations permits more internal constituent groups to perceive that they have power in this area than over other policy decisions.

### Implications for organization theory

The arguments above have many implications for theory and research on organizations other than schools. Our arguments seem quite plausible in terms of the literature on school organization, but some of them are sharply at odds with the theory of organizations (for a more detailed suggestion, see Meyer and Rowan, 1977). Perhaps organization theory is imperfect. It seems unlikely that educational organizations are so extremely unusual. Indeed, a most fundamental observation in research on all sorts of organizations is that rules and behavior – the formal and the informal – are often dissociated or inconsistent. This is the same observation we have been making about schooling organizations, and it may be time to stop being surprised at it. The surprise arises, not because the observations are novel, but because researchers take too limited a view of formal organizations. They see formal structure as created to actually coordinate production in the case of market organizations and conformity in the case of political bureaucracy (see Thompson, 1967; Scott, 1975). Consequently, they are surprised when formal structure and activity are loosely linked.

It is true that production requires some coordination, as political structure demands some conformity, but it is also true that the myth or social account of production and conformity is critical. Much of the value of what we purchase lies in intangibles. Much of the value of social control and order inheres in the faith that is generated. Put differently, organizations must have the *confidence* of their environments, not simply be in rational exchange with them. Those that have this confidence and legitimacy receive all sorts of social resources that provide for success and stability. That is, organizations must be legitimate, and they must contain legitimate accounts or explanations for their internal order and external products. *The formal structure of an organization is in good part a social myth and functions as a myth, whatever its actual implementation.* In small part, it is a mythical account that the organization attempts to institutionalize in society. In much greater part, the formal structure is taken over from the accounts already built into the environment. Incorporating the environmental myth of the organization's activities legitimates the organization both externally and internally (Dowling and Pfeffer, 1975) and stabilizes it over and above the stability generated by its network of internal relations and production. Organizations integrate themselves by incorporating the wider institutional structures as their own.

Thus, if systematic safety problems are 'discovered' by the environment, safety officers are invented: their existence explains how the organization has 'taken into account' safety problems. (Who actually deals with safety is another matter.) So also with pollution control, labor relations, public relations, advertising, affirmative action, or research and development. Some of these activities may, in a day-to-day sense, actually get done. Our point here is that incorporating them in the formal structure of the organization has the function of legitimating myths and that such myths may be created quite independent of the activities they index. All these units represent the formal incorporation by the organization of environmental definitions of activities that then become part of the firm's account. Incorporating them deflects criticism from internal coalitions. It also legitimates the organization externally: banks led money to *modern* firms. Role handles are provided: other organizations have someone inside the firm 'with whom they can deal.' The legal system may require such forms of accountability. Firms often incorporate external values in a very explicit way by attaching units and products 'shadow prices' derived not from any production function but from market prices external to the firm.

The formal structure of an organization incorporates (and in some respects *is*) an environmental ideology or theory of the organization's activity. As the environmental ideology changes, so does the formal structure. It is no wonder that the formal structure may be poorly adapted to the actual ongoing activity, which has to coordinate internal exigencies of its own.

A critical aspect of modern structure arises from the rationality of modern society and of organizations as myths. Formal organizational structures represent more than mere theories of activity: they must represent *national functional* theories. The structural account they present to society must give every appearance of rationality. Much of the irrationality of life in modern organizations arises because the organization itself must maintain a rational corporate persona: We must find planners and economists who will waste their time legitimating plans we have already made, accounts to justify our prices, and human relations professionals to deflect blame from our conflicts. Life in modern organizations is a constant interplay between the activities that we need to carry on and the organizational accounts we need to give.

This discussion generates several implications for organization theory. First, formal organizational structure reflects and incorporates prevailing environmental theories and categories, often without altering activity. These environmental rules constitute taken-for-granted understandings in the organization. Organizational actors are constantly in the business of managing categories abstracted directly from environmental theories.

Second, organizational structure has two faces: It conforms to environmental categories and categorical logics, and it classifies and controls activity. Organizational actors must take into account both what they are doing and the appearance of what they are doing.

Third, to accommodate both appearance and reality, organizational structure must always be partly decoupled from actual activity. Special managers may arise to adjudicate relationships between the categories of the formal structure and actual activities. Personnel officers classify persons and jobs into categories; registrars and admitting physicians institutionalize official diagnoses, accountants organize activity into budgets and budget categories, and so on. Linking the organization as a formal structure with the organization as a network of activities is a major task, and it tends to introduce inconsistencies and anomalies into both domains.

This view of organizations as constituted and coordinated at every point by taken-for-granted environmental understandings is considerably different from most prevailing views. Both closed-systems and open-systems views of organizations tend to see them as encountering the environment at their *boundaries*. We see the structure of an organization as derived from and legitimated by the environment. In this view, organizations begin to lose their status as internally interdependent systems and come to be seen as dramatic reflections of – dependent subunits within – the wider institutional environment.

## Note

This chapter is a revised version of a paper presented at the annual meeting of the American Sociological Association (ASA), San Francisco, August 1975. The work reported here was conducted in the Environment for Teaching Program of the Stanford Center for Research and Development in Teaching, under a grant from the National Institute of Education (NIE; grant number NE-C-00-3-0062). Views expressed here do not reflect NIE positions. Many colleagues in the Environment for Teaching Program, the NIE, the Organizations Training Program at Stanford, and the ASA work group on organizations and environments, offered helpful comments. In particular, detailed substantive suggestions and comments were provided by Albert Bergesen, Charles Bidwell, Terry Deal, John Freeman, Paul Hirsch, James March, Barbara Payne, Jeffrey Pfeffer, Phillip Runkel, and W. Richard Scott; and Betty Smith provided much editorial assistance.

## References

Acland, H. 'Parents Love Schools?' *Interchange*, 1975, *6*, 1–10.

Bailyn, B. *Education in the Forming of American Society*. Chapel Hill: University of North Carolina Press, 1960.

Bendix, R. *Nation Building and Citizenship*. New York: Wiley, 1964.

Bidwell, C. 'The School as a Formal Organization.' In J. G. March (Ed.), *Handbook of Organizations*. Chicago: Rand McNally, 1965.

Blau, P. M., and Duncan, O. D. *The American Occupational Structure*. New York: Wiley, 1967.

Callahan, R. E. *Education and the Cult of Efficiency*. Chicago: University of Chicago Press, 1962.

Cohen, E. G., and others. 'Organization and Instruction in Elementary Schools.' Technical Report No. 50. Stanford, Calif.: Center for Research and Development in Teaching, Stanford University, 1976.

Coombs, P. H. *The World Educational Crisis*. New York: Oxford University Press, 1968.

Corwin, R. G. *Militant Professionalism*. New York: Appleton-Century-Crofts, 1970.

Cubberly, E. P. *Public School Administration*. Boston: Houghton Mifflin, 1916.

Deal, T. E., Meyer, J. W., and Scott, W. R. 'Organizational Influences on Educational Innovation.' In J. V. Baldridge and T. E. Deal (Eds), *Managing Change in Educational Organizations*. Berkeley, Calif.: McCutcheon, 1975.

Dornbusch, S. M., and Scott, W. R. *Evaluation and the Exercise of Authority: A Theory of Control Applied to Diverse Organizations*. San Francisco: Jossey-Bass, 1975.

Dowling, J., and Pfeffer, J. 'Organizational Legitimacy: Social Values and Organizational Behavior.' *Pacific Sociological Review*, 1975, *18*, 122–136.

Dreeben, R. 'The School as a Workplace.' In R. M. W. Travers (Ed.), *Second Handbook of Research on Teaching*. Chicago: Rand McNally, 1973.

Fantini, M., and Gittell, M. *Decentralization: Achieving Reform*. New York: Praeger, 1973.

Field, A. 'Educational Reform and Manufacturing Development, Massachusetts 1837–1865.' Unpublished doctoral dissertation, University of California, Berkeley, 1972.

Goffman, E. *Interaction Ritual.* Garden City, NY: Doubleday, 1967.

Hobbs, N. (Ed.). *Issues in the Classification of Children: A Sourcebook on Categories, Labels, and Their Consequences.* San Francisco: Jossey-Bass, 1975.

Holt, J. C. *How Children Fail.* New York: Pitman, 1964.

Illich, I. *Deschooling Society.* New York: Harper & Row, 1971.

Katz, M. *The Irony of Early School Reform.* Boston: Beacon, 1968.

Lortie, D. C. 'Observations on Teaching as Work.' In R. M. W. Travers (Ed.), *Second Handbook of Research on Teaching.* Chicago: Rand McNally, 1973.

McCall, G. J., and Simmons, J. L. *Identities and Interactions.* New York: Free Press, 1966.

March, J. G., and Olsen, J. P. *Ambiguity and Choice in Organizations.* Bergen, Norway: Universitetsforlaget, 1976.

Meyer, J. W., and Rowan, B. 'Institutionalized Organizations: Formal Structure as Myth and Ceremony.' *American Journal of Sociology,* 1977, *83,* 440–463.

Meyer, J. W., and Rubinson, R. 'Education and Political Development.' *Review of Research in Education,* 1975, *3,* 134–162.

Meyer, J. W., and others. 'The Impact of the Open Space School Upon Teacher Influence and Autonomy: The Effects of an Organizational Innovation.' Technical Report No. 21. Stanford, Calif.: Center for Research and Development in Teaching, Stanford University, 1971.

Miles, M. B. 'Planned Change and Organizational Health.' In J. V. Baldridge, and T. E. Deal (Ed.), *Managing Change in Educational Organizations.* Berkeley, Calif.: McCutcheon, 1975.

Parsons, T. 'Suggestions for a Sociological Approach to the Theory of Organizations, I.' *Administrative Science Quarterly,* 1956, *1,* 63–85.

Perrow, C. 'Departmental Power and Perspective in Industrial Firms.' In M. N. Zald (Ed.), *Power in Organizations.* Nashville, Tenn.: Vanderbilt University Press, 1970.

Perrow, C. *Organizational Analysis: A Sociological View.* Belmont, Calif.: Wadsworth, 1970.

Ramirez, F. O. 'Societal Corporateness and Status Conferral.' Unpublished doctoral dissertation, Stanford University, 1974.

Rogers, D. *110 Livingston Street.* New York: Random House, 1968.

Rubinson, R. 'The Political Construction of Education.' Unpublished doctoral dissertation, Stanford University, 1974.

Scott, W. R. 'Organizational Structure.' In A. Inkeles (Ed.), *Annual Review of Sociology.* Vol. 1. Palo Alto, Calif.: Annual Reviews, 1975.

Thompson, J. D. *Organizations in Action.* New York: McGraw-Hill, 1967.

Tyack, D. B. *The One Best System.* Cambridge, Mass.: Harvard University Press, 1974.

Udy, S. H., Jr. *Work in Traditional and Modern Society.* Englewood Cliffs, NJ: Prentice-Hall, 1971.

Webster, W. 'Organizational Resistance to Statewide Educational Reform.' Paper prepared for Conference on Schools as Loosely Coupled Systems. Palo Alto, Calif., November 21, 1976.

Weick, K. E. 'Educational Organizations as Loosely Coupled Systems.' *Administrative Science Quarterly,* 1976, *21,* 1–19.

Woellner, E. H. *Requirements for Certification.* Chicago: University of Chicago Press, 1972.

# Individuals and organizations

# 7

# The decline and fall of science in educational administration

**Thomas B. Greenfield**

The study of educational administration is cast in a narrow mould. Its appeal stems from a science of administration whose experts claim that an objective view of the social world enables them to conduct value-free inquiry. They claim to possess knowledge that enables them to control organizations and to improve them. But such large claims appear increasingly unsound, for the science that justifies them rests on methods and assumptions that dismiss the central realities of administration as irrelevant. Those realities are values in human action. If administrative science deals with them at all, it does so only in a weakened or spuriously objective form. For this reason, scholars in educational administration are now called to consider whether their way forward is still to be defined, as it has been for a generation or more, by a single path called 'the way of science.' The alternative path would seek to understand administrative realities within a broader conception of science – a conception recognizing that values bespeak the human condition and serve as springs to action both in everyday life and in administration. But values are subjective realities, and people bind them inextricably to the facts in their worlds. Thus, an adequate new science may no longer be content to split facts from values, and deal only with the facts.

Promoters of the science of administration claim to have found a rational basis for human decision-making and a value-free technology for increasing the effectiveness and efficiency of organizations. Within a critical perspective, I will examine the basis of those claims and their mobilization on behalf of what Halpin (1970) called the 'New Movement' in educational administration. My aim is, first, to describe the intellectual and ideological development of this once revolutionary movement. Second, I will examine the consequences and offer a critique of the scientific approach to understanding the problems of administration. Third, I will suggest an alternative to

116   *Thomas B. Greenfield*

New Movement science in educational administration. And finally, I will speak about the problems of administrative studies in education today and suggest how those who are concerned to improve such studies might approach them in the future.

## The rise of science in administration

Self-conscious science entered administrative studies through the work of Herbert Simon. Published in 1945, *Administrative Behavior*[1] constituted a wholly new approach to the understanding and study of administration. His thinking transformed the field. Simon offered a totally new conception of the nature of administration, and, more importantly, a new set of rules for inquiry into administrative realities. From that time forward, his vision, his *Weltanschauung* of the world of administration , has dominated the field.

What Simon offered was a method of value-free inquiry into decision-making and administrative rationality. This method severely limited what could be considered as 'administration' or 'administrative decision-making,' but its great advantage was that it brought the force of science to buttress any claims that might be made about the nature of administration or about the best means for improving organizations and life within them. Thus, the unfortunate consequence of Simon's work has been to shift attention from questions about the nature of administration to an obsessive concern for the methods of inquiry into it.

Simon's critique of older knowledge in administration was that it offered little more than practitioners' prescriptive judgments on their experience. Simon's vision called for a knowledge of administrative realities founded on and validated by the power, objectivity, and utility of science. This transformation in administrative thought is perhaps worthy of being called a 'Revolution,' for it stands for the belief that only the methods of science can yield reliable insights into the realities of administration.

With the publication of Simon's seminal work in 1945, the methods of positivistic science were established as the only ones by which scholars might gain reliable knowledge of administrative realities. Following this bias, scholars of contemporary thought in administration, like March (1965, pp. x–xii), have classified as 'old' any knowledge created before 1950. This presentist bias stems from the ahistorical outlook of positivism and is seen in March's designation of his own and Simon's work as 'adult' and 'most fashionable.' But for March and other advocates of the science of administration, what most powerfully distinguishes old knowledge from new – and useless knowledge from useful – is that new and reliable knowledge can stand only on a foundation of empirical science.

Simon's achievement was to overthrow the past wisdom of the field – a wisdom that derived from the experience, observation, and reflection of writers who were administrators, not scientists. The practitioner-scholars, such as Taylor, Urwick, and Fayol, regarded their knowledge as scientific. But their wisdom was expressed as 'principles,' and the truth of what they claimed rested more upon insight and assertion than upon science. Noting that the principles of administration occurred only in pairs, Simon (1957, p. 20) damned them as nothing more than mutually contradictory proverbs. Such knowledge suffered, he said, from 'superficiality, oversimplification, lack of realism' (p. 38). To correct these errors, Simon set out to build a theory of administration on scientific knowledge, and his lasting contribution was to convince both scholars and practitioners that he had realized his vision. What is striking is how easily he appeared to have won the battle.

The work of Chester Barnard (1938), another of the scholar-practitioners, stands in dramatic contrast to Simon's. Bernard was essentially a moralist, and for him the heart of administration lay in the leader's creation of cooperative effort and commitment to institutional purpose among members of an organization. Yet Barnard was apparently dazzled by Simon's claim to have science on his side. He wrote a preface to *Administrative Behavior* in which he acknowledge Simon's 'important contribution' as 'a set of tools . . . suitable for describing an organization and the way an administrative organization works' (Simon, 1957, p. xli). But he also expressed confidence that these tools would simply confirm his belief in the abstract 'principles of general organization' and the importance of experience (such as his own) in understanding administration. In fact, Simon's science undermined the interpretation of experience as a means for understanding organizations, and it deflected attention from the moral questions about purpose and commitment highlighted by Barnard.

Unlike the scholar-practitioners, Simon did not attempt to provide a prescription for administrative action. Instead, he made minimal assumptions about the nature of administration and narrowed the limits of inquiry. Simon set out to build a 'vocabulary of administrative theory,' a vocabulary that would say nothing that could not be expressed in 'operational definitions' (pp. xlvi, 37). Such theory and its vocabulary would then be open to validation according to the norms of truth recognized by positivistic science. Simon's starting point for a scientific theory of administration was a single proposition: 'Decision-making is the heart of administration.' From this vantage point, he set out to explore 'the logic and psychology of human choice' (p. xlvi). The flaw in this definition is not so much its narrowness, for choice is certainly a fundamental and unavoidable dynamic in the making of organizational and administrative realities. Rather, the weakness stems from Simon's own choice to explore only the *factual basis of choice* and to ignore value and sentiment as springs of human action. Because science could not speak to the 'ethical content' of decisions, Simon eliminated values from his putative science of administration. Thereafter he was content with his struggle to predict and control decisions purely from their 'factual content':

The question of whether decisions can be correct and incorrect resolves itself, then, into the question of whether ethical terms like 'ought,' 'good,' and 'preferable' have a purely empirical meaning. It is a fundamental premise of this study that ethical terms are not completely reducible to factual terms. . . . Factual propositions cannot be derived from ethical ones by any process of reasoning, nor can ethical propositions be compared directly with the facts – since they assert 'oughts' rather than the facts. . . . Since decisions involve valuations of this kind, they too cannot be objectively described as correct or incorrect. (Simon, 1957, p. 38)

Simon's great contribution was his recognition that making decisions is the essence of administration. In a way not found in previous studies, he saw that decisions are taken by human beings, not by boxes drawn on an organization chart. He knew that principles founded on such abstractions would be impotent:

To many persons, organization means something that is drawn on charts or recorded in elaborate manuals of job descriptions, to be duly noted and filed. Even when it is discussed by some of its most perceptive students – for example, Colonel Urwick – it takes on more the aspect of a series of orderly cubicles contrived according to an abstract architectural logic, than of a house designed to be inhabited by human beings. (Simon, 1957, p. xvi.)

Simon's great failure was his own decision to focus exclusively on the factual basis of decisions and to regard as irrelevant all the other forces that shape them but which his science could not predict or control. And so the science of administration defined by Simon retreated in the face of the intractable powers and imponderable choices that make up the realities of life.

### Simon and positivism in administrative science

Since positivism dominates Simon's conception of science, it seems fair to use science in this discussion to mean positivistic inquiry. As Phillips (1983), Eisner (1983), and Culbertson (1983) suggest, positivism is both a philosophy of empiricism and a set of rules for determining what constitutes truth. The force of the assumptions of this method of inquiry dispenses with any knowledge not based upon objective and empirical observation. Such inquiry must therefore deny the world of value. It must abjure as proper subjects for scientific study all of what Halpin (1958, p. xii) called 'social philosophy' and all questions pertaining to 'right human conduct.' The positivist argument is, however, a powerful one. It reduces all internal states, all perceptions, feelings, and values to epiphenomena, to an unspeakable affect, to an externality that, as Hodgkinson (1983, p. 43) points out, 'one can only rebut . . . by referring to one's own phenomenological and, therefore, unverifiable experience . . . and by taking a position outside the limits of positivist discourse.'

There is, of course, a broader conception of science in which the scientist is not only an observer but also an interpreter of reality. This view acknowledges that human interest and its possible biases are inextricably interwoven in what we call scientific truth (Bauman, 1978; Giddens, 1976; Rabinow and Sullivan, 1979; Toulmin, 1983). Such broader conceptions of science should, I believe, be accommodated within the study of educational administration, and, indeed, they are beginning to be expressed there – at least by the minority voices in the field who are advocates of alternative approaches. Fortunately, these can now be found in the increasingly comprehensive and powerful statements of scholars such as Hodgkinson (1978b, 1983), Bates (1983, 1985b). Foster (1985), Gronn (1983, 1985a, 1985b, 1985c, in press), and Lakomski (1984, 1985a, 1985b, 1985c).

Simon's conception of administration as decision-making and his dedication to the belief that the methods of positivistic science could be used to understand and improve the rationality of administrators' decisions have powerfully shaped the modern field of study. From these theoretical points of departure, he constructed a model of rationality – the limited, sufficing rationality of 'administrative man' who makes only decisions that are 'good enough.' Simon's administrative man 'satisficed' as opposed to omniscient economic man who maximized and made the best possible decisions. Simon's view of administration thus retained the assumptions of the economic model but modified them to accommodate a less than perfect rationality. What is perhaps not so readily apparent is that he also retained the assumptions so dear to systems theorists – that administration is a function in a productive system and that this function is open to manipulation in the same way as other independent and objective conditions. For Simon, administration was simply an element or function in a productive system; as such, it could be regarded as operating in precisely the same manner as all other technical variables of a productive system.

### The failure of administrative science

My aim here is not so much to demonstrate the failure of administrative science in education, for I have been over that ground many times – too many times – before (Greenfield, 1975, 1978, 1980, 1985a, 1985b). Over the last decade or more, the continuing 'turmoil' in the field has been well chronicled elsewhere (Griffiths, 1979). And the implications of the furore have been drawn so fully and so clearly that only the obtuse or the uninformed could claim to be unaware of them (Gronn, 1983, 1985a). I have argued that administrative science has failed in education, but I believe its failure is equally apparent in the other subfields of administration as well. The difference in the subfields is perhaps best seen in the contrast between the journals *Administrative Science Quarterly* and *Educational Administration*

*Quarterly*. The former recognizes the Revolution may be in trouble, and its articles reflect a radically expanded view of administrative theory and empirical inquiry; the latter denies, or seems to, that there are any problems in the unfolding of the Revolution.[2] The predominating opinion in that journal continues to recommend more and larger doses of science largely in the form of improved methodologies, but still within the restrictive notions of theory and method that have pervaded the field since Simon blazed the revolutionary path.

The revolutionary goals that Modern Organization Theory promised generally for administration were echoed in Halpin's New Movement in educational administration (Greenfield, 1985b). Although the ideology of these movements still reigns supreme as a kind of Doctrine of the Revolution of Science in Administration, this revolution, in my view, has failed; it has been unable to answer why the science that Simon stipulated to solve administrative problems has notably failed to do so.

Mainstream thought in educational administration stands, though perhaps now with weakened conviction, on Simon's restrictive definition of administrative realities, embracing, *a fortiori*, his view of appropriate inquiry. For the most part, modern administrative theorists have heeded Simon's argument that the science of administration can be concerned only with means, not ends. The spirit of positivism, which is now pervasive, discourages historical inquiry, and so puts to flight any notion that scholars of administration should know their intellectual origins and the assumptions on which their field rests. But placed in the history of ideas, the belief that administration is (or can be) a science appears as a phenomenon of the mid-twentieth century. As we near the end of the century, this belief is beginning to appear as a misplaced faith. It is also becoming clear why it is an enormous error to conceive of administration as a science rather than as a moral act or as a political event.

Because positivistic science cannot derive a value from a fact or even recognize values as real, we have a science of administration which can deal only with facts and which does so by eliminating from its consideration all human passion, weakness, strength, conviction, hope, will, pity, frailty, altruism, courage, vice, and virtue. Simon led the science of administration down a narrow road which in its own impotence is inward-looking, self-deluding, self-defeating, and unnecessarily boring. These shortcomings are created by the blinkered view of choice and administrative action afforded by a narrowly empiricist science which lets us see but a pale and reduced reflection of the human will to achieve a purpose, to mobilize resources, to influence others – to do all that people in fact do as they make choices and strive to transform their values into realities.

The current overwhelming acceptance of positivistic science in administration has led theory and research to emphasize the epiphenomena of reality rather than the phenomenological force of that reality itself. This approach yields 'hard' but often impotent, irrelevant, or misleading data that are the only reality recognized by the hypothetico-deductive models favored in such science. In this science, only that which is quantifiable and calculable is real, for that is the only kind of reality consistent with the limited rationality that finds its ultimate expression in the linear workings of computers. What is lost in such approaches is human intention, value, commitment – human passion and potential. What is lost is human will and choice, the sheer power of people pursuing their purposes, a pursuit that brings what some may call good and others evil. Hodgkinson (1978b, p. 18) has shown, moreover, that administrative science has led us to focus upon the personality traits of administrators – upon the mere characteristics of administrators rather than upon their character. In consequence, the empirical study of administrators has elided their *moral* dimensions and virtually all that lends significance to what they do.

If this selective focusing is noticed in contemporary critiques of research, it appears only in Haller and Knapp's (1985) terms. Their response to the futility of research on the superficial characteristics of administrators is not to look more deeply, but to remove entirely the individual as a focus in administrative research. For them, a focus on the individual confuses 'the *questions* that are studied with the *subjects* . . . of the studies.' They recommend examining only the organizational production functions that administrators oversee. This position highlights the ultimate concern of administrative science – the effectiveness and efficiency of the organization which is, of course, conceived as an entity independent of human will, purpose, and values.

### What Simon omitted: right, responsibility, reflection

Simon's aim and hope were sweeping and daring: to enhance organizational efficiency and effectiveness by ensuring that administrators chose – within the limits of the rationality open to them – the best possible means to achieve a given end. But to fulfil the promise of the new science of productive rationality, administrative man had to disappear as a value-bearer and wilful and unpredictable choice-maker. Thus Simon's administrative man emerged in a devalued, dehumanized, and technologized form:

> Once the system of values which is to govern an administrative choice has been specified, there is one and only one 'best' decision, and this decision is determined by the organizational values and situation, and not by the personal motives of the member of the organization who makes the decision. Within the area of discretion, once an individual has decided, on the basis of his personal motives to recognize the organizational objectives, his further behavior is determined not by personal motives, but by the demands of efficiency. (Simon, 1957, p. 204)

So, if this view defines the limits of a science of administrative decision-making, it must be noted that some vital questions of administration lie beyond them. All that governs the choice of the values for the system is beyond it, as is the question of what objective reality could exist to keep the personal motives, character, or ideology of individual members from impinging upon the choices they make in pursuing the values of the organization.

The horror of Simon's neutered science appears only with the realization that it conforms, almost perfectly, to the view that administrators seem to want to have of themselves: that they are instruments of an objective, selfless rationality. Administrative science, as Simon conceived it, has done much to establish the belief that devalued, but rational, decision-making is desirable, attainable, and scientifically verifiable. This belief relieves the anxiety of decision-making and removes the administrator's sense of responsibility for his decisions. Scott and Hart (1979, pp. 46–7) show how a devalued rationality can help administrators deal with practical problems, but only at the price of desensitizing them to the values that must be engaged in making a difficult decision:

> The management of organizations is a practical and mundane effort. Implicit within the pragmatic rule is a warning against philosophizing. . . . Organizations are run by managers who must make decisions about goals, policies, and strategies of action that influence human values and behaviour, both within and outside the organization. . . . The vice president for personnel of a large company that must lay off five hundred employees is certainly not encouraged to consider the impact of this action on their lives. Instead, consideration is given to the health of the company.

A commitment to science in organizational affairs is not simply a commitment to rationality; it is, rather, a commitment to a restricted framework of rationality. Such a framework, called science, eases the sense of responsibility for powerful actors in organizational and administrative settings. It denies both responsibility and personal choice in the making of everyday decisions and in the making of decisions in the powerful world of organized reality. Such science takes sides in conflicts about the rightness of organizational purposes and about appropriate means for achieving them, but it denies it takes sides and claims to look dispassionately at such reality. As Hodgkinson (1978b, p. 163) says, 'Obedience or compliance can be construed as a way of abdicating responsibility.' In our society with its reverence for science and technique, obedience to a truncated concept of rationality has become a cover for the powerful administrator: science and rationality provide the ultimately persuasive and irrefutable excuse for the abdication of personal choice and responsibility.

To choose and to acknowlege responsibility for one's choice is often a risky way of living. It may require standing with those who are defined as heretics by powerful and possibly vengeful authorities. The safe course for administrators is suggested by Szasz's rueful observation: 'The Platonic maxim that "It is better to suffer wrong than to commit it" is fine for those to whom life is a spectator sport; the players, however, need something that gives them a little more protection in the clinches' (Szasz, 1976, p. 33).

The moral dilemma of the administrator whose best judgment leads him to stand on the wrong side of authority was noted nearly fifteen centuries ago by Boethius, 'the last of the Romans.' A scholar turned administrator, he tried to serve both the emperor and – as it turned out – the wrong pope. His reward for acting according to conscience was death at the hands of his master, Theodoric the Ostrogoth. The emperor, however, first placed Boethius under house arrest and thereby gave him time to reflect on his actions and to write *The Consolation of Philosophy*. There he makes the case that philosophy is the *only* consolation for a miscalculated risk. In his meditation, the figure of Philosophy appears to Boethius (1969, p. 53) and points out the high price of choosing to serve truth rather than sovereign power:

If you desire
To look on truth
And follow the path
With unswerving course
Rid yourself
Of joy and fear.
Put hope to flight.
And banish grief.
The mind is clouded
And bound in chains
Where these hold sway.

In organizational politics and administrative affairs, the acknowledgment of clearly chosen values can be dangerous. But as Boethius's life makes clear, acknowledgment enables us – both leaders and followers – to reflect upon our values. And in thinking about our lives, we may come to recognize that our decisions represent something beyond the decisions themselves; they bespeak a value and perhaps a commitment. As Hodgkinson (1978b, p. 172) points out, such commitment

is, of course, subject to critique from other philosophical positions but all that the proponents of these contending positions can do is to seek to persuade their audience by reason and rhetoric and all the powers at their disposal, that they have the better values. In the end the act of choice is individual; and if free and conscious, then moral.

*The infusion of science into educational administration*

Science emerged in public administration in 1945 with Simon's work and has dominated all parts of the field since then. The spirit of positivism spread to educational administration in the 1950s in a form Halpin (1970) called the

New Movement. This revolution began with a small band of social scientists who set out to redeem the older studies through science (Halpin, 1958; Campbell and Lipham, 1960). Halpin (1970, p. 161) describes the shock of the scholar-practitioners when advocates of the new science-based administration confronted them with the news that their knowledge was 'atheoretical and sloppy.' He also reports that the reception the practitioners gave this news was 'less than cordial.' But, by 1957, the New Movement scientists were in command, and they announced to a seminar held at the Midwest Administration Center of the University of Chicago the arrival of the scientific millennium in educational administration.

From that point onward, there began a remarkably rapid transformation of the theory, research, and graduate instruction in educational administration. Deaf to critical voices who warned against the founding of inquiry on a flawed and narrow foundation, scientists of the New Movement did not waver in their conviction. They justified their new understanding of administration with the claim that it brought research into line with the requirements of science and of rationality itself (Culbertson, 1983). Seeing the strategic advantage of having Science on their side, practitioners soon began to endorse New Movement assumptions and ideology. Under the banner 'Administrative Theory as a Guide to Action,' the Midwest Administration Center of the University of Chicago sponsored a second conference on theory, one that brought together social scientists and practitioners in the special mix that now marks so much of scholarly and professional endeavor in the field. Although Campbell warned the Conference that the millennium was not yet at hand, and although he cautioned that 'scientific knowledge offers maps, not prescriptions,' he also discouraged stragglers from the way of science by expressing the view that 'social science is principally the description of an intelligent, rational person in action' (Campbell and Lipham, 1960, pp. 175–6).

Halpin, however, was later torn by doubts concerning his role in promulgating a science that promised to enable the administrator to 'make wiser decisions' (Halpin, 1966, p. 285). He acknowledged that the ringing title of the conference invited administrators to believe in theory as a guide for action, when in fact there was 'no theory worthy of the name available to report' (Halpin, 1970, p. 157). But scholars and practitioners of the time were prepared to testify that the emperor called Science had clothes. Indeed, Marland, one of the superintendents at the 1959 conference (Campbell and Lipham, 1960, p. 34), told how practitioners awaited with interest the 'science of administration' and how they 'listen[ed] attentively to the counsel of social scientists.'[3] Marland compares the science-supported administrator to the bush pilot who

> now finds himself in the pilot's chair of a monstrous flying machine of untold power and dimensions. The social scientist tells us that there are buttons to push, levers to adjust, gauges to watch, beacons to reckon,

and codes to decipher. He tells us that one cannot fly this craft by the seat of the pants, but that certain buttons and levers, when actuated, produce specific and predictable results in the performance and the posture of the craft. (Campbell and Lipham, 1960, p. 24)

What has been called 'modern organization theory' (Haire, 1959; March, 1965) was created in close parallel with Halpin's New Movement in educational administration. Both may be seen as movements reflecting Simon's pioneering attempt to establish the study of organizations and administration on an objective scientific basis. Both began with a conscious break from previous studies that were viewed as mired in social philosophy (Halpin, 1958, p. xii). Both advocated that science, cast in an objective, positivistic mould, could save the field from the philosophers, moralists, and other subjectivists. Together they represented the deliberate founding of a new science of organizations which aimed to establish the experimental verification of hypothetico-deductive theory – an abstract, mathematically expressed theory that was held by its proponents to be the highest form of scientific knowledge. That there was no such theory of this kind in existence did not seem to deter advocates from seeking it, indeed, from launching research into organizations to test it. Such theory, it was held, would produce control over organizations in the same way that it permitted control over the physical world. The aim of the New Movement in educational adminis-tration was to generate such theory about schools, to place it in the hands of administrators, and to train them in its use. And so began the effort to train educational administrators in the science of organizations.

Convinced by a similar logic, Haller and Knapp (1985, p. 161) have more recently urged researchers not to focus on administrators, but rather to study relationships within organizations. They define educational adminis-tration as 'the study of the patterned relationships . . . with particular attention to the effects of those relationships on the transmission of subject matter to learners.' The image of organizations assumed here is that of a productive unit staffed by human beings who are subsidiary to the unit and largely independent of it. In this conception, it is relationships and structures that are important, not people themselves.

The scientific view of educational administration continues to recom-mend systems theory, a conception which sees the organization as a produc-tive unit striving under conditions of limited rationality to increase its output to a constraining environment. This view also continues to see the failure of science-based theories of administration as remediable by better and more powerful methodology. Such opinion thus reflects Simon's empiricism and his hope for improving the effectiveness and efficiency of the organization through rational decision-making. In these circumstances, it is not surprising to find that discussion of the failure of science-based theory and research soon reduces to technical issues – skewed distributions, outliers, Tukey's test, and box and whisker plots.[4]

## The Consequences of the New Science of Organizations

Despite the promise that the science of organization and administration was to be objective, quantitative, and value-free, the *images* of organization found in the theory-based research 'of the New Movement carry important values and philosophical assumptions. Taking these values and assumptions into consideration, four consequences of the movement should be noted.

### *The growing belief in adminstration as science*

The New Movement gave social validation to the belief that an objective science for guiding organizations had indeed been invented. With this belief widely accepted, so too was the idea that administrators should be trained in the science through programs of study in universities. Oftentimes, these programs have been state-mandated and tied to certification. Such programs teach the science of organization to administrators in the conviction it will enable them to do what they are supposed to do: direct organizations to achieve their goals in the most effective and efficient manner open to them. In this connection, the dominating metaphors of the science of administration are worth noting. Belief in the rationality of decision-making is prime among them, though this notion is closely tied to the systems concept that the organization is 'real' and exists in a natural balance with its environment. In the systems view, to study an organization scientifically means to study an aspect of natural reality – a reality that can be explored objectively and explained in the law-like, universal languages of mathematics and logic. Individuals disappear – and with them human agency, responsibility, and morality – and natural forces take over the conduct of human affairs. And so we have the language of abstraction – so common in the literature – that, for example, speaks of 'accommodating the organization to the reality demands of the environment and transforming the external situation' (Boyd and Crowson, 1981, p. 331).

To establish this science, it was necessary, as Hodgkinson pointed out, to commit the biological fallacy of endowing the organization with an ontological reality. The organization is conceived not only as real, but as more important than the people within it: 'and worse; the organization is not only reified, but deified. And the agent is not personally or morally responsible for the acts which are under the authority or *authorship* of the collectivity. . . . And outwardly benevolent organizations can become latent collective forces for evil' (Hodgkinson, 1978, p. 173).

And so another anomaly of scientific administration becomes apparent. Its emphasis falls not upon the phenomenological reality of administrators – neither upon the realities of those who wield power nor upon the perceptions of those who suffer its consequences. Such science chooses to study a greater reality, one that lies beyond the awareness of individuals: the reality of the organization itself. Even if we can assume the reality of the organization, and even if we assume that knowledge of that reality is in some way useful, we must still ask why administrative science has failed to explore the second of Simon's concerns: 'the logic and psychology of human choice.' The answer, as Hodgkinson (1978a, p. 272) suggests, is 'perhaps for the basic and stupefyingly simple reason that the central questions of administration are not scientific at all. They are philosophical.' Here Hodgkinson is using science to mean an objective, imperial Science that is presumed to live only within the limits that positivism has placed upon it: a limit that reduces values to epiphenomena and that precludes Science from speaking about values at all.[5] If such limits are accepted, then Science cannot presume to tell any of us that we should go to work today, let alone what we should do when we get there. But there is another and larger sense of science that sees it simply as truth, as reliable knowledge, and not as a particular method for arriving at knowledge (Schumacher, 1977). But what knowledge is reliable? Perhaps in the end we must be content simply with knowledge that lets us get through the day, preferably happily (Greenfield, 1983).

### The devaluation of administrative studies

The scientific movement is closely connected to the notion that a value-free science of administration is not merely possible but at hand. With the elimination of values, consideration of the conduct of organizations is reduced to technicalities. The substance of decisions is not important – only the manner of making of them. As Bates (1983a, p. 8) points out, this approach brings with it a separation of problems in administration from problems in education. It also brings, as Tipton (1985) argues, the isolation of theory in educational administration from other academic studies that bear powerfully on its professed concerns and interests. Many texts in the field bear the unimaginative title *Educational Administration*,[6] and from this emphasis one would expect that they should address uniquely educational issues. Not so. Readers look in vain for any substantive educational discussion. They may be told how to lead, motivate, communicate, develop morale, and maintain the organization in dynamic equilibrium, but they will find no discussion of an issue that they must bring to judgment. Radical and conservative critiques of school structure and curriculum, disputes over religion and language of instruction, the virtues of private versus public schools, class and cultural bias, unions, women, discipline, dress codes – of all these and the many other issues that beset education, there is no murmur of comment. Not even the major controversies about the meaning and reliability of administrative science are discussed in these tests.[7]

### Hidden values of administrative science

Despite its claim to objectivity, the science of administration is usually to be found on the side of the status quo. It starts from a standpoint of things as they are, and then asks why they are so. It does not question whether that which is ought to be. The argument here is not that conventional society or the status quo are necessarily wrong, but that positivist science cannot and *should not* attempt to validate social reality without revealing the weakness of its credentials for doing so. But despite its claims to neutrality, Science cannot seem to resist taking on the role of social validator and, in fact, is often well paid for its neutered conscience. This criticism has been launched against positivist social science generally, but in administration it has particular potency, for the state is the ultimate organization; it has almost unrestricted power over the individual – even the power that can ask for and get an individual's life. But if Science conceives the state (and all organizations of lesser puissance) as an objectified reality that is beyond question by the science of organization, then its students have no recourse but to serve their organizations with all the skill and devotion of which they are capable. In Hobbesian terms, the administrative scientist becomes a servant of the General Will – of the Sovereign. The General Will is, of course, to be interpreted by the Sovereign, not by the scientist whose role is limited to that of a technician skilled in applying a kind of physics of sociation – the impersonal and objective science of social organization and administration.[8]

A science of administration limited by the assumptions of positivism can produce experts in technique, not experts in value. If, however, the positivists are right, and values are merely an illusion or an affect that registers only in the psyche of individuals, then no real problem exists, for there is no objective way of expressing or arbitrating between competing claims of perceived value. The physics of sociation would then suffice as a basis for understanding and evaluating social reality. But if values are real, and if they are beyond the scope of positivist science, then a science of social order that claims to be value-free must remain silent in the face of the central issues of organizational and administrative life. But remain silent it does not. The mantle of objectivity permits scientists to intervene on behalf of values without seeming to do so and to move readily from commenting on the way things are to advocating the way they should be. In the contemporary field, such scientists are everywhere: for example, administrators who, following Hoy and Miskel (1982, p. vii), want to make their practice 'less of an art and more of a science,' the agent of educational change and implementation, the consultant on organization development who promises to improve the 'health' of the organization, and now the purveyors of excellence in organization and designs for effective schools. Indeed, all *experts* in organization theory who claim their prescriptions stand on objective Science are open to challenge, for their values, not their Science, constitute the real foundation of their knowledge.

The difficulty that arises from a belief in the possibility of a devalued notion of rationality and decision-making is well illustrated with a metaphor from Hodgkinson: the sandwich of rationality. Closely following his explication of three levels of reality and three types of values, Hodgkinson

(1983, 1985, 1986) draws attention to *levels* of reality and value in rationality itself. In this view, any human choice is made up of three elements. One is cognitive and limitedly rational in Simon's sense of the calculation of the factual relationship between ends and means. This calculation constitutes the 'meat' of the sandwich, but it is held in place by two slices of bread made up of subrational affect on the one hand and another slice made up of superrational ideology and transrational value. The sandwich metaphor thus recognizes that human beings are driven by their desires and fears, by their hopes and ideals, as much as by their rational calculations. And who is to say that such drives are not also a kind of rationality?

What the advocates of systematic reasoning and administrative science must comprehend is that issues great and small – whether to die for love of one's country, whether to close a school in the face of falling enrolment, whether to stop smoking today – are decided by people who bring all their belief, passion, habit, frailty, or nobility to the choice that faces them. Whatever the choice before them, they are unlikely to make it on the basis of a calculated, fact-driven rationality alone. Or as I have argued, facts *are*, but they do not tell us what to do (Greenfield, 1980, p. 43). Indeed, the facts alone decide nothing; it is we who decide about the facts. This realization comes as no surprise to historians and artists who deal with what men and women do, not with what the 'angels of reason' would have them do. But scientists of administration continue to be surprised, and spend much effort pointing out how the world would be better if people only behaved 'rationally.' This then is the failure of administrative science. Instead of providing, as it claims, an objective description of the world and of human choice, administrative science offers merely another value-driven prescription. Apparently despairing over the irrationality of the world, many otherwise encouraging critiques of administrative science offer expressions of hope that stronger research methodologies will yet plumb the depths of its mystery and find Simon's fact-only rationality at the bottom (see Haller and Knapp, 1985; Hoy, 1982).

### Science-validated training programs

New Movement science fosters and legitimates programs for training and certifying administrators. During the 1950s, a foundation-supported drive began in the United States to transform the old-style training programs into new ones based upon the assumptions of modern organization theory and administrative science (Tope *et al.*, 1965). These programs were designed to bring New Movement administrative science to bear upon the practical problems of education. Such programs have since spread through the proselytizing efforts of university-based advocates to other countries, notably the English-speaking Commonwealth countries, but increasingly to Third World countries as well.[9] To criticize the spread of such programs is not to suggest that the training of administrators is futile and unnecessary; rather, it is to argue that many university-based training programs, captured by a narrowly defined concept of administration, restrict the possibility of productive inquiry into administration.

Sovereign powers, in the form of state departments of education and other public and private authorities, have long had a role in the choice and validation of administrators for educational institutions. As Gronn (1985b) has shown, the selection of administrators is driven by a rationality that sweeps far beyond the logic of fact-driven choice. How could it be otherwise? Administrators are essentially value-carriers in organizations; they are both arbiters of values and representatives of them. Those who select and evaluate administrators are not so naïve as to ignore their surface characteristics. Indeed, they likely see all that meets the senses – dress, speech, custom – as expressions of the administrator's deeper values and commitments. But administrative science, holding up the ideal of the administrator as technician, is likely to argue otherwise. It offers the Sovereign the possibility of choosing the 'certified' decision-maker, the one who uses science to bring excellence, effectiveness, or efficiency – as though these conditions had no value content – to whatever organization employs him.

And so administrative science again plays into the hand of the social system. While the scientifically based training program claims to produce technicians skilled in decision-making and organization building, the Sovereign looks beyond such froth to the prospective administrator's values and character. But the froth is not irrelevant either; if for no other reason, it is politically advantageous to be seen standing with Science. Therefore, we see authorities increasingly turning to science-driven training programs. The result is a happy one for both sides of the bargain. The Sovereign can claim a scientific validation of its decisions, and Science gets privileged access to the benefits the Sovereign can bestow.

Callahan (1964) has identified four stages in the historical development of administrative programs for American school superintendents, and he shows how each stage was shaped by a characteristic ideal. In this development, we may also see the values that now generally pervade programs for the training of educational administrators in the United States. And – thanks to the international network that promulgates science-based training in educational administration – we may see these same values in similar programs in Canada and in many other countries as well. Callahan describes the stages through which the belief in the value of science-based programs for the training of educational administrators developed in the United States:

The superintendent as scholarly educational leader, 1865–1910.
The superintendent as business manager or school executive,
    1910–1930.
The superintendent as statesman in a democratic school system,
    1930–1954.
The superintendent as applied social scientist, 1954–present.

Khleif (1975) has reported an illuminating study of the socializing process and values of an exemplary program for the training of an élite cadre of educational administrators in administrative science. He found that more of the effort of the program was devoted to the inculcation of values than it was to the training of students in science. Indeed, he found that under the guise of training in social science, the neophyte administrators were offered a new persona and introduced to a set of values congenial to prospective employers. Students were carefully chosen for the program and schooled at length in their roles. After an appropriate time, the neophytes were certified as experts in the social scientific knowledge needed to administer schools and were introduced to mentors who then recommended them for jobs in the power system of education. Thus, particular social values were advanced under the guise of a training program dedicated to science.

As Khleif explains:

> The program is a high-speed course in social mobility. . . . The program is a school for statesmen or – if one is uncharitable – politicians. Candidates acquire an upper-middle class demeanor, dress, and presentability. Candidates become more socially polished, masters of small talk, alert politicians with – if necessary – a talent for intrigue and little arts of popularity. They become adept at self-manipulations and manipulations of others. (1975, p. 307)

With respect to the values in the four historical stages identified by Callahan, Khleif says the science-based program

> puts an emphasis on the three latter types of superintendency and definitely discourages or ignores the first type. Attention to school finances, a smooth facade of democratic leadership and pieties about it, and a realistic training in the ways of community power exemplify the historical heritage and current culture of this profession. (1975, p. 307)

It is not likely that training programs of the intensity and selectivity described by Khleif exist today. Such programs have been the victims of both a new stringency in university budgets and of a diminishing faith in the ideology that inspired them. But many programs of lesser purity and intensity undoubtedly remain, carrying on in the spirit noted by Khleif. Indeed, training programs for educational administrators have surely increased in number and enrolment over the past twenty years. They have consolidated their presence and have gained even stronger acceptance by sovereign powers. Such programs nurture Simon's conception of rational administration and decision-making. The pity of this situation is that such conceptions of administrative training block the development of programs that might deal more openly and helpfully with the value problems that confront all those who manage organizations. For administration is not a science in Simon's terms. It is better conceived by Hodgkinson: 'While it has at its disposal a managerial quasi-technology, it is essentially a philosophical endeavour, a kind of humanism. Its overriding mission is the civilization of power' (1978b, p. 100).

## The alternative

The criticisms I have made of the conventional practice of administrative science can be summed up in a few brief points. First, administrative science does not work as science; it has not brought us increased understanding and control of organizations. Yet this outcome is what both early and contemporary proponents of the science of administration claim to be its whole justification. Administrative science was to provide useful and powerful knowledge. This was the very criterion by which the fledgling science of administration rejected all previous knowledge in the field. Second, administrative science has ignored power relationships and has been content to deal with administrative problems that ignore substantive problems in education. Third, administrative science has focused its efforts not upon the phenomenological realities of administration – upon the experience of wielding power and making decisions – but upon the organization. It has been content to regard organizations rather than people as the real actors in society. And finally, administrative science has devalued the study of human choice and rationality. It has insisted that decision-making be dealt with *as though it were* fully explainable in rational and logical terms. This has allowed administrative science to deal with values surreptitiously, behind a mask of objectivity and impartiality, while denying it is doing so.

For these reasons, I believe it is a fair judgment to say that administrative science is in decline. Whether it has also fallen is a moot point. Some might argue that it does not matter whether the body of the science is dead or dying; it matters only that scholars and practitioners behave as though it were alive. Faith in administrative science certainly inspired the creation of the earliest models of science-based training programs (Khleif, 1975) and a similar if somewhat diminished faith surely continues to maintain them.

New directions are apparent in theory that again places value questions as central in administration (Hodgkinson, 1978b; Scott and Hart, 1979). What then is the alternative to a science- and fact-driven definition of the field? Though I have elaborated an answer elsewhere (Greenfield, 1983, 1985a), let me suggest again its dimensions.

1. Organizations are not things. They have no ontological reality, and there is no use studying them as though they did. They are an invented social reality of human creation. It is people who are responsible for organizations and people who change them. Organizations have reality only through human action, and it is that action (and the human will driving it) that we must come to understand. The alternative I am proposing rejects theory that explains human behavior as though a depersonalized

organization and its devalued, nonhuman environment *caused it*. The alternative theory grants a measure of free will to individuals, and so places a measure of responsibility upon them for their action. People do not exist in organizations. Organizations exist in and through individuals. The concept of organization should be understood as a moral order deeply embedded in each of us – an order that is arbitrary, nonnatural, and often backed by enormous power, even by violence. But that power may be redeemed by love, that is, by a dedication to better values.

2. Organizations are a nexus of freedom and compulsion. As invented social realities, they can not only be created but also manipulated. The creation and maintenance of this illusion is the root of what the world understands as leadership, although in less dramatic forms, it could as well be called administration. The metaphors of production and technical control, appropriate to systems, organisms, and other physical or biological unities, are not appropriate to understanding and administering organizations. We need new metaphors to describe organizations and administration. Perhaps most important would be to rid ourselves of the concept of an equilibriating system responding to benevolent environmental control. I suggest the metaphor of the bonsai tree. This image is particularly apt for education. The gardener does not let the young tree simply 'develop its full potential'. Instead, he acts upon his own view of what constitutes a proper expression of the tree's potential, and he keeps clipping and pruning until the tree manifests that form. Since in education the 'full potential' of a child (or of a teacher or administrator) could be anything from Charles Manson to Albert Schweitzer,[10] the gardener keeps pruning until the desired form is produced. The difference between the gardener's task and the administrator's, or the leader's, is that trees never learn. People do, and that is where organizations and human culture itself come from.

3. The world of will, intention, experience, and value is the world of organizations and administration. The building of a new science of administration will depend on our ability to understand these realities. It will require that we recognize their complexity (Hodgkinson, 1983, pp. 57–91) and their personal and subjective dimensions (Greenfield, 1985a). Such a science will require methods and instruments that are adequate to these realities. As Schumacher (1977, pp. 39–60) points out, the question of what constitutes adequate methods and instruments for understanding the world is essentially a philosophical one. And as Gronn (1982, 1984) has shown, our assumptions about adequate methods and instruments for studying administrators will not only reflect what we think administration is but also powerfully shape how we see administrators and understand what they do.

4. Conflict is endemic in organizations. It arises when different individuals or groups hold opposing values or when they must choose between accepted but incompatible values. Administrators represent values, but they also

impose them. Administrative science must come to understand these complexities if it is to speak meaningfully to the world of practice. Only then may it begin to help administrators understand and cope with the personal and existential stress of conflict. The texts of administrative science are suffused with metaphors that portray organizations in terms of equilibrium, stability, adjustment, and harmony. We need other metaphors to bespeak the reality of stress and conflict.

5. The ideas and insights of Barnard (1938), the scholar-practitioner, were largely swept aside in the rush to make the study of administration embrace the rationality of Simon's science. What Barnard focused upon was not rationality and the enhancement of it, but an essential value phenomenon in organizations: commitment. For him, the building of commitment was the fundamental task of administration. This view raises the question, 'How can administrators be moral?' rather than Simon's question, 'How can they be rational?' Simon would make the administrator a technician; Barnard would have him be a moral leader. Barnard speaks of the moral complexity of the leader. If we return to Barnard's view, we need again his insights as well as new metaphors to ground the science of administration. To help us begin to think of leaders in moral terms, we should recognize that they are representatives of values: indeed, they are both creators of values and entrepreneurs for them.

6. The ethical dimensions of administration come constantly to the fore once we free ourselves from the metaphors of harmony, optimism, and rationality that administrative science imposes upon organizational reality. What amazes in all of this is to read the science-based texts and to mark how positive and optimistic they are about human nature and the human condition. Administrative science lives in a world of pristine goodness, and so its knowledge can be of little use to those who face the perplexities of the world – perplexities that come readily to those who do no more than reflect upon their own experience or who simply read the newspapers or literary portrayals of life in organizations. Those, like Hodgkinson, who observe life in organizations in a clear-eyed fashion find that things often go wrong in them: they are beset by conflict, self-interested action, and the debasement of value through compromise. He lets us see the power of commitment, the pole-star quality of transcendent values, and the madness they may bring with them. He repeats Saul Bellow's simple but fundamental question: 'With everyone sold on the good, how does all the evil get done?' Of an earlier generation, Barnard speaks of the 'moral complexity' of the leader, by which he seems to mean the leader's wisdom in knowing when to raise moral issues and when to defuse them. Reflecting on such questions and building answers to them must become an essential and pervasive purpose of administrative studies. If Science cannot answer questions of what constitutes right action in social contexts – if it cannot speak of praxis – then it is time to begin again with a conception that sees administration as a set of existential and ethical issues. If inquiries launched

from this premise lead to an understanding of administration in moral terms, and if this knowledge helps administrators see themselves and their tasks more clearly and responsibly, we may then have reliable knowledge and a sound guide for action in the world. Although this is exactly the kind of knowledge that Simon found wanting and hoped to provide in a rational and control-oriented Science of Administration, could we not still call such knowledge 'science' in humbler form?

## An agenda for the future

Scholarship in administration has been bound for more than a generation by the power of Simon's thought. While a weakening of this remarkable uniformity is now apparent in all branches of the field, orthodoxy still struggles tenaciously to maintain its grip. In educational administration, defenders such as Willower (1985) meet the challenge by repeating positions only slightly modified from Simon's philosophical assumptions about the nature of administration and the proper means for inquiry into it. Most scholars will surely continue in the path that Simon pioneered, but others are now beginning to question that direction. They seek an alternative way and, therefore, an alternative conception of science to guide them. They, too, may call theirs the way of science, though they will likely abandon the assumptions and methods that Simon espoused as proper for scientific inquiry into administrative and organizational realities.

What is needed now in the study of educational administration is, first, the honesty to face the intellectual disarray of the field and, then, the courage to begin inquiry in a new mode. To guide such inquiry, we need only turn to an existing tradition of interpretive science that recognizes both subjectivity in the construction of social reality and the inevitability of interpretation in science. Though this mode of inquiry is still largely unknown and unused in administrative studies, it is at hand; it offers the best alternative to the narrow and increasingly sterile path of rationalism and positivistic science.

Administration is about power and powerful people. The study of administration must stand therefore upon a resolute examination of people as they strive to realize their ends. Administrative Science has too often yielded to the temptation of power and desired to wield it, not just to study it. Those who stand close to sovereign powers readily find reason to assist them. An adequate science of administration, however, must study power while resisting its pull. The new science of administration must be free to talk about the values that power serves, but free it cannot be if it is closely dependent upon the Sovereign (Ramos, 1981). To escape that dependency, the new science should abjure those activities that are most likely to endear it to the Sovereign – recognizing that the Sovereign, like the Devil, can take many forms. The certification of future administrators is one such endearing activity.

For more than a quarter of a century, a fact-driven model of decision-making and rationality has dominated training programs for educational administrators. To the extent that these programs embrace technically oriented notions of administration, they offer less than they espouse. They miss the meaning of human action and most of what saves the study of administration from inducing a state of ennui in its students. They oversimplify administrative problems and overstate the claim that science can solve them. Yet such programs recognize virtually no limit on what can be done through academic study to prepare candidates for administrative responsibility. Only by suffering through their perhaps intentionally boring training do students of science-based training come to glimpse the meaning of administrative power and its scope for good and evil (Greenfield, 1980, pp. 47–8).

A more fruitful training may be achieved through approaches that work with practising administrators and aim to give them deeper insights into the nature of their craft – into its dilemmas and possibilities – through study of its realities and through reflection upon them. We must seek new models for administrative training – ones that acknowledge responsibility, right judgment, and reflection as legitimately and inevitably part of administrative action. Such programs would lead the field of study toward what Scott (1985, p. 156) has called 'revolutionary moral discourse' and away, therefore, from instruction in a putative science of organization and administration.

When I first took up the study of educational administration, nothing I learned cast a scintilla of doubt upon the certainty and power of administrative science; its objectivity and probity were simply assumed as were the benefits that were supposed to flow from its application. Certainly I did not doubt these apparent truths. What then is to be said now? Would the world be the worse without an administrative science? Probably not. But the issue is not simply science versus something else – versus the humanities, philosophy, or doing nothing at all. The issue is rather 'What kind of science?' Toulmin (1983) has observed the progress of modern science and noted the transformation of the scientist from an observer of reality to a participant in its construction. Where scientists once worried only to do the measurement right, they now find an even greater problem: to do the right measurement – that is, to make the right observation. Thus the inevitability of subjective choice and interpretation enters science, and the possibility of a value-free science disappears. We must seek a new definition of science in administration – one that can accommodate the view that values pervade the entire realm of administration and, indeed, constitute the proper focus of study. Toulmin explains how a demand for neutrality in scientific method and observation came to limit the very kinds of problems that scientists could think of as proper for study:

> This demand for value neutrality played two separate roles in the sciences. On the one hand, it required the modern scientist to approach all the intellectual problems that properly fell within the scope of his

methods with a clear head and a cool heart. On the other hand, it served to demarcate those issues that were properly the subjects for 'scientific' investigation and discussion from those that were, rather, matters of human taste, choice, or decision. To begin with, these two aspects were not always distinguished in people's minds. (1981, p. 81)

If nothing else, we must understand that the new science of administration will be a science with values and of values.

What is required now is a transformation of the administrative scientist's attitudes toward the reality he studies. Scientists inspired by positivism approach administrators with the conviction that their theories and methods enable them to know administration in a way mere practitioners never could. The reverse assumption now seems a better point of departure: administrators know administration; scientists don't. The point of such inquiry would be to enable scientists to come to know what administrators know and to bring a fresh and questioning perspective to it. To accomplish this purpose, we might well return to one of Simon's original starting points and seek to understand the logic and psychology of human choice. But that will require the study of decisions, will, and intention in all their depth, perplexity, and subjective uncertainty. The new science will surely also require giving up the notion that decisions and organizations themselves can be controlled by science. Greater insight such science may offer, but greater control, no.

A possible research agenda of the new science is apparent:

1. How is the social reality of the organization built and maintained? What do administrators and others contribute to this process?
2. What is the role of language in the building of administrative reality? We might begin to answer this question by taking seriously Hodgkinson's propositions (1978b, pp. 199–222): Two of these state, 'Language is the basic administrative too!' and 'Language *has* power and cloaks power.'
3. The character of administrators is clearly of great importance. We may study it through biography and history.
4. Law is built upon the arbitration of value conflict. Let us emulate its methods and learn from the substance of its knowledge.
5. We must consider more fully such philosophical issues as the nature of value and the question of right values. What constitutes good or right in administrative affairs and how can administrators gain knowledge of it?
6. Questions of what constitutes good and right action in administration must be answered not simply for themselves, but in context and with specific educational issues and policies.
7. We must understand more deeply the administrative career. Who administers our schools? What motivates them to climb the ladder of administration? What happens to them as they do? What routes lead upward? In the recent past, there was truth in the dictum: women teach and men administer. What made that dictum true? Is there a better truth and how may it be realized?

8. We need to understand the existential realities of leading and following in organizations. We need to understand the wielding of power and the making of decisions when much is on the line. And we need to appreciate what it is to suffer the decisions of such power.

This is a minimal agenda for research but it stands in contrast with much of what has gone before. If we could achieve it only partially, we would have some basis to say a valid and valuable science of administration is emerging.

## Notes

1. I will refer to the 1957 edition and use the valuable perspective that Simon's 'Introduction to the Second Edition' provides on his work. The year 1957 also marks the beginning of New Movement science in educational administration.
2. Perhaps seeing language itself as the problem, the editors of *EAQ* recently announced a prohibition on first person pronouns. Ironically, they chose to begin their battle against the subjectivism of the world in a text dealing with *ethnographic intent*. So they extirpated 'I,' 'me,' and 'my' from Wolcott (1985), whose text thereby suffered a sea-change.
3. The attitude of the time is seen in Marland's deferential reference to 'scientist Halpin' (Campbell and Lipham, 1960, p. 34).
4. Among the many who call for better technique to shore up the sagging science of administration, see Willower (1979, 1980), Hoy (1982), Fields (1985), and Haller and Knapp (1985). Implicitly they defend the assumptions Simon made about appropriate theory and methods, though they never invoke his name.
5. I use 'Science' to denote the narrower but imperial inquiry that claims objectivity and value-neutrality and that stands in contrast to the broader search for reliable knowledge that characterizes all inquiry (Schumacher, 1977).
6. For example, Hoy and Miskel (1982).
7. Silver (1983) devotes not even a footnote to the controversies that have shaken educational administration for over a decade.
8. These ideas are elaborated in Greenfield (1984, pp. 147–51).
9. For further critique of this advocacy, see Riffel (in press) and Greenfield (1975, 1979/80).
10. Near one end of this continuum, there surely stands Jim Keegstra, the small-town Alberta teacher who until recently taught and examined his students on a history whose central 'facts' proved that Hitler's 'final solution' was purely a hoax perpetrated by Jewish conspiracy.

## References

Barnard, C. (1938). *The functions of the executive*. Cambridge, Mass.: Harvard University Press.

Bates, R. J. (1983a). *Educational administration and the management of knowledge*. Victoria, Australia: Deakin University Press.

Bates, R. J. (1983b). Morale and motivation: Myth and morality in educational administration. *Educational Administration Review* 3(1).

Bates, R. J. (1985). Towards a critical practice of educational administration. In T. J.

Sergiovanni and J. E. Corbally (eds.), *Leadership and organizational culture*. Urbana: University of Illinois.

Bauman, Z. (1978). *Hermeneutics and social science*. London: Hutchinson.

Boethius. (1969). *The consolation of philosophy* (V. E. Watts, trans.). Harmondsworth: Penguin Books.

Boyd, W. L., and Crowson, R. L. (1981). The changing conception and practice of public school administration. In D. C. Berliner (ed.), *Review of research in education: Vol. 9*. Washington: AERA.

Campbell, R. F., and Lipham, J. M. (eds). (1960). *Administrative theory as a guide to action*. Chicago: Midwest Center, University of Chicago.

Culbertson, J. (1983). Theory in educational administration: Echoes from critical thinkers. *Educational Researcher* 12(10): 15–22.

Eisner, E. W. (1983). Anastasia might be alive, but the monarchy is dead. *Educational Researcher* 12(5):13–24.

Fields, M. W. (1985). Exploratory data analysis in educational administration: Tempering methodological advances with a 'conservative note. *Educational Administration Quarterly* 21(3):247–62.

Foster, W. P. (1985). Towards a critical theory of educational administration. In T. J. Sergiovanni and J. E. Corbally (eds), *Leadership and organizational culture*. Urbana: University of Illinois.

Giddens, A. (1976). *New rules of sociological method: A positive critique of interpretive sociologies*. London: Hutchinson.

Greenfield, T. B. (1975). Theory about organization: A new perspective and its implications for schools. In M. Hughes (ed.), *Administering education: International challenge*. London: Athlone.

Greenfield, T. B. (1978). Reflections on organization theory and the truths of irreconcilable realities. *Educational Administration Quarterly* 14(2):1–23.

Greenfield, T. B. (1979/80). Research in educational administration in the United States and Canada: An overview and critique. *Educational Administration* 8(1): 207–45.

Greenfield, T. B. (1980). The man who comes back through the door in the wall: Discovering truth, discovering self, discovering organizations. *Educational Administration Quarterly* 16(3):26–59.

Greenfield, T. B. (1983). Against group mind: An anarchistic theory of organization. In R. L. Rattray-Wood (ed.), *Reflective readings in educational administration*. Victoria, Australia: Deakin University Press.

Greenfield, T. B. (1984). Leaders and schools: Wilfulness and nonnatural order in organizations. In T. J. Sergiovanni and J. E. Corbally (eds), *Leadership and organizational culture*. Urbana: University of Illinois.

Greenfield, T. B. (1985a). *Putting meaning back into theory: The search for lost values and the disappeared individual*. Paper presented to the Annual Conference of the Canadian Society for the Study of Education, Montreal.

Greenfield, T. B. (1985b). Theories of educational organization: A critical perspective. In T. Husen and T. N. Postlethwaite (eds), *International encyclopedia of education: Research and studies: Vol. 9*. Oxford: Pergamon.

Griffiths, D. E. (1979). Intellectual turmoil in educational administration. *Educational Administration Quarterly*, 15(3):43–65.

Gronn, P. C. (1982). Neo-Taylorism in educational administration? *Educational Administration Quarterly* 18(4):17–35.

Gronn, P. C. (1983). *Rethinking educational administration: T. B. Greenfield and his critics*. Victoria, Australia: Deakin University Press.

Gronn, P. C. (1984). On studying administrators at work. *Educational Administration Quarterly* 20(1):115–29.

Gronn, P. C. (1985a). After T. B. Greenfield, whither educational administration? *Educational Management and Administration* 13:55–61.

Gronn, P. C. (1985b). Choosing a deputy head: The rhetoric and the reality of administrative selection. *Australian Journal of Education* 29(3).

Gronn, P. C. (1985c). Notes on leader watching. In R. J. S. Macpherson and H. Sungaila (eds), *Ways and means of research*. Armidale, Australia: University of New England.

Gronn, P. C. (in press). *The psycho-social dynamics of leading and following*. Victoria, Australia: Deakin University.

Haire, M., (ed.). (1959). *Modern Organization Theory*. New York: Wiley.

Haller, E. J., and Knapp, T. R. (1985). Problems and methodology in educational administration. *Educational Administration Quarterly* 21(3):157–68.

Halpin, A. W., (ed.). (1958). *Administrative theory in education*. Chicago: Midwest Administration Center, University of Chicago.

Halpin, A. W. (1966). *Theory and research in administration*. New York: Macmillan.

Halpin, A. W. (1970). Administrative theory: The fumbled torch. In A. M. Kroll (ed.), *Issues in American education*. New York: Oxford.

Hodgkinson, C. (1978a). The failure of organizational and administrative theory. *McGill Journal of Education*. 13(3):271–8.

Hodgkinson, C. (1978b). *Towards a philosophy of administration*. Oxford: Basil Blackwell.

Hodgkinson, C. (1983). *The philosophy of leadership*. Oxford: Basil Blackwell.

Hodgkinson, C. (1985). *Confucius, Wittgenstein, and the perplexing world of administration*. Lecture, Ontario Institute for Studies in Education, Toronto.

Hodgkinson, C. (1986). *The value bases of administrative action*. Paper read to the Annual Conference of the American Educational Research Association, San Francisco.

Hoy, W. K. (1982). Recent developments in theory and research in educational administration. *Educational Administration Quarterly* 18(3):1–11.

Hoy, W. K., and Miskel, C. G. (1982). *Educational administration: Theory, research, and practice* (2nd edn). New York: Random House.

Khleif, B. B. (1975). Professionalization of school superintendents: A sociocultural study of an élite program. *Human Organization* 34(3): 301–8.

Lakomski, G. (1984). On agency and structure: Pierre Bourdieu and Jean-Claude Passeron's theory of symbolic violence. *Curriculum Inquiry* 14(2):151–63.

Lakomski, G. (1985a). *Critical theory and educational administration: Problems and solutions*. Paper read to the American Educational Research Association Annual Conference, Chicago.

Lakomski, G. (1985b). The cultural perspective in educational administration. In R. J. S. Macpherson and H. M. Sungaila (eds), *Ways and means of research in educational administration*. Armidale, Australia: University of New England.

Lakomski, G. (1985c). Theory, value, and relevance in educational administration. In F. Rizvi (ed.), *Working papers in ethics and educational administration*. Victoria, Australia: Deakin University.

March, J. G. (ed.) (1965). *Handbook of organizations*. Chicago: Rand-McNally.

Phillips, D. C. (1983). After the wake: Postpositivistic educational thought. *Educational Researcher* 12(5):4–12.

Rabinow, P., and Sullivan, W. M. (eds). (1979). *Interpretive social science: A reader.* Berkeley: University of California.

Ramos, A. G. (1981). *The new science of organizations: A reconstruction of the wealth of nations.* Toronto: University of Toronto Press.

Riffel, J. A. (in press). The study of educational administration: A developmental point of view. *Journal of Educational Administration*, 24:

Schumacher, E. F. (1977). *A guide for the perplexed.* New York: Harper & Row.

Scott, W. G. (1985). Organizational revolution: An end to managerial orthodoxy. *Administration and Society* 17(2):149–70.

Scott, W. G., and Hart, D. (1979). *Organizational America.* Boston: Houghton-Mifflin.

Silver, P. (1983). *Educational administration: Theoretical perspectives on practice and research.* New York: Harper & Row.

Simon, H. (1957). *Administrative behavior: A study of decision-making process in administrative organization* (2nd edn). New York: The Free Press.

Szasz, T. (1976). *Heresies.* Garden City, NY: Anchor/Doubleday.

Tipton, B. F. A. (1985). Educational organizations as workplaces. *British Journal of Educational Sociology* 6(1):35–53.

Tope, D. E., *et al.* (1965). *The social sciences view educational administration.* Englewood Cliffs, NJ: Prentice-Hall.

Toulmin, S. (1981). The emergence of post-modern science. In R. M. Hutchins and M. J. Adler (eds), *The great ideas today.* Chicago: Encyclopedia Britannica.

Toulmin, S. (1983). *From observer to participant: The transformation of twentieth century science.* Lecture, University of Toronto.

Wolcott, H. (1985). On ethnographic intent. *Educational Administration Quarterly* 21(3):187–203.

Willower, D. J. (1979). Ideology and science in organization theory. *Educational Administration Quarterly* 15(3):20–42.

Willower, D. J. (1980). Contemporary issues in theory in educational administration. *Educational Administration Quarterly* 16(3):1–25.

Willower, D. J. (1985). Philosophy and the study of educational administration. *Journal of Educational Administration* 23(1):7–22.

# 8

# A perspective
## on organization theory[1]

**H. L. Gray**

Every consultant and researcher has in his mind some kind of a model which influences the way he perceives the subjects of his investigation. For many people, the model is generalized, vague and below the level of logical consciousness, but nevertheless it exists and provides a perspective on the world under examination (Berger and Luckman, 1967). In education management the models generally in use and at a recognizable level of consciousness tend to be sociological, economic and political in concept and systems models in structure and logic. Such models have the advantage of a broad tradition of expository writing and a high level of apparent tangibility – they have 'measurable' elements which makes them generally acceptable by scientific criteria. Administrators tend to like such models because they permit decisions to be made on the basis of quantifiable data though they tend to assume the values of non-quantifiable (qualitative) data.

In recent years there has been a reaction against the hard line approach in management and administration and an interest in the so-called qualitative aspects of organizations. Within the broad stream of psychology, an important body of scholars has espoused the 'humanistic' cause and developed a concern for personal values as against laboratory criteria. Among social scientists an interest in New Paradigms for Research (Reason, 1977) has an increasing influence following on from interest in Action Research in its various forms (Clark, 1972). Action Research attempts to ensure the involvement of the client as an active participant in doing research.

Education management has tended towards a more conservative position as would be expected of a new field but after a long allegiance to a specific sociological school of thought (Greenfield, 1979) an interest in alternative methods of model building, researching and, as a consequence different models of consultancy, has grown and commands increasing support. The most significant event in the development of theory in the area of education management was Greenfield's paper at the International Intervisitation Programme (IIP) in Education Administration in the UK in 1974 (Greenfield, 1975). Controversy raged in the backwaters of education management theorists (hardly a mainstream group in the academic world) though comparatively little development occurred in spite of a general shift in opinion in support of Greenfield's basically phenomenological viewpoint (see *Educational Administration*, 1976 onwards). Largely ignored had been Dale's paper on Phenomenological Perspectives in the Sociology of the School published in 1973.

One reason for the apparent lack of activity in the new perspective was that in the European academic tradition, phenomenological approaches were comparatively well integrated into the general way of thinking. Europeans are perhaps more speculative and reflective than Americans who prefer action and visible evidence. Be this as it may, many writers in the UK at any rate have preferred to sit on the fence and have the best of both worlds – the phenomenological and the non-phenomenological – rather than help to develop a basically alternative approach to viewing organizations. One attempt was made by Gray (1980) in a paper entitled 'Organizations as Subjectivities' and it is broadly in line with this theory that the ideas in this chapter are developed.

A subjective theory of organizations provides a way of looking at organizations so that the uniqueness of individual perceptions is held in focus and becomes the major concern. Organizations exist effectively only in the experience of their members (i.e. those who experience them). A subjective theory is not very interested in whether organizations have objective existence or reality – they may or may not – the point is they can only be understood through the experiences individuals have of them. Because each of us is a different person (i.e. has a different self-concept, a different personality) each of us has a different experience of the same organization. Indeed, it might be claimed that each member belongs to a different organization because experiences of 'the same' are different.

This is not to deny the physical existence of organizations since they clearly do exist otherwise no one could experience them. But the tangible and measurable is not the essential organization; there is always something else other than what is measured. For example a hospital building may be turned into a college. Physically the building is the same but its changed purposes lead one to think differently about it though the casual passer-by may still see it as a hospital. Even when we reduce an organization to people only (like a crowd in a football match) that which is observable from without (or above) is only a facet of organization since much of what is going on organizationally (the football match is the organization – organizational behaviour is everything related to the creating and experiencing of the football match so long as its occurrence can be attributed to the central activity of a football game) is invisible because it is in the minds of the members of the game and the spectators. Although everyone is at the same match, everyone experiences the events of the afternoon differently.

It is these individual responses that are of interest in subjective theory (Poole, 1975). Instead of examining organizations as aggregations, summations or majorities, the subjective theorist seeks to understand the meaning an organization has for each individual member. Of course, there are enormous problems because organizational behaviour is by definition collective and so questions of agreement, consensus and control are problematical. One of the difficulties about Organization Development (OD) which as a technique for management appeals very much to individualists is that much of the emphasis appears to be on consensus and the avoidance of conflicting wishes in the greater interests of the organization or the collective good. But subjective theory does appear to provide a useful analysis of how individuals and collectivities or associations relate and no doubt OD and other management theories will respond.

If each individual has a different experience of a school, how can the school function when interests differ? There are two ways. One is for the organization to face up to the conflicts and resolve them in some way. Satisfactory resolution will lead to improved relationships; unsatisfactory resolution or avoidance will allow the conflicts to continue in some way. Of course, the organization does not do anything; the members do it, according to the way they have come to agree to work together. Usually this is in terms of the conventional positions that people hold such as manager, head, teacher, student, etc. These positions are expressed in terms of behaviour and a description of the behaviour is a role. Conventional and ritualized behaviours characterize role behaviour; that is, when there are common expectations about the appropriate behaviour for a position, that behaviour is ritualized as a 'role'. But all positions may be expressed in non-ritualized behaviour and in such a case an individual is often perceived as behaving inappropriately or denying his role (responsibilities). The rituals of organizations are explored in dramaturgical theories of organization (e.g. Mangham, 1978).

Another way of functioning is by doing everything to avoid conflict. In the normal way of things people manage to work together in an organization through a process of 'accommodation'. That is to say they reach agreement by default on all sorts of issues. In this way, two individuals of totally different personality with quite contradictory purposes may work together quite harmoniously because their differences just do not come into conflict; they can pursue their own lives as independently as passengers on a bus. The idea that individuals have to agree, have common purposes, objectives, values and so on is patently untrue although congruity in all these matters and others will lead to different and in some cases 'better' forms of association.

Relationships between individuals in an organization occur as psychological negotiations and contracts (Homans, 1961). In a perfect world these negotiations would be totally open but in practice they are generally constrained in some way. Nevertheless, all relationships are negotiated and the negotiations lead to some form of contract. Of course, these negotiations and contracts are unspoken, often subconsciously and for the most part unilaterally. Even mutual overt negotiations have a large element of unilateral reservation. When these psychological contracts are broken they are usually broken unilaterally and retrospectively. It is the unspoken nature of these negotiations that makes organizational life interesting because there is a constant element of surprise. Managers and administrators are disconcerted by these surprises because they upset their planning and control yet since they are one of the very essences of organizational behaviour a manager who is to be effective should be the kind of person to enjoy the unexpected rather than resent it.

If we pursue an interest in subjective theory, a fundamental concern is personality and how individuals develop a sense of themselves and give meaning to the world they live in (Hamachek, 1978). Personality theory is a confused area, but organization theorists will tend to fall into two groups: those who believe personality is socially conditioned and those who believe personality is pre-existent but develops in terms of social opportunity. This is not the place to examine personality theory, but on the whole, for a variety of reasons, organization theorists who are interested in subjective theory take a humanistic view of personality – humanistic or counselling psychology (e.g. Rogers, 1951). Much of their 'organization' theory is based upon their understanding of group behaviour, of group dynamics. My own position is akin to the latter. I see personality as a reflection of the self-concept; I believe the 'self' to be unique and pre-existent: I see organizations as oportunities for individuals to grow and develop through the process of self-discovery.

Formal organizations are simply one type of human organization but with all the characteristics of organization albeit formalized, ritualized and dramatized (Morris and Burgoyne, 1973). What happens in formal organizations happens essentially in informal organizations. Formal organizations are associations of individuals serving wider social purposes but at root having to deal with the requirements of individuals. Organizations are created by their members and do not have any inherent pre-existent form; they are not discovered, they are made and, being made by people, they are subject to people even when they are like Frankenstein's master and appear to be more powerful than their creators. They are always understood by their members differently, because they are experienced differently – a cause of perpetual exasperation to some managers.

Having very briefly outlined some of the more salient aspects of a subjective theory of organizations, I want now to deal with the implications for research and consultancy. If one views organizations from a phenomenological standpoint, there are certain quite clear imperatives for research and consultancy in which one will engage quite differently than if one has an alternative theoretical background. The presenting problems of organizations may appear the same but the explanations, solutions and approaches to solutions will be different. The researcher and consultant must approach his task with his theoretical perspective clearly in his mind or he will offer answers and explanations that are incompatible and inherently inconsistent.

I shall relate subjective theory to practice in terms of twelve propositions. Each of these represents an area of analysis and consideration and implies the terms in which an exploration will be expressed. Underlying them all is the idea that organizations exist for individuals only in terms of their experience and the understanding that comes from reflecting on that experience. Descriptions of organizational behaviour by an observer tell more about the observer than what he has observed. Interpretations and explanations are pictures created by the observer in terms that are consistent with his own intellectual framework. Objectivity is the understanding or meaning an experience has for another person in his terms not one's own interpretation of the same experience (Jehenson, 1973). What the subjective researcher and consultant is trying to do is to help his clients to understand their world better by exploring the terms in which they see it. The consultant is not explaining his own interpretation to them, though he may share his interpretations with his clients.

Such a client-centred approach has much in common with counselling and psychotherapy (Corsini, 1973). Indeed it may be called a counselling approach to consultancy (Gray, 1974) because the basic theory of the person is the same. The important element in the idea of counselling is that of listening to what the client has to say and the meaning he gives to the events and situations in which he is involved. In client-centred therapy the counsellor tries not to disturb the client's thoughts by substituting his own. That is what we need to try to do if we have a subjective theory of organizations because the solving of problems is dependent upon the correct insight into the self. Now for the propositions:

## 1. About order and disorder

*Order will always form and reform but in a different way.*

One of the deepest anxieties that people, especially managers, have about organizations is that somehow they will get out of control, that chaos will reign. Fear of losing control is pathological for some people but most managers justify strong controlling behaviour because they fear 'losing control'. Somehow 'being in complete control' is one of the expectations that managers have of themselves. The question is, what is the nature of order? In human terms there is no such thing as chaos. Chaos never reigns. Even when matters are 'beyond control' human behaviour is always purposeful. Those situations in which panic occurs are truly rare and quite special: they are not the general order of the day and, even when people panic, their behaviour becomes exceedingly purposeful.

All human behaviour is patterned in some way and responsive. When people gather together to do something they quickly organize themselves into some order. When the situation changes, they change their ordering. The problem with formal organizations is that they perpetuate a form of order suitable to a moment in time in their life and the need to perpetuate overrides other needs. There is no need to explain why this happens because it happens in many ways some of which are explained later, but the authority and/or power given by a group or organization to its first leader is a matter for exploration because power tends towards consolidation and leaders tend to seek to retain power even at the expense of their followers. The question is not whether without leadership control there will be 'chaos' (because there will not; simply a more appropriate structure will emerge) but why the leader is perceived to have the power he is given. And why do leaders insist that power is not 'personal' but 'of the office' when all their behaviour is personal (because, of course, it cannot be anything else)?

## 2. About structure

*Structure is a description of the behaviour of people.*

Many managers appear to be of the opinion that structure in organizations is pre-existent, that all organizations have a predetermined structure into which people must fit. This is not so. Structure is simply a description of what people do and how they relate; organization structure is a grossly simplified description of jobs and relationships. (Strictly speaking all 'organization charts' are little more than idealized representations.) A structure cannot be imposed on an organization, it can only derive from what people do. What people do is less determined by the nature of the job than the dispositions of the people doing it. Of course, some technical processes are highly deter-minative; there are a limited number of ways to stamp a die but most organizational tasks are complex and with increasing complexity there is a broadening of possible ways of doing things. No two people hold a pen in the same way or there would be no variation in handwriting.

To understand structure we need to explore not only what people are doing but what they believe they are doing and what kinds of explanations they give for their behaviour. It is not enough to observe people as if they were ants and to describe what the observer (believes he) sees – the problem with such writers as Desmond Morris who uses a biologist's perspective rather than a psychologist's (Morris, 1978). A headteacher will have an idea of what being a headteacher is and he will be attempting to reconcile that with the perceptions he has of himself. The conflict about position and self concept may not be observable from without yet in discussion the man may show himself to be in mental turmoil. The consequences of turmoil and uncertainty are certain forms of behaviour and a change in the individual's perceptions of role and self will lead to behavioural changes. To describe these changed behaviours is to describe the changed structures even though names of people and positions have not (apparently) changed.

### 3.  About objectives

*Organizations serve purposes, they do not have objectives.*

In subjective theory, because organizations have no corporeal existence apart from the experiences members have of them, there can be no 'objectives' for an organization only objectives for individual members. Furthermore, the nature of organizations as associations of people means that they are at best means to an end; that is they serve purposes. The purposes, however, are individual purposes – whatever members require the organization to do in order that something or other may be achieved.

But, more than this, individuals do not look to organizations to achieve simple and finite purposes. Human objectives are always negotiable. Whenever an individual fails in an objective, he substitutes an alternative – either an alternative solution, objective or retrospective expectation. People just do not reach a terminal point, point blank. So far as people are concerned, their contract with the organization is multiple, largely unexpressed, dependent on circumstances and on evaluation of experiences and outcomes and conditional upon the return being greater than the effort (a fair or generous reward; an unfair and punitive rebuff). To find out just what any individual wants (let alone wanted) of an organization is a difficult task because so many personal matters are involved but the answers have little or nothing to do with objective organizational goals or ascriptions.

### 4.  About the determinants of behaviour

*The critical dimension in human organization is human behaviour not technology.*

On the face of it, this must appear fairly obvious but it is too often forgotten especially by managers. Time and again problems in organizations occur because managers require colleagues to respond to material and technical demands as if they were totally immovable. It needs to be remembered that human beings have an advantage over physical objects, they can always go round them. Material and technical blockages are, from the standpoint of subjective theory, no more, or less, than personal interpretations of the situation. In practice alternative strategies are always available, however disagreeable they may be at first sight. Since no situation remains static it is only a matter of time before attitudes and standpoints change.

In many cases, the constructing of technological structures has become a total impediment to perceiving the true nature of organizational relationships. Education is the classic case of non-relevant technology being imported into the system. For the essential process of teaching (more properly of education) no technology is necessary other than those present in the need-to-learn situation. Teaching/learning is a personal exchange with no essential materials other than those that are present on the occasion. (That is to say, you cannot learn to ride a bike unless you have one but you do not need a computer to learn arithmetical processes.) The false objectification of organizations will always be an intractable problem to consultants who look for 'real', 'tangible' and 'concrete' problems. But phenomenological approaches will deal with the fundamental blockages in the individual and then he will be able to proceed to deal with the objects that have meaning for him.

## 5. About individual interests

*Individuals always behave in terms of what they believe to be their best interests. Altruism is best understood in terms of self-interest.*

This is the concept of negotiation and contract described earlier. Would anyone claim that members of organizations do things in what they believe to be their worst interests? Clearly not. Since such behaviour would be pathological, it cannot be said never to occur but emotional sickness is a different problem. Just how people perceive their best interest is very complicated. Some people go around in a perpetual state of confrontation while others seem never to have a row with anyone. Observe the changeover from one trade union representative to another and the blockages of years can be cast away in seconds. Negotiating skills are not like steps in a dance or movements on the stage, though they often have those same surface characteristics, rather they derive from a disposition within the individual and the ways he conceives of himself.

One of the biggest lies in management is that a manager has only the interests of the organization or his colleagues at heart. Such statements are no more than attempted blackmail. The reality of self-interest is that it cannot be pursued without due consideration for self as well as others. Claiming altruistic interest is often no more than a consequence of identification of self and organization, a form of megalomania unfortunately not uncommon in organizations. True self-interest includes regard for others, generosity, care and affection but they arise out of a sense of contentment, with an acceptance of self. The consultant must explore the regard individuals have for themselves and how it conditions the regard for others. It cannot be done by observation, certainly not by aggregated data, but only by a mutual exploration of the meaning that collective activity has for the individual. Leaders are especially at risk because they may assume a responsibility for others that is only in the interests of the leader's self esteem not the good of his colleagues. Difficulties in counselling leaders often arise from their attempt to depersonalize and objectify their relation with the organization.

## 6.  About subjectivity and objectivity

*Organizational experience is always subjective.*

By definition experience is subjective, though clearly the extent to which one is aware of others varies enormously. But being aware of others is not itself objective. This is not the place to argue the true nature of objectivity because the pragmatism of consultancy deals with a different relationship between the two concepts (objectivity and subjectivity). The individual's perceptions of organization are always richer in that they are subjective because reflection on one's own experience is possible but reflecting on another's is impossible. Of course, we all have views and opinions about others and we can make shrewd guesses about what they think and what they feel but we can never 'know' how they think and feel.

If the consultant is to help a manager, say the principal of a college, to deal with a problem with staff colleagues, he can best do this by helping the principal to understand why he sees a problem, how he constructs the problem, and interprets it, how it fills certain expectations about problems that he habitually employs, and how he perceives acceptable solutions. Obviously information about and from others in the problem situation can be obtained and discussed (many OD skills may be used such as feedback and paraphrasing) but the essential task is to help the principal to understand the way in which he perceives the situation because the problem is uniquely his; to anyone else it is uniquely different.

## 7.  About reality

*Organizations are personal constructs, artefacts or fantasies, existing only in the imagination of individuals.*

Obviously, all organizations exist in themselves – though I am not very clear what that means – but each individual creates his own organization as an experience which consolidates in reflection. This proposition means that effectively two people working in the same school may well attend two irreconcilable institutions. I have used the term 'collective fantasy' (Gray, 1980) to describe this situation. One consequence is that the organization is capable of almost infinite development within the mind of an individual since we are all sharing a different reality in our membership. Our reality is our experience and no one's reality is greater than anyone else's.

For the consultant it means that he must help each individual client to explore what kind of an organization he has created. Many of the problems that managers have are a result of their expecting others to conform to their organizational expectations. They believe that the only permissible objectives and purposes are their own and that the validity of these expectations is directly related to position in the (fantasy) hierarchy of the organization. For some individuals a high level of fantasy is essential if the otherwise appalling reality is to be surmounted – that is, their belief that 'reality' is appalling. (This statement might be seen to imply that no level of fantasy would be 'reality'. In fact reality would be a state of maximum agreement between individual perceptions. There would always be other realities for other people. Reality is not an absolute state but a degree of congruity.)

## 8. About organizational change

*Organizational change occurs only as a consequence of changes in the individual self-concept. It is the individual's view of himself that changes, not the organization.*

Organizations do change in a lot of ways – they start up, close down, amalgamate, enter into new areas of activity. Conventional management theory is about such changes. But we need to know how and why change begins to occur. We explained earlier (proposition 4) that technical considerations are secondary variables. If a school building falls down, the 'school' may move into new accommodation. A company that starts off as a travel agent may finish up as an international bank. Such material changes still require explanation. From a phenomenological viewpoint the fabric and material is not the primary area of interest but rather the perceptions individuals have about the organization and their organizational perceptions are direct correlations of the self-image.

If we define the self-concept (the self-image) as what an individual believes about himself, what he believes himself to be (the answer to the question, who am I?) then the organization to which he relates (i.e. which he experiences will be experienced in terms of his self-concept because imaging self and others are part of the same world creation. Thinking about oneself and thinking about other than self are aspects of the same process. This is not to say the correlation between perceptions is direct and clear. An individual who likes himself may like or dislike other people according to other elements in his make up, the complexity of reasons for high self-regard. High self-regard may be selfish or unselfish in its effects and only deep analysis can uncover what is there.

The consultant and researcher concerned with organizational change can only deal with individuals anyway; there are no tangible organizations to deal with. Even when dealing with small groups, the *effective* changes occur in individuals never in the group. Group or collective dynamics are a different, even if closely related, dimension to individual behaviour, and indeed there are many problems in working with groups when the individual emphasis is lost sight of.

By and large individual change occurs at what can conveniently be called the affective level of perception. That is to say cognition is a consequence of affective response. In group work it is customary to talk of 'feelings', 'gut reactions' and 'intuition' to refer to the psychological condition in which an individual says: 'Ah, now I see'. Invariably, this means he responds positively (i.e. by accepting) some feelings in his current experience and, as a consequence, sees himself differently with the further consequence that he sees the situation or organization differently. I have explained this process more fully in 'Training people to understand organizations: A clinical approach' (Gray, 1980).

## 9. About organizational functioning

*Organizations function as expressions of collective value systems and are inherently in a state of conflict.*

Much of this is inherent in what I have said already, though the emphasis on values is expressed very adequately in a book by Christopher Hodgkinson (1978). On the face of it, however, it may appear to conflict with the idea of individual functioning. But each individual behaves on the basis of a personal value system, not expressed verbally but in behaviour – the underlying value system that relates to the self-concept. The strange position is that values are very often ignored as a major feature of organizational behaviour, as if values were trawled up after an expedition rather than being the very expression of relationships. In subjective theory the interest is in the variety and incongruence of individual value systems and the fantasies about organizational values. Organizational values, of course, just do not exist as an entity, only the value systems of dominant individuals, a point which Hodgkinson makes very clearly.

The consultant and researcher will find considerable evidence of pervasive value systems in organizations but his first task will be to discover how they arise and which individual they reflect. The objective is not to seek common values but rather to discover what discordance there is. Value systems are highly personal and exceedingly complex and no two individuals share the same. Problems arise as individuals express personal values in behaviour with more than usual force or commitment. In organizations, as a general rule, accommodation takes place with regard to normal behaviour but, once behaviour changes, it changes the 'profile' of personal values, hence the need for renegotiation and new contracting. Inherent in this process is a realignment of values – changes in what is and is not acceptable. The ways in which individuals permit conflicts to be resolved depend on personal value systems – an aspect of organizational behaviour usually neglected because too personal and therefore too risky (Gray, 1975).

## 10. About causation

*Activity is generated in terms of psychological exchanges between members.*

Changes within the individual's self-concept bring about a changed perspective on other people and a consequent change in the nature of psychological exchanges. The point here is just that the consultant needs to be clear about causation in organizations. It is not enough to say, for example, that changes in resources lead to changes in management practice. No doubt there are chains of causation that can be described in material or visible terms, but the nature of the energizing mechanisms must be uncovered. For example, the reason why a manager dismisses workers when he has a cash-flow problem may be because he perceives the need to maintain the company in business as a preference to borrowing more money to tide him over a lean period. But why is he able to make such a choice? Had those to be dismissed been closely involved with him at a personal level the decision might have been different. But what makes it different? The phenomenologist tries to look for explanations in terms of the psychologically negotiated relationships and to uncover the nature of exchanges, rewards and punishments perhaps in the area of personal self-esteem.

In other words, a phenomenological stance to consultancy leads the consultant to work at as deep a psychological level as is possible and to understand organizational phenomena through some form of psychological analysis. In many cases, this leads him to embark on a psycho-therapeutic relationship with his client rather than a technological one, though technological knowledge may be used to facilitate the problem-solving processes.

## 11. About authority and leadership

*Organizations distribute roles and status without respect to individuals.*

There is an apparent paradox here, but the idea is that activities such as leadership are 'functions of the organization' rather than the individual. What happens in organizational terms is that situations require appropriate behaviour for their resolution, and this can only be done by those best fitted to deal with them irrespective of their formal position or status in the organization. Does this mean that the organization does in fact function as a separate entity? Not so, because the very functioning is a consequence of the nature of personal relationships, themselves functions of individual behaviour determined by the self-concept. A group forms itself around an individual in affective terms but that does not mean that all initiatives and all authority are confined to that single individual. As relationships develop, so everyone is brought into making important contributions and leadership is passed around and shared. One of the problems with charismatic leaders is that they do not allow the sharing to take place and so de-power their colleagues to the extent of incapacitation.

The consultant and researcher dealing with leadership and authority looks for the ways in which members of an organization regard each other and facilitates the sharing that goes on. He helps individuals both to accept and discard leadership behaviour according to the needs of the members of the organization.

## 12. About management

*Managers can only react to events, they cannot anticipate them.*

Of course, much organizational activity is predictable in a broad sense, but that is not the same as total prediction. But if an organization is running well, there is no need for any one individual to 'manage' others. Management is a form of control or (preferably) facilitation and support. Hence managerial behaviour (sc. leadership) is required only when problems arise – not only crises but the continual sequence of low level problems that are of the essence of relationships. Everyone in the organization is required to respond to problems as their skills and dispositions are appropriate. Individuals do not decide what others shall do, they can only work along with them in collective decision-making, a continuous collegiality. Sailing a boat may be a suitable analogy because sailing is a response to wind, tide and the characteristics of the boat, the captain having to be aware of what is at that moment going on every bit as much as being aware of where he wants to go. And when conditions change, he changes his objectives, he does not abandon the boat and walk.

The consultant and researcher is concerned with discovering the prevailing condition of the organization, dealing with what is 'here and now' without being distracted by substitute and alternative desires that are an avoidance of present realities.

These, then, are twelve propositions about organizations that are important in a subjective theory of organizations. They are outlined only briefly and incompletely but provide useful questions to ask about organizations and the people who make them what they are. One idea, at least, has been left untouched; that is the idea of pathological behaviour, though the term has been mentioned. I would define pathological behaviour as self-induced behaviour which leads to the destruction of an individual or an organization. Some individuals and some organizations do seem to bring destruction on themselves and many more seem to want to. Pathological behaviour is not the same as bringing an organization to a useful end – it may often be the contrary, a stark refusal to terminate association. Much of the 'angst' of organization life is healthy and exciting and to resent and reject it is not nearly so helpful as dealing with it. In the end organizations only exist for their members and for their greater happiness. Presumably research and consultancy is about making people feel better – but that seems to be never mentioned in the literature, let alone the practice.

## Notes

1. Many of the ideas in management applied to education are concerned with the tangible and measurable aspects of educational organization. There would appear to have been a great need for theorists to work on the basis of objective models and to develop theories of administration. Unfortunately, most organizational problems have to do with people and there are few technological problems in the organization of education because there is no basic technological process even though various technical systems like timetables and syllabuses have been invented.

   In his chapter on a 'subjective theory' (some would call it a phenomenological theory) Gray tries to explore some of the practical implications of a perspective on organizations that sees them as essentially personally and individually constructed artefacts. The problem up to now with phenomenological theories is that they have inevitably fallen short in suggesting methods of application. In his twelve propositions, Gray tries to move some way to indicating how subjective theory can be applied in practice.

## References

Berger, P. and Luckman, T. (1967). *The Social Construction of Reality*, Harmondsworth, Allen Lane.

Clark, P. A. (1972). *Action Research*, London, Harper & Row.

Corsini, R. (1973). *Current Psychotherapies*, Masca, Ill., F. E. Peacock Pubs.

Dale, Roger (1973). 'Phenomenological perspectives in the sociology of the school', *Educational Review* 25(3).

*Educational Administration* (1976, *et seq.*). 'Symposium and follow up on Barr Greenfield and organization theory' 1(1) (*et seq.*), Coombe Lodge, Bristol.

Gray, H. L. (1974). 'Counselling and management', *Education and Development* 15(1):26–34.

Gray, H. L. (1975). 'Exchange and conflict in the school', in Houghton, V., McHugh,

R. and Morgan, C. *Management in Education: the Management of Organizations and Individuals*, London, Ward Lock Educational/OU.

Gray, H. L. (1980). *Management in Education*, Driffield, Nafferton Books.

Greenfield, T. B. (1975). 'Theory in the study of organizations and administrative structures: A new perspective', in Hughes, M. G., *Administering Education: International Challenge*, London, Athlone Press.

Greenfield, T. B. (1979). 'Research in educational administration in the US and Canada: An overview and critique', paper presented at BEAS Research Seminar.

Hamachek, D. E. (1978). *Encounter with the Self*, New York, Holt, Rinehart & Winston.

Hodgkinson, C. (1978). *Towards a Philosophy of Administration*, Oxford, Basil Blackwell.

Homans, G. C. (1961). *Social Behaviour*, London, Routledge & Kegan Paul.

Houghton, V., McHugh, R. and Morgan, C. (1975). *Management in Education: the Management of Organizations and Individuals*, London, Ward Lock Educational/ OU.

Hughes, M. G. (Ed.) (1975). *Administering Education: International Challenge*, London, Athlone Press.

Jehensen, R. (1973). 'A phenomenological approach to the study of formal organization', in Psathas, G., *Phenomenological Sociology*, Chichester, John Wiley, Interscience.

Mangham, I. L. (1978). *Interactions and Interventions in Organizations*, Chichester, John Wiley.

Morris, D. (1978). *Manwatching*, St Albans, Triad Panther.

Morris, J. F. and Burgoyne J. (1973). *Developing Resourceful Managers*, London, Institute of Personnel Management.

Poole, R. (1975). 'From phenomenology to subjective method', *Universities Quarterly*, Autumn, pp. 412–40.

Psathas, G. (1973). *Phenomenological Sociology*, Chichester, John Wiley, Interscience.

Reason, P. (1977). 'Notes on holistic research processes and social system change', Centre for the Study of Organizational Change and Development, University of Bath.

Rogers, C. (1951). *Client-Centred Therapy*, Boston, Houghton-Mifflin.

# 9

# Meanings and contexts: the problem of interpretation in the study of a school

**P. M. Ribbins, C. B. Jarvis, R. E. Best and D. M. Oddy**

One of the weaknesses of much educational administration research is its failure to consider seriously what key activities actually mean for those who are supposed to perform them. As a result, 'academic', 'pastoral' and other structures of roles ('subject departments', 'houses', etc.) in schools and colleges are all too often taken at face value, and the tensions involved in the dynamic relationship between different dimensions of the institutional structure, and between the formal role positions and the unique individuals who fill them, are ignored. To explore these tensions it is necessary for the researcher to delve into the meanings which teachers attach to the roles, structures and practices which constitute different aspects of the educational provision of particular institutions. However, it is easier to recognize this as necessary for an adequate analysis of the life of a school or college, than it is to say precisely how it is to be done. This paper is an attempt to show one possible approach to the problem through the example of a recently completed five-year study of pastoral care in a comprehensive school.

### Teacher definitions of 'pastoral care'

One part of our investigation took the form of a depth-study of pastoral care provision of 'Rivendell', a mixed 11–18 comprehensive in the south-east of England (Best *et al.* 1979, 1980). In the context of that study we asked teachers to define 'pastoral care' and to make statements about the 'pastoral care' philosophy of the school. Many produced answers which accorded both with the sentiments of the 'conventional wisdom' of the literature (see Best *et al*, 1977) and with the official statements of the school's public documents. Thus teachers' definitions included such statements as:

> Pastoral care is making it possible for every child within the school to feel perfectly at home with the surroundings and to know there is somebody, initially the form tutor, who they can go to with a problem, however slight, and know they will get a sympathetic ear

while others chose to use anecdotes of individual counselling sessions to exemplify what 'pastoral care' meant for them. Many teachers described the school as having a strong caring philosophy: 'This is a genuinely caring school concerned with the welfare of children.' Senior staff gave the same assurance to parents of prospective first-year pupils to allay their fears about the transition from primary to comprehensive school: 'we make sure that the pastoral care of the child is taken care of'. But other interviews with staff and our observations of them in action in less public situations, led us to question to what extent these definitions of 'pastoral care' are actually implemented in teacher practice.

### Accounts in context

It should not be surprising to find teachers employing a 'conventional wisdom' which has such public currency in the literature, in the context of official documents stating the school's policy, in statements to parents (particularly prospective parents), and in response to particular kinds of questions posed by educational researchers. Furthermore, many senior teachers have powerful vested interests in depicting their schools as 'caring' institutions. The pursuit of a favourable public image is understandable enough under normal conditions but is even more so when a school is in the position of Rivendell, battling against what the staff rightly believe to be an unjustifiably poor reputation in the local community, and faced with what staff believed to be fierce competition from neighbouring schools for the area's dwindling supply of children. Given these circumstances it would have been remarkable indeed if senior staff had not sought to present the pastoral arrangements of the school to prospective parents in the most favourable light. No doubt similar statements were being made by the senior staff of other schools at recruitment meetings with their prospective parents.

The principle which these points seem to establish is that what a teacher *says* has to be interpreted in the light of the *context* in which he says it. Thus a teacher may say one thing in the context of a parents' evening but say something quite different in another context where the interests he holds are better served by different sorts of statements. This raises a fundamental problem for anyone attempting, as we were, to get at what 'pastoral care' (or any other educational activity of similar magnitude) *means* for teachers, how they perceive and evaluate pastoral structures and teacher roles, and how they construe particular situations and the interaction that take place within them. Whilst we accept the force of the argument that to explain any social phenomenon it is necessary to establish the subjective meanings which relevant actors attach to that phenomenon, it is difficult to see how one can establish *meanings* in any hard-and-fast way. 'Meanings' are not directly observable in the world as physical objects are, and it would be folly to imagine that imputing meanings to actors or situations is something a researcher can easily do.

One obvious 'solution' is to ask relevant actors about what they think is happening in given situations, and what they mean by the particular words they use to explain what is going on. By asking a teacher (or anybody else) what he does and why he does it, it is possible to extract from him his '*account*' of the situation or incident the researcher is seeking to understand. Such 'accounts' may be seen as giving *sense* to, or making *sense* of, the particular phenomenon, by describing it in terms which make it comprehensible to the questioner. But they may also be seen as the teacher's attempt at a *justification* for his actions on that occasion, demonstrating to the questioner that there were good reasons why he acted as he did. In other words, when asked to account for his actions, the actor does so by describing the situation in terms of its constituent parts, but *also* by indicating the *motives* behind the action and, perhaps, seeking the approval of the questioner by establishing the purity of his (the actor's) *intention*.

Although at Rivendell many senior staff spoke warmly and support-ively of the school's 'pastoral care' arrangements at meetings of 'feeder school' parents, this was not necessarily the case at other times. In the context of interviews and informal discussions with researchers, some of those teachers showed themselves capable of a criticism of the school's pastoral arrangements to which their statements in more public situations gave no clue. These discrepancies can be made perfectly understandable when we place their performance at the feeder schools in the *context* of a school struggling to survive – i.e. by making these statements '*accountable*' in terms of the *motives* of Rivendell staff – but there are still problems in doing this. For *motives* are no more accessible to simple observations than are *meanings*: they can only be 'identified' by the researcher who is prepared to *infer* them from observed behaviour, or by the actor specifying them in an 'account' offered to a questioner. In the first case, there is the danger that the researcher is imputing motives to the actor which he may not in fact have and in the second case, there is the danger that the teacher's account takes a certain form and admits to certain motives *only* because it is given in the context of an interview with someone he knows to be an educational researcher. In other words, the interview situation is itself a *context* which gives a particular significance to the interaction which takes place and against which the researcher has to interpret the teacher's account and, inescapably, infer the motives. If all this is correct, there is no context in which the researcher can ever escape the necessity of making his *own* interpretation of the meaning and truth of the statements which the actors he is studying make.

The problem is, then, that an interview with an (educational) researcher does *not* represent a neutral encounter for an actor. It is a *context* like any other, and is therefore a *setting* to which both teacher and researcher bring certain expectations and in which their interests may be best served by a particular sort of *performance*. The researcher simply cannot avoid speculating about the motives of those he observes or interviews. It is arguable that anything and everything a teacher says to a researcher is suspect because he enters the interview with a more or less clear expectation of the sorts of things the researcher wants to hear. Thus, as Keddie (1971) has argued in her analysis of 'classroom knowledge', the accounts teachers give of their actions depend significantly upon the context in which that account is produced. A particular philosophy or doctrine may be expounded in an *educationist* context (for example, explaining the school's policy on some issue to an outsider), but may be flatly contradicted by what is said in the *teacher* context (for example, staffroom gossip) (Best *et al.* 1980). For the purposes of this discussion, the researcher needs to recognize that the teacher sees the interview situation as an *educationist* context, in which the 'rules of the game' to be played include certain *norms* about the kind of topics to be discussed – educational matters – and the kind of language, the educationist jargon, which is to be used. But the *motives* of the teacher are also important: he may wish to impress the researcher with his erudition, his knowledge or the up-to-date progressive-ness of his educational philosophy. Or he may wish to demonstrate to himself (or others) his own superiority by 'putting one over' the researcher either by deliberately misleading him or by 'playing the Philistine' and intentionally rejecting everything which smacks of 'theory'. And there will be others, of course, who will wish to avail themselves of the opportunity to tell the researcher a few 'home truths' about research, researchers, lecturers, local councillors, modern teacher training, or almost anything else, regardless of what the researcher might actually be asking him. Finally, there will be those who genuinely want to assist the researcher by answering his questions as fully and honestly as possible.

If all teachers were in the latter category, the work of the researcher would be straightforward (and a good deal less interesting!) but they are not. Whether he likes it or not, the researcher is forced to make judgements about the *reliability* of the accounts which he gets from individual teachers. The alternative, (and this is something to which sociologists' fears about impos-ing their *own* interpretations on the actors can lead), is to treat the teacher's account as sacrosanct: if an action is to be explained in terms of the actor's reasons, and these are the reasons he has given the researcher, then there is really no more to be said. This is a view which we find unacceptable. Following Douglas (1976), we believe that although some kind of interpret-ation and evaluation of the reliability of actors' accounts is inescapable, there are ways in which this can be achieved which minimizes the subjective factor. (Best *et al.* 1979, pp. 57–60). For one thing, a researcher can spend so long with a teacher that it becomes increasingly unlikely that the latter could maintain a bogus *front* which he might have adopted at the beginning. After a while the mask inevitably begins to slip. We found that teachers tended to relax a little more each time we interviewed them and to talk less in educationalist jargon, and more about their own feelings and attitudes as *people*. It is arguable that weekly, sometimes daily, contact between teachers and researchers over a period of months, or better still years, in formal interviews, semi-formal staffroom discussions and even informal chats at the 'local', create an intimacy and spontaneity in interaction in which the accounts teachers give can be reasonably assumed to have some authenticity. Moreover, on some issues – 'factual' matters such as the commitment or adequacy of a particular head of house – the account which one teacher gives can be 'checked out' against the account which others offer. If the great majority of the teachers interviewed give the researcher a similar account, then it seems reasonable to suppose that the truth lies with the majority and that the small 'deviant' minority are not reliable witnesses in this case.

But such a 'triangulation' or 'cross-checking' of accounts is not the only method of *evaluating* what teachers say. There are other grounds upon which such an evaluation can be made, and upon which even 'majority' accounts might be discounted. For it is possible to 'check out' what a teacher says against not only what others say, but against what the researcher himself *observes*. Moreover, when a teacher's account concerns what he does, the reliability of his 'evidence' can be at least partly determined by looking to see whether he actually does what he *says* he does. Sometimes the discontinuity between the 'words' and the 'deeds' of individual teachers can become apparent to the researcher in particularly dramatic ways. For example, we once interviewed a fairly senior member of staff who spent some time telling us how much he cared for children and how the 'interests' of his pupils came first with him. At this point a lower-school boy knocked, and without waiting for permission, entered the room. He was immediately subjected to a diatribe of impressive proportions and sent from the room to 'wait to be dealt with later'. Once the boy had left, the teacher took up his account exactly where he had left it before the interruption, but to two researchers, who were now a good deal more sceptical than they had been a few minutes before!

At the end of the day, of course, the researcher *may* be imposing his own interpretation on what he *observes*, but this is simply unavoidable. So, too, is some element of subjective assessment of the teacher as a 'reliable' or 'unreliable' witness: there is no point in denying that the researcher senses, rightly or wrongly, that some teachers are 'taking him for a ride' while others are 'coming clean'. Occasionally, this may be confirmed in unexpected ways. In one instance a head of house had given us the most elegant, eloquent and extended answers to our questions, and yet we felt that somehow we were not really being told a great deal. Our suspicions were confirmed when he was overheard to say to a junior member of staff, 'All you have to do with these people is talk a lot and say nothing.' In our research we spent two years in all at Rivendell, interviewing all but a few of the eighty plus staff, some as many as eleven times, and observing teachers in a wide variety of situations, including form periods, parents' evenings, staff meetings and visits to feeder schools. These have provided an invaluable background against which to evaluate the accounts teachers gave in interview situations. At the same time, we were able to compare the accounts of each teacher against those of others, and the different accounts the same teacher gave on different occasions. Where there were inconsistencies within and between teachers' accounts, or where their accounts did not match up with what we observed, further interviews were held to 'follow up' the discrepancy. In this way, we were able to reach a position in which we could be fairly confident of the validity of the interpretations we finally made. To reach a position of such confidence, there is simply no substitute for spending a good deal of time over an extended period with the people who are being studied.

## The educationist context

Although all our interviews with Rivendell teachers could be said to take place in the 'educationist' context, in some this was made fairly explicit by the questions we asked. In particular, we asked a number of teachers two questions which might have signalled to them that an 'educationist' answer was 'expected': 'Would you say that the school has a general philosophy or policy on pastoral care, and if so what is it?' and 'If I ask you to give me a definition of "pastoral care" what would you say?' We have already seen that it is possible to interpret responses to these questions as drawing upon the vocabulary of the 'conventional wisdom' of the literature, and as concurring with the official statements of the school's policy documents. Thus expression was often given to the idea of 'caring' for the 'welfare' of the 'whole child', with every teacher a 'pastoral teacher'. But further insights can be gained from answers to these questions.

Although teachers were willing to give expression to the indivisibility of the 'pastoral' and the 'academic' in the school's provision, and of the individual pupil into the 'learner' and the 'child', some teachers did identify 'pastoral care' as something distinctive and separate: something that had to do with the welfare of the child as a *child* rather than as merely a pupil who might have academic problems. Thus a female member of staff without major pastoral responsibilities argued that pastoral care was about 'caring for the child, knowing about its home background and really problems they have in school which aren't academic'. In this respect some teachers at least did see 'pastoral care' as having a distinctive *person*- or *child*-orientation.

In answering these 'educationist' questions, other teachers identified pastoral care with the *structures* which existed, supposedly to implement it. Typically, this took the form of seeing pastoral care as the *roles* that make up the 'pastoral system', e.g. 'form tutor', 'house head', and 'counsellor'; and thus with the *activities* or *practices* associated with those roles. As one member of staff, who, at first was unable to think of a definition of 'pastoral care' suddenly said, 'Of course, there are people like [the school counsellor] who did try to help people with problems. Oh yes, that's another answer to what pastoral care is, isn't it?' In these accounts, 'pastoral care' is to be seen in the role-related practices of identifying children's problems, facilitating problem-solving by having an appropriate relationship with the child, and, finally, of taking such steps as are necessary to correct the causes of the problem. Although 'pastoral care' is seen as embodied in the practices of teachers in particular *roles* in the organization, the focus of attention is neither the teachers or the role, but the *child*, for it is the child, after all, who has the problem.

We can describe this kind of response as one which is *child-centred*. However this orientation may be largely attributable to the fact that 'edu-cationist' answers with a 'child-centred' flavour are to be expected in response to 'educationist' questions, in the apparently 'educationist' context of the interview situation. But, whilst the formal interview might be, *prima facie*, an 'educationist' context, by no means all the answers given to the questions we asked fitted neatly into an educationist, child-centred category. Rather, some of the things we were told seemed to square readily with the kinds of things we overheard teachers saying about pastoral care in the 'teacher' context. While we continue to believe that there is some force in Keddie's (1971) argument, that the accounts teachers give of their actions depend to some extent upon the context in which the accounts are produced, we would also argue that it represents an over-simplification. For it is false to consider that the teacher never expresses other than 'educationist' views in an interview setting or that there is only one 'teacher' context. On the contrary, we found that in so far as there are various facets to the teacher's role, interviewees could be thought of as speaking and acting in disciplinary-, administrative-, instructional-(etc.) contexts, rather than in a single teacher context such as Keddie perceives. The significance of this is not to be underestimated. (Best *et al.* 1980, pp. 255, 256).

## Teacher perspectives

As we have noted, the accounts teachers give in an interview situation are to some extent a function of the kind of questions which the researcher asks. For this reason questions have to be carefully thought out and phrased. We tried to ask a good many questions which were open-ended to allow teachers a reasonably free rein in deciding what they wanted to talk about. This enabled teachers to range quite widely in the issues they chose to discuss, albeit in the context of an interview they knew to be part of a research project on 'pastoral care'. However, more direct and even 'pointed' questions were used in subsequent interviews in order to 'follow up' or 'check out' points of interest or discrepancies between or within accounts and between accounts and observations. In the event, teachers used this setting to talk about a wide variety of topics including the curriculum, grouping practices, the school as an administrative structure, and problems of teacher discipline and classroom control. In analysing our field notes and interview transcripts we found a number of distinct *perspectives* emerging.

Some teachers accepted a *child-centred* perspective reminiscent of the 'conventional wisdom' of pastoral care as presented in the literature, orientating their answers towards the emotional, physical and social well-being of the individual child. Others orientated their answers towards the child, but not so much as a person as in his role as a 'learner', i.e. their responses reflected a *pupil-centred* perspective rather than a *child-centred* one. Others answered a variety of questions and talked at considerable length, and with some feeling, about their problems of classroom control and pupil discipline, viewing even the pastoral system from a *discipline-centred* perspective. Yet others adopted an *administrator-centred* perspective, seeing the school and its members as units and groups to be more or less efficiently managed. Finally, there were teachers whose perspective was *subject-centred*, perceiving their role as centrally that of a subject-specialist working in a particular curriculum area (Best *et al.* 1980, pp. 257–62). Beginning with these we have subsequently developed a more general typology of teacher perspectives to pastoral care and have located these in relation to the variety of *sub-roles* the teacher may have to play and in terms of the dominant *interests* which are being served.

### Multiple realities and shared meanings

The emphasis which our approach has given to the meanings which teachers give to their daily experience, and the opportunities given them to take some initiative in determining which aspects of that experience they wish to discuss, has led to some wide-ranging discussions of what goes on in Rivendell Comprehensive. Had we taken a more deterministic and less open-ended approach to the study, we could not have hoped to appreciate let alone interpret the variety which teacher attitudes and actions display. *The point to grasp here is that the school is not the same 'reality' for all its teachers.* Each teacher brings a perspective to the school, and to his place within it, which is to some extent unique. There are, if you like, as many 'realities' as there are teachers, and it is arguable that any kind of categorization of perspectives, even one grounded in the 'accounts' which teachers themselves offer, does unacceptable violence to the subtlety and uniqueness of each teacher's understanding of his world.

There is, however, some order in the world, and at Rivendell some common, shared meanings gave order to existence. Some generalizations are therefore justified and are in any case necessary if research data is not to be left as a 'buzzing confusion' of specifics. It needs to be put into a form which will be useful for the understanding of the deeper structures which underlie teachers' accounts. The identification of different teacher perspectives in the language and emphasis of teachers' comments is a helpful first step towards the creation of such generalizations, and sets the scene for locating teacher attitudes in the wider context of teacher roles, styles and ideologies. Using these conceptual tools to explore the meanings, motives and actions of teachers, it is possible to gain an insight into pastoral care (or any other educational activity) which is both more complex and more true to reality than those presented from other methodological persuasions.

Greenfield's seminal paper (1975) persuaded many of the need for a phenomenological approach to organizational analysis, but said little about the methodological procedures necessary to translate such an approach into action. This paper points to one way in which such an analysis has been undertaken. The degree to which the categories and models through which coherence is given to interview/observational data are predetermined by the theoretical predispositions of the researcher is, of course, a difficult question to which we have elsewhere given our attention. In this paper we have been at pains to point to the impossibility of the researcher avoiding at some stage a phase of interpretation from the 'researcher-perspective'. However, with this caveat, there is a sense in which the typologies used in our own work 'emerged' from the accounts of teachers themselves not as pre-givens but in an inductive way of which phenomenologists would presumably approve. That they were refined and systematized in the research-context may not, of course, find the same measure of support. Be that as it may, the prescriptions of social phenomenology must accommodate some initiative from the researcher, lest they lead to the solipsistic reification of the actors' accounts.

## Note

Thanks are due to the Social Science Research Council and the Faculty of Education, Arts and Humanities of Chelmer Institute for funding the project referred to in this paper. We would also like to acknowledge the work of Dorothy Smith of the Pastoral Care Research Unit.

## References

Best, R. E., Jarvis, C. B., Ribbins, P. M. (1977). 'Pastoral Care: Concept and Process', *British Journal of Educational Studies*, Vol. XXV (2).
Best, R. E., Jarvis, C. B., Ribbins P. M., (1979). 'Researching Pastoral Care', in Hughes, M. G. and Ribbins, P. M. *Research in Educational Administration,* Vol. 8 (1).
Best, R. E., Jarvis, C. B., Oddy, D. and Ribbins, P. M. (1980). 'Interpretations: Teachers' Views of 'Pastoral Care' in Best, Jarvis and Ribbins (eds) (1980) *Perspectives on Pastoral Care*, Heinemann.
Douglas, J. (1976). *Investigative Social Research*, Sage Publications.
Greenfield, T. B. (1975). 'Theory and Organisation: A New Perspective and Its

Implications for Schools', in Hughes, M. (ed.) *Administering Education*, Athlone Press.

Keddie, N. (1971). 'Classroom Knowledge' in Young, M.F.D. (ed.) (1971) *Knowledge and Control*, Collier-Macmillan.

# Measurement, meanings and cultures

# 10

# The second stage: towards a reconceptualization of theory and methodology in school effectiveness research

**D. Reynolds and K. Reid**

Earlier chapters have presented reports of work in progress and outlined the state of thinking about particular areas within the general field of school effectiveness studies. Our aim in this concluding chapter is somewhat different. Whilst summaries of research conducted to date may be useful, they are available elsewhere (Rutter, 1983; Reynolds, 1982) and hardly need repetition. We are concerned instead to identify the principal problems – of theory and methodology – that the 'first stage' of work over the last seven or eight years has revealed. These gaps in our knowledge, inadequacies in our theoretical conceptualizations and deficiencies in our methodologies will all be explored in some detail. Before this, though, it is necessary to outline what insights the first stage of work has generated.

This work – by Rutter *et al.* (1979), Reynolds (1976, *etc.*), Gray (1981) and Galloway *et al.* (1983) – has begun to indicate that there are substantial differences in the effectiveness of different schools. Although the effects of the school seem to be small by comparison with those of the home, the difference of seven or eight points in verbal reasoning scores which seems to be gained by attending an 'effective' rather than an 'ineffective' school is clearly not inconsiderable.

British studies in this field seem to indicate that variables such as pupil/teacher ratio, class size, quantity of resources spent per child and quantity/quality of physical plant in schools do not have major effects upon outcomes (see Rutter, 1983, and Reynolds, 1982, for more detailed reviews). Likewise, the formal organizational structure of the school appears to be less important in determining effectiveness than the informal, unstructured world or 'ethos' that the school possesses. High levels of pupil involvement in running the school, a balance between using alienating controls and weakly permissive use of minimal controls, a headteacher role that combines firm leadership with some teacher participation and a system of reinforcement that emphasizes rewards for good behaviour rather than punishments for bad seem to be associated with being an effective institution.

This first stage of work in Britain, although it has clearly brought us much interesting and useful information, now seems (perhaps inevitably) to have generated more questions than it has produced answers. Although schools have effects and although we are beginning to understand the processes that are responsible for those effects, the gaps in our knowledge that the early work has revealed indicate to us the need for a 'second stage' programme of work that focuses particularly upon ten discrete areas of work.

## I. Sampling strategy

It is axiomatic that existing samples of schools have been too small in number, since regression analysis of samples of eight (Reynolds) or twelve (Rutter) is likely to generate highly unreliable estimates of variance because of the effects of outlier or rogue schools upon overall relationships. We also need more representative samples of schools – the South Wales secondary modern schools in the Reynolds (1976, etc.) work are atypical compared with the national pattern of comprehensive scools. The Irish samples of schools utilized by Madaus *et al.* (1980) are also atypical (which is particularly unfortunate since this is the only study to show school effects as greater than home effects). Even the Rutter *et al.* (1979) London comprehensives are atypical in their resource availability, for example. Whilst it may well be likely that the Sheffield comprehensives used by Galloway *et al.* (1983) are the most 'representative' of all the samples, the limited range of information upon the processes of the schools collected in this study reduces its usefulness. Recent Scottish data (Gray *et al.*, 1983) must be viewed with the greatest caution since, as one study on ability grouping (Tibbenham *et al.*, 1978) reported, 'the outstanding feature to emerge is the difference between the situation in Scottish comprehensives and that in the rest of Britain.'

As well as ensuring 'representativeness' of sample composition, it is important not to miss the full *range* of school types, since only the full range of school factor differences can reveal the full power of the school variables. The relative homogeneity of the Rutter and Reynolds samples – which makes their reported school effects perhaps even more convincing – should be avoided in future work.

There is also a need for studies of primary schools to be conducted along the lines of the potentially impressive set of data collected in the ILEA study outlined earlier by Mortimore and his co-workers. There is, of course, greater accord between the findings of research on primary and secondary schools in the United States than in Britain. The lack of British research into the institutional effects of primary schools also hinders comparative study, hampers secondary school work and makes it impossible to test the important suggestion of Jencks *et al.* (1971) that ineffective primary schools served ineffective secondary schools, generating an additive disadvantage for some pupils. It should be remembered that this amounted to 5 or 6 per cent of the differences between individuals.

## 2. Concerning intakes

In many ways we believe that second stage work must rediscover the importance of pupil intakes. The current emphasis upon the school as a determinant of pupil outcomes stands in danger of neglecting the important role played by intakes in determining outcome and the crucial interaction between school, child and family that determines school effectiveness. Whilst the current emphasis upon school factors is necessary to displace conventional psychological paradigms attributing causation to home and family factors, the assertion of the *independence* of the school may prove damaging if it prevents us from seeing the interaction between pupils from specific home backgrounds and certain specified features of their schools, as in the South Wales study where *working-class* pupils find school rules governing 'dress, manners and morals' irksome because of their essentially *middle-class* nature (Reynolds, 1975). Outcomes cannot merely be seen as being produced by effective or ineffective schools without an assessment of which pupils, from which families and for which communities they are held to be effective or ineffective. As well as being *independent* in their effects on pupils, schools (and their levels of effectiveness) must also be seen as *dependent*. That is, they must be seen as dependent upon outside school factors for the determination of their effectiveness as educational institutions.

The 'rediscovery' of intake importance needs to be pursued in other ways too. More intake variables than the two used by the Rutter team are potentially important, a point frequently made over the last few years (Reynolds, 1981; Gray, 1981). Also, we need to discover a sense of the history of school institutions and of the complex interactive process between school and catchment area. Many expectations of, opinions of and attitudes to a school may exist in a community but not be tapped by any measurement of verbal reasoning score. These perceptions need to be measured and analyzed.

Two final problems concerned with intake factors have only recently emerged with the passing of the 1981 Education Act's regulations on the publication of examination results. First, it is possible that intake are now being directly affected by apparent output quality. Whilst the number of parents choosing to send their children to one school or another on the basis of public examination performance probably remains small, since most parents continue to opt for their neighbourhood school, there are hints that it is a growing practice.

If and when this practice escalates and assuming that it is higher ability pupils who are being moved to apparently higher performance schools, it is bound to intensify differences between those schools situated in 'good' and 'bad' catchment areas. Whilst schools with poor catchment areas are not necessarily (adjusting for their intake quality) any less effective than others, it may well be that the changing academic and social balance of poor catchment area schools will have 'knock-on' group effects on academic performance greater than would be predicted merely by knowledge of these pupils' individual academic abilities. At sixth-form level, for example, the removal of quite a small number of high-ability pupils may have quite dramatic effects on the academic and social mix of the classes in certain subjects. Below certain levels of intake quality, then, it may be very difficult to be an 'effective' educational institution, and it may well be that the operation of the 1981 Education Act is making such schools more common by changing pupil intellectual balance *and* mean intake ability.

The second effect of the 1981 Act is to make largely redundant cross-sectional studies of the kind used by Reynolds, Brimer and others since, because of parental choice, intake quality at certain schools may be changing quite rapidly over time. Using intake scores as a surrogate for the intake scores of output cohorts that are not available may be unwise, since the former are no longer as valid a guide as they once were to the scores of the output cohorts when they were intakes.

### 3. Concerning process

We still do not have a clear idea *which* school factors are associated with outcome, nor do we have any real idea as to *how* the process factors actually generate outputs, which may be through effects upon peer group processes or upon individual self-conception, for example. We still do not know what creates the factors, themselves, whether they be personality factors, prior educational experience of the headteacher or more idiosyncratic factors concerned with the past biographies of school staff. Although there are hints that output quality in turn directly affects process (perhaps through affecting the expectations of teachers), the strength of this influence is unclear. If past school success or failure does perpetuate itself in this way, we need to know far more about the mechanisms through which the process may operate.

Some of the confusion about conceptualizing school outcomes that Strivens notes earlier seems to be self-inflicted damage, easily remediable by the adoption of a paradigm that sees school organizations as both objective reality and yet subjectively perceived. We are consequently still very weak in terms of our understanding of key areas of within-school life. Curriculum in both a formal sense (the knowledge 'quantity' and 'content') and an informal sense (the more covert verbal and non-verbal cues that accompany the formal curriculum) has not been a major focus, as Wilcox reminds us earlier. The pastoral care system has not received the same attention as has the academic system, as Galloway noted. The headteacher and his or her effect upon teachers, pupils and the school in general has also been neglected as a factor, as have teacher/teacher relations. All these areas seem urgently in need of further work to improve our meagre understanding of within-school life.

## 4. Concerning outcomes

It is clear from the recent Scottish material that outcomes may not be so highly interrelated as both the Rutter and the Reynolds work had suggested. Intercorrelations of above o.6 in the latter two studies between their three or four outcome measures (delinquency, academic attainment, attendance, behaviour) drop in the Scottish work (Gray *et al.*, 1983) to only o.2 between attendance and O-level attainment for one sample of sixty-nine uncreamed comprehensives. The South Wales studies' averaging of school performance in different areas generating an 'overall' school position seems in the light of this evidence a somewhat undesirable practice.

As well as separating outcomes for independent analysis, the generation of further outcome measures is a major task. The British educational system has a multiplicity of social, moral, cultural, aesthetic and sporting goals that is probably unique amongst industrial societies. Explicitly, only two-thirds of school hours are actually used for academic purposes; the rest are spent on sport, religion and various cultural pursuits, all of which would be separate from normal school life in societies such as France or Germany. Although the 1981 Education Act only specifies that parents should be provided with information on 'cognitive' outcomes, information on the within-school social processes that will probably generate differential social outcomes is also published for parents. There are numerous hints that parents do in fact assess schools on their social processes and on such factors as 'tone' or social reputation as well as on academic results, and there is overwhelming evidence that schools themselves aim for social as well as cognitive outcomes (see, for example, Morton-Williams and Finch, 1968).

The generation of new outcome measures to tap 'affective' rather than cognitive outcomes is important because there are hints from some American studies (see the review in Reynolds, 1982) of substantial school effects upon social or affective outcomes, such as students' perception of their ability to master fate. Also, there is evidence of difference between the selective and non-selective systems of education in social outcomes, such as behaviour, truancy and attitudes to school in the recent Children's Bureau studies (Steedman, 1980). Social outcomes are also important because they are the only gains for those children – roughly 14 per cent in Britain – who attain no measurable cognitive outcomes through examination passes at CSE or at O-level. For the other 10 per cent of children who merely attain a grade 5 CSE pass and the large number of children who will attain the same 'points' score in calculations of examination passes, it is only *social* outcomes that will generate variation between individuals that cannot be shown on scales of mere academic attainment.

What exactly these social measures should be remains a matter of considerable speculation. No doubt some measures should attempt to tap those goals that schools have always aimed for – sporting achievement, job getting and holding, the possession of self-esteem, favourable locus of control and positive self-conceptions. Perhaps now racial tolerance, non-sexist attitudes, coping skills, survival skills and the other more recent goals that have been given to the educational system also need to be tapped. Since these goals will entail moving away from mere behavioural social outcomes (such as rates of delinquency and attendance), the complexity of the necessary attitudinal measures that can tap the deep structure of pupil attitudes and perceptions makes this whole area one of quite awesome difficulty.

One last point needs to be made about outcomes. The possible rise in their number only increases the need to conceptualize and measure more school process factors, since we have been very unsuccessful in finding school process items that are linked with social outcomes. In the Rutter *et al.* (1979) work, for example, only seven process items could be found that correlated with delinquency, whereas fourteen were correlated with academic attainment. Whatever within-school factors are associated with the social outcomes, we seem a long way from discovering them. The discovery of more *social* outcomes would merely increase the pressure on us in this area of work.

## 5. Disaggregating pupils and schools

One of the principal handicaps in the work on school differences and school effects has been the treatment of the pupils as unitary groups. The emphasis has been upon how whole cohorts of pupils are affected by their schools. In view of hints from American work that schools are differentially important for different groups of pupils (as in the case of the Coleman Report, 1966, and its findings of large school effects for low social class blacks), we need to analyse separately for boys and girls, older and younger pupils, higher and lower social class pupils, and ethnic minority and 'host culture' children.

Disaggregating the pupil group in this way also helps us to move towards the disaggregation of 'the school' as a unitary concept. All studies so far treat the school and its factors as being a common experience for all pupils, since school factor scores on, say, rate of physical punishment, or 'time on task' in the classroom are global averages of the experience of all pupils in the school, an experience that probably very few pupils will actually have gone through. Disaggregation of the school could in theory be taken as far as looking at the individual pupil's school, in terms of the actual classroom, year, departmental and school experience of each pupil, as in using, say, the individual's rate of corporal punishment or the individual pupil's time on task during an average school day.

There are, of course, major practical difficulties with the collection of pupil-specific school factors. It would be hugely time-consuming, involving the collection of data on perhaps forty or fifty school factors that would be unique to each child. Secondly, it would be methodologically difficult to cope with analyses where there is such huge variation in pupil factors, pupil home background factors and pupil school factors, since large sample sizes would be required to generate more than a mere handful of cases in each 'cell'. Thirdly, the weighting of each pupil's classroom experience, 'year experience' and school experience that would be necessary – in view of the different time and importance of each level in the life of the pupil – would also be difficult. Fourthly, such work as this could have no direct educational policy implications, since pupils are always treated as members of collectivities and never as individuals in overall educational policy-making.

Perhaps the answer to these difficulties may be to move away from school-specific school factors to class-specific school factors, year-specific school factors or department-specific school factors, where each of these school sub-units would have its own rating on the usual thirty or forty school factors. However it may be done, breaking down the unit of the school is important because of:

1. the presence of more variance within the school than between schools means that with our present analyses we are explaining little of the variance on any dependent variable we use;
2. the need to dispose of the allegation that school process is merely the sum total of all within-school classroom processes – an allegation which, if it is true, renders redundant the use of the school as a unit of analysis;
3. the need to have more sensitive descriptions of within-school processes than those available at present;
4. the urgent need for school-based research to be linked with the bodies of knowledge on teacher effectiveness, classroom processes and the psycho-social structure of the classroom as a learning environment. There is a clear need for studies of classroom processes to look outside the classroom at the teacher in the wider world of the school (as attempted in Murgatroyd and Reynolds, 1984) and for school-based studies to look also at the classroom;
5. the need to integrate the work on primary school processes, most of which utilizes the classroom as the unit of analysis, with the work on secondary schools, most of which uses the school as its unit of analysis.

## 6. Concerning change

In addition to our earlier points concerned with the epidemiology of schools as learning environments, we need experimental work to see how modifiable school regimes are in their processes and in their effects. We can gauge the effects of naturally occurring experiments such as the appointment of a new headteacher, a change of building or a change of streaming organization. We can also deliberately intervene with planned experiments, such as consultancy models of change, 'top down' models of change or approaches which lie mid-way between such extremes, such as the GRIDS project in institutional development at Bristol. Most important of all, we should try to understand which within-school factors hinder or potentiate the effects of these outside interventions. We have only a tenuous idea of the school factors important in affecting outcome – we have virtually no idea of the school factors associated with willingness or ability to change.

## 7. Concerning methodology

We now need a methodology appropriate to these major tasks of description and explanation of school life outlined above. To use Bronfenbrenner's (1979) analogy, we have been caught in our methodology between a rock and a soft place – the rock being the rigour of conventional positivist empiricism and the soft place being some of the excesses of participant observation found in parts of the 'new' sociology of education.

A middle position that combines the strengths of both methods seems to be required. This could involve use of positivist methodology to *generate* relationships, combined with use of 'softer' data to *explain* relationships. Alternatively, the approach could involve moving towards hardening 'soft' data, through introducing more checks on participant observers, use of 'blind' observers or increased use of triangulation. Using the different approaches to bolster each other in a collaborative methodology seems more preferable than continued competition between them (see Evans, 1983, and Reynolds, 1981, for further discussion of this theme). The methodology necessary to understand *how* schools are as they are and *how* they have their effects is likely to be very different from that which has been necessary to show that they *have* effects.

## 8. Concerning theory

We believe that we need to immerse ourselves more in theory. Much of the early work in this field has been highly atheoretical, as authorities such as Hargreaves (1981) have observed. The Rutter *et al.* (1979) work was atheoretical, as was the work of Brimer (1978), Madaus *et al.* (1980) and

Gray *et al.* (1983), who can perhaps be excused from criticism since he possessed no process data to relate to theory in any case. The work of Reynolds (1976, etc.) seems distinctly eclectic in its use of theory.

The reasons for this are not difficult to understand. Much of the British work grew out of attempts to test the hypotheses of Jencks and Coleman and therefore tended to work within the same paradigm of traditional atheoretical empiricism as they. We have customarily lacked adequate process data to relate to theory in any case. Also, many of us have probably seen ourselves as *opposed* to any dominant theoretical paradigm, regarding them as grossly flawed in their emphasis upon family factors or socio-structural factors as determinants of school outcomes.

The problems caused by our atheoreticism, however, are now numerous. No piece of work is cumulative, either set against work from the past or against other work in the present; the field is, therefore, not integrated. Work is not testable in theoretic terms and does not generate any middle-range theory, which is the building block of any attempted construction of meta-theory. In the absence of such attempts to relate work to theory, the field of school differences is unrelated to any current theoretical position except that of 'grubby empiricism'. The marginality of the work within the British educational research community is clearly related to our theoretical marginality.

## 9. Concerning analysis

Instead of current methods of analysis which give a snapshot of the intake/process/outcome interaction at a point *in* time, we urgently need dynamic models which show interaction *over* time. We need to be able to see the dynamic interaction between intake and process, outcomes and intakes (as above), and between outcomes and intakes as affected by the provisions of the 1981 Education Act. We need to see how decisions are made within the schools, how resources are distributed and how school factors are produced and reproduced by everyday decision-taking. Whilst it may be possible to generate 'nested' statistical models which can handle the mutual interaction and feedback between intake, process and outcome, it seems likely that quantitative analysis on its own is unlikely to generate the insight into these dynamic processes that is required. Only a more mixed methodological position as outlined above would seem to be adequate for fully dynamic analysis.

## 10. Concerning the additive nature of school and family effects

We have so far in the field been concerned to establish the independent nature of the school influence without establishing the directionality of influence.

School influence may operate in the same directions as family influence (to depress working-class children's performance) or in different directions (to depress highly achieving middle-class children's performance, for example).

There are strong suggestions from a number of data bases (the Scottish Data Archive, the Sheffield schools study of Galloway *et al.*, 1983, and the ILEA data bases (Mortimore and Byford, 1979) that schools with poor catchment areas do worse than would be expected from a knowledge of their intakes and from knowledge of the overall relationship for all schools between intakes and outcomes. Ineffective schools, then, would seem to be serving more disadvantaged catchment areas in an *additive* relationship whereby initial disadvantage is confounded, confirmed and increased by school effects.

Aside from the importance of this thesis merely in its intellectual pay-off and furtherance of our understanding, it is the policy implications of the thesis that are of major importance. It has always been difficult to place evidence that schools have independent effects against other overwhelming evidence that suggests school reform as having had minimal effects upon the wider class structure (e.g. Halsey *et al.*, 1980). The notion that school influence is additive but *dependent* on the influence of wider social structures and ultimately reinforcing of them integrates at a stroke two apparently opposite bodies of findings.

### Enabling the strategy

Delivering programmes of work that attempt to move us forward and learn from the manifold defects of first stage work is clearly a difficult task; cut-backs in research funding intensify this problem. Three strategies seem to be practicable at present.

1. School change strategies and programmes of action research may generate more knowledge about school processes than they generate change, since in order to understand something fully it may be necessary to attempt to change it. Change attempts are likely to show the interrelationships between variables, the pathways that relate the levels of the school and the facilitators or inhibitors of change that are likely to be school factors of major importance (as in Phillips' work reported earlier).
2. Using existing databases – on the lines of the Contexts Project reported earlier by Gray – may be fruitful also, since a large amount of information on school intakes and outcomes is already collected. Whilst there must remain doubts as to the representativeness of such data – since only certain LEAs collect them routinely – and whilst there must remain doubts as to their quality, use of these data seems a fruitful way forward.
3. Using 'teacher-researchers', as in various centres within South Wales, would seem to be another useful initiative.

The teacher-researcher concept is based upon the hope that the teacher, through conducting research into his or her own classroom or school, could both improve his or her own professional practice *and* generate useful research data that would be of wider interest. Lawrence Stenhouse (1975) argued vigorously in favour of teacher conducted research, viewing it as more concerned with developing professional practice than with the generation of 'objective' knowledge about schools. Since then, a considerable argument has developed over the merits and demerits of the concept (Hamilton and Delamont, 1974, Pring, 1978; Adelman and Alexander, 1982). There have been charges of bias, contamination of data, lack of rigour and subjectivity (see the collection of articles in *Interchange*, Vol. II, No. 4, 1981), yet those in favour of the concept accepted these problems as the inevitable price of personal and professional growth.

More recently there have been attempts – most notably in South Wales – to develop the concept of the teacher-researcher as *researcher*, not merely as teacher. The courses in behaviour and learning problems at University College, Cardiff, and the various in-service courses at the West Glamorgan Institute have attempted to utilize teachers as data-gatherers about within-school processes. In these courses, teachers undertake a school-based study of a certain issue or problem within their own school, taking the particular empirical material and relating it to the wider body of academic literature concerned. Whilst most of these studies contain a substantial amount of qualitative data on school factors, school processes and within-school life in general, many of these data (on whether schools stream, pastoral care provision, size, option arrangements, etc.) are likely to be specific enough to have reasonable validity. Data of a more quantitative nature on outputs, such as attendance, delinquency and examination success, are likely to be 'hard' enough to be other than observer-specific.

If such data – which in South Wales cover probably over 100 schools – can be utilized, perhaps with some additional checks on validity provided by the use of teachers as checks upon each other's observations, then a potentially large data base on processes and outputs is practicable, needing only the addition of data on intakes to make it more or less ready for systematic analysis. As a means of obtaining maximum data at minimum cost, the use of teachers in this way would seem to be another development to enable the strategy outlined in our earlier points, particularly since teachers may well be highly sensitive observers of within-school practices.

## References

Adelman, C. and Alexander, R. (1983). *The Self-Evaluating Institution*, London, Methuen.

Bronfenbrenner, U. (1979). *The Ecology of Human Development*, Cambridge, Mass, Harvard University Press.

Coleman, J. (1966). *Equality of Educational Opportunity*, Washington, DC, US Government Printing Office.

Evans, J. (1983). 'Criteria of validity in social research: Exploring the relationship between ethnographic and quantitative approaches', in Hammersley, M. (ed.) *The Ethnography of Schooling*, Driffield, Nafferton.

Galloway, D. *et al.* (1983). *Schools and Disruptive Pupils*, London, Longman.

Gray, J. (1981). 'Towards effective schools: Problems and progress in British research', in *British Educational Research Journal* 7(1), pp. 59–69.

Gray, J. McPherson, A. and Raffe, D. (1983). *Reconstructions of Secondary Education*, London, Routledge & Kegan Paul.

Halsey, A. H. *et al.* (1980). *Origins and Destinations*, Oxford, Oxford University Press.

Hamilton, D. and Delamont, S. (1974). 'Classroom research: A cautionary tale', in *Research in Education* 11(1), pp. 1–16.

Hargreaves, D. (1981). 'Schooling for delinquency', in Barton, L. and Walker, S. (eds), *Society, Schools and Teaching*, Lewes, Falmer Press.

Jencks, C. *et al.* (1971). *Inequality*, London, Allen Lane.

Madaus, G. F. *et al.* (1980). *School Effectiveness*, New York, McGraw-Hill.

Mortimore, P. and Byford, D. (1979). *School Examination Results in ILEA., 1977 (CRS 735/80)*, London, Inner London Education Authority.

Morton-Williams, R. and Finch, S. (1968). *Enquiry 1*, London, HMSO.

Murgatroyd, S. J. and Reynolds, D. (1984). 'Leadership and the teacher', in Harling, P. (ed.) *New Directions in Educational Leadership*, Lewes. Falmer Press.

Pring, R. (1978). 'Teacher as researcher', in Lawton, D. *et al.*, (eds) *Theory and Practice of Curriculum Studies*, London, Routledge & Kegan Paul.

Reynolds, D. (1975). 'When pupils and teachers refuse a truce', in Mungham, G. and Pearson, G. (eds), *Working Class Youth Culture*, London, Routledge & Kegan Paul.

Reynolds, D. (1976). 'The delinquent school', in Woods, P. (ed.), *The Process of Schooling*, London, Routledge & Kegan Paul.

Reynolds, D. (1981). Review of M. Rutter *et al. Fifteen Thousand Hours*, in *British Journal of Sociology of Education* 1(2), pp. 207–11.

Reynolds, D. (1981). 'The naturalist methods of educational and social research – A Marxist Critique', in *Interchange (Journal of the Ontario Institute for Studies in Education)* 11(4), pp. 77–89.

Reynolds, D. (1982). 'The search for effective schools', *School Organization*, 2(3), pp. 215–37.

Rutter, M. (1983). 'School effects on pupil progress – findings and policy implications', in *Child Development* 54(1), pp. 1–29.

Rutter, M. *et al.* (1979). *Fifteen Thousand Hours*, London, Open Books.

Steedman, J. (1980). *Progress in Secondary Schools*, London, National Children's Bureau.

Stenhouse, L. (1975). *An Introduction to Curriculum Research and Development*, London, Heinemann.

Tibbenham, A., Essen, J. and Fogelman, K. (1978). 'Ability grouping and school characteristics', *British Journal of Educational Studies* 26(1).

# 11

# Beyond the subject monolith: subject traditions and sub-cultures

## Ivor Goodson

A number of studies have confirmed the central role which subject sub-cultures and subject specialisms play in the preparation of teachers. In 1970 McLeish's research on college students and lecturers found that: 'The most remarkable differences in attitude of any in the total sample appear to be between subject specialists.'[1] Developing a more differentiated model of 'subject sub-cultures', Lacey noted in 1977 that 'the subject sub-culture appears to be a pervasive phenomenon affecting a student-teacher's behaviour in school and university, as well as their choice of friends and their attitudes towards education.' This leads on to arguing the case for 'considering the process of becoming a teacher as a multi-stranded process in which subject sub-cultures insulate the various strands from one another.'[2]

Whilst studies of teacher preparation have thereby pointed up the part played by subject specialisms and sub-cultures, these have often been presented as 'undifferentiated epistemological communities sharing knowledge and methodology'.[3] This paper will contend that a variety of 'traditions' exists within subject sub-cultures. These traditions initiate the teacher into widely differing visions of knowledge hierarchies and content, teacher role and overall pedagogic orientation.

To understand subject sub-cultures as a 'pervasive phenomenon' in teacher preparation, the major 'traditions' within these sub-cultures need to be identified and studied. We shall see that just as 'there are important differences within subject boundaries of the same order as the differences between subjects',[4] so also are there certain major 'traditions', which exist with varying degrees of articulation and allegiance, *within* most school subjects. It is these subject 'traditions' which act as the main agency of teacher initiation into subject communities, so that they are at the sharp end of the 'pervasive phenomenon' of the subject sub-culture.

The study of school subject 'traditions' should focus on the intentions and forces which underpin such traditions. Hopefully, it will be possible to discern certain patterns underlying subject traditions, and this paper argues that by studying school subjects and subject cultures in evolution certain historical imperatives can be identified. The forces which lead school subjects to follow broadly similar patterns of evolution are inevitably related to the forces which intrude on each individual teacher's judgement of how his career and material interests are pursued during his working life. However, the focus of this paper is on academic subject cultures and as a result teachers involved in mainly pastoral careers are not considered. Above all, the paper follows the aspiration voiced in an earlier paper from Mardle and Walker which viewed the location of classroom processes 'as part of a patterned historical framework' as a way of developing links between current micro and macro levels of analysis.[5]

## Subject tradition and sub-cultures

School subjects are made up of groups and individuals with varying identities, values and interests. One is often reminded of Bucher and Strauss's characterization of professions as: 'loose amalgamations of segments pursuing different objectives in different manners and more or less delicately held together under a common name at particular periods in history.'[6] The study of school subjects in evolution discerns a close relationship between the promotion of certain 'traditions' and sub-cultures and the pursuit of status and resources. Layton's study, *Science for the People*, traces a number of traditions in nineteenth century science which sought to relate science to people's lives.[7] The book generates a number of hypotheses as to why this version of science was ultimately replaced by a more thoroughly academic version pursued in laboratories and defined in new textbooks and syllabuses. The focal role played by subject associations in this pursuit of more academic status is documented by Hanson with reference to the Society of Art Masters.[8] The Society showed great concern for the academic dress and titles which bestow, or appeared to bestow, high status on other knowledge categories.

Dodd has recently reviewed the history of design and technology in the school curriculum, following earlier work on design education by Eggleston. A major theme in the work is the desire among teachers of the subject for higher status:

> Heavy craft activities have been referred to by a number of different titles as their nature and contribution has changed. Concealed in this ongoing discussion is the matter of 'status' and 'respectability', and although the most recent change from Handicraft to Design and Technology reflects a change of emphasis, there is something of the

former argument. 'Practical' describes quite adequately an essential part of the subject, but it is an adjective which is little used because in the terms of the Crowther Report, it is an 'emotionally charged word'. As the subject has developed there have been efforts made to encourage its acceptability by participation in certain kinds of external examinations (which have not always been the best instruments of assessment), the use of syllabuses (often malformed to make them acceptable by other institutions), and by euphemisms like the 'alternative road', but these have failed to hide the underlying low status which practical subjects have by tradition.[9]

Among more general studies of the history of curriculum, Raymond Williams' brief work relating educational philosophies to the social groups holding them is deeply suggestive. He writes: 'an educational curriculum, as we have seen again and again in the past periods, expresses a compromise between an inherited selection of interests and the emphasis of new interests. At varying points in history, even this compromise may be long delayed, and it will often be muddled.'[10] This view of the history of curriculum has been recently extended by Eggleston who contends that 'The fundamental conflicts are over the identity and legitimacy of the rival contenders for membership of the groups who define, evaluate and distribute knowledge and the power these confer.'[11]

Banks' study of *Parity and Prestige in English Secondary Education* written in 1955, though even more out of date than Williams' work, is a valuable complement. The same theme relating curriculum to social class emerges. Williams had noted that the academic curriculum was related to the vocations of the upper and professional classes. The curriculum related to the vocations of the majority was slowly introduced, and Banks notes that 'as the proportion of children from artisan and lower middle class homes increased, it was necessary to pay more attention to the vocational needs of the pupils, and even to amend the hitherto academic curriculum to admit subjects of vocational nature.'[12] But the subjects related to majority vocations were persistently viewed as of low status. Banks quotes a TUC pamphlet which in 1937 maintained: 'School time used for vocational training not only gives a bias to study but takes up valuable time and effort better employed in a wider and more useful field. Moreover, it stamps at an early and impressionable age the idea of class and inferior status on the scholar, which it is the aim of a noble education to avoid.'[13]

Viewed in this way, vocational training is seen not to refer to the pervasive underlying objective of all education as preparation for vocations but to the low-status concern of preparing the majority for their work. The academic curriculum is, and has historically been, in purpose vocational, but the preparation is for the high-status professions. Indeed, Banks' study concludes that 'the persistence of the academic tradition is seen as something more fundamental than the influence, sinister or otherwise, of teachers and administrators. It is the vocational qualification of the academic curriculum which enables it to exert such a pressure on all forms of secondary education.'[14]

Layton has analysed the evolution of science in England from the nineteenth century, and suggests a tentative model for the evolution of a school subject in the secondary school curriculum. Layton has defined three stages in this evolution. In the first stage:

> the callow intruder stakes a place in the timetable, justifying its presence on grounds such as pertinence and utility. During this stage learners are attracted to the subject because of its bearing on matters of concern to them. The teachers are rarely trained specialists, but bring the missionary enthusiasms of pioneers to their task. The dominant criterion is relevance to the needs and interests of the learners.

In the interim second stage:

> a tradition of scholarly work in the subject is emerging along with a corps of trained specialists from which teachers may be recruited. Students are still attracted to the Study, but as much by its reputation and growing academic status as by its relevance to their own problems and concerns. The internal logic and discipline of the subject is becoming increasingly influential in the selection and organisation of subject matter.

In the final stage:

> the teachers now constitute a professional body with established rules and values. The selection of subject matter is determined in large measure by the judgements and practices of the specialist scholars who lead inquiries in the field. Students are initiated into a tradition, their attitudes approaching passivity and resignation, a prelude to disenchantment.[15]

Whilst the conflict between vocational and academic traditions is studied in Williams, Banks, Dodd and Eggleston, Layton's work points towards a more complex and differentiated model of subject traditions. Layton's first stage clearly shows the 'pedagogic' as well as vocational origins of school subjects: not just 'utility' but also 'relevance to the needs and interests of the learners'. The concern with pupil relevance constitutes another tradition, and a continuing one, in the definition of the subject's content. In short, Layton's model warns against any monolithic explanations of school subjects and leads us towards identifying the motivations behind certain traditions and to studying the fate of these traditions as school subjects evolve over time.

## Defining subject traditions: academic, utilitarian and pedagogic

The historical study of school subjects defines certain 'traditions' which can often be related to the social class origins and occupational destinations of their pupil clienteles. Hence the curricula of public and grammar schools aimed mainly at the middle and upper classes preparing for professional life were primarily academic; whilst the elementary schools educating the majority stressed vocational training.

Writing of the 'traditions' in English primary education, Blyth discerned three different trends: the preparatory, the elementary and the developmental. The preparatory tradition was 'almost exclusively related to what we now call grammar school education, which developed in its turn mainly as an upper middle class phenomenon', the elementary tradition 'with its characteristic emphasis on the basic skills' was aimed at the lower classes. 'For those who were unfortunate, indolent or culpable enough to be poor, the minimum of education was proper and sufficient.' The third tradition, the developmental, bases its principles on concern with each child along the lines recommended by Rousseau or Pestalozzi. Broadly speaking Blyth's three primary traditions can be equated with the three traditions discerned within secondary education: the academic, utilitarian and pedagogic traditions.[16]

The definition of public and grammar school subjects in the nineteenth century, established in the 1904 Regulations and confirmed in the School Certificate Examinations, clearly followed the aims of education as a preparation for professional and academic life. Eggleston, commenting on the early nineteenth century, states:

> A new and important feature of the time that was to prevail, was the redefinition of high-status knowledge as that which was not immediately useful in a vocation or occupation. The study of the classics now came to be seen as essentially a training of the mind and the fact that a boy could be spared from work long enough to experience this in full measure was in itself seen as a demonstration not only of the high status of the knowledge itself but also of the recipient – the mark of a 'gentleman' rather than a worker.[17]

Eggleston's last sentence points up the contradiction: it was not so much that classical liberal education was non-vocational but that the vocational were only those fit for upper-class gentlemen. 'As educational history shows', Williams reminds us, 'the classical linguistic disciplines were primarily vocational but these particular vocations had acquired a separate traditional dignity, which was refused to vocations now of equal human relevance.[18]

For this reason we have avoided the use of the terms 'vocational education' or 'vocational knowledge'. Instead, we refer to the subject-based curriculum confirmed by the examination system as the *academic* tradition and to low-status practical knowledge as the *utilitarian* tradition. Utilitarian knowledge thus becomes that which is related to those non-professional

vocations in which most people work for most of their adult life. In addition
to the basic skills of numeracy and literacy, this includes commercial and
technical education.

Neither commercial nor technical education was ever seriously considered as a new dimension which could be added to the existing classical
curriculum. It was specialized training for a particular class of man, and its
confinement to low-status areas of the curriculum has remained a constant
feature of English curriculum conflict. For example, Layton's research on the
development of science education in the nineteenth century has shown how
the emphasis was increasingly placed on abstract knowledge with a consequent separation from the practical world of work. Nevertheless, the alternative view of a narrowly utilitarian curriculum is still powerful, as is shown by
the constant pressure for utilitarian subjects in spite of their recurrent failure
to earn high status. The manpower needs of a changing industrial economy
demand that utilitarian training will be consistently advocated by many
industrialists. When widespread industrial failure is endemic the continuing
ambivalence of educational status systems causes serious concern and
pressure for change. The Great Debate was one symptom of this concern, and
as was recently argued in *The Times*:

> Strategies for furthering the inter-relationship between industry and
> the educational system need to address the complex question of status
> systems. The established patterns of status represent an enormously
> powerful historical legacy, a kind of indirect pressure group. Only if
> high status areas in the educational system such as the public schools
> and Oxbridge are willing to remodel their value systems do current
> strategies stand any chance of success.[19]

The low status of utilitarian knowledge is shared by the personal, social and
commonsense knowledge stressed by those pursuing a child-centred
approach to education. This approach with its emphasis on the learning
process can be characterized as the *pedagogic* tradition within the English
curriculum. Child-centred or progressive education does not view the task of
education as preparation for the 'ladder' to the professions and academia or as
an apprenticeship to vocational work but as a way of aiding the child's own
'inquiries' or 'discoveries', and considers that this is best facilitated by
'activity' methods.

The pedagogic tradition normally challenges the existing professional
identity of teachers at two levels: (1) as a 'specialist' in a school subject, for
which the teacher had normally been specifically trained; and (2) as an
all-pervading authority figure within the classroom. The Interdisciplinary
Enquiry (IDE) workshops run by Goldsmiths College in the 1960s clarify and
exemplify the dual nature of the challenge. The workshops were specifically
instituted as pilot courses for experienced teachers involved with those school
leavers staying on as a result of ROSLA.

The IDE booklets contained a series of stark messages for teachers of traditional subjects: 'We suggest that the subject based curriculum has fundamental educational disadvantages. The school day is fragmented into subject periods and time allocated to each subject is always regarded as insufficient by the subject specialist, as indeed it is.' Apart from the disadvantages in terms of time:

> The arbitrary division of knowledge into subject-syllabuses encourages a didactic form of teaching with the pupil's role reduced to passive assimilation. Any enquiry resulting from a keen interest shown by children in a section of work they are doing in a subject inevitably takes them over the boundaries of the subject into another, perhaps several others. Good teachers would like to encourage this evidence of interest, but they simply cannot afford the time, especially if their syllabus is geared to external examinations.[20]

As a solution to the problems engendered by the didactic teaching of traditional subjects Goldsmiths' team advocated organizing schemes of work around interdisciplinary enquiries.

Another curriculum project aimed at young school leavers underlined both the need to reappraise 'subjects' and to clearly define new pedagogic relationships. The Humanities Curriculum Project (HCP) began in 1967 with Lawrence Stenhouse as its director. HCP pursued the pedagogic implications of curriculum reform through the notion of 'neutral chairmanship'. This meant 'that the teacher accepts the need to submit his teaching in controversial areas to the criterion of neutrality . . . i.e. that he regards it as part of his responsibility not to promote his own view', and further that 'the mode of enquiry in controversial areas should have discussion, rather than instruction as its core.'[21]

The pedagogic tradition has been closely allied to the so-called 'progressive' movement in education. As Shipman noted in 1969, the more progressive curricula have come to be concentrated on those sections of the pupil clientele not considered suitable for O- and A-level examinations. In this way the pedagogic tradition has often suffered from the comparatively low status also accorded to the utilitarian tradition.

### Examinations and academic subjects

The connection between certain subjects taught in school and external examinations was established on the present footing with the birth of the School Certificate in 1917. From this point on the conflict over the curriculum began to resemble the contemporary situation in focusing on the definition and evaluation of examinable knowledge. The School Certificate rapidly became the major concern of grammar schools and because of the subjects thereby examined confirmed that academic subjects would dominate the school timetable.

By 1943 the Norwood Report assessed the importance of examinations in the following manner:

> A certain sameness in the curricula of schools seems to have resulted from the double necessity of finding a place for the many subjects competing for time in the curriculum and the need to teach these subjects in such a way and to such a standard as will ensure success in the School Certificate examination. Under these necessities the curriculum has settled down into an uneasy equilibrium, the demands of specialists and subjects and examinations being nicely adjusted and compensated.[22]

Despite the warnings, the academic subject-centred curriculum was strengthened in the period following the 1944 Education Act. The introduction of the GCE in 1951 allowed subjects to be taken separately at O-level (whereas the School Certificate was a 'block' exam in which the main subjects all had to be passed), and the introduction of A-level increased subject specialization in a manner guaranteed to preserve if not enhance the largely 'academic' nature of the O-level examination. There was little chance that a lower-status examination, such as the CSE, which was introduced in 1965, would endanger the academic subject-centredness of the higher-status O- and A-levels.

Indeed, it has proved remarkably adaptive to maintaining the status differentiation noted by Shipman and has even extended it. A recent study by Ball shows four bands within a comprehensive school allocating pupils as follows: Band 1 to subject-based O-levels; Band 2 to subject-based CSE Mode 2; Band 3 to integrated or watered-down subjects (e.g. Maths for Living) for CSE Mode 3; and Band 4 to non-examined 'remedial' classes.

The hegemony of the academic subject-based curriculum for O-level candidates was confirmed by the organizational structure of the Schools Council. An early role for the Council in the examinations field was advising the Beloe Committee set up to consider the proliferation of examinations in secondary modern schools. Beloe employed the subject-based framework of the Secondary School Examination Council, set up in the inter-war years to ensure uniformity of examinations, mainly at O- and A-levels. As Robert Morris, one of the two founding Joint Secretaries, explained:

> You can now see why the Schools Council developed a committee structure based on subjects. It was simply logical . . . we just inherited the structure of the Secondary Schools Examination Council who had already developed a pattern for examinations in academic subjects. (personal interview)

The attempts of interest groups to promote new subjects have focussed since 1917 on the pursuit of high-status examination and qualifications. Subjects like art, woodwork and metalwork, technical studies, book-keeping, type-writing and needlework, domestic science and physical education have consistently pursued status improvement by arguing for enhanced examinations and qualifications. But as we have seen, few subjects have been able to challenge the hegemony of the academic subjects incorporated in the 1904 Regulations and 1917 School Certificate. This academic tradition has successfully withstood waves of comprehensive reorganization and associated curriculum reform. The upheaval of the Great Debate is a reminder that this survival appears to have been at the expense of certain 'dominant interests' in the economy.

## Academic subjects, status and resources

The historical connection between academic subjects and external examinations is only partly explained because of 'the need to teach these subjects in such a way and to such a standard as will ensure success in the School Certificate examination'.

The years after 1917 saw a range of significant developments in the professionalization of teachers. Increasingly with the establishment of specialized subject training courses teachers came to see themselves as part of a 'subject community'. The associated growth of subject associations both derived from and confirmed this trend. This increasing identification of secondary teachers with subject communities tended to separate them from each other, and as schools became larger, departmental forms of organization arose which reinforced the separation. Thus the subject-centred curriculum developed to the point where the Norwood Report in 1943 expressed considerable concern:

> Subjects have tended to become preserves belonging to specialist teachers; barriers have been erected between them, and teachers have felt unqualified or not free to trespass upon the dominions of other teachers. The specific values of each subject have been pressed to the neglect of the values common to several or all. The school course has come to resemble the 'hundred yards' course, each subject following a track marked off from the others by a tape. In the meantime, we feel, the child is apt to be forgotten.[23]

Norwood summarizes the position by saying that 'subjects seem to have built themselves vested interests and rights of their own.' In explaining the continuing connection between external examinations and academic subjects the part played by the vested interests of the subject groups needs to be analysed. The dominance of academic subjects with high-status examination credentials would need to be in close harmony with the vested interests of subject groups to explain the strength of this alliance over so long a period.

The 'subject' label is important at a number of levels: obviously as a school 'examination' category, but also as title for a 'degree' or 'training course'. Perhaps most important of all the subject defines the territory of a 'department' within each school. The subject is the major reference point in the work of the contemporary secondary school: the information and knowledge transmitted in schools is formally selected and organized through subjects. The teacher is identified by the pupils and related to them mainly through his subject specialism. Given the size of most comprehensive schools, a number of teachers are required for each subject and these are normally grouped into subject 'departments'. The departments have a range of 'graded posts' for special responsibilities and for the 'head of department'. In this way the teacher's subject provides the means whereby his salary is decided and his career structure defined.

Within school subjects there is a clear hierarchy of status. This is based upon assumptions that certain subjects, the so-called 'academic' subjects, are suitable for the 'able' students, whilst other subjects are not. In her study of resource allocation in schools, Eileen Byrne has shown how more resources are given to these able students and hence to the academic subjects:

> Two assumptions which might be questioned have been seen consist-ently to underlie educational planning and the consequent resource allocation for the more able children. First, that these necessarily need longer in school than non-grammar pupils, and secondly, that they necessarily need more staff, more highly paid staff and more money for equipment and books.[24]

Byrne's research ended in 1965 before widespread comprehensivization, and therefore refers to the tripartite system. However, referring to the now comprehensive system, she wrote in 1974:

> There is . . . little indication that a majority of councils or chief officers accept in principle the need for review and reassessment of the entire process of the allocation of resources in relation to the planned applica-tion, over a period of years, of an approved and progressive policy, or coherent educational development.[25]

Hence it is likely, if Byrne's judgement is correct, that the discrimination in favour of academic subjects for the able pupils continues within the comprehensive school.

That comprehensive schools do place overwhelming emphasis on academic examinations, in spite of the growth of 'pastoral systems', has been recently confirmed by Ball's study of Beachside Comprehensive. He notes that 'once reorganised as a comprehensive, academic excellence was quickly established as a central tenet of the value system of the school.'[26] He provides a range of qualitative and statistical indicators to confirm this contention and concludes that 'while the division is less clear-cut and stark than in the grammar school' none the less it is evident that 'the teacher-resources within the comprehensive school are allocated differently according to the pupil's ability.' Thus the most experienced teachers spend most of their time teaching the most able pupils. This is a reflection of the fact that the social and psychological rewards offered by the school to its pupils accrue to those who are academically successful and that academic achievement tended to be the single criterion of 'success in the school'.[27]

Through the study of Beachside Comprehensive considerable evidence is assembled to prove Marsden's prediction that 'if we give the new comprehensive the task of competing with selective schools for academic qualifications, the result will be remarkably little change in the selective nature of education. Selection will take place within the school and the working class child's education will still suffer.'[28]

The importance of different curriculum traditions for each ability band of pupils is central in confirming these selective patterns. After the first term we learn 'the increasing differences of syllabus and curriculum which develop between the bands mean that band 2 or band 3 pupils would have to perform exceptionally well if not brilliantly to overcome the limitations placed upon them by the organisation of the syllabus.'[29] Ball notes that the pattern of curriculum differentiation is 'not unlike that made in the Norwood Report for fourth and fifth year pupils.'[30] At the top of the hierarchy of subjects are the traditional O-level subjects like maths, English, the languages, sciences, history and geography. These high-status subjects have 'an academic orientation in common; they are concerned with theoretical knowledge. They are subjects for the brighter, the academic, the band 1 pupil. Below these in status come O-levels in practical subjects like technical studies and metalwork. For band 2 and 3 pupils there are traditional CSEs and lowest of all in status new Mode III CSEs.'[31]

In a detailed and illuminating study of how the option system works it is possible to discern how curriculum categories and pupil clienteles (and futures) are 'matched' by the teachers. Ball shows how this works for two classes – the band 1 class 3CU and the band 2 class 3TA. After the option system has worked the '3TA pupils have been directed away from the "academic" to the practical, while the reverse has happened for the 3CU pupil'.[32] The study shows clearly that working-class pupils concentrate in bands 2 and 3 and further that the 'differentiation of access to high-status knowledge with high negotiable value is crucially related to socio-economic status.' He concludes:

> Option-allocation is a point at which school careers become firmly differentiated and at which the informal differences between pupils in terms of social reputation and their experiences of the curriculum lower down the school are formalised into separate curricular routes and examination destinations. It is here that the stratified nature of the occupation structure is directly reflected in the ability stratification within the school.
>
> Both the differential status of the knowledge areas in the curriculum and the access to the sixth form that certain courses provide are aspects of the selection of pupils for further and higher education and the

occupation market. The selection process and negotiation of meanings that go to make up the option-allocation procedure are part of the structural relationships within the school which label pupils with different statures and educational identities.[33]

But the study of internal process in an individual school can only take us so far. Reflecting the reality of the teacher's views inside the school, such a study takes the differentiated curriculum traditions which play such a central part in pupil differentiation as given. Truly 'men make their own history but not in circumstances of their own choosing.' The comprehensive school has had to accept the 'circumstances' of curriculum traditions derived from the tripartite system and earlier.

A number of studies confirm the status hierarchy of subjects. Warwick reports that a 1968 survey showed that over 7 per cent of male teachers who had studied within the languages and literature group (forming just over 19 per cent of the total sample) had become headteachers, compared with less than 1 per cent of those who had studied in the field of technology and handicraft (who formed just over 11 per cent of the total sample). Similarly, among male teachers 'former students of languages and literature had apparently four times as many chances as former students of music and drama, and one and a half times the chances of former students of science and mathematics of becoming headmasters.'[34]

The hierarchy of subjects is clearly derived from traditional grammar school preferences. Stevens reports that here 'English, Science, Languages and Mathematics are in general the subjects in which success or lack of it is significant for the children. The fact that practical subjects come low on the scale does not in itself support an assumption that more intelligent children are weak, even comparatively, at practical subjects. . . . The figures are rather as indicating the degree of importance with which several people, but chiefly the staff, invest subjects for the children.'[35]

### School subjects and teachers' interests

Three major subject traditions have been identified: the academic, utilitarian and pedagogic. The link between external subject examinations for the able student and the flow of status and resources has been clearly demonstrated. Conflicts between separate subject traditions have to be viewed within this context of status and resource allocation.

The aspirational imperative to become an academic subject is fundamental and very powerful and can be summarized as follows: school subjects comprise groups of people with differing interests and intentions. Certain common factors unite these sub-groups, most notably that the material self-interest of each subject teacher is closely connected with the status of the subject in terms of its examinable knowledge. Academic subjects provide the teacher with a career structure characterized by better promotion prospects and pay than less academic subjects. Most resources are given to academic subjects which are taught to 'able' students. The conflict over the status of examinable knowledge is above all a battle over the material resources and career prospects available to each subject community or subject teacher.

The definition of a subject as an O- and even more as an A-level examination postulates acceptance of the academic tradition. Even subjects with clear pedagogic or utilitarian origins and intentions such as art, craft (in aspiration design and technology) and rural studies (in aspiration environmental studies/science) have had to present themselves as theoretical academic subjects if A-level status is to be seriously pursued. Of course, once granted, A-level status, alongside acceptance as a university discipline, ensures 'establishment'. Layton's profile brings out the often contradictory directions in which pupil relevance and teacher and pupil motivation move as against the pursuit of academic status and the consequent definition of subject content by scholarly academics. The fate of subject traditions is clearly exhibited in close linkage with knowledge patterns and classroom pedagogy: the historical imperative in the case of science is clear but so also are the implications in terms of teacher preparation.

A more recent historical study (Layton's model was devised in 1972) has allowed some of the tentative assertions he made from the case of science to be tested for geography, biology, and rural studies.[36] In the case of geography, the subject was initially dominated by utilitarian and pedagogic arguments: 'we seek to train future citizens' and the citizen 'must have a topographical background if he is to keep order in the mass of information which accumulates in the course of his life.'[37] At this point the subject was largely taught by teachers untrained in geography. In 1903 Mackinder had outlined a strategy for the improvement of geography: the first demand was that 'University Schools of Geography' be established 'where geographers can be made.'[38] By this time the Geographical Association, which had been formed in 1893, was actively promoting the subject's academic potential, so much so that when the Hadow Report came out in 1927 it contended that 'The main objective in good geographical teaching is to develop . . . an attitude of mind and mode of thought characteristic of the subject.'[39]

By that time the university schools of geography demanded by Mackinder were being established for, as Wooldridge noted: 'It has been conceded that if Geography is to be taught in schools it must be learned in the universities.'[40] However, not until after 1945, Garnett tells us, were most school departments of geography directed by specialist-trained geographers. As a result of this training, she noted, 'most of the initial marked differences and contrasts in subject personality had been blurred or obliterated.'[41]

In fact, for several decades university geographers were plagued both by the image of the subject as essentially for schoolchildren and by the idiosyncratic interpretations of the various university departments, especially

in respect to fieldwork which encapsulated many pedagogic and utilitarian objectives. Thus, while establishment in universities solved the status
problems of the subject within schools, within the universities themselves the
subject's status still remained low. The launching, in the 1960s, of 'new
geography' with aspirations to full scientific or social scientific rigour is
therefore to be largely understood as a strategy for finally establishing
geography's status at the highest academic level. New geography stressed the
'scientific' and theoretical side of the subject at the expense of 'fieldwork' and
'regional studies'.

The history of biology, from low-status origins in elementary and
secondary schools to establishment in universities, is similar to that of
geography. The utilitarian and pedagogic elements in biology which so
retarded its progress were mainly confirmed by the fieldwork aspects of the
subject. Hence, the development of field biology ran counter to the pressures
for status escalation. Status through a vision of biology as 'hard science' was
increasingly pursued in the 1960s through an emphasis on laboratory investigations and mathematical techniques. In 1962 Dowdeswell had conceded
the crucial importance of laboratories as status symbols and had directed
much of the Nuffield Foundation's money and resources towards their
development.[42] The rise of molecular biology with the work of Crick and
Watson finally confirmed biology as a laboratory-based hard science. As a
result, the subject was rapidly expanded in the universities (themselves
expanded apace). With the training of a new generation of biology graduates
the subject's incorporation as a high-status O- and A-level school subject was
finally assured.

The case of rural studies provides a different pattern of evolution. The
origins of the subject were clearly and avowedly utilitarian, and pedagogic
arguments for the subject were continuous, but academic arguments were
never seriously entertained or deployed. After 1944 the subject was almost
exclusively confined to the secondary moderns, and with the growth of
comprehensives in the 1960s it was faced with extinction as schools were
reluctant to teach an ex-secondary modern subject with no examination
status. As a result the newly formed rural studies subject association began to
promote the subject as an 'academic discipline'. The name was changed to
'environmental studies' and a protracted battle ensued to have the subject
accepted at A-level. Unfortunately, although one board did accept the
subject at A-level, there was never any possibility of a university base and
hence no specialist scholars to define the discipline for broad-based A-level
acceptance. Lacking this university base, status passage to academic
acceptance has been denied to environmental studies.

Whilst aspiration to academic status has been discerned by Layton for
science and confirmed in the case of biology and geography and (unsuccessfully) in the case of rural studies, utilitarian and pedagogic traditions and
sub-groups owe their existence to radically different visions about the
assumptions and intentions which underpin school subjects. Despite the

continuing support for these traditions, the flow of resources and attributions of status plainly operate against them and in favour of the academic tradition. The implications of this imperative for the individual teacher's specialization and career pattern are fundamental and wide-ranging, affecting his view of his role and associated pedagogic predictions. In the study of the history of geography the author concluded:

> To further their own material self-interests school subject teachers must hand over control of their subject to those who are given the power to define 'disciplines'. Inevitably the subject is now defined by university scholars for their peers and students in line with the pervasive theoretical and scientific vision which characterises our academic institutions . . . whatever the original intentions or content areas of that subject may have been. [43]

In the evolution of the subject and through the promotion of different traditions over time the teacher's role therefore moves (following Layton) from an initial stage as 'an untrained specialist' to a final stage where as 'a professional' he is trained to teach pupils an examination subject defined by university scholars and examination boards. The stark differences in the teacher's role and associated pedagogy reflect the different visions embodied in the various subject 'traditions'.

### Conclusion

Sub-cultures, as well as initiating teachers into particular subject traditions, also offer arenas wherein those teachers can redefine and redirect educational patterns. But the direction in which school subjects move towards the culminating academic tradition is a reflection of the patterns of material interest and career aggrandizement which receive support inside the educational system and which crucially influence an individual teacher's assessment of the sub-cultural tradition which gains his allegiance.

The material interest of subject teachers is closely connected with the status of the subject in terms of examinable knowledge. 'Academic' subjects provide the teacher with a career structure characterized by better promotion prospects than less academic subjects. More resources are given to those academic subjects which are taught to 'able' children.

Hence the historical imperative is towards socialization into and acceptance of the academic tradition within subject sub-cultures. This tradition predicates fundamental assumptions about teacher role, pedagogic orientation, hierarchies of knowledge and the fabric of relationships which underpin these. We have noted that Layton sees the academic tradition as the prelude to disenchantment for pupils; likewise Witkin has shown how working-class pupils actively prefer and choose lessons they can relate to the everyday world; and Halsey's recent research shows the radical difference between working-class recruitment to technical schools (utilitarian tradition) and the far lower take-up of grammar schools (academic tradition). Plainly, the historical imperatives which lead teachers into acceptance of the academic tradition will be at the expense of other aspirations encapsulated within pedagogic and utilitarian traditions.

We have noted the recurrence of challenges to the dominance of the academic tradition and to the emergence of 'pastoral' careers within schools. At the present time, under the threat of falling rolls, some education authorities are reviewing their fundamental assumptions about curriculum planning. In some areas this has led to a concern for 'whole curriculum needs' which leads to planning according to the range of subjects required by all pupils. Were this questioning of assumptions to become more general, it would clearly question the mechanisms which currently maintain the academic/able pupil alliance.

Detailed consideration of subject traditions, together with an appraisal of the benefits and costs of each for the individual teacher, might seem a useful perspective from which to begin teacher preparation. By focusing on these themes teacher trainers could ensure a discussion about teacher roles, pedagogies and relationships which were closely related to actual choices with which the teacher will be confronted in his or her working life.

## Notes

1. McLeish, J. (1970). *Students' Attitudes and College Environments*, Cambridge, quoted in Lacey (1977), p. 64.
2. Lacey, C. (1977). *The Socialisation of Teachers*, London, Methuen, pp. 63–4.
3. Ball, S. J. and Lacey, C. (1978). 'Subject disciplines as the opportunity for group action: A measured critique of subject sub-cultures', paper presented at the SSRC Conference, Teacher and Pupil Strategies, St Hilda's College, University of Oxford, September.
4. *Ibid.*
5. Mardle, G. and Walker, M. (1980). Introduction to book on Teacher Preparation, mimeo.
6. Bucher, R. and Strauss, A. (1976). 'Professions in process', in Hammersley, M. and Woods, P. (eds) *The Process of Schooling: A Sociological Reader*, London, Routledge & Kegan Paul, p. 19.
7. Layton, D. (1973). *Science for the People*, London, George Allen & Unwin.
8. Hanson, D. (1971). 'The development of a professional association of art teachers', *Studies in Design Education*, 3 February.
9. Dodd, T. (1978). *Design and Technology in the School Curriculum*, London, Hodder & Stoughton.
10. Williams, R. (1961). *The Long Revolution*, London, Penguin, p. 172.
11. Eggleston, J. (1977). *The Sociology of the School Curriculum*, London, Routledge & Kegan Paul.
12. Banks, O. (1955). *Parity and Prestige in English Secondary Education*, London, Routledge & Kegan Paul, p. 5.

13. TUC (1937). *Education and Democracy*, London, TUC.
14. Banks (1955). *op. cit.*, p. 248.
15. Layton, D. (1972). 'Science as general education', *Trends in Education*, January.
16. Blyth, W. A. L. (1965). *English Primary Education: A Sociological Description*, Vol. 2, London, Routledge & Kegan Paul, pp. 21, 30, 124–5.
17. Eggleston (1977), *op. cit.*, p. 25.
18. Williams (1961), *op. cit.*, p. 163.
19. Goodson, I. F. (1978). 'Why Britain needs to change its image of the educated man', *The Times*, 14 February.
20. University of London, Goldsmiths College (1965). The Raising of the School Leaving Age: Second Pilot Course for Experienced Teachers, Autumn Term.
21. *The Humanities Project: An Introduction* (1972). London, Heinemann, p. 1.
22. The Norwood Report (1943). London, HMSO, p. 61.
23. *Ibid.*
24. Byrne, E. M. (1974). *Planning and Educational Inequality*, Slough, NFER, pp. 29, 311.
25. *Ibid.*
26. Ball, S. J. (1981). *Beachside Comprehensive*, Cambridge University Press, p. 18.
27. *Ibid.*
28. *Ibid.*, p. 21.
29. *Ibid.*, pp. 35–6.
30. *Ibid.*, p. 138.
31. *Ibid.*, p. 140.
32. *Ibid.*, p. 143.
33. *Ibid.*, pp. 152–3.
34. Warwick, D. (1976). 'Ideologies, integration and conflicts of meaning', in Flude, M. and Ahier, J. (eds) *Educability, Schools and Ideology*, London, Croom Helm, p. 101.
35. Stevens, F. (1972). *The Living Tradition: The Social and Educational Assumptions of the Grammar School*, 3rd ed., London, Hutchinson, pp. 117–18.
36. Goodson, I. F. (1982). *School Subjects and Curriculum Change: Case Studies in Curriculum History*, London, Croom Helm.
37. Council of the Geographical Association (1919). 'The position of geography', *The Geographical Teacher*, 10.
38. Mackinder, H. J. (1903). 'Report of the British Association meeting, September 1903', *The Geographical Teacher*, 2. pp. 95–101.
39. Board of Education (1927). *Report of the Hadow Committee*, London, HMSO.
40. Quoted in David, T. (1973). 'Against geography', in Bale, J. *et al.*, *Perspectives in Geographical Education*, Edinburgh, pp. 12–13.
41. Garnett, A. (1969). 'Teaching geography: Some reflections', *Geography*, 54, November, p. 368.
42. W. H. Dowdeswell as Director of the Nuffield Biology Project.
43. Goodson, I. F. (1981). 'Defining and defending the subject', paper presented at St Hilda's Conference, September.

# 12

# The symbolism of effective schools

**Terrence E. Deal**

In the world of education, a combination of research findings and commission reports has created the effective schools movement, a movement that may be different from past efforts to improve schools. In the past, we have had either answers without a pressing question or an immediate problem without apparent solutions. Now we appear to have both a crisis and a direction (Cohen 1985). The combination has resulted in significant interest in educational reform at the national, state, and local levels.

The question is whether educators can harness the zeal for reform and create new practices or transform old ones. If teachers and administrators use this opportunity to revitalize or reshape public schools, the effective schools movement will be a landmark event for education. As McDonnell notes in the January 1985 issue of the *Elementary School Journal*, crisis is a prime generator of innovation.

However, if energy is unchanneled and efforts are unfocused, the result may not be so favorable. A wave of public disaffection could result in a further withdrawal of support for public education. The implosion of dashed hopes among teachers and administrators could leave schools even more spiritually hollow than they are often depicted. In the past, other efforts to change schools have backfired. Failures have been documented at the classroom level (Artley 1981), at the school level (Charters and Jones 1975: Deal 1975; Packard 1975), at the district level (Krist 1983), and in postsecondary education (Bennis 1975). Other case studies of changes that fall short are included in Baldridge and Deal (1975, 1983). Because of its strong momentum, the effective schools movement could explode if we do not apply the lessons learned from our previous experiences.

## The symbolism of effective schools

In the January 1985 issue of the *Elementary School Journal*, a fine collection of papers summarizes the policy implications of effective schools research and outlines how we might proceed on various fronts. Most of the papers occasionally refer to the role of symbolism in school improvement: to language and ideas that describe a spiritual and moral essence of schools, to the idea that objects or activities often have implicit meaning and serve important hidden purposes, and to an awareness that schools do far more than produce learning.

In her paper highlighting research on principals, for example. Manasse (1985) mentions vision and symbolic presence as qualities of effective principals. Other papers also contain ideas that reflect a departure from rational imagery and language. Fullan (1985) discusses the importance of looking at how effective schools evolve and create meaning for the people inside. He mentions intense interaction, leadership 'feel,' values, and other ideas atypical in rational formulations of schools. Fenstermacher and Berliner (1985) stress the importance of organizational dynamics and context as potent factors that affect staff development. Darling-Hammond and Wise (1985) contrast the culture of teaching with the culture of bureaucrats, arguing that reforms conceived outside the profession often undermine important internal values and beliefs. Purkey and Smith (1985) move into the symbolic realm even more explicity by arguing that 'the school is the focus of change, and culture is the target.'

In this article I wish to build on these ideas by examining in even more detail the symbolism of reflective schools and the larger cultural significance of the movement as a policy-making activity. How can administrators use the opportunity to reshape and revitalize the culture of local schools? How can we avoid the turmoil and disappointment that have accompanied past efforts to change schools?

The article is built on a key proposition: understanding the symbols and culture of a school is a prerequisite to making the school more effective. Schools are judged by external constituencies as much on appearance as on results (Meyer and Rowan 1983). The faith and belief of teachers and administrators, as well as outsiders, are rooted more in perception than in tangible experience. Perception is based on shared values and symbols. Unless improvement strategies and programs are guided by a sensitive awareness of the role played by school culture, the effective schools movement could collapse under its own weight (Deal and Kennedy 1983). We now have a language to describe the symbolic side of schools and change. The purpose of this paper is to help policymakers and educators think about the symbolic components of effective schools and how the current momentum can be harnessed to revitalize – perhaps to reshape – the culture of schools. As Farrar, Neufeld, and Miles (1983) note, effective school programs are typically 'process reforms that strive to capture the imagination of school faculties, to revitalize those who are demoralized, and to generate enthusiasm for joint work on common goals' (p. 11).

This observation describes another meaning of the effective schools movement – a symbolic activity designed to serve deep cultural needs. At policy levels, improvement should affect how citizens view public schools. Utilized sensitively, commission reports and research results should also improve the public's views of schools as well as 'professionals' views of themselves. However, the effective schools movement also presents a unique opportunity for professionals to strengthen, reinforce, and rebuild the culture of educational organizations.

### Educational policy

In education, the primary operating units are classrooms and schools – the places where learning occurs. Policymakers at various levels attempt to shape activities inside schools to reflect various interests outside. Locally, boards of education try to influence the behavior of teachers and principals by formulating policy and delegating operating authority to a superintendent of schools. State and federal policymakers attempt to serve the public interest by sponsoring legislation and pursuing other activities to move schools in desired directions. Through policies, the citizens attempt to assure that schools will serve social mandates. In the words of Darling-Hammond and Wise (1985), policies are developed to 'maximize good and to minimize evil.'

There is, however, a recurring problem with the rational mind-set that sees a linear connection between policy and results. Desired connections between policies and practices are difficult to find. Policies are seldom carried out to the letter (Lipsky 1980; Murphy 1971). They often do not achieve intended results even if they are implemented. Formal incentives and penalties only occasionally dictate how people actually behave. Formal evaluations cannot always measure what policymakers desire.

Research studies and emerging theories of organization support a more 'loosely coupled' view (Weick 1976) of the link between policies and behavior at lower levels. In this interpretation, policy-making (Edelman 1977), evaluation (Floden and Weiner 1978), and research (Weiss 1981) serve as important rituals, ceremonies, or symbols. Their importance derives from what is signaled, expressed, or represented rather than from what is accomplished (Meyer and Rowan 1977). They happen when events seem worrisome or out of control and play a different role in human experience than many would imagine. In this view, policy-making is social drama played to a wider audience of citizens, as well as to interested spectators in local communities. A symbolic approach to organizations would characterize the effective schools movement as an important symbolic activity – the commissions as high ceremony, the research as a potent symbol.

A number of blue-ribbon panels and commissions have dramatized the problem of educational ineffectiveness and have formulated recommendations that are a mixture of practical, costly, unfeasible, and revolutionary suggestions. Many of the recommendations will not be suited to conditions in a specific community. Most will be discounted and lost in local dialogue and action. Yet in the drama, the American people will have rediscovered and reclaimed some important values and beliefs about public schools (Deal 1985). The succession of ceremonies already seems to have rekindled the faith of the American public in education. Findings from a Gallup Poll conducted in 1984 (p. 24) support this interpretation:

> Americans are more favorably disposed toward the public schools today than at any time in the last decade. In this year's survey, more Americans (42%) grade their local schools A or B for their performance than at any time since 1976 – with an 11-point increase just since last year. Virtually the same dramatic increase occurs among the parents of public school children – with a 10% rise since last year in the percentage giving the local schools an A or B rating.
>
> Americans have also become significantly more favorably disposed toward public school teachers and administrators. In 1981, 39% gave teachers a grade of A or B, whereas today the figure is 50%. Moreover, the A or B grades given to principals and administrators have risen from 36% to 47% during this same three-year period.
>
> A final indicator that reveals an increase in favorable feelings toward the schools is the public's increased willingness to pay the price for public education. The percentage of Americans who say that they would be willing to pay more taxes for education has risen from 30% to 41%.

Opinions shifted before anything had changed. Commissions have succeeded before specific recommendations have been considered, let alone become part of everyday behavior. The curious link is hardly rational; it is demonstrably symbolic.

The symbolic importance of the commissions is similar to the documented role that ritual and ceremony play in other sectors and activities: presidential campaigns (Edelman 1977), administrative agencies of the federal government (Edelman 1977), the Polaris Missile Project (Sapolsky 1972), and collective bargaining (Blum 1961). Cultural ceremonies are important for what they express, and how they dramatize or transform important values (Moore and Meyerhoff 1977). Policy-making as ceremony is not fully intended to affect directly the inner workings of classrooms or schools. Although it may ultimately affect lower levels, policy-making has its chief influence by changing or revitalizing collective sentiments, values, or beliefs.

The symbolic importance of the effective schools movement does not end with commissions. It recasts the value of research studies. (See January 1975 issue of the *Elementary School Journal* for a synthesis of various studies.)

The findings of the effective schools research may be more important as symbols than as facts. Our society presently places more faith in science than in ordinary knowledge or common sense. Conclusions of researchers have more value than the judgment of practitioners. Although educators have claimed all along that schools make a difference, the Coleman Report (Coleman *et al.* 1966) demonstrated empirically that they did not. The facts overwhelmed the opinions of professionals, even though other social scientists hotly contested the facts. Coleman's method of proof was challenged by others who themselves believed in quantitative research. Despite the challenges, the facts fractured the faith. It took new quantitative evidence that schools can make a difference to shore up belief and confidence dampened by previous findings. One of the main contributions of the effective schools research is to restore the myth of education lost in the 1960s and 1970s. As a symbol in the policy arena, the effective schools literature has been immensely helpful.

As general research findings meet specific realities at the local level, however, many of the same problems arise as when commission recommendations are used as literal guides for action. As others have also mentioned, the results of research are based on associations between characteristics and effectiveness, not a direct cause-effect linkage (Purkey and Smith 1985). These associations are susceptible to influences from an unmeasured group of variables that may actually be more potent determinants of school achievement.

Despite limitations of the research, local schools will use the effective schools findings to relabel old initiatives and as new labels for existing practices, as ammunition in political fights among different constituencies, and as new measures of excellence. These are well-documented and potentially powerful ways of using research results (Weiss 1981).

As educators begin to rekindle and reshape local practices, they need to give considerable attention to another potentially influential, but largely unmeasured and unmentioned, factor in academic performance: school culture. Commissions and research findings pave the way for local initiatives to revitalize and reshape the character of schools. However, unless local educators understand and reckon with the existing culture of each school, the introduction of commissions' recommendations or characteristics of effectiveness will probably not work: it may even do more harm than good. Such action could erode still further the faith and confidence of administrators, teachers, parents, students, and members of the community. If the effective schools movement is to have a lasting effect, the ceremonies at the national and state levels need to be reconvened in local communities. Commission recommendations and effective schools research need to be debated locally by persons who call attention to educational values and renegotiate expectations for public schools. Professionals inside schools need to listen to and participate in these important dramas. They then need to look inward – to reexamine, revitalize, and possibly revise school culture.

## Shaping culture: lessons from effective businesses

Among the criticisms leveled at public schools is the popular charge that they would work better if run more like businesses. To most people, operating like a business entails planning, setting specific goals and objectives, measuring performance, linking costs to results, and evaluating programs and the performance of employees regularly and systematically. For several years schools tried to emulate business practices, usually with mixed results (Kirst 1983).

What many advocates of rationalizing schools missed was that many of the criticisms leveled at schools are also being aimed at businesses. Also, business productivity is off. Public confidence in business has been nearly as low as public faith in schools – especially within certain industries. It was not clear whether management techniques and approaches promising improvement were working any better than older approaches. This disaffection paved the way for a series of books about management: *Theory Z* (Ouchi 1981), *The Art of Japanese Management* (Athos and Pascale 1978), *Corporate Cultures* (Deal and Kennedy 1982). The One Minute Manager (Blanchard and Johnson 1982). *The General Managers* (Kotter 1982), and *In Search of Excellence* (Peters and Waterman 1982).

Each of these books attempts to articulate a softer, people-oriented, symbolic strategy for raising productivity. A shared premise is that successful companies, here or in Japan, have special internal qualities that distinguish them. A strong performance is dependent on a cohesive culture – a set of shared values that motivates and shapes behavior inside the company and inspires commitment and loyalty from customers or clients. The real lesson that schools can learn from business refocuses attention on the culture of the school. It is a lesson that most educators have already learned from experience but often devalue in the face of a barrage of rational ideologies. The following examples from business are offered to restore educators' faith in wisdom, intuition, and administrative lore – time-tested concepts that have been eclipsed recently by theories of modern management.

Culture is an expression that tries to capture the informal, implicit – often unconscious – side of business or any human organization. Although there are many definitions of the term, culture in everyday usage is typically described as 'the way we do things around here.' It consists of patterns of thought, behavior, and artifacts that symbolize and give meaning to the workplace. Meaning derives from the elements of culture: shared values and beliefs, heroes and heroines, ritual and ceremony, stories, and an informal network of cultural players. Effective businesses typically show a remarkable consistency across these cultural elements (Deal and Kennedy 1982).

### Shared values and beliefs

In effective businesses, slogans, written philosophies, and symbols express core values. These values are shared across the company and shape behavior across levels.

In Mary Kay Cosmetics, a group of part-time typists at a large convention articulated why working for the company was special: 'It's all there in the bumblebee.' They said, 'It cannot fly, but doesn't know it. The bumblebee represents the 'you can do it' spirit that makes this a meaningful place to work – even on a part-time basis.'

In Anheuser-Busch, a worker cleaning the vats admitted that working conditions were difficult but added, 'It's a good company.' When asked what that meant, he mentioned quality and pride – two values that have governed the successful beer company for more than a century. When pushed about the meaning of quality, he told a dramatic story about August Busch III, chairman of the board. The story illustrated vividly and concretely what quality meant at Anheuser-Busch.

At Johnson and Johnson, the discovery of the tainted Tylenol capsules raised a serious dilemma. Do we pull the product from the shelves, or do we take the chance that all the poisoned capsules have been recovered? The decision to remove the product was made by James Burke, Johnson and Johnson's CEO, relying heavily on their 'Credo' – a short statement of the company's philosophy that puts the customers first and shareholders fourth.

These values narrow a company's mission and offer guidelines for the behavior of employees and decisions of top executives. Values evolve from a company's experience, sorting practices that work from those that do not. Over time the values are summarized in symbols, slogans, and philosophies. They are widely known and informally reinforced across the company from boardroom to factory floor.

### Heros and heroines

Effective businesses anoint and celebrate heros and heroines, human beings whose thoughts, deeds, and personal qualities represent core company values. Within IBM, stories of Thomas Watson, Sr, founder of IBM are legendary. Employees who join the company learn of Watson's philosophies and exploits, even though Watson. Sr, has been dead for years.

The president of Nissan of America, Marvin Runyon, is known by every employee in the large truck-producing factory. Runyon wears blue coveralls with 'Marvin' written across the left-hand pocket. As he walks through the factory, people's faces light up. He talks to them about their work: they tell him the truth. They know that if they are experiencing difficulty, they need to find help, not try to bury the problem. They know Runyon cares about them: they also know that Marvin will not tolerate anything less than a near-perfect truck. In story and in person, Marvin Runyon's presence speaks the values of quality and people.

Mary Kay Ash of Mary Kay Cosmetics exemplifies the struggle for success. She founded a company to sell top-quality cosmetic products, employing a sales force composed primarily of women. Her husband was to be a partner but died just before the company was launched. Mary Kay went ahead, made her mistakes, and through her successes has built a multi-million dollar company. 'I have bloodied my knees more than any human being I know. My success comes from my willingness to get up and try again: you can do it too,' she tells her beauty consultants. She exemplifies the spirit that motivates and inspires employees and managers.

In successful companies, a pantheon of heros and heroines representing the status quo (sacred cow or hunker-down types) as well as innovation (compass and outlaw types) provides role models and tangible expressions of values for other employees. These heroic figures are extolled in everyday lore and rewarded and celebrated formally and informally.

### Ritual

Effective companies have distinctive rituals of work, management, and personal exchange. Much of the day-to-day behavior in any company is ritualistic. People have regular ways of doing their work. In many accounting firms, for example, the way an audit is conducted follows standard procedures outlined by the profession but also reflects the specific values of the culture.

In a company like Boeing, meetings give much more attention to detail than in a sales company, where a particular decision does not have as far-reaching effects. The management rituals of a company reinforce the core values of the culture.

Rituals of greeting and exit also vary across companies and usually reinforce the basic tenor or ethos of the workplace. The more conservative culture of Procter and Gamble encourages more formal interchanges among employees than a more creatively oriented, competitive company such as Young and Rubicom, where conversations are playful and very straightforward.

In ritual, managers and employees of a company come together, bonding with each other and with core values and shared symbols. When the far-flung, diversified subsidiary companies of Johnson and Johnson come together, for example, well-known rituals permit members of very different subcultures to communicate effectively with one another.

### Ceremony

Effective companies have regular ceremonies that dramatize and reinforce core values and beliefs. In most high-performing companies, key employees assemble annually or semiannually for a conference, retreat, or meeting. At these events the culture of the company is put on stage to be experienced, celebrated, and transformed. As an illustration, the general managers of Hyatt Hotels assemble once a year to reinforce the Hyatt way of service. The managers talk directly with Pat Foley (the president) and J. Pritzker (chairman of the board), two of the heros revered within Hyatt. General managers examine the linkage between values, details, and service. They tell stories and have a good time but in the process regenerate their commitment to the company.

### Stories

In effective companies, managers and employees freely discuss positive stories about philosophy, exploits of heroes or heroines, and the success of distinctive practices. These shared stories carry company values.

In a visit to Hyatt's general managers' meeting, four people greeted my arrival. For 20 minutes they told me stories about the exploits and daring of the company's two heros: Pat Foley and J. Pritzker. Once they felt I knew what the company was all about, I was permitted to join the cocktail party. In a recent visit to Hyatt's Airport Hotel in Los Angeles, I asked a waitress if she knew any good 'Foley' stories. She replied, 'All stories about Pat Foley are good ones.' She then told me many of the same stories I had heard at the general managers' meeting.

### Informal network of cultural players

In effective companies, an informal network of priests or priestesses, gossips, storytellers, and other cultural players keeps the culture alive and intact and acts as a barrier to change. In most strongly performing companies there is an informal collection of people whose chief function is to keep watch over the culture, to carry and reinforce the values. In one large company, I came upon a person who could recite the company's history and philosophy verbatim. He knew all the old-timers by name and worked to bring new employees into the fold. A recent change in top executive positions has pitted this man against his boss. He knows of the tension but notes that 'someone needs to keep reminding the newcomers what the company is all about.' He takes confession. He is summoned when something goes wrong. He is there to bless anything that goes right. He is the informal priest of the culture.

In another company, an older man pulled me aside. 'See this card,' he said, handing me a business card, 'What do you think?' 'You're rumor control?' I responded after reading his title. 'Yes,' he said, 'When people want to validate a rumor, they call me. I confirm or disconfirm the rumor – or try to check it out. I get more calls than the boss.' The man is the company gossip. Priests, gossips, storytellers, and other cultural players, such as spies or whisperers, are a natural, and usually well-appreciated, group in a solid company.

What can be learned from business is something educators have known all along: the importance of building a strong cohesive culture – a well-developed network of cultural players, to be sure. However, in addition, schools need widely shared values, instead of a lengthy statement of goals that few people know; a well-known and amply rewarded pantheon of heros and heroines, instead of anti-heros or people whose exploits go unnoticed; meaningful rituals of teaching and managing, instead of meaningless routine; regular and inspiring ceremonies, instead of lifeless gatherings; memorable and widely told positive stories, instead of cold facts and figures. Strong cultures do not develop overnight; they evolve over years. Cultures grow through human interactions; thereafter they shape human experience. In schools where diverse expectations, political vulnerability, and the lack of a tangible product make values, beliefs, and faith crucial in determining success, the development of a solid culture is even more important than it might be in business. Behind effective schools, like high-performing businesses, there is a strong culture that encourages productivity, high morale, confidence, and commitment. Making schools more effective requires building and reshaping the hidden, taken-for-granted rules that govern day-to-day behavior.

## School culture: revival and elaboration of an old idea

The publication of *Corporate Cultures* (Deal and Kennedy 1982) and *In Search of Excellence* (Peters and Waterman 1982) made culture a preoccupation with many businesses. Companies across all sections of the economy – banks, insurance companies, hotel chains, and airlines – are now struggling to identify, revitalize, and reshape their cultures. It is difficult to attend an executive retreat, annual conference, or business seminar without hearing the term used, misused, or abused. The concept of culture in corporate America has become a powerful management tool: it is on the brink of becoming a management fad.

In the field of education, the idea of culture has not become as popular yet as it has in business. School administrators continue to emphasize climate or effective schools' characteristics as guiding concepts. This is ironic because the momentum for studying culture was stimulated, in part, by research in public schools (Cohen, Deal, Meyer, and Scott 1979; Deal, Meyer, and Scott 1983; Meyer and Rowan 1977). Culture and symbols have played – and will continue to play – a major role in school performance, both actual and perceived.

As noted earlier, both results and appearance are focal points in judging educational effectiveness. In the absence of one, the other becomes even more important. An institution like Harvard is not asked to provide evidence of success: it is consistently reflected in its distinctive ways, nourished by a long history. By contrast, a new alternative high school (one that deviates from the profile of a typical school) must provide ample evidence of successful performance until its worth is proven or until the culture creates a persuasive myth and system of beliefs that can convey the meaning of new patterns to outsiders (Deal 1975, 1982). A school like Radcliffe can get by without either tangible results or typical appearance (no deans, classes, or students) because belief in the institution is so strong. In each case, the tenor or tone of the culture is the driving force in reinforcing collective identity and broadcasting a favorable image. A cohesive culture can produce better results. However, even in the absence of tangible gains or in the face of declining results, a strong organizational culture can provide justification for the continued faith and support of both participants and outside constituencies.

The concept of culture is not new to education. Waller (1932) focused on the importance of culture, beliefs, rituals, ceremonies, and values for the school as a social organization:

> Teachers have always known that it was not necessary for the students of strange customs to cross the seas to find materials. Folklore and myth, tradition, taboo, magic rites, ceremonials of all sorts, collective representations, participation mystique, all abound in the front yard of every school, and occasionally they creep into the more formal portions of school life. (p. 103)

Clark (1983) emphasizes the role of the organizational saga, which is a shared mythology rooted in tradition, reinforced by a charismatic leader, and possessing a cadre of faculty supporters, distinctive educational practices, a student subculture, and an external group of alumni and other believers. As internal and external groups share their common beliefs, a saga creates links across internal divisions and organizational boundaries. With deep emotional commitment, believers define themselves by their organizational affiliation, and in their bond to other believers, they share an intensive sense of uniqueness. In an organization defined by a strong saga, there is the small, sanctified world of the lucky few and the large routine world of others outside the chosen flock. Such an emotional bond turns the membership into a community, even a cult (Clark 1983).

Sarason (1971) documents the power of school culture, defined as behavioral regularities and shared assumptions, in successfully resisting and redefining educational innovations such as the new math. Deal (1982) and Swidler (1979) demonstrate the importance of culture or shared symbols in the formation and operation of alternative schools. As Swidler (1979, p. viii) observes:

> Watching teachers and students in free schools, I became convinced that culture, in the sense of symbols, ideologies, and a legitimate language for discussing individual and group objectives, provides the crucial substrate on which new organizational forms can be exacted. The ability to make altered patterns of social control effective depends on the development of new cultural resources. Even the most personal, charismatic forms of influence depend ultimately on a shared ideology. Organizational innovations and cultural change are consistently

intertwined, since it is the culture that creates the new images of human nature and new symbols with which people can move one another. Organizations, in turn, are the contexts within which cultural meanings are used, tested, and made real.

Each of these sources suggests why the culture of schools is important, but none specifically links culture to performance. In businesses (and hospitals) the connection between culture and performance is presently built on theoretical argument and examples.

The same argument can be made and supported by examples of exemplary schools. Effective schools are those that over time have built a system of belief, supported by cultural forms that give meaning to the process of education. Just as with businesses, these schools will display shared values and beliefs, well-known and widely celebrated heros and heroines, well-attended and memorable rituals and ceremonies, positive stories, and a dedicated informal group whose members work diligently to maintain and strengthen the culture. The Exemplary Center for Reading Instruction (ECRI) Program, which Fullan (1985) describes, is a superb example. It primarily focuses on building a belief system around teaching practices. In one elementary school, for example, the introduction of ECRI created a strong belief system and sense of community. Its heros and heroines were well known (example: the teacher who got polyps in her larynx from enthusiastic classroom lessons). A unique teaching ritual was observed across different classrooms, even though individual teachers varied enormously in personal background and style. Positive stories of individual student accomplishments (example: a foreign student whose achievement gains were especially significant in a short time span) were told repeatedly by teachers, administrators, and parents (Deal, Gunnar, and Wiske 1977). These characteristics are strikingly different from patterns in typical elementary schools.

In addition to anecdotes and examples, the case for a link between culture and performance in schools can be inferred from two empirical sources. The first of these consists of school climate studies that attempt to measure the effects of social atmosphere on educational outcomes or example. McDill and Rigsby (1973) document some interesting linkages between school climate, student achievement, and student educational aspirations. Similar findings are evident in school effectiveness studies, where both climate and ethos are consistently connected to measures of performance. (Again, see the January 1985 edition of the *Elementary School Journal.*) Although the conceptual match between climate, ethos, or culture has not been specified, it is clear that something intangible about a school – style, tone, or social atmosphere – is related somehow to student performance.

A second empirical source involves the effects of subcultures on performance. School cultures, like any others, contain subcultures:

The culture of the school is a curious melange of the work of young artists making culture for themselves and old artists making culture for the young; it is also mingled with such bits of the culture as children have been able to appropriate. In turning to more concrete materials, we may notice certain aspects of tradition in a school. It will illustrate well the mingling of cultures if we divide the tradition which clusters about the school into three classes: tradition which comes entirely or in part from outside the school, tradition which in part is indigenous, and tradition which is almost entirely indigenous. It is roughly true that tradition of the first class exists in the community at large, that of the second class among teachers, and that of the third class among students. (Waller 1932, p. 108)

Subcultures are clearly evident to anyone who visits a school, walks around, and talks to various persons and groups inside. Students have their own subculture, often formed in opposition to that of teachers. Within this subculture are a number of smaller subcultures or 'gangs,' each with its own values, norms, language, patterns of dress, and informal rules for acceptable behavior. Differences among student subcultures are easily observed, especially in high schools where separate collections of 'rah-rahs,' 'greasers,' 'pot-heads,' and 'brains' are well delineated (and the effect of subculture membership on behavior is obvious). Less obvious, but well documented, is the effect of subcultural membership on educational outcomes. Peer groups, for example, influence scholastic performance and educational aspirations (McDill and Rigsby 1973). In the wider student subculture, student leaders, or heros, significantly affect the scholastic tone of a school – and subsequently, student behavior and performance (Gordon 1957).

The values, rituals, language, and beliefs of the teachers' subculture are also well documented in the literature. For example, norms – or informal rules – of autonomy and equality dictate how teachers relate to one another and undermine efforts to introduce innovations such as open-space architecture, team teaching, or performance-based salary plans. The teaching subculture can directly influence teacher expectations or the amount of time teachers spend on instruction and thus can also influence student performance and achievement.

The administrative subculture – of which principals are a part – has its own informal rules and procedures. As Wolcott (1973) convincingly notes, the administrative subculture had often become preoccupied with accountability, control, and change. These values frequently place principals in direct conflict with teachers – a factor that can erode teachers' motivation and their effectiveness in the classroom. Most studies of effective schools show that the principal plays a key role in how well students perform. However, the effect can go either way. The values and beliefs a principal brings to the job are influenced by the administrative subculture. Unless bureaucratic values are balanced with professional ones, the principal's influence may encourage procedural conformity rather than inspirational creativity in the classroom. It is easy to see how the administrative subculture can affect the tone and performance of local schools – one way or the other.

Outside the school are the values and traditions of parents and the local community. In many communities different values are championed by different interest groups or subcultures. External values affect the culture of the school, shaping what goes on inside. Orientations of both parents and the community, for example, have been linked to student performance (McDill and Rigsby 1973).

Subcultures can play a very positive role in school performance. Both theory and research demonstrate the effects of subcultures on behavior and, through behavior, on performance. Yet these influences can also undermine schoolwide values, create subcultural battles, or neutralize each other. This is particularly true when subcultures, in the absence of schoolwide cultural influences, vie constantly for supremacy and attention. For any school to perform effectively, shared values must keep various subgroups pulling in roughly the same direction. Otherwise subculture influences will predominate, and both cohesion and performance will fall victim to a cacophony of diverse voices and special interests.

The concept of school culture introduces another dimension to the effective schools literature. Every school has a culture, although the sense of tradition and shared direction vary significantly from school to school. Beneath the well-accepted organizational characteristics of effective schools are cultural elements that influence the behavior of administrators, teachers, and students. By influencing behavior, culture affects productivity – how well teachers teach and how much students learn. By projecting an image of what the school stands for, culture affects perceptions and confidence of parents and the community.

Table 1 outlines the characteristics of effective schools and strong organizational cultures. A quick scan across the columns suggests some similarities between the characteristics of effective schools and the attributes of strong organizational cultures. However, the comparison also highlights differences in terminology and underlying assumptions. The effective schools research reflects a strong rational and technical emphasis: goals, leadership, planning, meetings, and training. The cultural approach shows a definite symbolic emphasis: values, heros and heroines, rituals, and beliefs. The differences are important because they represent divergent ways of depicting the core attributes of effective schools and identifying for policymakers and practitioners what is needed to help less successful schools improve. Others emphasize the more technical approach both in what schools should do as well as how they should do it. In the remainder of this paper, I suggest how language and concepts of culture can be applied to local school improvement efforts. Rather than only trying to emulate the characteristics of effective schools, the approach encourages schools to look back on their own histories and inward on the elements of their cultures: shared

**Table 1**   Characteristics of effective schools and strong organizational cultures

| *Characteristics of effective schools* | *Characteristics of strong organizational cultures* |
|---|---|
| Coherent ethos with agreed-upon ways of doing things; agreement on instructional goals | Strong culture with shared values and a consensus on 'how we do things around here' |
| Importance of principal as leader | Importance of principal as hero or heroine who embodies core values or who anoints other heroic figures |
| Strong beliefs about teaching and learning | Widely shared beliefs reflected in distinctive practices or rituals |
| Teachers as role models: students with positions of responsibility | Employees as situational heros or heroines who represent core values |
| Staff training on schoolwide basis | Rituals of acculturation and cultural renewal |
| Effective meetings to plan jointly and solve problems | Potent rituals to celebrate and transform core values |
| Orderly atmosphere without rigidity, guilt without oppression | Balance between innovation and tradition, autonomy and authority |
| Joint participation in technical decision making | Widespread participation in cultural rituals |

values, heros and heroines, rituals and ceremonies, stories, and the informal cultural network. Efforts on the local level, as well as efforts of policymakers, can be strengthened if approached symbolically as well as rationally.

## Revitalizing and reshaping the culture of schools

How strong are the cultures of public schools in general, and how do school cultures fit the demands of the educational environment? These two questions are at the heart of the effective schools issue. For a number of reasons, many public schools today have become pockets of mediocrity and places of despair and disinterest rather than of hope and enthusiasm. In most cases forces outside the schools have stimulated the erosion. Identities have been weakened by a number of social trends, and images tarnished by a constant stream of social criticism, culminating in the 1983 report of the National Commission on Excellence in Education, *A Nation at Risk*. Some speculation about the effects of external forces on schools is outlined in this section.

### The weakening of social myths

There was a time when attending school automatically was seen as a prime pathway to virtue and success in later life. It was a deeply ingrained and widely shared belief, akin to our faith and confidence in modern medicine.

For a variety of reasons, these beliefs have given way to doubts. In the absence of a collective myth, special-interest groups – teacher unions, taxpayer associations, state departments of education – have tried to remake schools in a multitude of molds. Difficulties with the schools' culture are tied strongly to the fragmentation of American society's culture.

### Change agents

During the 1960s, a new breed of educators challenged existing philosophies and practices and shaped new ones. Their aim was to make schools more responsive, flexible, and humane. They replaced old wisdom with new ideas and innovations in governance (parent involvement), curriculum (the new math) and instruction (individualized teaching) – thus reweaving the basic fabric of schools. As the form of education changed, the faith of those who were not caught up in the innovative spirit crumbled. The gains of innovators represented losses to persons with more traditional views. Traditionalists' questions found few answers, and in many communities teachers sought haven in their classrooms, and communities demanded a return to old practices. Many parents and residents ultimately withdrew support from schools.

### Research

In the 1960s, a coalition of university professors and policymakers espoused the belief that answers to the problems of American education could be solved by the production, development, and dissemination of scientific research findings. This activity focused attention away from the insights and intuition of local educators, replacing the authority of tradition and experience with the authority of researchers' and consultants' expertise.

### Accountability and evaluation

Coupled with the emphasis on research, a new breed of people entered the public schools to examine systematically the link between instructional activities and educational outcomes. Evaluation became a commonly accepted activity, producing disparate results – usually of failure, occasionally of success. These mixed reviews further eroded public faith in schools and practitioners' confidence in their own abilities.

### Hyperrationalization

Many of the innovations and reforms of the 1970s were designed to make school operations more rational – Program, Planning, and Budget Systems (PPBS). Management by Objectives (MBO), goal setting, and clarification of goals (Wise 1983). Evaluation was part of the package. Schools were also encouraged to adopt more specialized divisions of labor, to focus on the technical aspects of instruction and administration, and to engage in systematic planning and problem solving. These activities diverted time and attention from important tasks such as instruction or making sure the buses were on time. The role of tradition and intuition took a secondary place in decision making.

### Unionization and teacher militancy

Since 1960, professional associations of teachers (occasionally of administrators) have become highly vocal and have cultivated ties with or emulated the practices of labor and trade unions. Their militancy, coupled with collective bargaining procedures, has increased the tangible rewards and benefits of teaching. At the same time, many of the best teachers have identified with the unions rather than with their own districts, schools, colleagues, or clients. Overall, teachers (in the perceptions of the public) have sacrificed their traditional authority in favor of short-term financial rewards, and in many communities, contracts have replaced informal agreements and pacts with specific procedural rules. Stronger unions often unknowingly have weakened the culture of the schools.

### Policy and regulations

In the 1960s and 1970s, local schools were hit by an endless stream of state and federal regulations. Many of these were tied to additional funds. Some policies and regulations were voluntary, others mandated. In a variety of ways, courts, state education agencies, and intermediate service agencies sought to change local schools. Local values fell victim, real or imagined, to external policies and larger political forces.

### Turnover

Because of the structure and working conditions of teaching, a number of teachers have either taken other employment or retired early.

### Other events

Of course, other events impinged on public schools during these turbulent decades. Desegregation has often achieved racial balance at the expense of neighborhood schools. Courts have enforced student rights at a cost to local discipline standards. New approaches tailored for one group of students are outmoded and ineffective for another. The combined influence of all these forces is both powerful and complex. Generally, however, these developments have eroded the traditions, moral order, and historical practices of local schools. This, in turn, has undermined the faith and support of local communities.

While social forces weakened the culture of schools, recent shifts in the educational environment raised questions about how appropriate existing cultural patterns are for the challenges that lie ahead. In past times, schools have been seen as low-risk industries (Do they really make a difference?) where results are difficult to pinpoint (How would we ever know anyway?). The combination of low risk and ambiguous feedback encourages a process mentality in which form, details, and job security are desirable attributes. The main task is to manage details and to keep day-to-day activities standardized and running smoothly. The world of schools, in this respect, is similar to that of banks, insurance companies, and many government agencies. How things are done is important, not why. Caution, procedures, and seniority are emphasized, rather than risk taking, improvement, and performance. Although process values equip organizations to manage the day-to-day details and to keep the process running smoothly and punctually, they are not values that emphasize productivity or innovation.

In recent months, however, the educational environment has experienced some fundamental changes. Education is now receiving widespread attention as a central social and economic function. To fail in educating our youth will threaten the core of our society. Further, the recent commission report, *A Nation at Risk*, indicates that our educational system is failing. To fail with any child, in any school, is a significant loss. To fail with many pupils, in numerous schools, raises issues about whether our way of life will continue. Day-to-day teaching tasks or routine school-management decisions have thus become increasingly important to our society. The perceived level of risk associated with a poorly educated population has risen.

In addition, the accountability movement in schools has sharpened measures of performance and criteria for evaluating practices and procedures. Teachers and administrators often use achievement scores, for better or worse, as education's bottom line. Scores are seen as a prime indicator of instructional success. New programs launched at the beginning of one year are often judged – and either dropped or modified – before the year is over. Achievement tests may not measure a significant part of education. However, test results make life considerably different for both teachers and administrators by providing a concrete indicator of performance.

Powerful forces over the past decade have weakened the culture of schools, and changes in the educational environment have raised questions about whether existing cultural patterns are equal to new demands. By capitalizing on the momentum of the effective schools movement, what can policymakers or local practitioners now do to restrengthen and reshape the culture of schools?

The previous barrage of changes from outside and from nonbelievers within education did little to improve public education and much to damage the culture of schools. It is at this critical juncture that we can choose, through the effective schools movement, whether to make the same mistakes again. An understanding of the symbolic side of organizations permits us to use the opportunity to rebuild the integrity and identity of schools and at the same time to rekindle our social commitment and faith in public education.

Policymakers need to reexamine assumptions and the imagery that links policy directly with behavior in schools. They need to entertain the possibility that commission reports and research results serve as powerful ceremonies or symbols, creating a drama that can indirectly revitalize and reshape deep values at the national, state, and local levels (Deal 1985). Around these events, expectations are formed, and coalitions are forged. New energy is created, and efforts are refocused.

Policymakers also need to encourage local versions of national commissions. The dialogue of the national commissions was much more rich than the reports or recommendations summarizing the deliberations. Convening local commissions will make the issues and voices of educational improvement accessible to local residents and practitioners. The drama will influence indirectly how practitioners respond to local expectations and mandates.

Most important, policymakers need to consider how proposed reforms will affect the existing culture of schools. As noted, past efforts have often weakened schools as organizations rather than produced the desired improvement. Although policymakers always intend to improve local schools, effects of policy are often negligible and sometimes counterproductive. By their nature, policymakers respond to political pressures and timely ideas. The result is that they often ask schools to sacrifice long-standing traditions for untested innovations. And in the midst of trying new approaches, schools are monitored to ensure compliance. When they have yet to understand, accept, or believe that new practices are much better than past ones, they are asked to produce evidence of how well they are doing. Although it would be foolish to argue that policy should not encourage innovations and visions beyond those in particular settings, it is equally absurd to expect that state and federal policies can dictate local values, patterns, and practices. By combining rational, philosophical directives with local incentives and resources, it is possible to promote discussions that may result in slight changes in school practice. The key point is to delineate differences between accepted practices and new approaches. Adaptations will vary from school to school, but they will assure that practices and values continue to have meaning within local cultures.

The main message of this paper is that the pathway to educational effectiveness is inside each school. It exists in the traditions and symbols that make a school special to students, teachers, administrators, parents, and the community. Policymakers can lay the groundwork, but the people in each school will dictate through words and deeds what happens next. Here are some possible steps toward that end.

A beginning point is to explore and document a school's history. Each school has its story of origin, the people or circumstances that launched it, and those who presided over its course thereafter. Through evolutionary development – crises and resolutions, internal innovations and external pressures, plans and chance occurrences – the original concept was shaped and reshaped into an organic collection of traditions and distinctive ways. Throughout a school's history, a parade of students, teachers, principals, and parents casts sustaining memories. Great accomplishments meld with dramatic failures to form a potentially cherishable lore. This legacy needs to be codified and passed on.

As an example, the Urban Coalition (New York City Public Schools 1981, 1982, 1983) coached a group of New York City elementary schools in developing their histories, a shared sense of a school's past. Teachers, administrators, parents, and residents came together to reconstruct a school's experience, to weave private recollections and interpretations into a common story. The history-building exercise was part of a larger effort to help a school community bring its historical roots into a shared vision of the future. Subsequent improvements across all measures of performance – achievement, morale, truancy, and vandalism – were dramatic. Schools need to develop a core set of values shared by students, teachers, administrators, parents, residents, and others. However, shared values evolve from experience and have historical analogues. Values detached from history rarely have meaning. Reconstructing a school's history can help a school arrive at values that are attached to the past but equal to the challenges of the present or future. The articulation of values provides a common banner for the various constituencies of a school to rally behind.

A second strategy is to anoint and celebrate heros and heroines. Such figures are tangible examples of values and provide role models for others to emulate. In any school there are people – teachers, students, staff, administrators, and alumni – who embody and represent a school's core values: a teacher who turned down a corporate offer to stay in the classroom close to students: a student who learned to read despite major learning handicaps; a custodian who knows each student by name; a principal who successfully fought the district superintendent and initiated a new program for parents; or a former student who once struggled with math and caused trouble and now is a well-recognized physicist. Potential heros and heroines exist in any school. The problem is that they are rarely anointed or regularly celebrated.

In a recent interview, a veteran teacher blandly described her participation in a new district evaluation program. She was going through the motions, but her heart was obviously not in the task. Suddenly, she began to talk about her teaching, the students, and how exciting it was to see them grow. She waxed eloquently and enthusiastically for nearly 20 minutes. When asked why she had not shared these thoughts before, she remarked to me, 'They told me you were from Harvard and I thought you wouldn't care. Why should you? Nobody here cares anymore.' A heroine, unappreciated, unanointed, and unrecognized.

In a recent meeting of Peabody College at Vanderbilt's Roundtable (those who donate sizable sums to the college), members were asked to bring along their most memorable teachers. The teachers were introduced with stories that communicated their specialness. Each received a crystal apple as a symbol of the accomplishment. One teacher remarked at the end: 'This was so wonderful. But I wish someone in my school would recognize me in the same style.'

Heros and heroines need to be recognized – for themselves and for the values they represent. Otherwise, anti-heros (teachers who are bitter, resentful, or retired on the job: students who are nonproductive or destructive) will fill the void.

A possibility is to review a schools' rituals. The art of teaching is a sacred ritual, important for what it dramatizes and expresses as well as for what is accomplished. In a classroom, surrounded by well-known artifacts such as globes and blackboards, teachers and students come together in an age-old exchange. Partly the teacher is there to transmit knowledge, but mostly the teacher is there to represent and inculcate basic values, to provide a guidepost along the pathway of growing up. A teacher's zeal, enthusiasm, and love for learning and life are important signals. Principals provide similar signals and models in the way they administer the school. Living and meaningful rituals convey cultural values and beliefs. Rituals that have become routine dampen the human spirit. A thoughtful inventory of what classroom and management rituals say to students and others can open some interesting avenues of school improvement.

A fourth strategy for building school culture is through ceremony. Pep rallies, assemblies, sports contests, and graduation have long been recognized as forces that promote school spirit. Individuals experience cultural values through ceremonies. However, the ceremonial life of a school is not restricted to assemblies and pep rallies. It includes retirement parties, parents' night, PTA meetings, and other episodic events where people gather to negotiate and celebrate the meaning of a school. In some schools, symbolic events are mandatory exercises, in others sacred occasions. The former add nothing of value to a culture; the latter are a primary source of cultural values and renewal.

Recently, a group of interested parents in Massachusetts decided to host a celebration in honor of teachers in Concord High School. They decorated the cafeteria and put silver candle holders on tables covered with white linen. Each teacher received a corsage on arrival bearing the terms: guru, mentor, guide, and teacher. Parents and teachers sang songs together around a piano bar, drinking wine and eating cheese. Dinner was potluck; each parent brought a dish. After dinner, speeches and choral music from students completed the evening. A representative of the National Association of Independent Schools (himself a parent) remarked at the conclusion: 'People wonder what private schools have that public schools often lack – this is it!' An important ceremony with deep and powerful messages. An inexpensive way of honoring teachers that could be expanded to other aspects of life in school.

A fifth route available to teachers or administrators who want to revitalize a culture is to tell good stories. Stories carry values. Yet the rhetoric of modern education is often dull and lifeless. Systematic information is a preferred mode of communication. Words such as impact, implementation, interaction, and programmatic evaluation dominate the language – a statement of values in itself. These terms need to be supplemented or replaced by vivid stories of memorable events and accomplishments. Each day in schools, there are countless moving and dramatic events and stories. Properly told, the stories inspire those inside and convey to outsiders what school is really about. Consider three stories recently told to me.

In a well-known university, a teacher was promoted to full professor with tenure, based primarily on his record of scholarly accomplishments. A year later, the president learned the vita was, in part, a fabrication. She summoned the professor to a meeting of representative groups to announce how she had decided to handle the situation. 'You may keep your rank and tenure,' she told the professor, 'but for three years you can't talk to a student. That is the most severe penalty I can levy on a teacher.'

An elementary teacher faced a decision this summer. He had been offered a highly paid position in a well-known corporation. Although the position was everything he had wanted, he kept postponing the decision. In late August, he was shopping in a local market. A former student ran into him. 'Oh, Mr Jones. I just heard that my sister Rhonda will be in your class this year. You'll be her favorite teacher just as you were mine won't you?' The teacher paused for a moment to reflect on his important decision then said, 'Yes, I will, Julie. You bet I will.'

A group of teachers in the Brookline schools recently took exception to, 'I'm just a teacher' – a phrase teachers too frequently use in response to the question: What do you do for a living? They coined a new phrase: 'I'm just a great teacher!'

Stories like these remind us all of what education is really about. Similar stories need to be told to broadcast and reinforce the values of general education as well as the values of a particular school.

Finally, the cultural network of a school needs to be strengthened rather than resisted, officially rewarded rather than silently despised. People often wonder why the school secretary, custodian, or elderly teacher seem to have so much power. Their power usually derives from their unofficial role as priestess, gossip, or storyteller. Schools need to identify these people, to integrate them into the mainstream of activity, and to reward them for the important positive contributions they make. A principal who fights the informal network usually loses; one who works with the cultural cast of characters can have a powerful effect on a school.

Priests or priestesses need to attend important functions. They need to be summoned when something goes wrong or to be in attendance to bless something that has gone well. Advice from the primary keeper of the culture needs to be sought whenever a key ritual or ceremony is planned. The priest or priestess should be a part of the official orientation of newcomers. Otherwise the powerful figure will conduct an unofficial rite to counteract the messages received in the formal socialization program.

Storytellers need to be encouraged. They should be prominent features at parties or ceremonies, and they should be given opportunities to share stories with parents and the community as well as with insiders. Storytellers always need material and have a natural ear for a good story. Woven into the form of a story, policies, values, decisions, and successes will be greatly enjoyed and widely circulated.

Gossips also need to be encouraged. They serve as an important communication link between individuals within a school: community gossips carry themes to parents and residents outside. Meetings and memos are notoriously ineffective for communicating information. That is one reason why gossips are so important. To perform their unofficial job effectively, they need good material and people's attention. To ignore the gossip is to remove oneself from the primary communications network.

Cultural networks are often devalued and demeaned for their negative influence on a school. Their negativity often results from mistreatment or neglect rather than from malice. Actively used and positively rewarded, the informal network can make a substantial contribution to school effectiveness.

These few ideas are a beginning. They show how a school can begin to build or reshape its culture. The strategies are primarily symbolic. They are powerful, and they can work to revitalize a school.

The effective schools movement offers an opportunity for all schools to improve. The hoopla in policy circles creates favorable external encouragement. By looking backward on its history and inward on its symbols and rites and by using cultural players, a school can revitalize or transform itself through the combined efforts of its people (Ruane 1984). The effective schools movement thus sets the stage for schools to broadcast their virtues, celebrate their quirks, and transform mediocrity into positive educational values and performance. In the midst of rhetoric and reform, we need to remember that above all else, schools are places where teaching – one of the most sacred of all human activities – is performed.

### References

Artley, A. (1981). Individual differences and reading instruction. *Elementary School Journal* 82:143–51.
Athos, T., and Pascale, R. (1978). *The art of Japanese management*. New York: Simon & Schuster.
Baldridge, J., and Deal, T. (1975). *Managing change in educational organizations: Sociological theories, strategies and case studies*. Berkeley, CA: McCutchan.
Baldridge, J., and Deal, T. (1983). *The dynamics of organizational change in education*. Berkeley, CA: McCutchan.

Bennis, W. (1975). Who sank the yellow submarine? In J. Baldridge and T. Deal (eds), *Managing change in educational organizations*. Berkeley, CA: McCutchan.

Blanchard, K., and Johnson, S. (1982). *The one minute manager*. New York: Berkeley Books.

Blum, A. (1961). Collective bargaining: Ritual or reality? *Harvard Business Review* 39(6):63–9.

Charters, W., Jr., and Jones, J. (1975). On neglect of the independent variable in program evaluation. In J. Baldridge and T. Deal (eds), *Managing change in educational organizations*. Berkeley, CA: McCutchan.

Clark, B. (1983). The organizational saga in higher education. In J. Baldridge and T. Deal (eds), *The dynamics of organizational change in education*. Berkeley, CA: McCutchan.

Cohen, E., Deal, T., Meyer, J., and Scott, W. (1979). Technology and teaming in the elementary school. *Sociology of Education* 52:20–33.

Cohen, M. (1985). Introduction to special issue on effective schools. *Elementary School Journal* 85(3):277–9.

Coleman, J. S., *et al.* (1966). *Equality of educational opportunity*. Washington, DC: Government Printing Office.

Darling-Hammond, L., and Wise, A. (1985). Beyond standardization: State standards and school improvement. *Elementary School Journal* 85(3):315–36.

Deal, T. (1975, Spring). An organizational explanation of alternative school failures. *Educational Researcher* 4(4):10–16.

Deal, T. (1982). Alternative schools: Struggle for identity. *Changing Schools* 10(2):8–9.

Deal, T. (1985, February). National commission reports: Blueprints for remodeling or ceremonies for revitalizing public schools. *Journal of Education and Urban Society* 17(2): in press.

Deal, T., Gunnar, H., and Wiske, S. (1977). *Linking knowledge to schools: The process of change in six sites*. Andover, MA: The Network.

Deal, T., and Kennedy, A. (1982). *Corporate cultures*. Reading, MA: Addison-Wesley.

Deal, T., and Kennedy, A. (1983). Culture and school performance. *Educational Leadership* 40(5): 14–15.

Deal, T., Meyer, J., and Scott, W. (1983). Organizational influences on educational innovation. In J. Baldridge and T. Deal (eds), *The dynamics of organizational change in education*. Berkeley, CA: McCutchan.

Edelman, M. (1977). *The symbolic use of politics* (5th edn). Urbana: University of Illinois Press.

Farrar, E., Neufeld, B., and Miles, M. (1983). *Review of effective schools programs. III: Effective schools programs in high schools: Implications for policy, practice, and research*. Cambridge, MA: Huron Institute.

Fenstermacher, G., and Berliner, D. (1985). Determining the value of staff development. *Elementary School Journal* 85(3):281–314.

Floden, R. E., and Weiner, S. S. (1978). Rationality to ritual: Multiple roles of evaluation in governmental processes. *Policy Sciences* 9(1), 9–18.

Fullan, M. (1985). Change processes and strategies at the local level. *Elementary School Journal* 85(3):391–421.

Gallup, G. (1984). The sixteenth annual Gallup Poll of the public's attitudes toward the public schools. *Phi Delta Kappan* 66(1):24.

Gordon, W. (1957). *The social system of the high school*. New York: Free Press.

Kirst, M. (1983). The rise and fall of PPBS in California. In J. Baldridge and T. Deal (eds), *The dynamics of organizational change in education*. Berkeley, CA: McCutchan.

Kotter, J. P. (1982). *The general managers*. New York: Free Press.

Lipsky, M. (1980). *Street-level bureaucrats*. New York: Russell Sage.

Manasse, A. L. (1985). Improving conditions for principal effectiveness: Policy implications of research. *Elementary School Journal* 85(3):439–63.

McDill, E., and Rigsby, L. (1973). *Structure and process in secondary schools*. Baltimore: Johns Hopkins University Press.

McDonnell, L. (1985). Implementing low-cost school improvement strategies. *Elementary School Journal* 85(3):423–38.

Meyer, J., and Rowan, B. (1977). Institutional organizations – formal structure as myth and ceremony. *American Journal of Sociology* 83:440–63.

Meyer, J., and Rowan, B. (1983). The structure of educational organizations. In J. Baldridge and T. Deal (eds), *Dynamics of organizational change in education*. Berkeley, CA: McCutchan.

Moore, S. F., and Meyerhoff, B. (1977). *Secular ritual*. Assen/Amsterdam: Van Gorcun.

Murphy, J. T. (1971). Title I of ESEA: The politics of implementing federal education reform. *Harvard Educational Review* 41:35–63.

National Commission on Excellence in Education. (1983). *A nation at risk*. Washington, DC: Government Printing Office.

New York City Public Schools, Office of Education Evaluation. (1981, 1982, 1983). [Project Evaluation Documents]. Unpublished data.

Ouchi, W. (1981). *Theory Z*. Reading, MA: Addison-Wesley.

Packard, J. (1975). Changing to a multiunit school. In J. Baldridge and T. Deal (eds), *Managing change in educational organizations*. Berkeley, CA: McCutchan.

Peters, T., & Waterman, R. (1982). *In search of excellence*. New York: Harper & Row.

Purkey, S., and Smith, M. (1985). School reform: The district policy implications of the effective schools literature. *Elementary School Journal* 85(3):353–89.

Ruane, P. (1984). Moving through and beyond transition: Barriers and bridges to a better quality of organizational life. Unpublished doctoral dissertation, Harvard University, Cambridge, MA.

Sapolsky, H. (1972). *The Polaris system development*. Cambridge, MA: Harvard University Press.

Sarason, S. (1971). *The culture of the school and the problems of change*. Boston: Allyn & Bacon.

Swidler, A. (1979). *Organization without authority*. Cambridge, MA: Harvard University Press.

Waller, W. (1932). *The sociology of teaching*. New York: Wiley.

Weick, K. (1976). Educational organizations as loosely coupled systems. *Administrative Science Quarterly* 21:1–19.

Weiss, C. (1981). Measuring the use of evaluation. In J. Ciarlo (ed.), *Utilizing evaluation: Concepts and measurement techniques*. Beverly Hills, CA: Sage.

Wise, A. (1983). Why educational policies often fail: The hyperrationalization hypothesis. In J. Baldridge and T. Deal (eds), *The dynamics of organizational change in education*. Berkeley, CA: McCutchan.

Wolcott, H. F. (1973). *The man in the principal's office: An ethnography*. New York: Holt, Rinehart & Winston.

# 13
# Organizational culture

## William G. Ouchi and Alan L. Wilkins

*Abstract*

The contemporary study of organizational culture reflects mainline concerns of the organizational sociologist. Though anthropology and cognitive psychology have made significant contributions to this new field, the study of organizational culture may be seen as a return to some of the most basic concerns about the nature of organizations and the appropriate methods for analysing them. We review current work on theory, empirical studies, and contributions – both theoretical and empirical – to the understanding of planned change of organizations. The contemporary study of organizational culture reflects several hotly contested concerns, among which are the following: Can culture be intentionally managed? Must culture be studied using the tools of the phenomenologist or the ethnographer, or does the use of multivariate statistics also have a place? Which social science paradigm is most appropriate for understanding organizational culture: phenomenology, symbolic interaction, semiotics, structural-functional anthropology, cognitive psychology?

## Introduction: the contemporary study of organizational culture

During 1983 three major collections of articles on organizational culture appeared. Since 1979 no fewer than seven review articles have been published on aspects of this topic, and the outpouring of work shows no signs of abatement. Few readers would disagree that the study of organizational culture has become one of the major domains of organizational research, and some might even argue that it has become the single most active arena, eclipsing studies of formal structure, of organization-environment research, and of bureaucracy.

What is perhaps most unusual about this development is that several books and articles by academics have been widely read by nonacademics, and a few have appeared on best-seller lists. At the same time, studies of organizational culture often compare western organizations to Japanese or other national organizations, thus bringing an unusual comparative international flavor to organizational research.

Indeed, some might observe that the rise of research on organizational culture came about because Japanese firms were during the late 1970s and the early 1980s widely considered to have superior operating characteristics, but the forms of organizational research dominant then emphasized formal structure and so failed to uncover any difference between Japanese and western firms. As a consequence, scholars began to examine the possibility that the different national cultures might have penetrated modern corporate forms, thus creating differences in organizational culture between, say, Nissan and General Motors. Several early studies gave credence to this approach, which led next to the possibility that even within a single national culture there might be local differences in the culture of firms, e.g. between Hewlett-Packard and ITT.

A casual inspection of the contemporary literature suggests that most of those who study organizational culture trace their intellectual roots to a few key anthropologists. Both the point of view and the method of the anthropologist might seem to have been heavily borrowed by the student of organization. It is undeniable that anthropological style and method have been a great, perhaps the single greatest, influence on these contemporary studies, but this new work owes a very major debt to the sociology of organizations as well.

We offer the view that the contemporary study of organizational culture may be best understood as a continuation of the main line of organizational sociology, which has always focused on the normative bases and the shared understandings that, through subtle and complex expression, regulate social life in organizations. Many younger scholars, trained to study those problems most easily subjected to multivariate statistical analysis, may have the impression that the study of organizational culture through participant observation is an aberration or a departure from the tradition of organizational sociology. Such a view does not withstand historical review.

As we trace the development of organizational sociology since Max Weber, we find a constant tension between those who prefer to study what is explicit about organizations and those who prefer what is implicit; a tension between those who emphasize the capacity of organizations to create order and rationality versus those who are struck by the sometimes chaotic and nonrational features of organizational life. The study of organizational culture grows out of that tension and represents, we believe, but the most recent stage of the intellectual cycle.

The preparation for writing a review article mostly involves reading a large number of books and articles, many of them not yet published. In many domains of scholarship that can be a chore. To read on organizational culture is more nearly a pleasure, in large part because the contemporary study of organizational culture relies upon bringing to life the richness and the vitality of people living and working together. The equations and statistics are few, the attempts to capture an ineffable essence are many. These studies recall the excitement, the passion, and the drama of social life, which were and continue to be central to the reason for the study of organizations.

## The intellectual foundations of organizational culture

*Heterogenous intellectual roots: a citation analysis*

The contemporary study of organizational culture appears to amalgamate several points of view, rather than to constitute one branch of a single disciplinary family of scholarship. There is no single dominant point of view or method but rather a rich mixture of ideas and of approaches. We attempt to characterize the most important of these. Our review is limited to the study of formal economic organizations, primarily business firms.

During 1983, three collections of articles on organizational culture appeared: an anthology on *Organizational Symbolism* (Pondy *et al.* 1983) and special issues of *Administrative Science Quarterly* (Vol. 28, No. 3) and of *Organizational Dynamics* (Vol. 12, No. 2). In all, these comprise thirty-two articles. A citation analysis reveals something of the diverse intellectual roots of this new field. Those sources cited six or more times are listed in Note 1.

These works, which provide the foundations of the field, are as heterogeneous as are most other aspects of the study of organizational culture. Of the seven most frequently cited works,[1] one was written by an anthropologist, three were authored or coauthored by sociologists, and three by management scholars (categorized by place of employment, rather than by training).

In all, a total of 103 works are cited in the thirty-two articles. Eleven authors are cited for three or four separate works each. Of these eleven, ten hold appointments in graduate schools of management.

*The influence of sociology on studies of organizational culture*

Many students of organizational culture would assert that their primary intellectual debt is to the anthropologist rather than to the sociologist. Most would also assert a debt to the social psychologist. Although this review will focus on the debt of organizational culture studies to sociology, we will begin with a brief review of the impact of anthropological tradition on this field, and end the section with the briefest of acknowledgments to social psychology as a coda.

### The influence of anthropology on organizational culture

Most of the currently 'popular' work on organizational culture (Ouchi 1981; Pascale and Athos 1981; Deal and Kennedy 1982; Peters and Waterman 1982) as well as other work written for management audiences and management scholars (Dandridge *et al.* 1980; Dyer 1982, 1984; Schein 1983a, 1983b; Martin and Siehl 1983; Wilkins 1983a, 1983b; and Wilkins and Ouchi 1983) draws upon the spirit if not the details of the functionalist tradition in anthropology. This influence can be further divided between two rather distinct forms of contemporary work.

Radcliffe-Brown (1952) and Malinowski (1961) represent a school of thought in anthropology that encourages the scholar to consider a group or society as a whole and to see how its practices, beliefs, and other cultural elements function to maintain social structure. Although organizational scholars rarely cite these sources, their work describes such cultural elements as employment practices, corporate ceremonies, and company legends in structural-functional terms. Malinowski and Radcliffe-Brown might be appalled by the explicitly promanagement and change-oriented bias of many contemporary scholars, but the impact of their organic, whole view of the structure and functioning of social systems on the contemporary study of organizational culture is undeniable.

Benedict (1934) and Mead (e.g. 1949) also represent an interest in groups or societies as a whole but tend to describe society as a large complex personality. This 'configurationist' position suggests that a culture 'selects' from a virtually infinite array of behavioral possibilities a limited set that may be interpreted as a particular configuration of related patterns. For example, Benedict (1934) described the Apollonian discomfort with excess and orgy and the Dionysian encouragement of psychic and emotional excess (see Sanday 1979) as opposing patterns found in many cultures. Some contemporary work on culture describes patterns of assumptions within organizations (Dyer 1982) in this tradition.

A second school of thought in anthropology is perhaps best represented by Clifford Geertz (1973), the most frequently cited of any scholar in the foregoing citation analysis. Along with other contemporary anthropologists such as Goodenough and Lévi-Strauss, Geertz emphasized the importance of discovering the 'native's point of view.' This approach has been called 'semiotic' for its focus on language and symbols as the principal tools for apprehending the native's perspective.

Geertz (1973:24) suggests that 'the whole point of a semiotic approach to culture is to aid us in gaining access to the conceptual world in which our subjects live so that we can, in some extended sense of the term, converse with them.' Accomplishing this purpose, according to Geertz, requires that the anthropologist be immersed in the complex clusterings of symbols people use to confer meaning upon their world. Anthropology is thus not a matter of precise method but requires instead that the anthropologist engage in an intellectual effort that is 'an elaborate venture in, to borrow a notion from Gilbert Ryle, "thick description"' (pp. 5–6).

By contrast, Goodenough (1971) and others have developed an approach labeled 'ethnoscience,' 'componential analysis,' or 'cognitive anthropology.' While their aim is similar to that expressed by Geertz, they differ considerably in method. Culture for ethnoscientists is the system of standards or rules for perceiving, believing, and acting that one needs to know in order to operate in a manner acceptable to the members of the culture. Anthropologists in this tradition have been strongly influenced by linguists (e.g. Chomsky 1972). They have in mind that just as a learned, and usually implicit, grammar helps people generate acceptable sentences, so cultural rules and categories and principles help people to generate acceptable behavior. Cultural description, according to Goodenough and others in this tradition, requires the discovery and writing out of systematic rules or algorithms that members of the culture implicitly use to generate acceptable behavior.

While most scholars currently working in the area of organizational culture refer to Geertz to suggest the need for 'thick description,' it appears that those who engage in empirical work instead use some variant of the methods suggested by Goodenough. Perhaps this is because the methods suggested by Geertz require a great deal of artistic ability and intuition while Goodenough's methods are more systematic and thus easier to learn. Sanday (1979) notes a similar tendency among practicing anthropologists to quote and admire Geertz but to follow the methods of Goodenough. Contemporary organizational scholars who have been influenced by the semiotic school include Pondy (1978), Smircich (1983), Gregory (1983), Barley (1983a), Evered (1983), Van Maanen (1979), and Frost and Morgan (1983).

The elements that comprise a culture to an anthropologist, such as language, ritual, and social structure, develop over decades or centuries. These cultural elements represent specific solutions to what often are universal problems or needs of social life and of survival, and in this sense culture is to the anthropologist both a dependent variable (shaped by a unique time and place) and an independent variable (shaping the beliefs and behavior of individuals). As we shall see, the contemporary student of organizational culture often takes the organization not as a natural solution to deep and universal forces but rather as a rational instrument designed by top management to shape the behavior of employees in purposive ways (Lammers 1981). The study of organizational culture typically takes culture as the independent variable, rarely attending to the environmental forces that have shaped the culture of, say, IBM or Sony and instead concentrating on a description of those critical elements of the firm's culture and on the patterns of employee behavior that they guide. Despite these differences, the study of organizational culture owes a great debt for point of view and method to anthropologists.

## The influence of organizational sociology on organizational culture

The influence of sociology on the study of organizational culture has been broad and direct. As a consequence, it is difficult to characterize a few main streams of effect. The several streams of work that have been most influential – the study of myth and ritual, symbolic interaction, ethnomethodology, and the study of organizations as institutions – are so interrelated that we have chosen to recount their effects in the form of an interpretive history rather than as separate schools of thought.

This historical approach leads us to conclude that the contemporary study of organizational culture is perhaps best understood as only the latest turn in the struggle between explicit and rational views of organization on the one hand and implicit, nonrational views on the other. This tension has long been a central feature in the sociology of organizations, and we can expect that the approach of organizational culture will have its day and then recede in importance, to rise yet again in modified form.

### *The explicit versus the implicit features of organization*

Perhaps the most pervasive effect has been Durkheim's emphasis on the importance of myth and ritual as the counterpoint to the study of social structure. Durkheim asserts that concrete symbols, such as myths, are necessary for solidarity because 'the clan is too complex a reality to be represented clearly in all its complex unity' (1961:220, from French). This suggestion that simple, symbolic representations of a complex social reality are fundamental to collective life has had a pervasive effect on the study of organizational culture. Durkheim suggested that this symbolic structure can be apprehended through the study of those myths and rituals that lie on the surface of social life and that provide clues to the deeper strains and forces. This method has also become a central feature of the study of organizational culture. Finally, Durkheim (1893), like Weber (1968) and Toennies (1957), drew a distinction between the explicit and the implicit features of social life and regarded the study of both as essential. This dual interest in the objective and the subjective features of organizational life has consistently been a central theme in the sociology of organizations and has become central to the study of organizational culture.

A later school of sociology came to emphasize not only that the objective and the subjective features of social life are separable, but that the two sides may be disconnected from one another more often than was supposed, and even that commonly understood symbols may be manipulated for the purpose of deceiving a social partner. Thus Goffman (1959) found more meaning in what is implicit than in what is explicit in the presentation of self, and Garfinkel (1967) asserted that juries engage in sense-making of their decisions only after the fact and that this constitutes a form of social deception. Berger and Luckman (1966) offered a legitimating sociology of knowledge to which many students of organizational culture resort in emphasizing ethnographic method in a field that has in recent years been dominated by multivariate statistics.

This line of work was also characterized by a critical anti-establishment tone that sought to expose the taken-for-granted social reality that, it was argued, had been largely fostered by the ruling classes for their own benefit (Gouldner 1970). A remnant of that critical strain remains in the contemporary study of organizational culture, but it has found an inhospitable environment in schools of management.

*Rational versus nonrational features of organization*

A brief historical review suggests that the current managerial view of organizational culture is only the latest in a series of pretenders vying for control of how organizations shall be understood. During the 1950s and the 1960s, organizational sociologists sought to explore the informal relations that regulate organizational life. However, they never strayed very far from ideas of bureaucratic administration. They sought to understand how informal relationships and beliefs modified the demands of the formal system or provided a means to cope with its pressures. Furthermore, their search was strongly motivated by an underlying belief that the fundamental contribution of large-scale economic organizations is to bring 'rationality' to an otherwise overwhelmingly complex reality. This predisposition can be attributed to the emphasis by Weber (1968:223) on the rational properties of bureaucracy:

> Experience tends universally to show that the purely bureaucratic type of administration . . . is, from a purely technical point of view, capable of attaining the highest degree of efficiency and is in this sense formally the most rational known means of exercising authority over human beings. It is superior to any other form in precision, in stability, in the stringency of its discipline, and in its reliability. . . . The choice is only between bureaucracy and dilettantism in the field of administration.

While the ethnomethodologists and symbolic interactionists of the 1950s and 1960s sought to emphasize the nonrational aspects of organizational life, the mainstream organizational sociologists tried instead to discover the rational basis of organizational life (thus choosing to ignore Weber's emphasis on the importance of charismatic leadership), and the next twenty years of scholarship reflected this tension. We shall describe that contest in some detail because it contains the central forces that today motivate the various approaches to the study of organizational culture.

In 1937 Gulick and Urwick published their *Papers on the Science of Administration* and established the school of 'Administrative Rationality.' Among the collected papers in that 1937 volume was one by Graicunas which pointed out that as the size of a small group increases, the number of possible interactions grows so rapidly that no manager could oversee more than five or six workers effectively. Thus was born the study of formal organizational structure and the attempt to discover the bases of organizational rationality.

In 1938 Chester Barnard published *The Functions of the Executive*. He emphasized the overwhelming ambiguity of organizational life and suggested that it is the role of the executive to provide the overarching point of view that brings meaning and order to corporate life. In 1939 Roethlisberger and Dickson published the Hawthorne Studies, in which they described the informal norms of workers that successfully frustrated the productivity goals of the management. Each of these themes – organizational rationality, formal structure, leadership under ambiguity, and informal organization versus formal purpose – was subsequently developed. For example, though he wrote of leadership in a slum, Whyte (1943) described how informal leadership always formed within a social group and influenced group behavior. However, the predisposition that dominated the field was to find that large, complex organizations can be made orderly, responsive to top management, and 'rational' in serving the purposes of their owners. The problem was that, as anyone could see, no large organization was in fact so orderly. How could we believe that organizations can be rational?

The legitimation for combining a belief in organizational rationality with the empirical observation of organizational nonrationality was offered by Herbert Simon in 1945. Simon argued that human behavior that appears contrary to organizational goals is in fact quite rational if one takes into account the imperfect and limited information-processing ability of human beings, who cannot understand all of the far-flung organizational consequences of their current actions. With this idea of 'bounded rationality,' Simon provided the basis for the coupling of the rational and the nonrational views of organizations. With that, the study of organizations exploded. It grew in part because large public and commercial organizations proliferated rapidly in the west during the twentieth century, and it grew because Simon had supplied the last necessary piece of a paradigm within which most features of organizational life could be understood.

For the next twenty years (roughly 1945–65), the main line of research juxtaposed the objective against the subjective, the formal purpose against the informal purpose, the explicit against the implicit in organizational life. The principal method of inquiry was the case study written from the point of view of the social scientist rather than of the native and interpreted to demonstrate why apparently irrational behavior was, in fact, rational or in concert with the goals of the owners and managers of the organization under the circumstances. The method was crystallized by Homans (1950), who interpreted the Hawthorne Studies to great effect. It was employed by Selznick (1949), Trist and Bamforth (1951), by Gouldner (1954), Blau (1955), Lipset, Trow and Coleman (1956), and by Crozier (1964). It must be said that these studies remain among the most informative, penetrating, and lively of all organizational literature.

The tension between rational and nonrational views of organization continued, but the rational view steadily gained the upper hand. Observing that executives, managers, technicians, and workers seem not to share a common purpose, Parsons (1956) offered a mainline theoretical rationale to explain why this was perfectly consistent with prevailing norms of rationality. Udy (1962), on the other hand, maintained that there must always be a tension between the rational goals of economic organizations and the nonrational goals of their social milieu and that this prevents organizations from ever attaining full rationality. Blau and Scott (1962) took perhaps the most trenchant position of all and produced a book that defined the field for more than a decade; it established the interpretation of a formal organization as a purposive aggregation of individuals who exert common effort towards a shared and explicitly recognized goal. In hindsight, it appears that the dominance of this view may have been but one expression of the major shift then taking place in the culture of US social science towards explicit, quantitative, computer-aided analysis.

### The period of comparative multivariate analysis

In 1944 the first computer, Mark I, was developed, and in 1946 the first commercial prototype, ENIAC, was introduced. By the late 1960s, 20,000 computers were in use worldwide (Ouchi 1984). This development had a great impact on the metaphor with which social scientists thought about organizations. For the first time, organizations were construed as information-processing systems rather than as status systems or systems of domination or of ritual.

Computers also had a great impact on the methodology of organizational research. In 1955 Terrien and Mills followed up the logical implications of Graicunas's (1937) article on the span of control. They found that the administrative ratio in school districts was positively related to number of employees and thus conjectured that this relationship would severely limit the maximum feasible size of such organizations. Anderson and Warkov (1961) found that organizational complexity mediates this size–administrative ratio relationship, and at that point a 'true science' of organization was off and running. For the first time, students of organization not only could adopt norms of rationality, they could subject their hypothesis to the sort of protorational test using the computer that had previously been accessible only to physical scientists. Subsequent studies by Hage and Aiken (1967), by Hall *et al.* (1967), Blau (1968), Blau and Schoenherr (1971), and a host of other organizational sociologists explored every subtlety of the paradigm. Particularly notable were the studies by the Aston Group in England: Pugh *et al.* (1969), Hinings and Lee (1971), and a steady stream of similar work, most of which involved the application of factor analysis to the study of organization. All of this research on the structure of formal organizations was done in the name of Max Weber, all of it represented attempts to represent operationally the elements of bureaucratic administration that Weber had described, but in the end it was an effort dominated by a methodology and by a computer rather than by a point of view.

The September 1974 issue of *Administrative Science Quarterly* included a letter to the editor from Cornelius Lammers, a Dutch sociologist playing the role of friendly uncle. Lammers visited eighteen US campuses, talked to faculties of sixteen sociology department and of twelve schools of management, and tabulated the responses of twenty leading scholars (including Aiken, Aldrich, Blau, Evan, Laumann, Selznick) to questions concerning the state of their field. The research trend mentioned most often as being strong at the time was 'comparative studies of organizational structure.' The trend most often evaluated as being 'bad' was 'comparative studies of organizational structure' (Lammers 1974:423). What had seemed a few years earlier to be the continuation of the mainstream of organizational sociology turned out instead to be an epiphenomenon, driven as much by the new computer technology as by any underlying conceptual force.

While this development in organizational sociology was dominating the attention of many sociologists, the principal heirs of Herbert Simon's (1945) work were following a path that had a similar history but a quite different ending. March and Simon (1958) attempted to place the study of organization within an explicitly rational metaphor, adopting a propositional form modeled on the hierarchy of operating systems and application systems of computer software. They developed the view that organizations economize on the bounded rationality of human beings, thus producing what, in the end, is a system in which goals and behavior are connected in a manner that is quite rational. Cyert and March (1963) took the computer metaphor to its logical if austere conclusion, while Thompson (1967) attempted a formal theory of organizational rationality. Although this approach seemed for a while to have the kind of promise that had been hoped for in the comparative study of organizational structure, it too subsided.

The period of the mid-1950s through the 1960s was marked not only by the dominance of the rational point of view in the study of organizations but also by a cleavage in method that clearly set apart organizational ethnographers from the multivariate statisticians of the Terrien and Mills (1955) school and from the applied mathematicians of the Simon (1945) school. The academic ethos of the time quite clearly granted the nod to those who were more quantitatively oriented, but the qualitative social scientists did not entirely disappear. In organizational sociology, the main line that had been represented in an earlier period by Selznick (1949) was carried forward in studies of construction firms by Stinchcombe (1959), of utopian communities by Kanter (1968), of 'skid row' communities by Spradley (1970), and of colleges by Clark (1970). All of these chose as their subject something other than large public or private organizations. They were substantively as well as paradigmatically on the fringes of organizational sociology, but they preserved a link to Durkheim's (1961) tradition while the Weberian (1968) point of view temporarily took center stage. This small but hardy family of scholarship was later to become a focal point for the development of organizational culture studies.

Also during this period, the method of ethnography and the point of view of symbolic interaction developed within the sociology of occupations. The work of Becker and Carper (1956), of Gouldner (1957), of Roy (1960), Janowitz (1960), and of Gertzl (1961) had barely penetrated the organizational sociology of the period, but it too was to become a central feature of the later study of organizational culture. Consider next how this intellectual setting gave rise to the contemporary study of organizational culture.

### Anomaly leads to evolution

Every scholar in the field may legitimately point to a book or article that he or she favors as the beginning of the study of organizational culture as we now see it. The beginnings, however, came not in the putting forward of a new scheme but rather in the form of several stirrings, none of which seemed at the time to be consequential for organizational sociology.

It was the resistance of school systems to bureaucratic interpretation that provided the major anomaly and brought an end to the study of formal organizational structure. Cohen, March and Olsen (1972) found that even the idea of bounded rationality failed to capture the weakly rational properties of school systems; these authors describe them instead as 'organized anarchies'. Dornbusch and Scott (1975) had a similar befuddling experience in applying the bureaucratic study to school districts and delayed the publication of their book for several years while they attempted to make sense out of the experience. Weick (1976) could describe them best as 'loosely coupled systems', and Meyer and Rowan (1977) saw in their formal structure nothing more than myth and ceremony, detached from the 'real' activities of teachers and of students. Becker and Gordon (1966) attempted to apply the paradigm, by then well developed, of comparative organizational structure to the analysis of hospitals but found that it did not effectively capture their essence.

Another significant anomaly at this time occurred as organizational sociologists attempted to apply the size–complexity–administrative ratio model to business organizations in Japan. Abegglen (1958), Dore (1973), McMillan *et al.* (1973), Tracy and Azumi (1976), Marsh and Mannari (1976), and Cole (1979) found that some stable results replicated in Japan, while others did not. Lincoln *et al.* (1978), in a study of Japanese-owned businesses in the United States employing expatriate Japanese and Japanese-Americans, found little difference in structure related to the ratio of Japanese ethnics to whites, but the authors were quite clearly frustrated at their inability to capture statistically what they experienced as a major organizational difference: 'We cannot describe adequately how different is the atmosphere in an organization where 50 to 80% of the personnel have Japanese origins, where Japanese is widely spoken and certain Japanese interpersonal customs are observed, from one employing few or no Japanese or Japanese-Americans' (1978:834).

The ground was thus prepared for a new approach to the study of organization. The paradigm of formal organizational structure had been found incapable of encompassing the anomalous forms of hospital and of school organization, nor could it effectively encompass the modern Japanese industrial firm, which had come to prominence in scholarship as well as in public affairs. The attitude among many organizational scholars was one of despair. If organizations are anarchies, if their social structure is a myth that is entirely disconnected from everyday behavior, then there is little that the mainline social scientist can bring to the study of them.

Groundwork for a solution came from the extensive sociology of careers and occupations. Kuhn (1970) observed that a socially constructed point of view strongly influences the behavior of scientists, and it tends to be consistent within professions and across organizations. Lodahl and Gordon (1972) demonstrated that this view was entirely compatible with mainline sociological tradition, and Imershein (1977) suggested that the idea of scientific paradigm might be applied to the organization rather than the profession as the unit of analysis, thus creating the idea of an organizational paradigm. Van Maanen and Schein (1978) described how the processes found in occupational socialization were also at work in organizations. Van Maanen (1973) reported on his year of living with a police force, thus bringing the method and point of view of the ethnographer squarely into the mainstream of management literature. Pfeffer (1981) elaborated the idea of an organizational paradigm and fleshed out the possibilities of the study of management as symbolic action.

The study of organizational culture is rooted more deeply in sociology than in any other intellectual tradition. Critical both to sociology and to the study of organizational culture is the idea of an organization as a social phenomenon that has its own features which distinguish it from an environment on the one hand and from the individual desires and predispositions of its members on the other. Whereas the sociologist will typically emphasize the organization as a dependent variable with respect to macrosocial forces, it seems organizational culture has instead treated the organization as an independent variable almost exclusively, paying attention to the effect of organizational culture on employee participation and morale.

At the moment, the study of organizational culture is dominated by behavioral scientists working in the 600 schools of management in the US. These management schools now produce a good deal more organizational work than do departments of sociology, which surely must be a reversal of the situation of twenty years ago. The sheer growth in numbers of management schools is largely accountable for this difference, but there is a difference of intellectual domain as well. When sociologists became disenchanted with the multivariate studies of organizational structure in the 1970s, they simply took their intellectual curiosity and methodologies and migrated to the study of community structure, of occupational structure, of the structure of health care, and so on. Those who are employed in schools of management, however, are rather permanently committed to the study of business firms. As a result, they maintained their focus on business organizations but sought new points of view and new techniques with which to revitalize the study of those specific institutions. In that transition was created the study of organizational culture. Perhaps it is through culture, rather than formal structure, that large firms can be bent to the will of their masters and rendered predictable, 'rational.'

It was a curious turnabout, to say the least, in which the study of informal organization as the opponent of organizational rationality was thus transformed into the study of organizational culture as the basis for organizational rationality.

We should mention at least briefly some developments in social psychology that have had an important bearing on the development of the study of organizational culture. Many organizational scholars have been influenced by the tradition in psychology of studying the disjuncture between expressed intention and observed behavior (e.g. Festinger 1957; Kelley 1977). Variously developed as the study of cognitive dissonance, of persuasion, and of attribution, this tradition has consistently drawn attention to the nonrational features of individual behavior. For example, cognitive psychologists have shown systematic biases in the way people assess causality and make decisions (Kahneman and Tversky 1979). People tend to use story or single-case information more than multiple observations to make judgments (Borgida and Nisbett 1977). They also engage in self-serving rationalizations of the past, attributing success to their own efforts and failure to external forces beyond their control (Weiner *et al.* 1971). Apparently, organizations similarly attribute success to managerial skill and poor performance to a poor economy or other external forces (Staw *et al.* 1982).

The import of these ideas for organizational scholars has been to bolster the view that decision-making in organizations is not consistently rational. Goals are often discovered or created after the organizational activities they are supposed to direct (Weick 1979). Popular stories may have more influence on decisions and commitment than rules and statistics (Martin and Powers 1983).

A second significant line of social psychology for the study of organizational culture has been the study of organizational climate (Forehand and Gilmer 1964; Tagiuri 1968). Studies of climate have been sometimes indistinguishable from some current studies of organizational culture. The method of those studies, however, was that of survey research rather than of ethnography, and survey methods were under heavy attack within social psychology as lacking in the precision of experimental method. Two broad critiques of the climate studies appeared in one year (Hellriegel and Slocum 1974; James and Jones 1974) and effectively diminished the activity in that area of study. We shall also see that the use of survey methodology is seen by many current scholars of culture as being too much the product of the social scientist's rather than the participant's point of view and therefore inappropriate as a method for measuring culture. There are thus many scholars who are aghast that anyone would label climate studies as studies of culture even though some of the underlying ideas are the same.

### A review of current theory, empirical research, and practice in organizational change

The historical review just concluded attempted to relate some older themes to the contemporary work, thus providing an ordering of the contemporary approaches. In this section, we offer a second and more complete attempt to bring order to this new work, making use of categories that occurred to us as we sifted through several score of books, articles, and working papers.

We begin with current theoretical work on organizational culture. Then we consider current empirical work. Finally, we consider work on the planned change of organizational culture. The interested reader may also wish to pursue other recent reviews by Burrell and Morgan (1979), Sanday (1979), Smircich (1983), Gregory (1983), Louis (1983), and Morgan *et al.* (1983).

#### *Theoretical studies of organizational culture*

The currently developing theory may be assigned in a rough way to the category of either macroanalytic or microanalytic approaches to culture in organizations. The macroanalytic theories have in common an attempt to understand the culture of a whole group or subgroup, the functions that culture performs in maintaining the group, or the conditions under which the group and its culture and subcultures develop. The microanalytic theories present culture as something that resides within each individual and can be understood through the cognitive processes of sense-making, learning, and causal attribution, or by probing the unconscious mind.

#### *Macroanalytic theories of organizational culture*
Most of these exhibit a functional logic reminiscent of the anthropologists Malinowski and Radcliffe-Brown. For example, in studying the rites and ceremonies of organizations Trice and Beyer (1984; see also Trice 1983) developed a typology of rites (rites of passage, of degradation, of renewal, of

integration, etc.) and suggested that these rites fulfil both manifest and latent social functions (e.g. to socialize, integrate, assign social identity). Wilkins (1983a) suggests that popularly told stories about founders and other key organizational actors in some organizations perform integrative and control functions by serving as persuasive and instructive exemplars of managerial paradigms.

A second group of studies has adopted the view that the study of organizational culture should be closely related to some aspects of institutional microeconomics. In this view, both the form and content of culture are interpreted as consequences of the needs of the firm for efficiency. Wilkins and Ouchi (1983) argue that a homogeneous corporate culture performs organizational control functions but that it will develop only under certain conditions (e.g. long and stable membership, interaction across functional/ hierarchical boundaries, and an absence or discrediting of institutional alternatives). In a similar vein, Jones (1983) suggests that the content of an organizational culture results from the particular economic conditions (property rights structures, etc) in which organizational participants find themselves. He suggests three types of cultures that may result: production, bureaucratic, and professional. Barney (1984) extends these ideas to suggest that in some organizations culture can become a 'firm-specific asset,' which can produce 'supernormal returns.'

The study of occupational groups as cultural forms is now a lively and active field for both theory and empiricism. Van Maanen and Barley (1984) review an extensive occupational literature and assert that we are much more likely to find shared understandings and values among members of a same occupational group than among the functionally differentiated and spatially dispersed members of an organization. Others who have raised this problem of subcultures or lack of shared organization culture – though with differing suggestions for subunits and how to select them – include Louis (1983), Martin and Siehl (1983), Gregory (1983), and Wilkins (1983b).

. By and large, these studies attempt to describe the purpose and function of patterns of belief, language, and symbol in organizations. They tend to present these elements of organizational culture as necessary to order and stability, and to regard them as resistant to explicit attempts at manipulation owing to their natural or evolutionary character. Rarely, however, do they attempt to explain the relationship between an organization's internal culture and its larger cultural or socioeconomic environment. At this moment, the diversity of approach seems to be vigorously wide.

### Microanalytic theories of organizational culture

Attempts to develop theories of organizational culture from a psychological point of view are small in number and tend to be mid-range rather than grand abstractions. Existing works can be separated into two general categories – one for those that tend to use psychological notions of attribution or social learning and one for those that point to the unconscious or underlying assumptions that give meaning to the surface manifestations of culture.

In the first category, Pfeffer (1981) exemplifies the use of theories that emphasize the lack of coupling between attitudes and behavior. He suggests that organizational symbols are decoupled from actual outcomes, which are primarily mediated by environmentally determined, resource-dependency relationships. Schein (1983a) argues that culture is the sum of what individuals have learned of their organizational world, based on (*a*) the observed consequences of past action, and (*b*) the success or failure of attempts to cope with needs for anxiety avoidance. This learning ultimately yields a few commonly shared organizational beliefs. A similar approach is taken by Martin *et al.* (1983), who present a typology of organizational stories that serve to resolve or express psychological tensions.

The second class of psychological theories suggests that culture is best understood by going beyond surface manifestations. Some follow Freudian or Jungian psychoanalytic approaches, while others subscribe to a more linguistic, 'deep structure' approach (Chomsky 1972). Mitroff and his colleagues (see Mitroff 1983, Mitroff *et al.* 1983, and Dandridge *et al.* 1980) present a Jungian concern for archetypes or other meaning-structures to help them characterize deeper layers of meaning in organizational life. Walter (1983), following Lasch (1979), points out the neurotic aspects of organizational culture in a psychoanalytic vein. Pondy (1978, 1983), on the other hand, uses a linguistic approach to 'uncover meaning.' He sees leadership as a language game, the meaning of which can only be understood by getting at underlying 'grammar' or rules and standards in people's minds from which they generate appropriate behavior.

It seems natural to seek the cognitive analogues of organizational belief, as some of this work does. What is more interesting, however, is that this line of work seeks explicitly to join the psychology of individual cognition with the organizational setting that provides much of the cognitive field. When studies of formal structure dominated organizational research, there were few obvious opportunities for developing the social psychology of organizations, and the distance between organizational sociologists and organizational psychologists grew. Through the study of organizational culture, that distance may be diminished.

*Empirical studies of organizational culture*

The issues, problems, and methods of research on organizational culture have been discussed in several recent reviews (e.g. *Administrative Science Quarterly* 24:4; Spradley 1979; Martin 1983; Van Maanen 1979; Louis 1984; Burrell and Morgan 1979). Each of the reviews presents a unique view of the field. Some argue that quantitative techniques have no place in empirical studies of culture, while others assert that multiple methods, both quantitative and qualitative, are necessary. The range of methodologies is broad, with much borrowing from linguistics, survey research, participant observation, ethnomethodology, and symbolic interaction.

We have divided the empirical work into categories that follow from the principal intellectual traditions described above. These are: (1) *holistic studies* in the tradition of Radcliffe-Brown and Malinowski; (2) *semiotic* or *language studies*, which follow Geertz and Goodenough; and (3) *quantitative studies*, which use surveys or experimental manipulation.

*Holistic studies of organizational culture*

The exemplar in this category is the work by Rohlen (1974), who presents an ethnographic description of his participant observation in a Japanese bank. More recent examples of ethnographic descriptions of organizations include Krieger's portrait of a San Francisco rock music station (1979), Van Maanen's (1973) description of the socialization of police recruits, Manning's (1979) study of the world of detectives, Dyer's (1982) description of a computer company, Wilkins's (1983b) study of subcultures in an electronics company, the examination by Trice and Beyer (1985) of two social movement organizations routinizing the charisma of their founder, and Barley's (1983b) study of the evolution in organizational roles accompanying the introduction of CAT scanning technology in two hospitals.

These studies vary greatly in their degree of overt analysis and of theorizing. For example, Krieger (1979) avoids theoretical interpretation while Trice and Beyer (1985) use their observations of contrasts between the two organizations over a the twenty-year period to generate a rough theory of routinization of charisma. While some of these studies employ quantitative methods such as content analysis (Martin *et al.* 1984) or surveys (Barley 1983a), most rely upon field observation for periods of six months to twenty years (off and on). They tend to be rich and interesting descriptions of organizational life and provide a sharp contrast to the statistics typical of the structural view of organizations.

One major subset of holistic studies relies on archival, historical, or other public documents rather than field observation to arrive at an understanding of a social group. One example is Clark's (1970) study of organizational 'sagas' at Antioch, Reed, and Swarthmore colleges; he relied upon historical documents supplemented with interviews to recreate the past. Similarly, Dyer (1984) studied cultural evolution at 'Brown Corporation' during the years 1922–83 through a combination of interviews, public records (e.g. annual reports, minutes of stockholder meetings), internal reports (e.g. minutes from Board of Directors meetings, financial and personnel records) and industry reports.

Boje (1983) has used public histories combined with field observation to study changes in the folklore of the commerical printer since 1400. He finds that with recent rapid technological change the previously traditional and longstanding culture has been virtually destroyed. Kanter (1968) and Martin and Siehl (1983) relied upon secondary histories or other books as their primary sources. While the potential limitations and biases associated with such sources are obvious, the use of public and historical documents has encouraged a longitudinal perspective that is otherwise almost impossible to obtain. While these holistic studies embody the spirit of Radcliffe-Brown and of Malinowski, they employ an amalgam of methods both old and new to study the modern business firm and are thus quite distinct from any earlier body of work.

*Semiotic studies (focus on language and symbolism)*
The ethnoscience approach mentioned earlier is exhibited clearly in recent studies by Gregory (1983) and Barley (1983a). Gregory interviewed seventy-five professionals from several companies and studied several companies in depth in Silicon Valley. Her analysis of the language of these professionals suggested several taxonomies that enable the natives to make sense of their multifaceted and rapidly changing industry. Barley (1983a) studied the language of funeral directors to understand the implicit categories and taxonomies they use to make sense of their work. He spent some time observing a funeral home and then conducted several in-depth interviews, which were transcribed and later used for the linguistic analysis.

Other studies have focused on language but without the overtly ethnoscience approach. Pondy (1983) used ethnographic accounts of Communist China and of an African tribe (the Nuer) to illustrate the role of metaphor in helping participants in a culture to use the past to understand the uncertain or complex future. Huff (1983) examined public documents in a graduate school of management to show how the language of different subgroups was first couched in terms preferred by a new dean but then changed as the groups became increasingly independent. Pondy and Huff (1983a) have also traced the decline of one frame of reference used by policy makers and the rise of another by following the language used in public documents and recorded interviews over a several year period. They have documented (Pondy and Huff 1983b) the use of rhetoric by an administrator to prepare the way for a goal of computer literacy in public schools.

These semiotic studies appear to have been quite directly influenced by the tradition in anthropology. They typically require painstaking effort both in the collection of transcripts and in analysis, and they sometimes resemble exercises in methodology as much as anything else. As the techniques become more widely disseminated, however, the approach seems likely to expand rapidly.

*Quantitative studies*
Some studies of culture seem to be very much like the previous studies of organizational climate as we noted earlier. For example, Ouchi and Johnson (1978) employed questionnaires to characterize the differences in the cultures of companies 'A' and 'Z' (see also Ouchi 1983). O'Reilly (1983) distributed

questionnaires in seven high technology companies in Silicon Valley to test the association between the presence of a 'strong culture' and employee identification with the firm. He found general support. Bowditch *et al.* (1983) used a standard climate survey with an original culture survey to study the effect on culture and climate of the merger of two banks. Friedman (1983) reports on the use of content analysis of projective measures to reveal subcultures in one particular firm. He is careful to note that the procedure requires qualitative observation and data collection to assist in the interpretation of results. Beck and Moore (1983, 1984) report studies that use a variety of projective measures in order to illuminate the relationship between broader social norms and the firm-specific culture of Canadian banks.

Meyer (1982) used both questionnaires and content analysis of stories collected through open-ended interviews to examine the creation of shared ideologies. Finally, Zucker (1977) subjected the theme of institutionalization to laboratory experimentation, and Martin and Powers (1983) report the use of experimental manipulation to demonstrate that facts embedded in organizational stories are more vivid and persuasive than are quantitative summaries.

### Summary: empirical studies

The empirical studies of organizational culture involve a combination of the technology of the organizational social scientist with the interests of the cultural anthropologist. Since the organizational scholars of management schools have highly developed skills in the multivariate analysis of survey and experimental data, it is not surprising that they approach the study of organizational culture with these techniques. However, most of these studies also employ to varying degrees the techniques of participant observation, which have long been absent from organizational research. An ethnographer might assert with some justification that this new line of work is nothing but a mongrelization of the study of culture, and perhaps in the end the studies of this sort will be evaluated as having been a fad. At the moment, we can only observe what appears to be new 'hybrid energy' flowing from the confluence of several established methodologies with a variety of approaches to the idea of organizational culture. This confluence is producing a quite novel form of organizational scholarship.

### Work on planned change related to organizational culture

The prescriptive work in this area can be conveniently divided into two general categories: (*a*) case descriptions of planned change efforts; and (*b*) advice to executives. Both are natural developments in the milieu of a school of management.

#### Case descriptions

Although management scholars may seek to find useful prescriptions that can guide managers, their inquiry is nonetheless guided by more traditional rules of science, and their predisposition towards claims of simple organizational change is one of skepticism. The descriptions of efforts to change culture are not encouraging to those who believe culture can be a tool for management control. For example, Van de Ven (1983b) documents, with pre- and post-interview and survey data, the failure of a charismatic black minister to integrate into a single organizational culture several semiautonomous entities. Bowditch *et al.* (1983) describe how the attempted cultural merger of two banks resulted instead in the domination of one culture by the other. Trice and Beyer (1985) point out that the founder of Alcoholics Anonymous was able to institutionalize his organization through a set of quite unique circumstances, which another similar organization was unable to duplicate. These studies might properly be regarded as a subset of holistic studies of organizational culture, particularly because they are few in number. However, these studies have typically found that organizational cultures are not easily altered in intentional ways, and they have often turned to an examination of environmental factors to explain this result. Studies of change are thus typically more inclined to see organizational culture as a dependent variable than are the other approaches, and they are of particular interest for that reason.

### Advice to executives

Much of the advice to executives seems quite distant from the detached tone of typical academic writing. This area seems to proceed directly from the popular success of descriptions of already successful corporate cultures (Ouchi 1981, Pascale and Athos 1981, Deal and Kennedy 1982, and Peters and Waterman 1982) to general recommendations about how to influence corporate culture. Most authors in this genre present the view that the culture of a successful company can be emulated, although with difficulty.

Some of the most popular advice to executives comes from consultants or business school professors who offer recommendations about how to influence attitudes, opinions, and beliefs. Peters (1978, 1980) suggests that executives can effectively signal changes in values by the way they spend their time, what they ask questions about, and what they include on their agenda. Sathe (1983) uses a social psychological model to suggest how managers can help participants interpret events and can use hiring and training to influence beliefs.

Other approaches in this area follow the lead of Selznick (1957). For example, Van de Ven (1983a) suggests that the primary role of executives should be to articulate and embody a mission and role for the organization. Ouchi and Price (1978) suggest that executives should articulate a philosophy of management that describes organizational goals.

Some are less sanguine about the possibility of changing an organizational culture but suggest that it is useful to have culture in mind because it delimits efforts at change. For example, Schwartz and Davis (1981) suggest that executives should consider the 'cultural risk' of proposed new strategies.

In their view, the organizational change implied by new business strategies should be compared to the cultural orientations of the organization in order to determine the degree of potential resistance.

Schein (1983a), as noted above, has forcefully argued that much of an organization's culture represents the ways people have learned to cope with anxiety. Thus attempts to change culture are tantamount to asking people to give up their social defenses. We should consider the ethics of such a course, according to Schein. We should also be aware that threats to such social defenses are only likely to meet with success when the culture is under considerable challenge.

## Concluding thoughts

The large commercial organization is a recent phenomenon, which developed only after the introduction of rail transport and telegraphy. It is therefore to be expected that scholars will continue for some time to try one intellectual template after another before finding one that adequately captures its essence. On the other hand, the business firm is just one special case of a much older class of large and complex social structures, and it is therefore to be expected that many inherited scholarly tools will be useful in studying it. This review suggests both that the study of large firms is in a period of experimentation and that it draws upon many insights that anthropologists, sociologists, and psychologists have developed in the study of other forms of social organization.

We have treated the contemporary study of organizational culture as a cultural phenomenon as much as a scholarly development. As a cultural phenomenon, this field exhibits two facets of particular interest. First is a struggle among academics over which of many points of view will dominate the study of organizations, and second is the impact of multivariate statistics on the study of organizations.

Several points of view are now in active contention for dominance among students of organizational culture. One contest is over whether culture is a dependent or an independent variable. Among those who prefer to study organizational culture as a dependent variable, some take a natural-systems point of view and conclude that the culture of a firm is the natural outgrowth of its particular time and place and is not subject to human attempts at manipulation, while others assert that critical features of organizational culture may be systematically altered by a determined management. Those who view culture as an independent variable tend to ignore these possibilities and instead seek to explicate the variety of forms through which the subtle and implicit features of organization influence the thoughts, feelings, and behavior of individual participants.

A second contest is over the appropriate methods of study. Some hold that the method of lengthy field observation must be employed, while others assert that the whole point of the contemporary study of organizational culture is to go beyond the method of the anthropologist by applying multivariate statistical analysis to these issues. Although rarely written in journal articles, it is often said by those who are statistically inclined that organizational culture has become the refuge of the untrained and the incompetent, who will degrade this new field if they are not rooted out.

This review has consistently taken a historical point of view in attempting to achieve perspective on the study of organizational culture, and it is with a historical perspective that our review will conclude. The study of organizations, like any field of study, grows only through a constant intellectual tension that yields thesis and antithesis. During the 1960s, the multivariate studies of complex organizations had just begun to invade a domain that had long been dominated by field studies. The sociology of prisons, armies, slums, and gold coasts had been rich with the participants' point of view. Those who first championed the 'comparative' (that is, large-sample) point of view were passionate about the inherent superiority of intellectual rigor in their approach. The struggle often produced research that manifested elements of various approaches, research that raised scholarship to new heights.

During much of the 1970s, the struggle ceased. The multivariate approach dominated the leading journals, and those who preferred qualitative approaches established their own journals, meetings, and subculture. In the absence of conflict, there was a flowering of sub-branches and of sub-subbranches dealing on the one hand with abstract representations of networks of interorganizational relations and on the other hand with Jungian archetypes of corporate personality. Neither, as of this moment, has amounted to much. It is difficult to resist the interpretation that conflict and confrontation are good for research and that they are essential for good research. It is on these grounds that the contemporary study of organizational culture shows promise. This new field is rich with confrontation between those who feel that the statisticians continue to be too powerful and those who feel that the phenomenologists have sapped the scientific rigor of the field. Those who study occupational cultures argue passionately that any attempt to describe the culture of a firm with its many occupational subcultures is superficial, simpleminded, and cheap. The disputes are deeply felt and hotly contended, as are the more basic intellectual commitments on which they rest.

In a way, the study of organizational culture is a return. Much of the contemporary writing on organizational culture is accessible to the educated layman and is of interest even to the press. This was true of an earlier period of urban sociology, of industrial social psychology, and of cultural anthropology. There is in the field a return to a concern for the whole of the organization, an interest in knowing not only about that which can be captured in a standardized regression coefficient, but in knowing also what can be described only in a lengthy quotation that reveals the native's point of view. There is a return to a dual interest in description and in prescription, which typified the social sciences after the Second World War but which became unbalanced in a single-minded allegiance to description twenty years later. With the return to these earlier, perhaps more complete, approaches to organization come also the old tensions between points of view, tastes, and methods that do not make natural bedfellows. For the moment, at least, we can expect the study of organizational culture to be marked both by dissension and by creativity.

## Notes

We would like to thank several people whose thoughtful comments have improved this paper. They include Jay Barney, W. Gibb Dyer, Jr, Connie Gersick, Mitchell Koza, Barbara Lawrence, J. B. Richie, Harrison Trice, and the members of the UCLA interdisciplinary organization discussion group (Lynne Zucker, chair). We are grateful for the financial support of the Office of Naval Research and the Hank Marcheschi Entrepreneurship Fund.

1. Most frequently cited works: C. Geertz, *The Interpretation of Cultures.* 1973 – ten citations; P. Berger, T. Luckman, *The Social Construction of Reality: A Treatise in the Sociology of Knowledge*, 1966 – seven citations: Burton Clark, *The Distinctive College: Antioch, Reed, and Swarthmore.* 1970 – seven citations; Terrence Deal, A. Kennedy, *Corporate Cultures*, 1982 – seven citations; William G. Ouchi, *Theory Z*, 1981 – six citations; A. M. Pettigrew, 'On Studying Organizational Culture,' *Admin. Sci. Q.* 24:570–81, 1979 – six citations; Karl Weick, *The Social Psychology of Organizing*, 1979 – six citations.

## References

Abeggglen, J. 1958. *The Japanese Factory*, Glencoe, Ill., Free Press.
*Administrative Science Quarterly.* 1979. 24(4):519–671.
*Administrative Science Quarterly.* 1983. 28(3):331–502.
Anderson, T., Warkov, S. 1961. Organizational size and the functional complexity: A study of administration in hospitals. *Am. Sociol. Rev.* 26:23–28.
Barley, S. 1983a. Semiotics and the study of occupational and organizational cultures. *Admin. Sci. Q.* 28:393–413.
Barley, S. 1983b. *The evolution of roles in a technological subculture: A case from CAT scanning.* Presented at the Conf. on Interpretive Approaches to Study of Organ., Alta, Utah.
Barnard, C. 1938. *The Functions of the Executive.* Cambridge, Mass: Harvard Univ. Press.
Barney, J. 1984. *Economic profit from organizational culture.* UCLA Grad. School Mgmt. Working Paper.
Beck, B., Moore, L. 1983. *Influence of corporate image on manager's styles: The example of five Canadian banks.* Presented at the Conf. Organ. Folklore, Santa Monica, Calif.
Beck, B., Moore, L. 1984. *Linking the host culture to organizational variables.* Presented

at the Conf. Organ. Culture and Meaning of Life in the Workplace, Vancouver, Canada.

Becker, H. S., J. W. Carper. 1956. The development of identification with an occupation. *Am. J. Sociol.* 61:289–98.

Becker, S., Gordon, G. 1966. An entrepreneurial theory of formal organizations, Part I. *Admin. Sci. Q.* 11:315–44.

Benedict, R. 1934. *Patterns of Culture*. New York: Houghton-Mifflin.

Berger, P., Luckmann, T. 1966. *The Social Construction of Reality: a Treatise in the Sociology of Knowledge*. New York: Anchor.

Blau, P. 1955. *The Dynamics of Bureaucracy*. Chicago: Univ. Chicago Press.

Blau, P. 1968. The hierarchy of authority in organizations. *Am. J. Sociol.* 73:453–67.

Blau, P., Schoenherr, R. 1971. *The Structure of Organizations*. New York: Basic.

Blau, P., Scott, W. R. 1962. *Formal Organizations: A Comparative Approach*. San Francisco: Chandler.

Boje, D. 1983. *The fraternal spirit and folklore of the commercial printer*. UCLA Grad. School Mgmt. Working Paper No. 83–27.

Borgida, E., Nisbett, R. E. 1977. The differential impact of abstract vs. concrete information on decisions. *J. Appl. Soc. Psychol.* 7:258–71.

Bowditch, J., Buono, A., Lewis, J. III. 1983. *When cultures collide: The anatomy of a merger*. Presented at the Acad. Mgmt. Mtgs. in Dallas, Tex.

Burrell, G., Morgan, G. 1979. *Sociological Paradigms and Organizational Analysis*. London: Heinemann.

Chomsky, N. 1972. *Language and Mind*. New York: Harcourt, Brace, Jovanovich.

Clark, B. 1970. *The Distinctive College: Antioch, Reed, and Swarthmore*. Chicago: Aldine.

Cohen, M., March, J., Olsen, J. 1972. A garbage can model of organizational choice. *Admin. Sci. Q.* 17:1–25.

Cole, Robert. 1979. *Work, Mobility, and Participation*, Berkeley, Calif: Univ. Calif. Press.

Crozier, M. 1964. *The Bureaucratic Phenomenon*. London: Tavistock.

Cyert, R., March, J. 1963. *A Behavioral Theory of the Firm*. Englewood Cliffs, NJ: Prentice-Hall.

Dandridge, T., Mitroff, I., Joyce, W. 1980. Organizational symbolism: a topic to expand organizational analysis. *Acad. Mgmt. Rev.* 5:77–82.

Deal, T., Kennedy, A. 1982. *Corporate Cultures*. Reading, Mass: Addison-Wesley.

Dore, Ronald. 1973. *British Factory, Japanese Factory*. Los Angeles, Calif: Univ. Calif. Press.

Dyer, W. G. Jr. 1982. *Culture in organizations: a case study*. MIT Sloan School of Mgmt. Working Paper.

Dyer, W. G. Jr. 1984. The cycle of cultural evolution in organizations. In *Managing Corporate Culture*, ed. R. Kilmann *et al.* San Francisco: Jossey-Bass. In press.

Dornbush, S., Scott, W. R. 1975. *Evaluation and Authority*. San Francisco: Jossey-Bass.

Durkheim, E. 1893. *The Division of Labor in Society*. Transl. G. Simpson, 1933. New York: Free Press (from French).

Durkheim, E. *The Elementary Forms of Religious Life*. Transl. J. Swain, 1961. New York: Collier (from French).

Dyer, W. G. Jr. 1982. *Culture in organizations: a case study*. MIT Sloan School of Mgmt. Working Paper.

Dyer, W. G. Jr. 1984. The cycle of cultural evolution in organizations. In *Managing Corporate Culture*, ed. R. Kilmann *et al*. San Francisco: Jossey-Bass. In press.

Evered, R. 1983. The language of organizations: the case of the Navy. See Pondy *et al.* 1983 pp. 125–44.

Festinger, L. 1957. *A Theory of Cognitive Dissonance*. Stanford, Calif: Stanford Univ. Press.

Forehand, G., Gilmer, B. 1964. Environmental variation in studies of organizational behavior. *Psychol. Bull*. 22:361–82.

Friedman, S. 1983. *Cultures within cultures? An empirical assessment of an organization's subcultures using projective measures*. Presented at the Acad. of Mgt. Mtgs., Dallas, Tex.

Frost, P., Morgan, G. 1983. Symbols and sensemaking: the realization of a framework. See Pondy *et al.* 1983, pp. 207–36.

Garfinkel, H. 1967. *Studies in Enthnomethodology*. Englewood Cliffs, NJ: Prentice-Hall.

Geertz, C. 1973. *The Interpretation of Cultures*. New York: Basic.

Gertzl, B. G. 1961. Determinants of occupational community in high status occupations. *Sociol. Quart*., 2:37–40.

Goffman, E. 1959. *The Presentation of Self in Everyday Life*. New York: Doubleday.

Goodenough, W. 1971. *Culture, Language, and Society*. Reading, Mass: Addison-Wesley Modular Publ., No. 7.

Gouldner, A. W. 1954. *Patterns of Industrial Bureaucracy*. Glencoe, Ill: Free Press.

Gouldner, A. W. 1957. Cosmopolitans and locals: toward an analysis of latent social roles, Parts I, II, *Admin. Sci. Q*. 2:281–306, 3:444–80.

Gouldner, A. W. 1970. *The Coming Crisis of Western Sociology*. New York: Avon.

Graicunas, V. A. 1937. Relationship to organization. In *Papers on the Science of Administration*, ed. L. Gulick, L. Urwick, pp. 183–7. New York: Columbia Univ. Inst. Publ. Admin.

Gregory, K. 1983. Native-view paradigms: multiple culture and culture conflicts in organizations. *Admin. Sci. Q*. 28:359–76.

Gulick, L., Urwick, L., eds. 1937. *Papers on the Science of Administration*. New York: Inst. Publ. Admin., Columbia Univ. Press.

Hage, J., Aiken, M. 1967. Relationship of centralization to other structural properties. *Admin. Sci. Q*. 12:72–92.

Hall, R., Haas, E., Johnson, N. 1967. An examination of the Blau-Scott and Etzioni Typologies. *Admin. Sci. Q*. 12:118–39.

Hellriegel, D., Slocum, J. Jr. 1974. Organizational climate: Measures, research and contingencies. *Acad. Mgt. J*. 17:255–80.

Hinings, C. R., Lee, G. 1971. Dimensions of organization structure and their context: replication. *Sociology* 5:83–93.

Hirsch, P. 1972. Processing fads and fashions: An organization-set analysis of cultural industry systems. *Am. J. Sociol*. 72:639–59.

Homans, G. C. 1950. *The Human Group*. New York: Harcourt, Brace, World.

Huff, A., 1983. A rhetorical examination of strategic change. See Pondy *et al.* 1983, pp. 167–83.

Imershein, A. W. 1977. Organizational change as a paradigm shift. *Sociol. Q*. 18:33–4.

James, L., Jones, A. 1974. Organizational climate: a review of theory and research. *Psychol. Bull*. 81:1096–112.

Janowitz, M. 1960. *The Professional Soldier*. Glencoe, Ill: Free Press.

Johnson, R., Ouchi, W. G. 1974. Made in America (under Japanese management). *Harv. Bus. Rev.* 52(5):61–9.

Jones, G. 1983. Transaction costs, property rights, and organizational culture: an exchange perspective. *Adm. Sci. Q.* 28:454–67.

Kahneman, D., Tversky, A. 1979. On the psychology of prediction. *Psychol. Rev.* 80:237–51.

Kanter, R. 1968. Commitment and social organization: a study of commitment mechanisms in utopian communities. *Am. Sociol. Rev.* 33:499–517.

Kanter, R. 1977. *Men and Women of the Corporation*. New York: Basic.

Kelley, H. 1977. Attribution in social interaction. In *Attribution: Perceiving the Causes of Behavior*, ed. E. Jones, *et al*. Morristown, NJ: General Learning.

Krieger, S. 1979. *Hip Capitalism*. Beverly Hills: Sage.

Kuhn, T. 1970. *The Structure of Scientific Revolutions*. Chicago: Univ. Chicago Press.

Lammers, C. 1974. The state of organizational sociology in the United States: Travel impressions by a Dutch Cousin, *Adm. Sci. Q.* 19(3):422–30.

Lammers, C. 1981. Contributions of organizational sociology Part II. Contributions to organizational theory and practice – A liberal view. *Organization Studies* 2(4):361–76.

Lasch, C. 1979. *The Culture of Narcissism*. New York: Warner.

Lawrence, P., Lorsch, J. 1967. *Organization and Environment*. Cambridge, Mass: Harvard Grad. School Bus. Admin.

Lincoln, J. R., Olson, J., Hanada, M. 1978. Cultural effects on organizational structure: The case of Japanese firms in the United States. *Am. Sociol. Rev.* 43:829–47.

Lipset, S., Trow, M., Coleman, J. 1956. *Union Democracy*. Glencoe, Ill: Free Press.

Lodahl, J., Gordon, G. 1972. The structure of scientific fields and the functioning of Univeristy Graduate Departments. *Am. Sociol. Rev.* 37:57–72.

Louis, M. 1981. A cultural perspective on organizations: the need for and consequences of viewing organizations as culture-bearing milieux. *Hum. Syst. Mgmt.* 2:246–58.

Louis, M. 1983. Organizations as culture-bearing milieux. See Pondy *et al*. 1983, pp. 39–54.

Louis, M. 1984. *An investigator's guide to workplace culture: assumptions, choice points, and alternatives*. Presented at the Conf. on Organ. Culture and Meaning of Life in the Workplace. Vancouver, Canada.

Malinowski, B. 1961. *Argonauts of the Western Pacific*. London: Routledge & Kegan Paul.

Manning, P. 1979. Metaphors of the field: varieties of organizational discourse. *Admin. Sci. Q.* 24:660–71.

March, J., Simon, H. 1958. *Organizations*. New York: Wiley.

Marsh, Robert, Mannari, Hiroshi. 1976. *Modernization and the Japanese Factory*, Princeton: Princeton Univ. Press.

Martin, J. 1983. *Breaking up the mono-method monoplies in organizational research*. Stanford Grad. School Bus. Working Paper.

Martin, J. 1984. *The elusiveness of founder effect on culture*. Stanford University Grad. School Bus. Working Paper.

Martin, J., Feldman, M., Hatch, M., Sitkin, S. 1983. The uniqueness paradox in organizational stories. *Admin. Sci. Q.* 28:438–53.

Martin, J., Powers, M. 1983. Truth or corporate propaganda: the value of a good war story. See Pondy *et al.* 1983, pp. 93–108.

Martin, J., Siehl, C. 1983. Organizational culture and counter-culture: an uneasy symbiosis. *Organ. Dynam.* 12(2):52–64.

McMillan, C., Hickson, D., Hinings, C. Schneck, R. 1973. The structure of work organizations across societies. *Acad. Mgmt. J.* 16:555–69.

Mead, M. 1949. *Coming of age in Samoa.* New York: New Am. Lib.

Meyer, A. 1982. How ideologies supplant formal structures and shape responses to environments. *J. Mgmt. Stud.* 19(1):45–61.

Meyer, J., Rowan, B. 1977. Notes on the structure of educational organizations. In *Studies on Environment and Organization,* ed. M. Meyer, San Francisco: Jossey-Bass.

Mitroff, I. 1983. Archetypal social systems analysis: on the deeper structure of human systems. *Acad. of Mgmt. Rev.* 8:387–97.

Mitroff, I., Kilmann, R., Saxton, M. 1983. *Organizational culture: collective order-making out of an ambiguous world.* Univ. Calif. Working Paper.

Moore, L., Beck, B. 1983. Leadership among bank managers: A structural comparison of behavioral responses and metaphorical imagery. In *Managerial Work and Leadership: International Perspectives,* ed. J. Hunt *et al.* New York: Pergamon.

Morgan, G., Frost, P., Pondy, L. 1983. Organizational symbolism. See Pondy *et al.* 1983, pp. 3–38.

O'Reilly, C. 1983. *Corporations, culture and organizational culture: lessons from Silicon Valley firms.* Presented at the Acad. of Mgmt. Mtgs. Dallas, Tex.

*Organizational Dynamics.* 1983. 12(2).

Ouchi, W. G. 1980. Markets, bureaucracies, and clans. *Admin. Sci. Q.* 25:129–41.

Ouchi, W. G., 1981. *Theory Z.* Reading, Mass: Addison-Wesley.

Ouchi, W. G. 1983. Theory Z: An elaboration of methodology and findings. *J. Contemp. Bus.* 11:27–41.

Ouchi, W. G. 1984. *The M-Form Society,* Reading, Mass: Addison-Wesley.

Ouchi, W. G., Johnson, J. 1978. Types of organizational control and their relationship to emotional well-being. *Admin. Sci. Q.* 23:293–317.

Ouchi, W. G., Price, R. 1978. Hierarchies, clans, and theory z: A new perspective on organization development. *Organ. Dynam.* 7(2):25–44.

Parsons, T. 1956. Suggestions for a sociological approach to the study of organizations, Pt. I, II. *Admin. Sci. Q.* 1:63–85, 1:225–39.

Pascale, R. T., Athos, A. 1981. *The Art of Japanese Management.* New York: Simon Schuster.

Peters, T. 1978. Symbols, patterns, settings: An optimistic case for getting things done. *Organ. Dynam.* 7(2):3–23.

Peters, T. 1980. Management systems: The language of organizational character and competence. *Organ. Dynam.* 3–27.

Peters, T., Waterman, R. 1982. *In Search of Excellence: Lessons from America's Best-Run Companies.* New York: Harper & Row.

Pettigrew, A. M. 1979. On studying organizational culture. *Admin. Sci. Q.* 24:570–81.

Pfeffer, J. 1981. Management as symbolic action: the creation and maintenance of organizational paradigms. In *Research in Organizational Behavior,* ed. L. Cummings, B. Staw, 3:1–51.

Pondy, L. R. 1978. Leadership is a language game. In *Leadership: Where Else Can We*

*Go?*, ed. M. McCall, M. Lombardo, Greensboro, NC: Duke Univ. Press.

Pondy, L. R. 1983. The role of metaphors and myths in organization and in the facilitation of change. See Pondy *et al.* 1983, pp. 157–66.

Pondy, L. R., Frost, P. M., Morgan, G., Dandridge, T. C. 1983. *Organizational Symbolism*. Greenwich, Conn: JAI.

Pondy, L. R., Huff, A. 1983a. *Achieving routine*. Univ. Ill. Dept. Bus. Admin. Working Paper.

Pondy, L. R., Huff, A. 1983b. *Budget cutting in Riverside: Emergent policy reframing as a process of analytic discovery and conflict minimizing*. Presented at the Acad. Of Mgmt. Mtgs. Dallas, Tex.

Pondy, L. R., Mitroff, I. I. 1979. Beyond open system models of organization. In *Research in Organizational Behavior*, ed. B. Staw, Vol. I. Greenwich, Conn: JAI.

Pugh, D., Hickson, D., Hinings, C., Turner. C. 1969. An empirical taxonomy of work organizations. *Admin. Sci. Q.* 14:115–26.

Radcliffe-Brown, A. 1952. *Structure and Function in Primitive Society*. London: Oxford Univ. Press.

Roethlisberger, F., Dickson, W. 1939. *Management and the Worker*. Cambridge, Mass: Harvard Univ. Press.

Rohlen, T. 1974. *For Harmony and Strength: Japanese White-collar Organization in Anthropological Perspective*. Berkeley: Univ. Calif. Press.

Roy, D. 1960. Banana time: job satisfaction and informal interactions. *Hum. Organ.* 18:156–68.

Sanday, P. 1979. The ethnographic paradigm(s). *Admin. Sci. Q.* 24:527–38.

Sathe, V. 1983. Some action implications of corporate culture. *Organ. Dynam.* 12(2):5–23.

Schein, E. 1983a. *Organizational culture: A dynamic model*. MIT Sloan School of Mgmt. Working Paper No. 1412–83.

Schein, E. 1983b. The role of the founder in creating organizational culture. *Organ. Dynam.* 12(1):13–28.

Schwartz, H., Davis, S. 1981. Matching corporate culture and business strategy. *Organ. Dynam.* 10(1):30–48.

Selznick, P. 1949. *T.V.A. and the Grass Roots*. Berkeley, Calif: Univ. Calif. Press.

Selznick, P. 1957. *Leadership in Administration*. Evanston, Ill: Row, Peterson.

Simon, H. 1945. *Administrative Behavior: a Study of Decision-making Processes in Administrative Organization*. New York: Free Press.

Smircich, L. 1983. Concepts of culture and organizational analysis. *Admin. Sci. Q.* 28:339–58.

Spradley, J. 1970. *You Owe Yourself a Drunk: an Ethnography of Urban Nomads*. Boston: Little, Brown.

Spradley, J. 1979. *The Ethnographic Interview*. New York: Holt, Rinehart, Winston.

Staw, B., ed. 1981. *Research in Organizational Behavior*. Greenwich, Conn: JAI.

Staw, B., McKechnie, P., Puffer, S. 1982. The justification of corporate performance. Unpublished manuscript, Univ. of Calif. Berkeley.

Stinchcombe, A. 1959. Bureaucratic and craft administration of production. *Admin. Sci. Q.* 4:168–87.

Tagiuri, R. 1968. The concept of organizational climate. In *Organizational climate: explorations of a concept*, ed. R. Tagiuri, G. Litivin. Boston, Mass: Grad. School Bus., Harvard Univ.

Terrien, F., Mills, D. 1955. The effects of changing size upon the internal structure of an organization. *Am. Sociol. Rev.* 20:11–23.

Thompson, J. 1967. *Organizations in Action*. New York: McGraw-Hill.

Toennies, Ferdinand. 1957. *Community and Society*. Transl. C. P. Loomis, East Lansing, Mich: Michigan State Univ. Press (from French).

Tracy, P. K., Azumi, K. 1976. Determinants of administrative control: a test of a theory with Japanese factories. *Am. Sociol. Rev.* 41:80–94.

Trice, H. 1983. Rites and ceremonials in organizational culture. In *Perspectives in organizational sociology: Theory and research*, Vol. 4, ed. S. Bacharach, S. Mitchell. Greenwich, Conn: JAI.

Trice, H., Beyer, J. 1984. Studying organizational cultures through rites and ceremonials. *Acad. Mgmt. Rev.* 9:653–69.

Trice, H., Beyer, J. 1985. The routinization of charisma in two social movement organizations. In *Research in Organizational Behavior*, Vol. 7, ed. B. Staw and L. Cummings. Greenwich, Conn: JAI.

Trist, E. L., Bamforth, K. W. 1951. Some social and psychological consequences of the longwall method of coal-getting *Hum. Rel.* 4:3–38.

Udy, S. H. Jr. 1962. Administrative rationality, social setting, and organizational development, *Am. J. Sociol.* 68:299–308.

Van de Ven, A. 1983a. *Creating and sustaining a corporate culture in fast changing organizations*. Univ. Minn. Working Paper.

Van de Ven, A. 1983b. *An attempt to institutionalize an organization's culture*. Presentation at the Acad. Mgmt. Meeting, Dallas, Tex.

Van Maanen, J. 1973. Observations on the making of policemen. *Hum. Organ.* 32:407–18.

Van Maanen, J. 1979. The fact of fiction in organizational ethnography. *Admin. Sci. Q.* 24:539–50.

Van Maanen, J., Barley, S. 1984. Occupational communities: culture and control in organizations. In *Research in Organizational Behavior*, Vol. 6. ed. B. Staw, L. Cummings. Greenwich, Conn: JAI.

Van Maanen, J., Schein, E. 1978. Toward a theory of organizational socialization, In *Research in Organization Behavior*, ed. B. Staw. Greenwich, Conn: JAI.

Walter, G. 1983. Psyche and symbol. See Pondy *et al.* 1983, pp. 257–72. Greenwich: Conn: JAI.

Weber, Max 1968. *Economy and Society*. Berkeley, Calif: Univ. Calif. Press.

Weick, K. 1979. *The Social Psychology of Organizing*. Reading, Mass: Addison-Wesley. 2nd edn.

Weick, K. 1976. Educational organizations as loosely coupled systems. *Admin. Sci. Q.* 21:1–19.

Weiner, B., Frieze, I., Kullea, A., Reed, L., Rest, S., Rosenbaum, R. 1971. *Perceiving the Causes of Success and Failure*. Morristown, NJ: General Learning.

Whyte, W. F. 1943. *Street Corner Society*. Chicago: Univ. Chicago Press.

Wilkins, A. 1978. *Organizational stories as an expression of management philosophy: implications for social control in organizations*. PhD thesis. Stanford Univ.

Wilkins, A. 1983a. Organizational stories as symbols which control the organization. See Pondy *et al.* 1983, pp. 81–92.

Wilkins, A. 1983b. The culture audit: a tool for understanding organizations. *Organ. Dynam.* 12(2):24–38.

Wilkins, A., Ouchi, W. G. 1983. Efficient cultures: exploring the relationship between culture and organizational performance. *Admin. Sci. Q.* 28:468–81.

Zucker, L. 1977. The role of institutionalization in cultural persistence, *Am. Sociol. Rev.*, 42:726–43.

**Section V**

# Politics and power

# 14
# Micropolitics of educational organizations

**Eric Hoyle**

Both practitioners and theorists regard administration as an essentially rational process. Although the current emphasis on contingency theory recognizes that effective patterns of administration are relative to the contexts in which they are to operate, there remains the fundamental assumption that if plans are well conceived, clearly set out, and adequately communicated, then systems can be improved. Yet everyone working in organizations is all too well aware of their often idiosyncratic, adventitious, unpredictable and intractable nature when every day brings a new organizational 'pathology' to disrupt well laid plans. This uncertainty occurs at the highest levels of policy-making and implementation. In his much cited work on the Cuban missile crisis Allison (1971) showed that what had been interpreted as the outcome of carefully considered and rationally enacted policies could be viewed as the result of actors within a highly uncertain situation bargaining within their own camps as well as across national boundaries. In an interview, Zbegniew Brzezinski, President Carter's adviser on national security stated:

> My overwhelming observation from the experience of the last four years is that history is neither the product of design nor of conspiracy, but is rather the reflection of continuing chaos. Seen from the outside, decisions may often seem clear and consciously formulated . . . but one learns that so much of what happens . . . is the product of chaotic conditions and a great deal of personal struggle and ambiguity (Urban, 1981).

Policy-makers and administrators in the less lethal field of education will recognize the aleatory dimension of the institution – described by Kogan (1975) as 'pluralistic, incremental, unsystematic and reactive' – as they attempt to improve the service in conditions which appear to be perennially turbulent.

Evidence of the quirky and idiosyncratic nature of social institutions could lead one into a consideration of fundamental questions about the nature of the social sciences. However, this path will not be taken in this paper. The question to be considered is whether social scientists have explored suffic-iently all dimensions of institutions as a source of explanation of what, within the prevailing paradigms of social science research, appears to be irrational, adventitious and peculiar to a unique setting at one point in time. It is the purpose of this paper to suggest that there is one dimension of organizations which has been largely ignored in administration and organization theory. We can refer to this as the 'micropolitics of organizations'. It is an organiza-tional underworld which we all recognize and in which we all participate. We acknowledge it when we speak of 'organizational mafias', 'hidden agendas', 'playing politics' and 'Machiavellism'. It is a dark side of organizational life which provides the source of much staff gossip. Ironically, micropolitical activity is engaged in by the very administrators who profess a rational theory of administration. Yet it is very rarely made the focus of academic study. For enlightenment on micropolitics and for enjoyable confirmation of what we know of this dimension of organizations, we got to television serials, films, plays and novels:

> 'Wilt' does more than Weber can
> To reveal the FE world to man.

There may be good reason for the academic neglect of micropolitics. It is perhaps considered slightly unrespectable, or too self-indulgent ('the cute school of organization theory', Ouchi, 1981), or a threat to conventional administrative theory – which it is, or as having no practical application – which it may not. Or it may be that it simply is not a single dimension of organizations at all but a range of different processes each best handled separately through existing bodies of theory and research.

The purpose of this paper is simply to put the issue of micropolitics on the agenda. The sections which follow deal with the hypothesized domain of micropolitics, reasons for its omission from the major approaches to the study of organizations and their administration, the approaches to organiza-tion and administrative theory which deal to some degree with micropolitics, and implications of micropolitics for the training of administrators.

### The domain of micropolitics

Micropolitics embraces those strategies by which individuals and groups in organizational contexts seek to use their resources of power and influence to further their interests. The cynic might well say that this is simply a definition of administration. It is true that the relationship between administration and micropolitics is symbiotic in that in practice they are inextricably linked, but it can at least be hypothesized that there is some measure of independence. Administrative theory focuses on structures and the associated processes of power, decision-making, communication, etc. But the space between structures is occupied by something other than individuals and their motives. This 'other' consists of micropolitical structures and processes. It is characterized more by coalitions than by departments, by strategies rather than by enacted rules, by influence rather than by power, and by knowledge rather than by status. The micropolitical dimension may be largely shaped by the formal structure – which may well be the dimension which best accounts for organizational activity – but it is nevertheless worthwhile reversing the traditional approach by treating the micropolitical as the 'figure' and the administration as the 'ground' to explore whether this throws a different light on the operation of organizations. Such a procedure would lead to a focus on the major elements of micropolitics: interests, interest sets, power and strategies.

Politics is inevitably concerned with *interests*. Administrative theory *Interest* often underestimates the plurality of interests in organizations because it tends to be attuned to organizational goals as determined by the leadership. That there are interests other than those of organizational effectiveness has of course long been taken into account by most administrative theories, but they nevertheless tend to be treated as recalcitrant, a suitable case for leadership, or socialization or coercion. It is beyond the scope of this paper to offer a taxonomy of interests, but any classification would at least include personal, professional and political interests. Personal interests would include autonomy, status, territory and rewards. Professional interests involve commitments to particular forms of practice: curriculum, pedagogy, organization and so forth. Political interests involve a commitment to certain macro or party-political policies. It is easily seen that, taking these three areas of interest alone, it is difficult to disentangle the personal, the professional and the political at a substantive level. The tendency is perhaps for personal or political interests to be presented in terms of the professional, since normatively this is the most 'respectable' form of interest in education. Thus a proposed innovation which threatened the territorial interests of a teacher might well be resisted by mobilizing 'professional' arguments against it. Similarly, political interests can be presented as professional interests. However, it can be seen that here even the conceptual distinction is very difficult to sustain. In institutions other than education the distinction between personal and political interests is blurred. The conceptual difficulties are particularly acute when one considers 'the micropolitics of macropolitics', where the question is whether X is espousing a political interest *per se* or as a means of pursuing a personal interest in a political career. A large part of the fascination of Crossman's Cabinet diaries (Crossman, 1975, 1977) is his revelations about micropolitics within the Cabinet and the ambiguous relationship between personal and political interests.

*Interest*

Interests constitute the *content* of micropolitics but it can be seen that the area is fraught with conceptual and methodological difficulties. It is perhaps for this reason that those who have addressed themselves to micropolitics have tended to focus on strategies rather than content.

Interests are pursued by individuals but frequently they are most effectively pursued in collaboration with others who share a common concern. Some of these may have the qualities of a group in that they are relatively enduring and have a degree of cohesion, but others – which are perhaps best referred to as *interest sets* – will be looser associations of individuals who collaborate only infrequently when a common interest comes to the fore. Some interest groups will be coterminous with formal organizational groupings, e.g. departments or teams. These will be particularly strong. Others will transcend formal boundaries and will form when a common interest has to be pursued. The basis of group or set association may be age, sex, professional interests, politics, union activity, etc. Burns (1955) distinguished between *cliques* which are committed to sustaining the status quo and *cabals* which are committed to organizational change.

Coalitions have been the focus of attention of a number of writers. Selznick (1957) has made a sociological contribution to their study. Bacharach and Lawler (1980) review the major socio–psychological theories of coalitions before offering their own theory which is essentially a socio–psychological approach to the political dimension of organizations. They define a coalition as 'a grouping of interest groups which are committed to achieving a common goal'. In turn, interest groups are defined as 'groups of actors who are aware of the commonality of their goals, and the commonality of their fate beyond simply their interdependence with regard to the conduct of work'.

Some interest groups will be permanently mobilized; interest sets will mobilize as and when their interest becomes salient. Components of the formal structure will remain the most powerful set of groupings in an organization, but there is at least a case for viewing an organization in terms of the alternative structure of shifting interest sets which, in fact, interpenetrate with the formal organization at many points.

*Power* is one of those social science concepts which refer to an important social phenomenon but about which there are theoretical and empirical disputes which are likely to remain unresolved. Given the libraries of works on power produced by political scientists, philosophers, sociologists and social psychologists, it would be impossible to review the complex theoretical and methodological issues involved in this short paper. Thus the remarks made will be those of particular relevance to micropolitics.

*Power*

The distinction between two major aspects of power are important. *Authority* is the legally supported form of power which involves the right to make decisions and is supported by a set of sanctions which is ultimately coercive. *Influence* is the capacity to affect the actions of others without legal sanctions. The distinction is conceptually important but difficult to sustain empirically because, since authority can be latent, it is difficult to establish when control is exercised through influence or through latent power. However, the distinction between authority and influence remains potentially useful since the power deployed in micropolitics frequently takes the form of influence since interests sets will draw on resources other than those of authority to achieve their ends.

Administrative theory tends to focus on authority which has its source in the hierarchical structure of the organization. Micropolitical theory would give greater prominence to influence. Influence is derived from a number of sources, e.g. personality (charisma), expertise, access (especially to information) and resources (material or symbolic). Influence differs from authority in having a number of sources in the organization, in being embedded in the actual relationships between groups rather than located in an abstract legal source, and is not 'fixed' but is variable and operates through bargaining, manipulation, exchange and so forth.

The headteacher in Britain has a high degree of authority; but his exercise of this authority is increasingly modified as teachers' sources of influence through expertise, access to symbolic resources, etc., increases and thus involves the head in a greater degree of exchange and bargaining behaviour (Hoyle, 1981). These are the aspects of power which are the appropriate focus of micropolitics.

Micropolitics takes account of the *strategies* used by interest sets to attain their ends and gives these greater attention than formal procedures. Organizational politics has been insufficiently studied to yield a systematic taxonomy of such strategies although there are good individual studies. For example, Pettigrew (1973) identified four strategies used by a group of programmers to protect their interests: norms which denied the outsider's competence, protective myths, secrecy, and control over recruitment and training. Handy (1976) discusses a number of protective strategies such as the distortion of information, the imposition of rules and procedures, the control of rewards, etc. There is so little discussion of micropolitical strategies in educational organisations that it is perhaps appropriate to invent some examples: an FE college may have a 'collegial' structure, but the principal, caught in the dilemma of all who would manage pluralistic organizations, i.e. the reconciliation of legal authority and the expectation of participation, may indulge in micropolitics in order to cope with this dilemma. Thus he may attempt to handle situations by: 'losing' recommendations from working parties by referring them to other groups in the hope that they will disappear or become transformed, 'rigging' agendas, 'massaging' the minutes of meetings, 'nobbling' individuals before meetings ('I'm glad you see it my way. I hope you'll make your views known at the meeting'), 'inventing' consensus ('Well, we all seem to be agreed on that') when consensus has not been tested, 'interpreting' the opinions of outside groups ('The governors would never accept it'; 'The LEA wouldn't finance it') and so forth. As Noble and Pym (1964) discovered, 'collegial' organizations are characterized by a 'receding locus of power'. The course of power is difficult to identify in a collegial organization. The principal can draw on his resources of legal power, but other members of staff have their own resources.

Thus micropolitics involves a study of interests, interest sets, power and strategies. These are intimately related to the more formal aspects of an organization which is the main focus of much administrative theory, but the political dimension of an organisation constitutes an alternative focus for understanding organizational processes. However, from the brief discussions of these four components in this section it can be seen that it is likely to be a conceptually and methodologically complex area of enquiry.

## The neglect of micropolitics

Theories of organizations and administration are *relative*, i.e. products of their place and time, *partial*, i.e. in adopting one theoretical perspective others are inevitably excluded since a total perspective is not a possibility, and *normative*, i.e. to a greater or lesser degree they are infused with values.

The dominant paradigm in organizational and administrative theory is one in which political aspects do not easily fit. Although it is a great over-simplification to group all prevailing theories within one paradigm, and although it is impossible to do justice to the diversity of existing theories, some broad points can be made in order to illustrate the reason for the neglect of micropolitics.

Current organization theory has two origins: Weber's theory of bureaucracy and early theories of management. These two strands converge and diverge at many points in the development of theory. Sociological theory in the Weberian tradition is potentially concerned with understanding organizations; management theory is potentially concerned with improving them. However, theories of management need to be based on understanding if they are not to be merely recipe theories, and organization theory has not retained a detached purity since its protagonists have also been concerned with improving organizations in various ways: their efficiency, the quality of life of participants, and, hopefully, both. Hence they share a common paradigm which can be termed the *maintenance* paradigm.

It is impossible to give a detailed account of this paradigm let alone the variations within. Nevertheless, the following are its major lineaments: its metatheory assumes that the social world is to a greater or lesser degree, rational, amenable to scientific study and predictable. Its perspective on organizations follows from this in emphasizing the centrality of structure, the legal authority inherent in that structure, a relatively high degree of integration and systemness, participants who will continue to be committed given an appropriate mix of rewards and conflicts which are either 'creative' or arise from some malfunction of the structure or leadership. The associated management theory is concerned with the effective use of resources, maximizing

the fit between organizational goals and personal needs, and an organizational responsiveness to contingent conditions in the environment. The
theory of change inherent in the model is essentially that of planned change
whereby adaptation to a changing environment is handled by structural
changes and the retraining and resocialization of participants. Overall the
paradigm views organizations in a top-down manner.

The operation of the maintenance paradigm in education can be – again
in a gross over-simplification – summarized as follows. Educational organizations – schools, colleges, polytechnics and universities – have to cope with
changes in their environment: cultural, technological, economic and political
changes of various kinds. Political changes are initiated at the macropolitical
level and tend to focus on the allocation of resources, legal enactments and
overall structure with rather less focus on matters of curriculum and pedagogy. It is assumed that practitioners will interpret these external changes in an
attempt to keep in balance the interests of society and the interests of clients.
Hence the expectation is that innovation will be professionalized rather than
politicized. In order to equip institutions and practitioners to cope with the
professional demands of innovation, programmes of professional development, organizational development and the development of interpersonal
skills have emerged. The appropriate strategy of change, within the coercive
strategies of national and local government, is considered to be a mixture of
rational and re-educative approaches.

A major alternative is the *action* paradigm which again has a complex
history and embraces a wide range of perspectives so that to bring them
together under one heading is to oversimplify. Nevertheless the lineaments
of the action paradigm are as follows: its metatheory holds that the social
world is nothing other than the construction of the minds of men and hence
has no objective reality 'out there'. Social life is sustained because men,
through their daily interaction and their language, create intersubjectively
shared meanings. These meanings may be relatively persistent and perhaps
come to have the appearance of objectivity but, in fact, as men continue to
solve the problems of their daily lives, they can voluntarily construct new
meanings. It follows then in strict terms there can be no action theory of
organizations since organizations are not 'objects' but social constructs, and
the meanings attached to them, will differ according to one's perspective.
The action theorist is interested in activities within what are conventionally
termed organizations because he is interested in how participants construe
organizations and their processes. He treats as 'problematic' the organizational structure and administrative processes which organizational theorists
take for granted. As there can strictly be no organization theory, there can
likewise be no theory of management since management is only a constructed
label for a group of organizational processes dominated by those who have
resources of power which tend to become problematic only if treated
phenomenologically. It should follow that an action perspective is neutral in
relation to change since it is a paradigm more concerned with understanding

the world – or, more precisely, understanding others' understanding of the world, than with initiating change. Its active contribution to the change process is the assumption that social theorists of this persuasion should work with practitioners at any level of the organization helping them to clarify their own perspectives, helping them to question what had previously been taken for granted which then becomes potentially amenable to change. Thus it generally encourages an 'active' stance on the part of participants. This sounds rather like the process consultant operating within the maintenance paradigm but whoever the process consultant is, however independent of management he may profess to be, ultimately he is concerned with improving organizational functioning in relation to the goals of management. The action theorist tends to be orientated towards enabling the lower participants to perceive the possibility of reconstructing the organization in ways alternative to that perceived as 'effective' by management. In short, action theory, like maintenance theory is relative, partial and normative. Yet there is more potential within the action perspective for focusing on micropolitical activities since these are actions which can be made the strict focus of enquiries and not treated as pathological or deviant activities.[1]

What can be termed the *radical change* paradigm has political activity at its centre. It is concerned with understanding the social world in order to change it in accordance with a set of political beliefs. This perspective is strongly Marxist in orientation. Again, at the risk of great over-simplification the following are some of the main characteristics of this approach: the metatheory may, according to the particular view of Marx taken, share the same view of the world as the maintenance theorists, in that it is taken that there is an objective world out there which is amenable to scientific understanding and control via the manipulation of structures and the socialization of individuals, or of the action theorists. Essentially it is not an organization theory but a broad socio-political theory in which organizations are seen as arenas in which occur the clashes between the prevailing ideology and the alternative radical ideology. Thus the political transformation of organizations is a necessary step towards transforming society. This is captured in the phrase about 'the long march through the institutions' which became prevalent in the late 1960s. Thus there is no management theory as such, only a theory-in-waiting. Current theories of management are held to be simply theories supportive of the capitalist hegemony. There are theories about using 'the organizational weapon' in the period of transformation but only when the transformation occurs can a radical, egalitarian and democratic theory of organization – 'management' is perhaps a tainted word – emerge. Although this perspective certainly has political concerns, organizational politics are subsumed within macropolitics, with micropolitical activities which do not obviously contribute to the political transformation of the organization being regarded as pathological.

## Approaches to micropolitics

The chief elements of micropolitics: power, coalitions, strategies and in-terests have been the focus of studies in a number of social science disciplines. In social psychology there has been considerable study of interpersonal power particularly in group settings. However, the socio-psychological study of organizations has been largely concerned with problems of leader-ship and communication and is clearly located within the maintenance model. Weick (1979) is an exception to this trend in that he has concerned himself with the 'negotiation' of organizational order, but the focus has not been directly upon the micropolitical. The concern of political theorists has been games, choice and coalitions (Brams, 1975; Laver, 1981). They have tended to be concerned with establishing formal theories rather than with understanding political activity *in vivo*.[2] There are a number of sociological approaches which, though not focusing directly on micropolitics, are never-theless concerned with relevant issues. Of particular significance there is exchange theory which is predicated on the assumption that many aspects of social life are explained in terms of the implicit and explicit bargains struck between groups which, though they may be different in relation to the degree of relative power which each has, necessarily needs to reach an accommoda-tion with the other in order to serve their mutual interests. (Homans, 1958; Blau, 1964). Other sociological theorists of organisation, particularly Selz-nick (1957, 1966) and Gouldner (1954a, 1954b) attended to the 'dysfunc-tional' elements in organizations which were often the outcome of the pursuits of group interests rather than organizational interests via what we are here terming micropolitics. However, neither has pursued the implications of this in the direction of making micropolitics central to his analysis. Selznick resorted to classical functionalism, and although Gouldner was to come to adopt a radical view of social institutions, this was developed within a Marxist rather than a micropolitical framework.

In decision-making approaches to organization, Simon's (1964) notion of 'bounded rationality' is concerned with the boundary between rational and non-rational aspects of social behaviour. The 'non-rational' – which we would now, in these post-phenomenological days, refer to as 'alternative rationality' – relates to the activities which we have referred to as micropoli-tical. However, in the theories of March and Simon (1958) organizational analysis remains well within the maintenance framework in noting these aberrant behaviours as evidence that organizations do not in fact function according to the rational model.

Three organizational theories which are more directly concerned with micropolitics can be noted.

The first is the later work of March who now appears to have brought what was earlier considered to be 'non-rational behaviour' in the decision process, i.e. micropolitics, to the centre of the stage. In *Ambiguity and Choice in Organizations* (March and Olsen, 1974) he and his colleagues concentrate less on how decisions ought to be made if they are to conform to canons of rationality, than on how in fact they *are* made. What is described is how decisions, which are rarely the clear-cut events usually described, emerge out of a complexity of micropolitical activities. They advance what is now their well-known 'garbage can' model of decision-making:

> Although choice opportunities may lead first to the generation of decision alternatives, then to an examination of the consequences of those alternatives, then to an examination of the consequences in terms of objectives, and finally to a decision, such a model is often a poor description of what actually happens. In a garbage can situation, a decision is an outcome or an interpretation of several relatively independent 'streams' within an organization.

They consider four streams which might go into the 'garbage can':

*Problems:* These are the personal problems of participants as they relate to such matters as pay, status, promotion, personal relationships, families and even the problems of mankind.
*Solutions:* They reverse the normal view of solutions and see them as sometimes preceding problems. They cite the installation of a computer in an organization which may represent a solution to problems not yet conceived. In the educational context one could conceive a new curriculum or a plan for school-focused in-service training generating new problems rather than solving existing ones.
*Choice opportunities:* These are occasions such as those when a new member of staff is to be appointed or where a responsibility allowance is to be allocated which generate behaviour which can be called a decision.
*Participants:* Individuals come and go and their different attributes will shape the outcomes which are termed 'decisions'.

The rates, patterns of flow and confluence between these four streams shape certain organizational events which come to be labelled as 'decisions'. March and Olsen write of organizations 'running backwards' in the sense that organizational events are the outcome of bargaining, negotiating and exchange and only after they have occurred is their history 're-written' by managers to give them the appearance of having been the outcome of a rational decision-making process.

Michel Crozier (1964) has long been interested in how power and influence operate in organizations and has developed the view that organizational processes are best understood by focusing not on formal organization and power as a commodity but on the games which individuals and groups play in order to solve problems, and in which power is treated as a bargaining relationship. He argues for a change in paradigm. Thus the research problem is to explore how different systems of games can solve the problems which organizations face. He believes that the way forward is to learn more about current games in all forms of organization and the forms of regulation inherent in these games. This will be best approached by case and comparative studies at the present time with the prospect of formalization and measurement left until the future. He has written (Crozier, 1975):

> The dominant paradigm revolved around the basic question concerning the structure: how contextual variables determine the basic structural features of an organisation and how these features command the behaviour of the members and the performances of the organisation. The new paradigm emerges first around the idea that the contextual features of the organisation should not be considered as variables determining the structure of the organisation, but as problems to be solved, and second around the idea that structure is not the necessary nodal point of the organisation, but that the games with their rational mathematical features as well as their human parameters will be a much more concrete and rich focal point.

Bacharach and Lawler (1980) set out their concerns as follows:

> An understanding of organizational politics requires an analysis of power, coalitions and bargaining. The power relationship is the context for political action and encompasses the most basic issues underlying organizational politics. As the primary mechanism through which individuals and subgroups acquire, maintain, and use power, coalitions crystallize and bring to the foreground the conflicting interests of organizational subgroups. Through bargaining, distinct coalitions attempt to achieve their political objectives and protect themselves from encroachments by opposing coalitions. Power, coalitions, and bargaining, therefore, constitute the three basic themes in our theoretical treatise on organizational politics.

They review the existing literature and argue that in sociological studies there has been too great an emphasis on formal structure and power and that the traditional social psychology of organizations has tended to focus on motivation, leadership and so forth and have thus ignored the political nature of organizations. They therefore focus on the activities of *work groups*, e.g. departments, *interest groups*, i.e. groups of actors with common goals which are not necessarily coterminous with work groups, and *coalitions*, i.e. groups of interest groups who engage in joint actions against other interest groups. On the basis of a detailed analysis of power, authority, group formation, and bargaining, they develop a formal theory incorporating over 100 hypotheses.

In sum, there have been a number of approaches to the study of micropolitics, but at the present time they cannot be said to constitute a coherent body of theory. The question is whether such a coherence is likely to be achieved and, if so, what its contribution to the study of educational administration might be.

Empirical studies of micropolitics are extremely rare. Some exceptions are Thompson (1967) in the United States and in the United Kingdom

Pettigrew (1973) and Mangham (1979), but none of these studies was conducted in educational organizations.

## The prospects for micropolitical studies

This paper is based on the assumption that a considerable gap exists between the organizational world which is presented in theory and research and the organizational world which we all experience. This gap is acknowledged by administrators who perhaps gain little help from administrative theory because it is not of their world, or at least it relates to a rather sanitized version of the world in which they function. The gap is also increasingly recognized by theoreticians and researchers who have become somewhat disenchanted with the prevailing paradigm but are not wholly happy with the action and radical change alternatives. Thus the importance of the micropolitical world is existentially acknowledged. The question is: can it be captured by the theories and methods of the social sciences and, if so, will what is learnt be of value to practising administrators?

The answer to the first of these questions must remain tentative. There are two basic levels of answer. One relates to the fundamental problem of the social sciences of whether in principle a knowledge of the social world can be attained by the methods of objective enquiry. This is no place to rehearse the arguments yet again, except to note that of the three broad positions: a knowledge of the social world is in principle impossible, that it is possible only through an understanding of the meanings which actors ascribe to situations, and that the social world is in fact, knowable by the procedures of the natural sciences. If we make the assumption that it is, in principle, knowable, then we have to ask *how* it might be knowable. It could be argued that the micropolitical world is so ideographic, idiosyncratic, contingent and volatile that in practice it cannot be grasped. It could be further argued that it is indeed of this character but it can be grasped in its particular concrete setting via a detailed case study, but that generalizations are very difficult to achieve in practice. Or it can be argued that the micropolitical world is amenable to study by the methods of the social sciences which permit generalization.

If one takes the latter position, then two things have to be said. One is that 'the real stuff' of micropolitics is particularly elusive. As we have seen, different approaches focus on different components of micropolitics, so the interactive nature of power, coalitions, interests, and strategies is unclear. However, if studies to concentrate on one or other aspects in an effort to clear the way towards formal, testable theory, then the configuration disintegrates. Thus we are left, as we often are in the social sciences, with a choice between case studies providing rich data and formal studies providing – hopefully – generalizable findings. And one inevitably comes to the familiar conclusion that both approaches should proceed, if, indeed, it is worthwhile pursuing at all the study of micropolitics in education. It may be that it is not a viable area of study as a whole and that its components are better pursued independently.

If one concludes that it is worthwhile getting to grips with the micropolitics of educational organizations, by whatever method, one has to ask whether the outcome is likely to improve the practice of educational administration. Would it, in fact, provide theory-for-understanding or theory-for-improving? It would appear more likely to provide theory-for-understanding. Studies of micropolitics could well bring the area much more into the arena of open discussion, but it isn't easy to see in what ways this might improve the quality of administration or the quality of life in educational organizations for participants. It is even more difficult to see how the outcome of the study of micropolitics would feature in courses for practising administrators other than as a general mirror-raising component and as theory-for-understanding. In what sense could it contribute to improvement of skills? It could form the basis of various forms of simulation and games, but the degree of transfer from gaming to practical decision-making contexts must be somewhat dubious. And even if it were possible to teach micropolitical skills to practising administrators, this would – to say the least – generate some obvious moral issues.

It is clearly the case that micropolitics is difficult to embrace within the conventional theory, research and training patterns of educational administration since administrative theory is normatively oriented to rationalizing order and control and eliminating the alternative world of micropolitics. This paper offers no solutions. As stated at the outset, its purpose has been to put micropolitics on the agenda.

## Notes

1. Perhaps the best known protagonist of an action or phenomenological approach to educational administration is Greenfield (1975). For a recent interesting exchange between the relative merits of a phenomenological and a flexible system approach see Greenfield (1980), and Willower (1980). More generally on the potential of one action approach see Silverman (1970) and the same writer's more thoroughgoing phenomenological approach (Silverman and Jones, 1976). For a good review of current organization theories see Burrell and Morgan (1979).
2. The dramaturgical approach of Goffman (e.g. 1969, 1971, 1974) is difficult to classify, but the personal strategies which he identifies are those of the micropolitical actor.

## References

Allison, Graham T. (1971). *Essence of Decision: Explaining the Cuban Missile Crisis.* Boston: Little Brown.
Bacharach, Samuel B. and Lawler, Edward J. (1980). *Power and Politics in Organizations.* San Francisco: Josey-Bass.

Blau, P. M. (1964). *Exchange and Power in Social Life*. New York: Basic Books.

Brams, Stephen (1975). *Game Theory and Politics*. New York: Free Press.

Burns, T. (1955). 'The reference of conduct in small groups', *Human Relations* 8:467–86.

Burrell, Gibson and Morgan, Gareth (1979). *Sociological Paradigms and Organisational Analysis*. London: Heinemann.

Crossman, Richard (1975). *The Diaries of a Cabinet Minister Vol. I. Minister of Housing 1964–6*, London: Hamish Hamilton/Cape.

Crossman, Richard (1977). *The Diaries of a Cabinet Minister Vol. II. Lord President of the Council and Leader of the House, 1966–8*, London: Hamish Hamilton/Cape.

Crozier, Michel (1964). *The Bureaucratic Phenomenon*. London: Tavistock.

Crozier, Michel (1975). 'Comparing structures and comparing games', Hotstede, G. and Kassem, N. S. *European Contributions of Organisation Theory*. Assen: Van Gorcum, pp. 193–207. Reprinted in Lockett, Martin and Spear, Roger (1980). *Organizations as Systems*. Milton Keynes: Open University Press.

Goffman, Erving (1969). *Strategic Interaction*. Philadelphia: University of Pennsylvania Press.

Goffman, Erving (1971). *Relations in Public: Microstudies of the Public Order*. New York: Basic Books.

Goffman, Erving (1974). *Frame Analysis: an Essay on the Organization of Experience*. New York: Harper & Row.

Gouldner, A. W. (1954a). *Patterns of Industrial Bureaucracy*. Glencoe: Free Press.

Gouldner, A. W. (1954b). *Wildcat Strike*: New York: Antioch Press.

Greenfield, T. Barr (1975). 'Theory about organization: its implications for schools', in Hughes, M. (ed.) *Administering Education: International Challenge*. London: Athlone Press, pp. 72–99.

Greenfield, Thomas B. (1980). 'The man who comes back through the door in the wall: discovering truth, discovering self, discovering organisations', *Educational Administration*. Quarterly 16(3):26–59.

Handy, Charles B. (1976). *Understanding Organisations*. Harmondsworth: Penguin Books.

Homans, G. C. (1958). 'Human behaviour as exchange', *American Journal of Sociology* 63(6):597–606.

Hoyle, Eric (1981). 'The process of management', Managerial Processes in Schools, *Management and the School*, O. U. Course E 323 Block 3, pp. 6–51, Milton Keynes: Open University Press.

Kogan, Maurice (1975). *Educational Policy Making: a Study of Interest Groups and Parliament*. London: George Allen & Unwin.

Laver, Michael (1981). *The Politics of Private Desires*. Harmondsworth: Penguin Books.

Mangham, Iain (1979). *The Politics of Organizational Change*. London: Associated Business Press.

March, J. G. and Simon, A. A. (1958). *Organizations*. Wiley: New York.

March, J. G. and Olsen, J. (1976). *Ambiguity and Choice in Organizations*. Bergen: Universitetsforlaget.

Noble, Trevor and Pym, Bridget (1970). 'Collegial authority and the receding locus of power', *British Journal of Sociology* 21(4):431–45.

Ouchi, William G. (1981). 'A framework for understanding organizational failure', *Administrative Science Quarterly* 28.

Pettigrew, A. (1973). *The Politics of Organization Decision-Making.* London: Tavistock.

Selznick, P. (1957). *Leadership in Administration.* New York: Harper & Row.

Selznick, P. (1966). *TVA and the Grass Roots.* Berkeley: University of California Press.

Silverman, D. (1970). *The Theory of Organizations.* London: Heinemann.

Silverman, D. and Jones, J. (1976). *Organisational Work: The Language of Grading/The Grading of Language.* London: Collier-Macmillan.

Simon, H. (1964). *Administrative Behaviour: a Study of Decision Making Processes in Administrative Organization*, 2nd edn. New York: Collier-Macmillan.

Thompson, J. D. (1967). *Organizations in Action.* New York: McGraw-Hill.

Urban, George (1981). 'The perils of foreign policy: a conversation with Dr Zbigniew Brzezinski'. *Encounter*, May, pp. 13–30.

Weick, Karl E. (1979). *The Social Psychology of Organizing.* 2nd edn. Reading, Mass: Addison-Wesley.

Willower, Donald (1980). 'Contemporary issues in theory in educational administration', *Educational Administration Quarterly* 16(3):1–25.

# 15
# Rationality, experience and theory

**K. E. Shaw**

Von Molkte said:

> There are always three courses open to the enemy – and he usually takes the fourth! Only the layman believes that he sees in the course of a war the accomplishment of an idea conceived beforehand, considered in every detail and adhered to until the end. Logistic plans are to be detailed therefore, but operational plans purposefully vague to take account of the 'fourth course'. (Quoted in Pearson, 1982)

At a more general level Oakshott notes:

> How appropriate rationalist politics are to the man who, not brought up or educated to their use, finds himself in a position to exert political initiative or authority, requires no emphasis. His need of it is so great that he will have no incentive to be sceptical about the possibility of a magical technique of politics which will remove the handicap of his lack of political education. The offer of such a technique will seem to him the offer of salvation itself: to be told that the necessary knowledge is to be found complete and self contained in a book . . . will seem, like salvation, something almost too good to be true. (Quoted in Gellner, 1974.)

That this remains true if for rationalist politics we substitute rationalist administration, or for that matter, rationalist curriculum planning, I leave the reader to consider. Those whose own moment of reflection leaves them in doubt might ponder Wise's excellent analysis of the misapplication of rationality to educational planning (1977) or Wrong's much more celebrated paper (1961). The excessive application of rationality to complex problems of policy and planning runs headlong into two difficulties: people and change.

Experience rather than reasoning teaches that all too often people, in the form of pupils, students, parents or staff, if presented with three courses of action 'take the fourth' – or would do if not prevented by the system. So hindered, people may pursue courses one to three with reduced motivation, resignation or resentment, lack of commitment or merely notional assent, frequently endowing the missing fourth choice with romanticized advantages. Why can't I do history *and* geography if I do three sciences? Why must I do a third-choice A-level subject here when I could do A-level Computer Studies at the FE college? Why must my son go to school B when the bus passes the very gates of school A? Why must I teach five periods on the care course when I could be teaching that extra option group in my subject which had to be turned away to release me?

And change: changes in social preferences, in demography, in technology, in the economy. Von Molkte was prepared to accept the 'fog of war' in all its obscurity as it shrouds the future from our sight, and to leave plenty of room for manoeuvre instead of, as his nephew did, devising an inflexible technically constrained, rational plan, which encouraged plunging into the fog with unwavering determination, a kind of motorway madness. And yet at a time of unprecedented economic, technological and social change we are being invited to reintroduce vocational and prevocational training and education into the curriculum with every substantial cash inducements, when the man- and womanpower needs five years ahead are shrouded from our vision as never before.

This, I grant, somewhat rhetorical introduction is a prelude to a brief consideration of some central management concerns of school leadership and of attempts to conceptualize and research them. I shall begin with levels of decision. With heroic simplification, the tasks of school leadership reduce to making strategic policy decisions, bringing about the resource allocations and deployments which follow from such decisions, and arranging for, maintaining and monitoring the operating procedures which seek to deliver the policy intentions, within the limits set by resources, to the learners. The chief difficulties of school leadership are the problems of clarifying major policies and freeing them from contradictions; of achieving sufficient agreement and commitment in the spheres of allocations and deployment to liberate energies to the real tasks of the institution and not to personal preferences, resistance, distortions of purpose, sideshows and other perennial distractions; and finally of making the operating procedures deliberate and effective, not merely ritual, contrived performances or thoughtless habits based on tradition and energy conservation.

It is the third level, the day-to-day operating procedures, which benefits most from the conscious application of systematic rational planning. The teaching itself, since it calls for artistry and creativity in some aspects, has largely to be left to the practitioner, subject to safeguards about successful previous performance, length of experience, and degree of task related expertise. What tends to be underplayed in teacher training which stresses the artistic and creative aspects of the job, and in schools which place too much reliance on the teachers' own professional commitment, is that much of the work, however individual, is necessarily carried out within a framework of routines ranging from giving out textbooks to dealing with serious accidents. Getting the balance right between the well-trained teacher's professional autonomy and the need for a framework of reliable, stable, predictable routine is a subtler business than is commonly realized, especially if rather cheap and simple forms of accountability are demanded of the teacher and the institution. Insight and judgement are here as important as rationality. A great deal of consultancy work both in industry and in education comes down to persuading management to take careful thought of what they have preferred to take for granted. This is not something, however, that we can at once see when it is pointed out to us; it has to do with attitudes and values, to some extent culturally inculcated rather than taught or learned consciously which act as filters for perception and information. What else was so much of the human relations movement in management theorizing than an attempt to point out that the occupational sub-culture and the needs of the person in the workplace for security, protection of identity and retention of a degree of control over the work, led to practices which, if inconvenient for management and to some extent 'irrational', were nevertheless quite understandable, even necessary from the workers' viewpoint, and certainly not to be brushed aside except at the cost of disruption? If we are to make more progress at this day-to-day, humdrum, down-at-the-chalk-face level, neither pressure nor one-way explanation is enough. We must at least take seriously what the Cambridgeshire document (Duffett, 1982), written by an outside business-man, stresses, namely that an element of management expertise must be part of the professional equipment of all staff down to the least experienced probationer. This is still under-developed as an emphasis both in pre- and inservice education.

The second level of decision is that of allocating resources, including staff deployment. Foucault (1977) has reminded us that the timetable, like the bell it depends on, goes back beyond the factory system to the medieval monastery; the notion has deep cultural roots. The timetable, and latterly job-specifications are public documents; together with the instrument of government and the accounts (estimates, balance sheet including points allocation) which are normally less public, they constitute key charter documents of the school. Syllabus and curriculum pattern are rather less important since they are more like working guides subject to local renegotiation at least in the United Kingdom.

To be an insider is to know that within the not always clearly defined limits set by these documents (Shaw, 1980) the politics of the institution come into play. Needs are infinite, resources limited; a mechanism is called into being by which allocations can be made. It is hardly a democratic one since power, patronage and access to information are unevenly distributed; but it allows for bids, lobbying, negotiation and other well-known processes of partial adjustment which any complex institution needs, however strong the consensus on which it rests. What has to be allocated, nominally in relation to tasks, but in reality having regard to tradition, bargaining and social power, seniority, personality and the like, are chiefly facilities of varying degrees of desirability (rooms and equipment), money, time, say-in-decisions, professional skills and energy, rewards, and access to desired groups of pupils. The day-to-day operating level of the school or college rests quite substantially on this second level, of resource allocation; though there is increasing evidence that the performance of schools and the departments within them is not so dependent on the level of resourcing as some have thought, as witness the investigations into class size and pupil achievement. In addition, and here research is less developed, there is considerable variation in school structures and the resources allocations that sustain them, a response to differences in size, context, purposes and personalities. Witness again the great variation in time allocated to, say, science or craft. We are in no position to know what consequences such variation has. We can take note, though, that the particular settlement in any school or college is an invention, a working compromise, made by people and changeable by them. Rationality has some part in this, but since each party in disputes habitually appeals to it, at times for contradictory purposes, its scope must be limited.

Since all but the most ingenuous of staff have encountered it, it seems wise to come clean about the micropolitical aspect of resource allocation when dealing with staff development and training. This would involve admitting that the institution needs to seek a degree of consensus actively rather than assuming comfortably that it has a natural unity of purpose. It would probably involve facing up to the need for more genuinely consultative arrangements rather than those which merely generate consent. A valuable way to alert staff to this is to bring together staff from more than one school to pool experiences. DES/Regional type courses for middle-rank staff, in which realistic exercises and studies by participants of resource allocation in relation to policy and to operations figure prominently are well received, as a decade of experience in the south-west has shown.

The first level is that of strategic policy, the one task leadership cannot delegate. Policy gives the institution its sense of direction and links it to the wider society. It is the ground on which society is prepared to find the funds for the institution. The word 'discovery' almost implies that policy is hidden, like gold, to be found by prospecting around. Of course at any point after opening, schools and colleges have a policy, but it resembles a sheaf rather than a nugget. An older form of writing urged us to define the 'primary task' as an aid to clarification. Apart from the fact that in many cases the honest answer would be 'to survive in a quasi-competition with other local schools' (see Dawson, 1981) or 'to maintain subscription', the problem is that educational institutions have a cluster of tasks, not one. Except in conditions of convulsive change such as reorganization, most strategic policy turns on priorities within the tasks at *this* particular juncture, circumstances having (probably: information is seldom clear and reliable) subtly altered since the last general reappraisal. Much turns on different estimates of the significance of new information, on discrepant and sometimes self-interested interpretations by parties to the discussion, on differential access to information, and on discordant value systems and purposes. If the level of allocations has problems with people and their micropolitics (Burns, 1961) this third policy level has problems both with people and with change. Will the New Training Initiative reduce the need for careers education in school and the points it carries? Will generic vocational training at 16+ make specific craft training in woodwork and metalwork at 14+ obsolescent? Is the deputy head right when he says that the new 17+ examination will find no takers in school? How long can we go on trying to offer a curriculum based on the staffing for 6 fe now that we have fallen to 4½ fe?

Rational planning approaches such as the use of critical path analysis and the attempt to conceptualize what is happening by the adoption of systems theory have been proposed for this level. Their key weakness, however, is the implicit assumption that problems can be factorized and the discrete elements systematically rescheduled into a rational patterned order susceptible of being indicated in a systems diagram or algorithm. Frequently there is a strain to ascribe weighting, chronological sequence or numerical value to the factors. The natural home of such approaches is engineering, and there is more than a touch of scientism about them. Now the case of the military since 1914 shows that the adoption of strictly scientific approaches, operational research, and the application of technology to complex practical problems pays enormous dividends. But in education there has been no technological revolution since the invention of printed books: the classroom is conspicuously a low-technology area. Schools and colleges are relatively small, scattered, internally complex units, heavily responsive to their immediate local context: guerrilla warfare not guided missiles. In such circumstances policy, both strategic and tactical, is more likely to rest on complex synthetic judgements of the type needed in ethics, politics or diplomacy, not like those needed in engineering or economics. It is doubtful whether systems thinking has offered more than heuristic models and a new vocabulary when applied to the broadest levels of educational policy-making and decisions at any rate at the level of the school.

This is not to deny that rational, scientific approaches should be explored for their contribution. Technology alone cannot win wars but neglect of it can lose them. Rather I would advocate greater emphasis in two areas as likely to have more pay-off for managing schools. The first is staff development. Turn-over is now a tenth of what it was in the 1960s. The quick-in/quick-out problem of wastage has given way to over-stability; for the first time we can seriously transfer resources from initial to in-service training on a substantial scale. The lead task is retraining for the 16+ sector, but partial retraining for a much wider group of teachers is now a realistic matter. During expansion, teacher movement and turn-over was overwhelmingly the greatest adaptive mechanism open to educational institutions; now the essential lubrication must be supplied by in-service training and redeployment. Whilst an overall staff development plan might be ideal, the only realistic plan for schools in current conditions is opportunism: ad hocery with a sense of direction. Direction comes from seeing the problem in the round, and recognizing that development may be for the individual, for teams and for the school as a whole. There are tensions among these levels, for the development desired by an individual may contribute little, indeed contradict, the needs of the school; such tensions cannot be finally resolved without compromise, so that a degree of opportunism is essential. To handle it may need prior staff development on the part of the head; it calls for interpersonal competencies and political nous. One test of the maturity of an institution is whether it can deal confidently with its inner, often conflicting needs and tensions, and has standing means of doing so. Staff development is important amongst these means as part of the planned activities of the place. It might even be said that it is part of the curriculum – the hidden curriculum too! It is a school task and ought to be much more school based. Teachers, not unaided, must ultimately take responsibility for their own education, and do it on their own ground.

The second aspect has to do with theory. Policy statements by the DES in December 1982 foreshadow a substantial growth in management courses for teachers. To provide them with requisite credibility will call for greater sophistication in theory construction and the methodologies on which this must rest. The articles and discussion which followed Greenfield's (1975) publication have been in my judgement disappointing. They are tainted with theoretical parochialism. Some of the most spirited, readable and stimulating writing in philosophy over the last decade has been to do with what counts as evidence and the criteria for good theory in both the natural and social sciences, from the pens of, to name only the most impressive, Lakatos (1970), Gellner (1974), Mary Hesse (1980) and Roy Bhaskar (1979). More advanced teaching and research will have to confront these developments, the thrust of which, as I read it, is quite away from rationalist and engineering models.

Alongside these are very rapid and far-reaching developments in sociology which have important implications for research in the sphere of management. These have been touched on by Hoyle (1976) and Tipton (1977) but not in sufficient depth. What Greenfield made his central theme – not relations among variables but experiences of people in situations, as the central subject matter – is part of a wave that is sweeping through all the social sciences, breaking up older preconceptions, notably in the area of evaluation in education, already influencing psychology, but whose full force is still to be felt in writing about educational management and administration. Different facets of this go by different names: qualitative and case-study approaches in research, phenomenology and ethnomethodology as schools of writers, interactionism, the 'new', 'critical' or 'reflexive' sociology. Despite occasional grotesque manifestations, all have a core of shared ideas and press towards (amongst many other things) a revised view of how organizations work, in ways often more convincing to the organizational member.

It is understandable that a study for managers and administrators should cling to a safer, simpler, less politically involved, and methodologically more straightforward body of ideas derived essentially from theories and approaches that were dominant in the 1950s. We have only to look to the church to see what happens to organizations which cannot digest newer thinking and find their adaptive potential eroded. What von Molkte and Oakshott were criticizing is an inappropriate reductionist approach, not the attempt to think clearly, logically and even scientifically. Both note the yearning of the inexperienced for a golden key, 'a magical technique' when faced with complexity. That is why educational gurus and hasty borrowings from sister sciences on shaky philosophical foundations find a market. The maturity of this domain, as practice, as methodology and as theory will be promoted best when it stands on its own feet and uses other peoples' discoveries as tools rather than as crutches.

## References

Bhaskar, R. (1979). *The possibility of naturalism*. Brighton, Harvester Press.

Burns, T. (1961). 'Micropolitics', *Administrative Science Quarterly* 6: 257–81.

Dawson, P. (1981). *Making a comprehensive work*. London, Basil Blackwell.

Duffett, R. H. E. (1982). *Study of the devolution of managerial responsibility to heads of schools*. Cambridge, Local Education Authority.

Foucault, M. (1977). *Discipline and punish*, London, Allen.

Gellner, E. (1974). *Legitimation of belief*, Cambridge, Cambridge University Press.

Greenfield, T. (1975). 'Theory about organisation', Hughes, M. (ed.) *Administering Education*, London, Athlone Press.

Hesse, M. (1980). *Revolutions and reconstructions in the philosophy of science*, Brighton, Harvester Press.

Hoyle, E. (1976). 'Barr-Greenfield and organization theory: a symposium', *Educational Administration* 5:1–13.

Lakatos, I. (1970). 'Falsification and the methodology of scientific research programmes', Lakatos, I. and Musgrove, A. *Criticism and the growth of knowledge*. Cambridge, Cambridge University Press.

Pearson, M. (1982). *The Knowledgeable State*, London, Burnett Books.

Shaw, K. E. (1980). 'The timetable: a Bill of Rights?' *Teaching Politics* 9(2):111–20.

Tipton, B. (1977). 'The tense relationship of sociology and educational administration', *Educational Administration* 5(2):46–57.

Wise, A. (1977). 'Why educational policies often fail', *Journal of Curriculum Studies* 9(1):43–58.

Wrong, D. (1961). 'The oversocialized conception of man' *American Sociological Review* 26(2):183–92.

# 16

# Notes on a political theory of educational organizations[1]

## Samuel B. Bacharach

There was a shift in methodological and theoretical approaches to the study of organizations in the mid to late 1960s. Methodologically, the emergence of multivariate analysis and statistical packages allowed social scientists to deal with larger bodies of data, and for the most part the previously predominant case-study approach was left behind. Theoretically, the concern shifted away from an examination of the dynamics of organizations (i.e. strategy and change), toward a relatively static analysis of the structure of organizations. Thus in the 1960s and 1970s the sociological study of organizations was dominated by the comparative structural perspective (Blau and Schoenherr, 1971; Hage and Aiken, 1967; Pugh et al., 1969). The comparative-structural perspective emerged as a response to the earlier detailed case study approaches exemplified by Selznick (1949) and Gouldner (1954). While the case studies were concerned with how the behavior of organizations and their members idiosyncratically varied from a common theoretical reference point (i.e. Weber's model of bureaucracy) the comparative structuralists were primarily concerned with discovering common patterns across organizations.

An argument can be made that in its basic concern with the collection of large quantifiable data-banks, the comparative-structuralist reduced theory to the position of a legitimizer of methods rather than holding that methods are a tool of theory. The selective use of works of Max Weber exemplifies this phenomenon. Weber's ideal construct of bureaucracy emerged as a series of testable propositions while it was clearly never meant to do so (Hall and Tittle, 1966; Hall, 1963). Furthermore, Weber himself was cast as an aggregate structuralist who viewed organizations as based on the functional interdependence between various structures, for example size and differentiation (Blau and Schoenherr, 1971). The dynamic aspects of the Weberian perspective, viewing structure as contingent on historical and cultural setting and as determined by the conscious action of particular interest groups, was for the most part ignored by the comparative structuralists. Contemporary theoretical perspectives (March and Simon, 1958; Cyert and March, 1963; Thompson, 1967) were also selectively used by the comparative structuralists. The references made to these theoretical works ignored, for the most part, the dynamic aspects of the perspectives. For example, not until recently has the theme of coalitions and coalition behavior been viewed as integral to the empirical research while it is obviously of import to the theoretical volumes (Cyert and March, 1963; Thompson, 1967).

The rise of the comparative structuralist perspective may be due in part to its affinity with one of the primary tendencies of organizational behavior: the development of general, overarching theories with applicability to all organizations. The statistical analysis employed by the comparative structuralists are well suited to the development of general theory. Even the earlier case-study tradition tended to lose sight of the specifics of the empirical referents on which they were based, with emergent theoretical generalizations coming to the forefront. The comparative structuralists offered a more explicit and direct route to the same end, while sacrificing a significant degree of realism and practicality in the process.

Although not as extreme, this interplay between theory and methods is also apparent in educational administration. Through most of its history, educational administration has placed a heavy emphasis on practice. As a result, those in educational administration have tended to rely on detailed empirical descriptions of educational systems rather than the development of broad theories of organizations. There has been a heavy use of case studies or other intensive research techniques which tend to reveal the more idiosyncratic and dynamic aspects of school systems. One consequence of this has been the consistent lament among those in educational administration concerning the lack of theory (e.g. Cunningham, Hack and Nystrand, 1977; Immegart and Boyd, 1979; Boyan, 1981). There has been a call for the use of more refined methodological and statistical approaches to aid in the development of a more specific and quantified theory of educational administration.

The uncritical adoption of such an approach would have the same costs for the study of educational administration that the rise of the comparative structuralist perspective did for the study of organizations. The work of Bidwell and Kasarda (1980) most closely approximates the structural model and provides a good example of these costs. Like many other structuralists, Bidwell and Kasarda view schools and school districts[2] in terms of the economic context and morphological structure of these organizations. For example, organizational attributes are measured in terms of such dimensions as pupil–teacher ratio, administrative intensity, ratio of professional support staff to classroom teachers, and staff qualifications. Their analysis essentially consists of examining how these four 'organizational attributes' moderate the impact of environmental conditions such as school district size, fiscal resources, percentage of disadvantaged families, district population educational levels, and percentage of non-whites in a district on measures of student achievement. Like most organizational theorists they view organizations as an input–output system. However, like most aggregate structuralists, (e.g. Blau and Schenherr, 1971), they leave the process by which actors translate the impact of the environment unspecified. The environment's impact on structure is never viewed as mediated by the cognitions and calculative behavior of organizational actors. Environment is somehow transformed into structure, yet the process of transformation remains unspecified. Conscious actors, strategic decision-making, and open conflict are never considered. The discovery of static patterns occurs at the expense of the dynamics of practical reality. While this approach may produce a theory of educational administration, there is a distinct possibility that such a theory would be too far removed from the practice of educational administration to be of much use.

Obviously there is a need in both organizational behavior and educational administration for the generation of practical theory (Bacharach and Mitchell, 1981a). The development of practical theory requires that attention be paid to the common patterns that exist across organizations *and* the idiosyncratic realities of specific organizations. In recent years the structural perspective has come under attack from a variety of theoretical perspectives (Karpick, 1972a; Georgiou, 1973; Goldman and Van Houten, 1977; McNeil, 1978; Salaman, 1978; Bacharach and Lawler, 1980; Crozier and Friedberg, 1981; Weick, 1976). Curiously, there appears to be little interest in defending this approach to the study of organizations, with the consequence that there has been considerable experimentation with alternative perspectives such as the negotiated order perspective (Strauss, 1978); the Marxian perspective (Benson, 1977; Braverman, 1971; Heydebrand, 1977; Goldman and Van Houten, 1977); the ethnomethodological perspective (Manning, 1977); a renewed interest in the social action perspectives (Rose, 1974; Goldthorpe, 1968; Silverman, 1970; Touraine, 1971) and the political perspective (Pettigrew, 1973; Bacharach and Lawler, 1980; Pfeffer, 1980; Weiss, 1981).

Among the more potent critiques of the comparative structuralist perspective is March and Simon's (1958) notion of the loose coupling of organizations, recently elaborated by Weick (1976). What makes this perspective of particular interest is the fact that it represents an attempt by an organizational theorist to deal with the particular properties of educational organizations. In essence, the notion of loosely coupled systems characterizes organizations in a manner directly opposite that of comparative structuralist theory. Thus the objective focus on structure is replaced by a concern with the subjective aspects of cognition. As a consequence, the assumption of organizations as holistic or homogeneous gives way to a view of organizations as heterogeneous. Harmony is usurped by chaos. However, it is precisely at this point that the weaknesses of the loosely coupled metaphor becomes most apparent. Possible sources of order are left vague and unspecified. While Weick (1976) lists some possible mechanisms through which coupling may occur (e.g. authority, technology), it is not apparent at what point coupling occurs. Further, it is not apparent whether coupling occurs between individuals, groups, or organizations. Indeed, one of the primary problems with the loosely coupled systems approach is the fact that it is based on an individual phenomenological analysis, yet it is applied haphazardly to organizations as a unit.

Implicit in one or more of the aforementioned perspectives are a number of critiques of the comparative-structure approach to the study of organizations:

1. Comparative structuralists have reified organizations.
2. Comparative structuralists have anthropomorphized organizations.
3. Comparative structuralists have objectified organizations.
4. Comparative structuralists have viewed individual organizational members as passive.
5. Comparative structuralists have viewed organizational structures as constraining behavior rather than as emergent from behavior.
6. Comparative structuralists have assumed the existence of an aggregate organizational reality.
7. Comparative structuralists have ignored divergence in subgroup and individual cognitions and interests.
8. Comparative structuralists have failed to explain the dynamics of change and conflict in organizations.

What most of the critiques of the comparative structuralists have in common is a primary concern with the analysis of organizational dynamics and organizational change. They view organizations as systems of actions. Not coincidently, their development has been accompanied by a renewed interest in the use of 'qualitative' methods (*ASQ*, 1981). The problem with the various critiques offered of the comparative structuralists is that no one perspective has addressed all the points of criticism, nor have they shown an appreciation for the positive aspects of the structural approach. To that end, we have yet to see a theoretical perspective which deals with what must be viewed as the three critical issues of organizational theory:

1. How do organizational structures and processes emerge from the behavior and cognitions of individual actors?
2. How do organizational structures and processes stabilize without inhibiting the behaviors and cognitions of individual actors?
3. How do organizations change without being reduced to chaos? Specifically, how do organizations change while still maintaining their organizational identity?

To a large degree what Weick (1976) and others have failed to emphasize is that beyond the façade of loose coupling, there may exist the day-to-day calculative workings of a political reality. That is, at times one has the sense that the proponents of the loosely coupled are trapped by their own metaphor, failing to realize that what appears as loose coupling may indeed be the informal but highly predictable politics of organizational life. Indeed, the modes of coupling may be based on calculative decisions constrained by the structure and environmental content of organizations. While the structuralists fall to consider the internal dynamics of organizations, the adherents of the loosely coupled systems approach fail to consider the structural constraints that impinge on the individual actor's cognitions and actions.

It is my premise that a middle ground between the comparative structuralist and the loosely coupled systems approaches may be found in the political analysis of organizations. Unlike the political perspective offered by Marxists, I believe it is critical to emphasize not simply macro-institutional analysis, but the analysis of micropolitics (Pfeffer, 1979; Bacharach and Lawler, 1980). To the degree that a political analysis examines the cognitions and actions of actors within the context of specific organizational structure and environment, it may be seen as incorporating the strengths of both the structuralist and loosely coupled system approaches while not succumbing to the weaknesses of these approaches. That is, a political perspective incorporates structure, cognition, and action and as such, takes into account the structural constraints of an approach like Bidwell and Kasarda and the voluntarism implicit in a perspective such as Weick's.

The image of school organizations as political entities is not new. Indeed, an argument can be made that in the educational administration literature this has been a prevailing perspective (Charters, 1953; Eliot, 1959; Corwin, 1965; Ziegler and Jennings, 1974; Wirt and Kirst, 1972; Thompson, 1976). This perception of an existing political orientation stems, to a significant degree, from the use of detailed case studies and other intensive, descriptive methods in educational administration noted earlier. Most of these theorists, while offering an insight into the political analysis of organizations, fail to develop the conceptions of schools as complex political organizations. That is, for the most part, they concentrated on selective relationships such as the relationship between the superintendent and the school board (e.g. Ziegler and Jennings), or they concentrated on specific political roles such as the role of superintendent (Iannaccone and Lutz, 1970). Perhaps the most thoroughly developed analysis of schools as complex political organizations is that offered by Corwin. By identifying key actors and their interactions, in developing a differentiated view of the organizational environment, and by emphasizing the notion of bargaining and adaptive strategies, Corwin has taken an important preliminary step towards developing a political model of the school system and its environment that is more comprehensive in its scope than most earlier efforts.

Considering that the works of Corwin, Charters, Eliot, and so on, preceded theorists such as Bidwell and Kasarda, Weick, and Meyer and Rowan (1977), it is astonishing that the political perspective offered by students of educational systems has not been thoroughly incorporated in the analysis of educational organizations. In a sense, it is ironic that I propose a political approach to the study of educational institutions as a middle ground between structuralist and loosely coupled systems approaches.

A detailed analysis of schools and school districts suggests a political image of organizations accounting for the following:

(1) Educational organizations are best conceived as political systems, both internally and in their external relationships. In educational organizations, at all levels, constant tactical power struggles occur in an effort to obtain control over real or symbolic resources. Whether this struggles occurs between the superintendent and the school board, between the school board and the state, or between principals and teachers is not the important consideration. It is essential to accept the dynamics of power struggles over resources as integral to any organizational analysis.

(2) In educational organizations, participants can be conceived of as political actors with their own needs, objectives, and strategies to achieve those objectives. While there may be some apparent consensus regarding the normative goals of educational organizations (e.g. education), the weight given to different subgoals and the strategies used to pursue them will differ depending upon which actors are questioned. For example, a decision to cut an administrator of an affirmative action program may be viewed by the community as a serious threat to minority protections calling for public protest at school board meetings or letters to the editor of the local paper. The same issue may be coded as a budgetary necessity by the school board. Similarly, in discussions of class size, one finds administrators mentioning financial and child population statistics while teachers speak of pedagogical technique. Thus each group may argue not only the 'rightness' of its specific position, but will also define the issue in terms of its own function.

(3) The decision-making process is the primary arena of political conflict. Each subgroup can be expected to approach a decision with the objective of maximizing its specific interests or goals rather than the maximization of some general organizational objective. For example, in a choice between purchasing new school buses and multiplying the trips of current buses by staggering students' arrival and leaving times, citizens may be concerned with such things as the general traffic patterns in the community, costs, and students being out of school until mid-morning and arriving home after dark. For its part, the school board may be strongly committed to a staggered schedule because it believes that the costs of increased driver time and mechanical depreciation is significantly less expensive than would be the purchase of new buses and the subsequent need to hire more drivers. School administrators may be concerned with questions of congestion around the buildings and the disruption of classes as students arrive and depart. Teachers, as a group, may be entirely disinterested and attempt not to participate. Unless some aspect of the question involves their self-interest (e.g. a significant increase in the transportation budget will decrease the

monies available for salaries), teachers, or any other group, may decide not to become involved in a specific decision. For those who perceive an issue as related to their self-interest, however, the decision-making process becomes the arena in which to attempt to insure that the decision outcome reflects their self-interests.

(4) Each subgroup will also have a different view of who has the formal power (authority), who has the informal power (influence), or who should have the power to make organizational decisions. A group's efforts to have their point of view reflected in the decision outcome centers in large part around questions of authority and influence. Having one's viewpoint represented requires that others agree that your view should be considered; that is, that you should have influence over the decision. The level of agreement or congruence between parties over who has or should have authority and influence over various decisions is constrained by the structure of educational organizations, their work processes, and the different goals of groups. In regards to congruence and incongruence, four types of conditions can be considered (Bacharach and Lawler, 1980):

(i) Congruence (legitimate authority)
  (a) Centralized: superiors and subordinates concur that the right to make a final decision belongs to only the superior.
  (b) Decentralized: superiors and subordinates concur that subordinates have the right to make final decisions.
(ii) Incongruence
  (a) Shirking: superiors maintain that subordinates have the right to make final decisions but subordinates refuse to do so.
  (b) Usurpation: superiors maintain that subordinates do not have the right to make final decisions, but subordinates maintain that they do have the right to make final decisions.

(5) Given the importance of the decision-making process and groups' efforts to have their views reflected in decision outcomes, the nature of congruence with regard to where power lies in the decision-making process is consequential for the level of conflict and ultimately for educational quality. Obviously, the two congruent conditions will produce the least conflict and will enable decision-making to proceed as necessary. In contrast, the two incongruent conditions both pose a major threat to the integrity of the decision-making process. In one (shirking), efforts will be made to pass responsibility for the decision on to others. The passing of the sensitive issue such as school closings back and forth between the administration and school board would be an illustration of this. In the other incongruent condition (usurpation), a group's efforts to obtain authority or influence over a decision which others feel they are not entitled to may also stall the decision process. For example, if teachers, administration, the school board, and various community groups all attempted to become involved in a particular decision, the likelihood of

conflict is high and the chances for a speedy decision low. Disruption of the decision process, particularly when important educational issues are involved, will have a direct effect on the school district's program.

(6) The ability of a single individual or group to have its interests represented in the decision-making process is often limited. As a consequence, in educational organizations coalitions of actors emerge, identify collective objectives, and devise strategies to achieve those objectives. For example, the power of individual teachers or groups of teachers is limited, but the power of a coalition of teachers, that is the union, is often substantial. Should the teachers' union elicit the support of the PTA, an even more influential coalition could result. The formation of coalitions is constrained by organizational structures, ideologies, and environment. For example, the type of coalitions that emerge and the strategies which they follow will depend greatly on whether we are dealing with a large, highly bureaucratic school district or a small, non-bureaucratic school district; whether the community is liberal or conservative; or whether the district population is well educated or poorly educated. In other words, the coalitions which emerge, the collective objectives which they identify, and the strategies which they use to achieve these objectives will be determined to a large degree by the various combinations of structures, ideologies, and environment.

(7) In any school district, there are likely to be a number of different coalitions either in existence or capable of being formed. The dominant coalition is that coalition of actors which controls the authority structure and resources of the organization at a given point in time; their actions and orientations can be described in terms of their *logiques d'action* (perspective from the point of view of the observer that gives their actions meaning and coherence). For example, in one school district we observed (Bacharach and Mitchell, 1981b), the superintendent and a majority faction of the school board constituted the dominant coalition in the district. Although challenged by other groups such as the teachers and the minority faction of the school board, there was no single group or coalition of groups with sufficient influence to replace the dominant coalition in the district. This coalition had enough power through the superintendent's control over his administration and the majority factions control over school board votes to insure the district was run as they saw fit. Further, the strategies and tactics employed (such as the superintendent's control over information and the majority factions ties to the community élite) were consistent with their perception of their roles and responsibilities as school district officials in a particular school district. In a similar manner, those who challenged the dominant coalition also followed a consistent set of rules or expectations. As a consequence, there was an underlying logic to what often appeared to be a chaotic and conflictual state of affairs. The same reasoning can be applied to all school districts.

(8) Although a dominant coalition may remain in place for an extended

period of time either through astute political maneuvering or the relative quiescence of the district, no coalition is sacrosanct. A dialectical relationship exists between the organizational structures, ideologies, and environment and the emergence and aspirations of coalitions. Coalitions emerge in reaction to structures, ideologies, and environment and in turn reformulate and institutionalize structures, work processes, and ideologies which engender over time, a reaction from emergent coalitions. The rotation of coalitions on school boards illustrates this process. In one district we observed (Bacharach and Mitchell, 1981b), a taxpayer's group concerned over rising school costs was able to mobilize sufficient community support to gain a majority of seats on the school board. This coalition was able to oust the superintendent from office, alter the content and definition of other administrative roles, and to undertake a review of the district curriculum with an eye toward adapting a more fundamental or back-to-basics approach to education. Shocked by some of these actions, a rival coalition consisting of teachers, parent groups, and members of the community élite was formed and after intensive campaigning, was able to replace the taxpayer's group as the majority faction on the school board. This new coalition then proceeded to implement a series of its own changes in school district policy. The point is that educational organizations must be seen as political entities that shape and are shaped by their environmental and organizational context.

(9) The dialectic presented above as a critical component of a political analysis of schools occurs over time and within a specific context. This means that educational organizations are best understood in terms of a historical perspective and in terms of the specificity and structure of the institutional system of which they are a part.

At least two methodological issues emerge from this elaboration of the major points involved in an analysis of educational organizations as political entities. The first issue deals with the unit of analysis. A political analysis, due to its concentration on coalitions as the basis of action and change, envisions groups as the primary focus of a study of educational organizations. This perspective affords an empirical middle ground between a concentration on aggregate and individual data by examining collectivities of individuals within an organization. To date, the potential of the group model has not been fully realized. The group has been seen as a relatively formal entity whose activities within the organization are passive and of little interest to the researcher. What attention has been paid to them focuses on group autonomy, that is, with the group itself rather than the group's relationship with other work groups in the organization. Realization of the full potential of the group perspective requires that the dynamics of the group interrelationships become a focal point of future research. For example, properly conceptualized, a group model is well suited to examination of the administrative, educational, and political imperatives that confront school administrators as they are expressed in various group interactions. We believe that the proper application of the group model can be achieved if it is embedded in a theoretical approach that considers the organization as a political system.

The second methodological issue has to deal with the use of case studies versus large quantitative comparative studies with which we began our discussion. There, we argued that the choice of method has in many cases dictated the theoretical content of the research undertaken. One of the advantages of the political approach being advocated here is its ability to constructively utilize both methods, drawing upon their strengths without succumbing to their limitations. To elaborate, the major strengths of the large-scale comparative survey approach is the ability to generalize that it affords. It enables one to pinpoint the key variables and variable relationships which constrain the political process across school districts. The primary weakness is its inability to provide a sense of process and the specific information necessary for an in-depth analysis. In contrast, the strengths of a case study approach lie in its ability to explore how political processes unfold over time in a specific setting. Its principal weakness is its failure to provide a sufficient base for generalizing to other organizations. Together, the two methods complement one another and provide the basis for a thorough understanding of school districts as political systems, allowing one to determine which aspects of school districts are qualitatively unique, and which aspects are quantitatively recurrent.

Obviously, the key step here involves the creative design of research which can effectively utilize both approaches. For example, in our own research, we began a series of case studies to familiarize ourselves with how the issues we were concerned with were handled in school districts. The information collected from these case-study sites was then used to help in designing a survey for distribution to a larger sample of schools of which the case-study sites were a part. Having collected data using both approaches, it is now possible to use the results of the case studies to suggest potential analyses of the survey data, or to use the results of a survey analysis to characterize a case-study site and examine how a given profile of variable values is translated into action in an actual school district (Bacharach and Mitchell, 1981b). Other ways of interfacing the two types of data are also possible. The point is that drawing on the strengths of each approach insures that the results will both be abstract enough to allow for significant theoretical contributions, yet concrete enough to generate practical policy recommendations.

In closing, as I noted elsewhere, the interplay between theory, methods, and practice may arise in any area, and the difference in emphasis which characterizes organizational theory and educational administration as areas of activity has direct consequences for the establishment of a dialogue between these two fields (Bacharach and Mitchell, 1981a). The purpose of such an interaction is to insure that the theory that is generated is relevant and useful both to those in educational administration and in organizational behavior. For educational administration, this suggests a critical assessment of the concepts being proposed by organizational behaviorists; for organizational behaviorists, this prompts a step down from the heights of general theory and a focus on the specific properties of schools as well as a concern with how broader theoretical concepts unfold in educational settings. For both, the dialogue should be an exercise in the creation of practical theory. One example of the potential fruitfulness of this kind of a dialogue is in the political analysis of schools as organizations elaborated here (e.g. Bacharach and Mitchell, 1982). Recent theoretical developments in organizational behavior, when combined with the rich body of descriptive empirical literature in the areas of school politics and school organizations, results in a perspective which presents a realistic image of schools as organizations with direct implications for the development and refinement of theory, research, and practice.

## Notes

1. This paper is a revision of an invited talk originally presented during the meeting of Organization Theory Special Interest Group of the American Educational Research Association. Please do not cite or quote without the permission of the author. This material is based on work supported by the National Institute of Education under Grant number NIE G 78 0080, Samuel Bacharach, principal investigator. Any opinions, findings, conclusions or recommendations expressed in this report are those of the authors and do not necessarily reflect the views of the Institute or the Department of Education.
2. While Bidwell and Kasarda use school districts as the unit of analysis, the implication of their perspective holds for schools and school districts.

## References

Bacharach, Samuel B. (ed.) (1981). *Organizational Behavior in Schools and School Districts*, New York: Praeger.

Bacharach, Samuel B. and Edwrd J. Lawler (1980). *Power and Politics in Organizations*, San Francisco: Jossey-Bass.

Bacharach, Samuel B. and Stephen M. Mitchell (1981a). 'Toward a Dialogue in The Middle Range,' *Educational Administration Quarterly* XVII(3):1–14 (University of Rochester, University Council for Educational Administration).

Bacharach, Samuel B. and Stephen M. Mitchell (1981b). 'Critical Variables in the Formation and Maintenance of Consensus in School Districts,' *Educational Administration Quarterly* VIII(4):74–97.

Bacharach, Samuel B. and Stephen M. Mitchell (1982). 'Organizations and Expectations: Organizational Determinants of Union Membership Demands,' to appear in *Advances in Industrial Relations*, ed. David Lipsky, Greenwich, Conn.: JAI Press.

Benson, J. K. *Organizational Analysis: Critique and Innovation*, Sage Publications.

Bidwell, Charles E. and John D. Kasarda (1980). 'School District Organization and

288    *Samuel B. Bacharach*

Student Achievement,' *The Study of Organizations*, eds Daniel Katz, Robert L. Kahn and J. Stacy Adams, San Francisco: Jossey-Bass.

Blau, P. and R. Schoenherr (1971). *The Structure of Organizations*, New York: Basic.

Charters, W. W. (1953). 'Social Class Analysis and the Control of Public Education,' *Harvard Education Review* 23 (Fall).

Clark, Burton (1972). 'The Organizational Saga in Higher Education,' *Administrative Science Quarterly* 17 (June): 178–84.

Corwin, Ronald G. (1965). *A Sociology of Education*, New York: Appleton-Century-Crofts.

Crozier, Michael (1964). *The Bureaucratic Phenomenon*, Chicago: University of Chicago Press.

Crozier, Michael and Friedberg, Erhard., *Actors and Systems: The Politics of Collective Action*, 1981. University of Chicago Press.

Cyert, Richard M. and James G. March (1963). *A Behavioral Theory of the Firm* Englewood Cliffs, NJ: Prentice-Hall.

Edelman, M. (1971). *Politics as Symbolic Action*, Chicago: Markham.

Eliot, Thomas H. (1959). 'Toward an Understanding of Public School Politics', *American Political Science Review* 52:1032–51.

Hage, Jerald and Michael Aiken (1967). 'Program Change and Organizational Properties,' *American Journal of Sociology* 72 (March): 503–19.

Hall, Richard H. (1963). 'The Concept of Bureaucracy,' *American Journal of Sociology* 69(1):32–40.

Hall, Richard H. and Charles R. Tittle (1966). 'Bureaucracy and its Correlates, *American Journal of Sociology* 72(3):267–72.

Iannacone, L. and F. Lutz (1970). *Politics, Power and Policy: The Governing of Local School Districts*, Columbus, Ohio: Charles Merrill.

Kerr, Norman D. (1964). 'The School Board as an Agency of Legitimation,' *Sociology of Education* 38:34–54.

March, James G., and H. Simon (1958). *Organizations*, New York: John Wiley.

Meyer, J. and B. Rowan (1977). 'Notes on the structure of educational organizations', *Studies on Environment and Organization*, San Francisco: Jossey-Bass.

Pettigrew, A. M. (1973). *The politics of organizational decision-making*. London: Tavistock.

Pfeffer, J. (1979). 'Power and resource allocation in organizations', *The organization game*, eds R. H. Miles and W. A. Randolph, Santa Monica: Goodyear.

Pugh, D., D. Hickson, C. Hinings, and C. Turner (1969). 'The Context of Organizational Structures,' *Administrative Science Quarterly* 14:115–26.

Selznick, P. (1949). *TVA and the Grass Roots*, Berkeley: University of California Press.

Thompson, J. D. (1967). *Organizations in Action*, New York: McGraw Hill.

Thompson, J. and W. McEwen (1958). 'Organizational Goals and Environment: Goalsetting as an Interaction Process,' *American Sociological Review* 23:23–31.

Weber, M. (1947). *The Theory of Social and Economic Organizations*, New York, Oxford University Press.

Weick, Karl (1976). 'Educational Organizations as Loosely Coupled Systems,' *Administrative Science Quarterly* 21 (March): 1–19.

Wirt, Frederick M. and Michael W. Kirst (1975). *The Political Web of American Schools*, Boston: Little, Brown.

Zeigler, Harmon and Kent, Jennings (1974). *Governing American Schools*, North Scituate, Mass.: Duxbory Press.

# 17

# Talk as the work:
# the accomplishment of
# school administration

**Peter C. Gronn**

This article[1] provides a case study of administering a school, showing how talk is central to the achievement of control. Analysis of extracts of a transcript of talk by and with the principal shows school administrators trying to direct and control the deployment of personnel in conformity with their will and intents. A principal and his two immediate subordinates do this with their words in their talk with one another, in the corridor, the principal's office, and in the staff room. The analysis shows that not only do administrators spend much of their time talking and that this talk accomplishes administration, but that talk is used to do the work of tightening and loosening administrative control.

## Introduction

Various writers have suggested means by which administrators administer. Pocock (1973a) showed how tradition both circumscribed and legitimated activity. Weber (1970) wrote about the charismatic leader's mission and power. In a school context, Sir James Darling (1967:70) referred to 'dignity and a corresponding awe' and to the written memorandum or circular as 'government by notes and directives' (1967:65). Finally, there is Halpin's (1960:85) 'language of eyes and hands, of gestures, of time and status symbols.' At least one important resource missing from this list is talk. A great proportion of administrative activity consists of talk in interactional settings, yet talk remains a neglected dimension in accounts of leadership and administration (Pondy, 1978). Talk is significant in that it permits speakers to monitor each other by observing one another (Goffman, 1979). Thus, in conversing with staff, 'one can watch and suit one's words to the atmosphere' (Darling, 1967:65).

Control is an aspect of administration for which talk is a key resource, particularly for staff relations, and in schools, talk is a potential instrument of control for both principal and staff. Healey (1978) suggested that although the position of headmaster frequently affords domination, this is only by virtue of the confidence of the council, staff, parents, and pupils, and the influence of the old boys. Similarly, Fletcher (1937:236) questioned the myth that school heads are autocrats, stating that 'in particular his powers are limited by the traditions of the school as well as by the personalities of his staff.'[2]

To the extent that administrative control is accomplished by talk, school personnel become enmeshed in language games. This article presents a case study of a principal and his vice-principal grappling with staff allocation and deployment for the ensuing year. It shows that the two leading administrators use words to cloak their power. Transcribed extracts are included in the text to indicate the nature of the interaction. The sections that follow discuss the background to the investigation of talk in administration, the method used in obtaining the data for the case study, the setting of the study, the dimensions of control evident in the talk, and the way talk achieves control.

### Background

Eight recent studies that describe school administration have followed books by Mintzberg (1973) and by Wolcott (1973). Inspired by the central question of the Mintzberg study (1973:1), 'What do managers do?,' these eight accounts (O'Dempsey, 1976; Peterson, 1976; Duignan, 1980; Friesen and Duignan, 1980; Willis, 1980; Martin and Willower, 1981; Sproull, 1981; Thomas, Willis, and Phillips, 1981) point to the same frenzied and interrupted work routines experienced by Mintzberg's five chief executives. Furthermore, as Mintzberg (1973:38) wrote, 'Virtually every empirical study of management time allocation draws attention to the great proportion of time spent in verbal communication . . . [and] my own findings bear this out.' The same picture emerges in the school studies (Wolcott, 1973; O'Dempsey, 1976; Willis, 1980).

Elsewhere (Gronn, 1982) it has been argued that these eight studies, and indeed the Mintzberg approach known as 'structured observation,' show serious deficiencies and leave a number of questions unanswered. Six of the eight accounts indicate that between two-thirds and three-quarters of the total working time of a principal or superintendent is spent talking, yet none of these studies examines the interactants' words. Talk is presented as simple behavior, noteworthy of analysis as a form of social action. Nowhere is there any hint that the interactants' talk accomplishes administration.

Two earlier diary-based accounts point to this reliance on the spoken word. In a study of the interaction of four executives, Burns (1954) wrote that they spent 80 percent of the total recorded time (890 hours) in conversation, including telephone conversation. In a study of sixty-six middle managers, Horne and Lupton (1965) observed that half of the time of all the managers was spent in their own offices talking.

Another weakness of structured observational accounts is that they have focused attention solely on the top person, emphasizing only one party in what is an interactional activity (e.g. Mintzberg, 1973). Burns' account not only highlighted the group basis of managerial work and the centrality of talk within the group, but also showed what the four interactants took each other's talk to be about, or how they perceived it. For example Burns (1954: 95) stated.:

> Half the time, what the manager thought he was giving as instructions or decisions was being treated as information or advice. This result may be regarded as an aspect of status protection. The tendency for the three senior staff to treat instructions from the head of department as information or advice amounts to a rejection of the subordination implied in being instructed to take this or that action.

What all the structured observation studies do reveal is that talk *is* the work, i.e. it consumes most of an administrator's time and energy. The next step is to make clear the circumstances under which talk *does* the work, that is, to show how talk is the resource that school personnel use to get others to act (Austin, 1978). To see talk in such terms is to view it as an instrument or tool (Hodgkinson, 1978:204) for performing actions like influencing, persuading, manipulating, and so on. That words perform actions (Austin, 1978) can be seen in the following example: 'The bottle's half empty' versus 'The bottle's half full' (Blakar, 1979:111). Blakar comments that 'there is good reason to assume that the two expressions may well have quite different effects on the atmosphere.' Expanding this example to 'The bottle's *already* half empty' versus 'The bottle's *still* half full' (original emphasis), Blakar points out the different effect that each utterance could have on a party. The next example shows what happens when there is an interplay of differing definitions of the situation, and is an actual recorded doctor–patient exchange (Coulthard and Ashby, 1975:174):

*Doctor*: How many *attacks* have you had?
*Patient*: It's the first one . . . one.
*Doctor*: You've only had one in all?
*Patient*: Well as far as I know there's not been one this severe like.
*Doctor*: Yeah, and when do you get *these*?
*Patient*: It came on very suddenly last Wedensday.

If it is true, as Austin (1978:6–7) claims, that 'the issuing of the utterance is the performing of an action – it is not normally thought of as just saying something,' then two questions must be asked of administrative control that is evident in interaction. First, what is the nature of the control accomplished by the words of the administrator and those he administers? Second, how do the words accomplish that control? The rest of this article addresses these two questions.

## Method

Research on samples of participants' talk had been collected in school council settings (Gronn, 1979, 1981b) and had indicated how school principals and parents used their words to pursue their interests and to achieve their particular ends, so that an investigation of what principals and teachers did with their words and how they did this seemed warranted. Accordingly, in December 1980, the talk of a school principal and everyone with whom he spoke over two school days was received by an unobtrusive radio microphone attached to the principal's lapel and was transmitted to a tape recorder housed in a small outbuilding separate from the main school building (Soskin and John, 1963:230–1). Typed transcriptions of these recordings yielded in excess of 300 pages of scripts. From these, a segment that took place in three locations (the corridor, the principal's office and the staff room) on the afternoon of the second day was chosen for detailed analysis. Total recording time of this segment was 30 minutes. The author was present as an observer in the corridor and in the staff room. The typist's draft transcription of this 30-minute segment was refined to produce a final transcript of twelve pages (Gronn, 1981a: Appendix). Selections from this final transcript are reproduced in this article. Each part of the interaction is discussed in the order of its occurrence.

The transcript presentation in this article is conventional in form and conforms closely to the pattern used by Clegg (1975). Transcript production and presentation, quite apart from the question of its interpretation, has occasioned a good deal of recent discussion. The presentation here has benefited particularly from the arguments of Kress (1979), Ochs (1979) and Sacks, Schegloff, and Jefferson (1974). The number of symbols in the transcript has been deliberately minimized to ensure readability. Only limited evidence of stress, intonation, and nonverbal communication has been provided. Essentially, Ochs' (1979) injunction against strictly standard orthography has been adhered to in order to capture roughly how a lexical item was pronounced.

The following transcription symbols have been used:

| // | Overlapping talk from the first to the last slash. Utterances begin with an upper case letter and end with a full stop. |
| ... | A pause of one second or less within an utterance. |
| (1,1) | A pause of more than one second within an utterance or between turns, the numeral indicating the length of the pause. |

| ***** | A deletion. |
|---|---|
| [] | An explanatory insertion. |
| *italics* | A word or part of a word emphasized by a speaker. |
| ? | A question, marked by a rise in pitch. |
| ! | An exclamation. |

## Setting

Prior information about the school setting had been given by the principal who was a former student of the author and who agreed to be recorded for this investigation. The only contact with the school prior to the recording days took place when the author met the whole staff and explained the nature and purposes of the research. Assurance was given orally that only pseudonyms would be used when referring to the school or individuals in any published work. Staff were told that they could have the radio microphone turned off when talking to the principal. To the author's knowledge, this happened only once.

The staff and their positions follow:

| | | | |
|---|---|---|---|
| Alf Bennett: | principal | Keith Lamb: | grade 2 |
| Cecily Donald: | librarian | Merrill Nash: | grade 3 |
| Ellen Finch: | remedial teacher | Oliver Peters: | grade 4 |
| Grace Harvey: | prep. year | Quentin Rogers: | grade 5 |
| Ida Jones: | grade 1 | Steven Trigg: | vice-principal, grade 6 |

The school was a small state primary (i.e. elementary) school in the eastern suburb of Park, Melbourne, 12 miles from the city center. Park is a semi-rural area on the fringe of the city. Real estate subdivisions have recently replaced orchards, market gardens, and poultry farms. Burgeoning housing growth is beginning to swell enrolments. The primary school had an enrolment of just under 200 children at the time of the study.

All staff were on first-name terms with the principal and with each other. The smallness of the school meant that Bennett was very visible to the staff and constantly engaged in face-to-face interaction with all of them, whereas in a larger school (e.g. with a staff of 100) this frequency and intimacy of relationships would be missing.

The choice of teachers for different grades is an annual end-of-year concern of teachers and principals. It is of particular significance in terms of personal careers for individual teachers and, if not handled carefully by principals, can make for disharmony in staff relationships. In December, before the long Australian summer vacation, staffing is also of concern to parents who are often anxious to know who is to be in charge of their children. The recording was made two weeks before the end of the school year, and nobody knew what the staffing was to be. Yet, a number of people

were concerned, as was evident from frequent references to their concern in
these extracts. This dual concern of teachers and parents was compounded for
Bennett (who was to transfer to another school in the new year), because the
final decisions in this case were not his to make. As a servant of the state in a
government school, his only power was one of deployment. There were still
staff appointments for the next year to be made by state education department
officials.

### The process of control

*Corridor work*

The first part of the episode is illustrative of Rolland's dictum that 'a
headmaster's work consists mainly of interruptions to it' (Keith, 1977:111).
Early in the afternoon Bennett was conversing with Trigg outside Trigg's
classroom. Bennett was reporting on a meeting he attended over lunch, when
Trigg interrupted.

1. *Trigg*: I think one thing that it'd be very dangerous to disc keep discussing at the staff meeting is . . . is . . . classes and grades for next year.
2. *Bennett*: Oh I'm not gonna talk about that.
3. *Trigg*: I would I would just/
4. *Bennett*: /I'm not I haven't got it down.
5. *Trigg*: It's down [on the agenda].
6. *Bennett*: It's down is it?
7. *Trigg*: Hang on . . . um (2.5) it was put down Merrill [Nash] put it down.
8. *Bennett*: Mm.
9. *Trigg*: And I think that um (1.4) it's better to be forgotten about all all that needs to be said is it's still unde*ci*ded.
10. *Bennett*: Mm.
11. *Trigg*: You can say (3.5) I've got grade 6.
12. *Bennett*: Mm.
13. *Trigg*: Keith's got grade 2 Merrill's got grade 3 Grace has got prep they're the ones that we know for definite at the/
14. *Bennett*: /We know yeah/
15. *Trigg*: /at the present time.
16. *Bennett*: That's right yeah.
17. *Trigg*: And leave it at that.
18. *Bennett*: Leave it at that yeah till we know.
19. *Trigg*: And don't discuss any further cos it's not/
20. *Bennett*: /Except that they could oh they could question me.
21. *Trigg*: Well they can question you but I would.
22. *Bennett*: Just say well I'm sorry but/

23. *Trigg*: /I'd say that there's nothing has been nothing definite.
(Bennett agrees substantially with Trigg's assessment of the situation but queries his use of 'pressure.')
49. *Trigg*: Well I for one you know am not prepared to discuss it and I don't think we ought to discuss it (1.3) I think there's too much can get you that goes on in too much pressure.
50. *Bennett*: Yeah.
51. *Trigg*: After all.
52. *Bennett*: They can't apply pressure if there's nothing (1.3) *there* for it to be applied to.
(Bennett believes that all that could be done about the staffing situation has been done.)
69. *Trigg*: You as principal or you and me and Keith as vice-principals in the place ought to talk about these kinds of things and come up with a workable situation so that.
70. *Bennett*: Well we have/
71. *Trigg*: /We don't we don't have all these sort of things.
72. *Bennett*: We've tried we've tried to work it out we worked out the best that we can we can't work it out much more.
73. *Trigg*: See I think this little miss [Nash] is trying to put a lot of pressure on.
(Eventually he agrees that there might be something in what Trigg says.)
103. *Trigg*: Be very careful you know.
104. *Bennett*: Very interesting what you find out when you're about to go. (laughs) [Bennett is to transfer to a new school]
105. *Trigg*: Oh no I think you've known that a along.
106. *Bennett*: Yeah but I didn't realize that/
107. *Trigg*: /But you know these are the things that are starting to roll again and I think it's a pretty dangerous situation/
108. *Bennett*: /Do you want to have a discussion with Keith about it now so we know our stance or can you and Keith answer this situation when we have the staff meeting?
109. *Trigg*: Aw we'll get Keith and have a five minute talk.
110. *Bennett*: Aw well let's go down because we're gotta be prepared for it (2.1) [They begin walking] ah I think . . . I mean if she's★★★★★

The first point to note is the significance of architecture and territory in these exchanges. Corridors are crucial territories in most schools. Classrooms and offices open off them, so that a good deal of organizational work is done in corridors. There is constant movement between classes and at breaks, messages are transmitted from offices to teachers, and people always mingle and gather informally. It is common for a principal to put his or her head around a teacher's door to have a chat. The teacher leaves the class and comes over, and both individuals straddle the doorway between a bit of the school and the school as a whole. This may be the principal's respite from the telephone, but it is crucial to administering a school. Teachers and principals both know that what might appear as 'prowling' (Darling, 1967:64) is also a way of the principal showing the staff that he or she is around and keeping in touch with the pulse of the school.

In using the corridor in this way, the principal gets caught up in the staff's concerns. Being narrow and long, corridors seem to force individuals to gaze, smile at or greet one another as they go past. Such encounters afford the staff access to a principal that they might not have if he or she were ensconced in an office with the door shut. And although the corridor, a public thoroughfare, affords no guarantee of privacy, there is sufficient background noise for talk to be indistinct, so that any insecurity generated by being seen talking is tempered by the knowledge that others often cannot hear what is being said. Consequently, the corridor is the place where greetings are exchanged, contacts are made, initial forays are undertaken into a topic, and where arrangements are made to pursue the matter in quieter, more private surroundings. It is only later on, as part of the office work, that a topic can be deliberated on and examined more fully.

How is this administering? Where is the control? Just as children, in a sense, bring up their parents, and so are the active agents while the adults are those acted upon, so Bennett is the object rather than the subject of the relationship with Trigg. The concerns of the moment are Trigg's. The flow of events and their terms have been determined for, rather than by, Bennett. He adjusts to a definition of the situation that he did not author. He has been persuaded ('Do you want to have a discussion with Keith about it now . . . ?') If not to perceive the situation from within the same threat frame as Trigg, then at least to be warned to re-examine the matter ('so we know our stance,' 'we're gotta be prepared for it'). This incident illustrates Hodgkinson's (1978:81) comment that 'one man's power is another man's impotence if the latter must forego his will on behalf of the former.'

Contrary, then, to the image of the administrator in much of the management literature as directing, commanding, planning, etc., as if administering is a unilateral and unidimensional action directed at a set of employees, here is an administrator seemingly being controlled rather than being in control.

Another architectural feature that contributed to Bennett's informal relations with the staff and the staff's familiarity with each other was that all staff but one had to pass Bennett's door to enter the staff room and leave the building. There was no possibility that the aura and distance that many administrators enjoy could develop in such circumstances. These factors are evident in the talk, for there is, on the one hand, a kind of chumminess in the way the staff speak and, on the other, an insistence and persistence in manner (especially with Trigg), which would be less likely to manifest itself with a more remote principal.

*Office work*
The second exchange lasted about 17 minutes. A marked shift begins to take
place in the relative positions of Trigg and Bennett during what is a lengthy
but pivotal interlude between the corridor and staff room talk. Bennett
begins to assume control over the situation, whereas Trigg lets his initiative
slip away. Bennett tells Lamb about Trigg's concern.

111. *Bennett*: [to Lamb] (*sotto voce*) I'll just have a (1.3) little very small talk
about staffing for next year because it's down on the agenda for today
and (1.2) ah [they walk to Bennett's office] Steven thinks we should
have a united front on what we're (laughingly) going to say (10.5) (*sotto
voce*) Steven's got the feeling Merrill's going to bring up wants with the
demands as to (1.1) you know what the staffing situation should be well
(3.2) all we can tell her is what we know (1.1) and that is the . . . the fixed
(2.2) positions for next year which (1.7) at the moment would be Grace
(2.3) and yourself (2.7) and Merrill (2.2) and Steven . . . because
Quentin hasn't indicated yet that she's going to ah resign or stay (1.1)
Ellen Finch hasn't indicated whether she's going to resign or stay (1.6)
[Trigg enters] and . . . we've just got the one appointment coming in
which is the girl Veal.
(There are glimpses of Bennett's inner mental state evident in that
already, before Trigg joins Bennett and Lamb, Bennett has laughed off
Trigg's feeling (111) by parodying him 'Steven thinks we should have a
united front on what we're (laughingly) going to say.' The three of
them begin to talk about the subject at length in Bennett's office.)

112. *Trigg*: I saw the list that.
113. *Bennett*: There it is there/
114. *Trigg*: /It was put down grades and rooms for next year. (1.2)
115. *Bennett*: Yeah I want to I want to sort the grades and rooms/
116. *Trigg*: /I think it's a bit dangerous to keep talking about it and talking
about it and talking about it personally.
117. *Bennett*: Well see I've shut up about it I haven't said but they're talking
about it. (1.5)
118. *Lamb*: Well I spose everybody wants to know what they're doing . . .
but.
119. *Bennett*: Yeah.
120. *Lamb*: We really can't say at the moment can we?
121. *Bennett*: Well all we know/
122. *Lamb*: /We/
123. *Bennett*: /We/
124. *Lamb*: /put up a number of um . . . alternatives.
125. *Trigg*: Well we *tried* that and we came up against a *blank wall*.
126. *Bennett*: If we put up alternatives it still doesn't help them because er
they can't decide the issues you know it's between Steven you and me to
decide in the end.
127. *Lamb*: No what I mean by alternatives alternatives according to what-

ever set of circumstances arise as whether Steven's offered the job or whether we get another principal.

128. *Bennett*: I think they *know* this don't they we all all we can do is is retell them what we've told them before (exasperation) (1.1) and see we don't know until next February er we may not know till next February as to who's going to be principal here.
(They discuss all kinds of possible grade arrangements. Trigg continues to refer to 'pressure.')

183. *Trigg*: But there's already been moves (1.2) of pressure being brought on . . . Alf . . . about a certain person [Ellen Finch] taking grade 5.

184. *Lamb*: Yeah.

185. *Bennett*: By.

186. *Trigg*: By parents/

187. *Bennett*: /by parents/

188. *Lamb*: /Yeah yeah I know you told me.

189. *Trigg*: Now um (10.0) [they are interrupted by the bell monitors] I don't bow to that sort of pressure.*****
(Bennett here admits that he has been approached by parents.)

243. *Trigg*: If the you know someone's gonna keep pushing.

244. *Bennett*: Well they're got nowhere to push Steven there's nothing to push about.

245. *Trigg*: If there's nothing to push well we've gotta be organized ourselves so we know what's going but we don't know what's going/

246. *Bennett*: /No/

247. *Trigg*: /so there's no (1.1) I think it's dangerous to keep talking about it that's all.

248. *Bennett*: Hm but it's being talked about here it's not being talked about/

249. *Trigg*: /Oh no/

250. *Bennett*: /by us/

251. *Trigg*: Yeah but that particular person [Merrill Nash] is well known for getting/

252. *Bennett*: /For talking/

253. *Trigg*: /parental pressure.

254. *Bennett*: Is she? (1.5)*****

255. *Trigg*: You know she's always talking to parents and very good friends with parents. (1.4)

256. *Bennett*: That's right how friendly is she with Wilma Young [a parent]?'

257. *Trigg*: Very friendly/

258. *Bennett*: /Ya see/

259. *Trigg*: /they play tennis I think.

260. *Bennett*: Well Wilma Young was one who came in to discuss Ellen Finch and her mates.

261. *Trigg*: Yeah well she Wilma Young wouldn't have known who was going to take the grade 5 unless she was spec spec specifically told.

262. *Bennett*: Yeah yeah.

263. *Trigg*: Now I haven't told anyone because I haven't a clue.
264. *Bennett*: No it's come from outside/
265. *Trigg*: /We've discussed about it/
266. *Bennett*: /because I was absolutely sur*prised* when she walked in here and wanted to know who was going to take grade 5.
267. *Trigg*: The School Council have talked about it.
268. *Bennett*: They talked about it *after*wards.
269. *Trigg*: But they but they don't know who's actually going to take it.
270. *Bennett*: No.
271. *Trigg*: And they made the same comment that we've just said (1.6) thut if . . . Ellen takes the grade 5 you're going to get pressure from parents.
272. *Bennett*: The word deputation was tossed around. (laughs)
    (Trigg is then called away on a message.)
296. *Bennett*: But anyway well look . . . ah . . ˙ I think we're right we know what we're gonna say there's only a few positions permanent (3.0) permanent classes so.

To this point Bennett has shrugged off 'deputation' (272). Later on (316), he responds to the reported threat, 'she said we'll go as high as we can,' in a similar fashion. He has become impatient with Trigg and it shows on three occasions (117, 244, and 248). Lamb gives Bennett one other opportunity to vent his irritation (128).

In this first half of the office session quite different positions are taken compared with those in the corridor. Bennett, Trigg, and Lamb adopt dual postures, arbitrating the merits of their colleagues' interests while advancing interests of their own. They shift back and forth between articulating their own career concerns and talk for or on behalf of others. This movement is evident in changes in pronoun usage from 'I' and 'you' to 'we' and 'us' as opposed to 'them' and 'they.' After Trigg leaves (296), Bennett explains the parents' interest to Lamb.

314. *Bennett*: See yud have two unhappy teachers yud ave Una Veal in grade 5 you know eating her heart out because she wants to be in 1 . . . yud ave Ellen Finch in 1 wanting to be in 5 (1.6) now wh I ga I think we've got to take a risk somewhere here and I think poss we may have to put up with the parents' anger over Ellen Finch being back in grade 5 (1.8) but I think it's for us to decide and I think Ellen's gotta realize that ya know it'll be absolute *chaos* if she goes on confinement leave and if she's pregnant now and I don't know whether she is I think she should confide in us that she is pregnant . . . but I don't know whether she would . . . maybe she isn't maybe she's not gonna have any more children and maybe she would say to us well mind you own damn business. (laughs)
315. *Lamb*: Yeah.
316. *Bennett*: But see Wilma Young came in from that Parents' Club meeting with Amy Brown [another parent] and a couple of other vers of

others and uh demanded to know where Ellen Finch was going next year and I said grade 5 and she said well if she does there's gonna be a deputation to stop it you know well er if she she said we'll go as high as we can (6.6) (laughs) and now er g well guess the other thing is to . . . you know if we don't do that Ellen *Finch*'s gotta go in grade 1 and Quent's gotta go in grade 5 or she could go to grade 2 (1.2) and Id see if Ida stays she could go to 5 (1.6) there's about ten thousand alternatives at the moment.

The changed power status of the talkers evident in these stretches of talk derives from the shift in territory from the corridor to the privacy of the principal's office. No one person owns the corridor; all share territorial, i.e. proprietorial rights; however, while the principal moves around the whole site at will, the office is his personal domain, which allows privacy and which gives rise to the exchange of confidences. Intimate details of real lives and suppositions about career plans (see, especially, 314) together with data on enrolments (cited in 340), form an administrative knowledge stock.

The relative distribution of this knowledge proves crucial in shifting control from Trigg to Bennett. If there is anything to substantiate Trigg's case, it will come out in the confidentiality of this room. Bennett has put Trigg to the test (244, 248, 250) and his story has begun to look thin. The critical remark is 256 where Bennett brings his own knowledge and experience to bear (this is subsequently explicated in 316, after Trigg has left the room). For the first time Bennett has countered Trigg's facts with his own (267 and 268). Bennett continues to be unconcerned about the parents' interest.

340. *Bennett*: No it's not see we lost 20 [pupils] between July and December (1.2) so um (1.1) but a you know well we've tossed around the alternatives but we've got the answers for them [at the staff meeting] I don't I don't know I don't really see much pressure coming from there at all I think that it's just inquisitiveness and everybody's asking those questions aren't they yeah the parents are all asking too you see.

341. *Lamb*: Yeah.

342. *Bennett*: But um/

343. *Lamb*: /Just can't can't give any answers at the moment.

344. *Bennett*: Well see [an ex-staff member] always said that the parents have a lot to say in this school and this is one thing she's found over the years the parents are interested ah I wouldn't sa well they're quizzical without being sticky beaks . . . but they're just *inter*ested to know what's going on the school's small enough for them to be interested . . . yet up at [neighboring school] they wouldn't hear a thing because the school's big enough to keep them away but here (1.3) it's sort of ideal situation for parents to be interested and also they're going through parent-teacher interviews at the moment . . . and they're asking information before next year comes along.

This backstage maneuvering (Goffman, 1976b:114) ends with Bennett making manifest to Lamb his operating assumptions as a principal. In essence the norm at Park for parents is 'to know what's going on the school's small enough for them to be interested,' and the current events fit this norm.

### Staff meeting work

Staff meetings normally take place at the end of the day when classes have been dismissed. They are supposed to be an occasion when principals outline an agenda of topics and speak first on each item. It is a time when teachers relax, expecting to listen to the principal addressing them, and is not normally seen as an opportunity for discussion or debate. The convention, rather, is that staff will react or respond to the principal's remarks. This is a time for letting off steam, by griping, joking, and showing one's impatience if the meeting drags on. Moreover, such meetings are held in the staff room, the 'laughter arena' (Woods, 1979:211). Principals have to work doubly hard at keeping the meeting going by stifling interruptions and side chatter and by putting in their own thoughts and comments. One headmaster, A. H. Wood (1976:260), disliked staff meetings and stated that 'managing a staff meeting called for more tact and skill than any church meetings over which I have presided. I generally steered contentious issues away from an immediate decision and often resolved the matter afterwards.' In Bennett's case there was nothing exceptional in his mentioning staffing, as such, nor in talking about it as he did with 'the position is still unclear' (345).

In the staff meeting, Bennett began by stating the staffing position as he saw it:

345. *Bennett*: Um the other thing is grades and rooms for next year (2.3) (sighs) (1.5) the position is still unclear . . . now all we can say . . . at the moment is that Grace has got preps (3.0) grade 1 is not clear grade 2 at the moment will be Keith Lamb (1.2) grade 3 is Merrill Nash (1.5) grade 4 (1.1) is Quentin Rogers (3.0) grade 5 is not clear and grade 6 is Steven (1.6) and (2.4) if Steven gets the position as principal next year (1.8) he'll come outta grade 6 (1.5) Keith could go into grade 6 (1.2) which would leave grade 2 vacant (1.7) if Steven doesn't get it he stays in grade 6 (1.8) and (1.5) this is how we are at the moment now (2.2) uh (2.8) we could put . . . Una Veal in grade 1 and we can put um Ellen in grade 5 (2.0) Cecily stays as librarian (1.1) ah it all depends . . . on who gets the principal's job as to what's gonna happen with the staffing.
346. *Trigg*: But Ida could also stay.
347. *Bennett*: Id I'm sorry Ida/
348. *Trigg*: /It depends on numbers.
349. *Bennett*: Ida could stay it depends on numbers.
350. *Trigg*: She's got a position unspecified but she/
351. *Peters*: /But she cud be she cud be if you get the principal's job.

352. *Trigg*: Yeah but ya know she might still stay so that's a different thing again.
353. *Someone*: Ida could be principal.
354. *Donald*: That's right Ida could be principal.
355. *Bennett*: (laughs) Well see it's/(general laughter)
356. *Harvey*: /Ida can't hear you.
357. *Peters*: That is a completely different principle.
358. *Bennett*: Now if Ida stays/
359. *Donald*: /That'd be alright Ida/
360. *Bennett*: /right, if we/
361. *Donald*: /we'd follow Ida's directions.
362. *Bennett*: /if we hold our (general laughter) (2.3) come on . . . if we hold our numbers we have as we have a withdrawal or remedial teacher you know the position available if we hold our numbers if we don't Ida goes (3.1) right so that these are our options.
      (Bennett ends the discussion with a brief summary of his opening statement.)
456. *Bennett*: Well there's our options (2.6) now the only people who are fixed are the ones I told you . . . the prep the 2 . . . the the 3 and the 4 (3.1) it's all we can tell you so if parents ask you at parent–teacher interviews you really don't know you really (2.0) unless you're in those grades.

The staff meeting tossed the topic round for seven minutes. What the transcripts disclose is standard, unspectacular, and mundane, and replicated in hundreds of staff rooms across the state school system. An administrator has directed his staff to see part of the organizational world in his terms. He has defined the situation and they are expected to fall into line with that view.

### Analysis of control

The way to appreciate how control is brought about is to examine how each recipient reacts to an immediately preceding speaker. From Goffman's (1976a: 280) distinction between 'response' (category) and 'reply' (instance of the category), the following subtypes of replies can be distinguished.

i. **talk *to***: an utterance directed to the immediately preceding utterance, or if there are three interactants, the immediately preceding utterance but one.
ii. **talk *at***: an utterance not spoken in direct reference to the immediately preceding utterance.
iii. **talk *with***: an utterance emitted while someone is already speaking and in supportive reference to what is being said.
iv. **talk *over***: an utterance emitted while someone is already speaking, but not always in reference to what is being said.

v. **talk *instead of*:** an interrupting utterance, replacing the utterance being emitted, which gives the speaker the floor.

vi. **talk *again*:** an utterance that repeats a speaker's words while he or she is speaking or after the initial speaker has finished.

vii. **talk *for*:** utterance spoken on behalf of others who may not be present.

In addition, there are two distinct levels of control talk evident in the extracts: talk *of* control and talk *about* control. The talk *of* control is about being *an* authority on the matter of staffing. This is mostly face-to-face talk, but occasionally the speakers shift their alignment and the talk becomes face-by-face (Spiegelberg, 1973:134). Talk *about* control is about being *in* authority. This talk is disputation about authoritative action as such, rather than disputation on the particular topic in hand which is what the talk *of* comprises (Pocock, 1973b, 1981).

## Talk of Control

Forester's (1980) distinction between listening and hearing is used to sub-divide the first six reply types into two categories of attentiveness. When replying *to* (i), *with* (iii), or repeating (*again*, vi) an immediately prior utterance, a next-in-turn speaker may be described as listening. The replies are being called forth by what he or she has just taken in. But when replying *at* (ii), *over* (iv), or *instead of* (v), the next-in-turn speaker is more concerned with dictating rather than being dictated to. The transcribed extracts show that Bennett adopted a listening posture in the corridor, the office, and the staff room. His replies *to*, *with*, and *again* outnumber the corresponding replies for Trigg and out-number his own *at*, *over*, and *instead of* replies.

The prime mover in the corridor sequence is Trigg with his advice (1). Subsequent utterances are oriented to this one. But for this utterance the subsequent interactions in the office and staff room would not have taken place exactly in the form they did. Trigg's later utterances reiterate his initial concern or are offered in defense of it. Bennett is prepared to listen to the advice, querying the grounds or justification for it and attempting only minor amendments to the reading of the situation he is given, but, as is learned later on, he makes up his own mind and does not take the advice. How are the shifts in these two postures, adviser and advisee brought about?

Bennett's first reply to Trigg is to affirm that he will not talk about the matter to staff (2). He is surprised (6) that Nash intends to raise it. Trigg reiterates his initial advice (9) and provides possible replies (9, 11, 13, 15, 17, 19) that Bennett might use. Then Bennett interposes with a supposition (20) which, while it does not reformulate the topic of the talk, obliges Trigg to frame a different set of replies (21, 23). With only one exception (20), Bennett's utterances in the initial part of the conversation are brought forth by the immediately preceding ones of Trigg, yet, in only three instances (5, 7, 21) are Trigg's choice of words direct replies to what Bennett has said. Trigg is talking *at* Bennett, while Bennett is talking *to* Trigg.

Then, Bennett puts forward an emphatic denial (52), which disputes Trigg's framing of the topic. Up to this point no dire consequences or threats have been implied in Trigg's advice to keep quiet about staffing. He has simply used the adjective 'dangerous' (1) and the noun 'pressure' (49) to which Bennett is objecting. The denial compels Trigg to explicate his use of 'pressure.' Trigg outlines an instance of it (73). Confident that his point is made, Trigg exhorts Bennett to be careful (103) and clinches everything he has said to that point by alluding once more to danger (107). They agree to formulate a position (109, 110).

After the first twenty-three utterances Bennett continues to talk *to* rather than *at* Trigg (except for 52), and although Trigg frequently still talks *at* Bennett (49, 69, 73, 103, 107), his later utterances are directed *to* Bennett. Bennett talks *with* Trigg on one occasion (14). They occasionally interrupt each other and get the floor. Thus, Bennett talks *instead of* Trigg three times (4, 20, 108) and Trigg three times *instead of* Bennett (23, 71, 107). These are minor breaches in an otherwise largely conciliatory stretch of talk.

Trigg attempts to claim his facts as *the* facts of the matter throughout all the talk in the office (including that not quoted here). Of eleven utterances in which he does this, only two are 'talk to' replies, four are 'instead of' replies and four are 'talk at' replies. By contrast Bennett's facts tend to be reports of information to which he is privy. Furthermore, of the 185 utterances between the opening (111) and Trigg's departure (296), about one half are 'talk to' replies (the majority are Trigg's), with Bennett talking *over* Trigg and Trigg interrupting Bennett on about a dozen occasions in each case.

From Trigg's departure to the end of the office sequence (296–344) Lamb and Bennett talk mainly *to* each other. During these utterances Bennett's initial reassertion of his own position (296) is temporarily ignored. By elaborating on his grounds for it, he tries to get Lamb to support his summary of the situation (314 and 316). Bennett finally returns to his initial point (as at 296) in utterance 340, opposing Trigg's framing of the topic in terms of parent pressure and suggesting instead parents' 'inquisitiveness.' There follow two utterances by Bennett at the staff meeting directed *at* preceding speakers (355 and 358) and only two instances of *instead of* utterances (375, 393). His ten other utterances (excluding occasions in which he uses 'we') are 'talk to' replies.

The face-to-face talk *of* control examined here shows Bennett and Trigg vying, with divergent definitions of the situation, for the status of being an authority. Authority here (in this case, on staffing) 'is possessed by virtue of demonstrated knowledge, skill or expertise concerning a subject matter or activity' (Flathman, 1980: 16). Both speak, stake a claim to know, and have an equal claim to be authoritative. However, only one person can formally speak as *in* authority in a school; that is the principal, the most senior person. Flathman (1980:17, original emphasis) writes:

*In* authority is a property of rules and offices created by rules. Individuals possess it by virtue of holding an office in an organization. . . . Although we say that persons in such positions have authority, the authority they have is not their own in the sense of belonging to them as a piece of property or in the more plausible sense of being in virtue of their personal attributes. Rather, the authority belongs to the office they occupy and does nothing to set them as persons above anyone else.

Throughout the extracts Bennett and Trigg (and Lamb) employ utterances couched in 'talk for' terms. The first-person plural pronoun 'we' is mostly used, but occasionally 'our' is used. This appears to be *in* authority talk; that is, not we who know best, but we who ought to decide. While a superior (Bennett) and a subordinate (Trigg) do use 'we', which implies an equality of status, closer analysis reveals this to be what Spiegelberg (1973:133) calls the 'we' of an in-group of 'mutually understanding partners.'

Trigg's first use of 'we' is in the corridor (13). He uses it three other times (49, 71, 109) and then four times in the office with Bennett and Lamb (125, 245, 265, 271). He uses 'we' to refer to either himself and Bennett, or to himself, Bennett, and Lamb. This is the 'we of co-presence' (Spiegelberg, 1973:132). Such a use of 'we,' as a form of social address with those present, says Spiegelberg (1973:133), 'tries to make them (a) listen and (b) realize that they are appealed to as partners.' Significantly, Trigg does not use 'we' in front of the whole staff. Trigg's (and Lamb's) use of 'we' is presumptuous. He takes it upon himself to talk face-by-face with Bennett only when out of general earshot.

Bennett uses 'we' in all three locations: there are seven times in the corridor (14, 18, 70, 72, 108, 110, 111), nine times in the office (121, 123, 126, 128, 248–250, 296, 314, 316, 340) and four times at the staff meeting (four times in 345, once in 360, seven times in 362 and twice in 456). Cutting across his use of 'we' in a co-presence sense is his use of 'we' to refer to the staff as a whole (final use in 111, fourth use in 128, and first use in 340), Spiegelberg's (1973) 'absentee we.'

Bennett does not dispute Trigg's use of 'we.' Trigg's 'we know' (13) is immediately repeated by Bennett (14). He is talking with Trigg. The school year is to end in a fortnight, and the staff all know that Bennett will not return in the new year, as is clear when he describes himself as 'about to go' (104). Trigg, as next most senior person, may be principal (127). This uncertainty about the incumbency explains why Bennett is prepared to talk (108) either in terms of 'our stance' (at the staff meeting) or to give Trigg an option of his own. He says 'can you and Keith [Lamb] answer this situation?' (108). While still formally in authority, he is both winding down for the year and easing himself out of the school, so that he has nothing personal to lose in letting Trigg and Lamb do the talking. However, Trigg does not want the opportunity he is offered (108), and he prefers the security of 'we [three]' in his reply (109).

### Talk about *control*

In the instances just discussed the speakers flirt with or *presume* to speak collaboratively about *in* authority; however, there are two instances prior to the staff meeting where the speakers try to *formulate* who can speak in such a way. Once, in the corridor, Trigg says (69, emphasis added) 'You as principal or you and me and Keith as vice-principals in the place *ought to talk about* these kinds of things and come up with a workable solution. . . .' Then, in the office, Bennett says (126, emphasis added), 'If *we* put up alternatives it still doesn't help *them* because er *they can't decide* the issues . . . it's between Steven you and me *to decide in the end.*'

The most extensive attempt to formulate who can talk as *in* authority comes at the staff meeting. There, to 'come up with' (69) and who 'it's between' (126) are transformed into who 'it's up to' to make a decision about class size and the 'right' of the new principal:

366. *Jones*: Yes did Mrs Alan come up and see you about enrolling Ian?
367. *Bennett*: Yeah she did and I didn't rea even know there was a young Alan what's our numbers Ida at the moment for preps was it twenty-nine? (general laughter) (laughs) sorry Grace sorry Grace (general laughter) (4.1) [He has asked the wrong teacher] Grace what are our numbers for next year do y with th twenty-nine?
368. *Harvey*: No.
369. *Bennett*: Thirty?
370. *Harvey*: I told you yesterday if that other little girl stays it's thirty and then there'll be (1.0).
371. *Donald*: Ian.
372. *Harvey*: Thirty-one.
373. *Bennett*: Well it's up to you to decide whether you want thirty-one or whether you/
374. *Harvey*: /No it isn't/
375. *Bennett*: /yes it is or whether you want some of those preps taken out into the grade 1 and have a composite prep and 1.
376. *Trigg*: That that's not fair on Grace it's not up to her.
377. *Harvey*: It's not up to *me*.
378. *Bennett*: Well . . . what's the staff think about it?
379. *Trigg*: It's not up to the staff it's up to the principals.
380. *Bennett*: Well I may not be here next year so it could be the principal who's coming in February next year to decide it.
381. *Donald*: At the moment you're the you are this year aren't you but you're the principal at the moment.
382. *Trigg*: Yeah but that does that's not mandatory.
     (Lamb supports Bennett in this.)

387. *Lamb*: /Alf can make suggestions as to what happens next year but it'll be up to whoever has the principal's job/

388. *Harvey*: /I've got a few leaving I'm sure there's only about twenty-three going up.

389. *Bennett*: What's that?

390. *Lamb*: I'm saying you could make suggestions/

391. *Bennett*: /Yeah I can make suggestions/

392. *Lamb*: /as to what you feel it should be next year but as soon as someone comes in who's principal they have the/

393. *Bennett*: /Right to decide/

394. *Lamb*: /right to rearrange the school the way they want it.

Gibb (1961:144) suggested that 'speech which is used to control the listener evokes resistance.' Bennett precipitates (373) resistance from Harvey (374, 377) and then from Trigg (376) with his insistence (375) on Harvey deciding about grade numbers. Next, Trigg says (379) it's 'up to' the current and future incumbents (i.e. the principals), one of whom, of course, may be Trigg (127) if no appointment is made from outside to replace Bennett. Donald and Lamb speak in support of Bennett (381, 387, 390, 392, 394), offering counter-resistance to Trigg. Donald's words (381) 'at the moment' point up the administrative interregnum that the school has entered. These words mean that Bennett's *in* authority formally holds good but will only do so for another fortnight. When Trigg says 'that's not mandatory' (382), in reply to Donald, he is indicating that whatever Bennett says has only the effective or *de facto* force of suggestion or recommendation, since a newcomer in the new year will decide *de jure* anyway. Thus, they have formulated *who* can speak and for *how long*. In following up with 'suggestions' (387, 390) Lamb has formulated *how* that same person can speak.

## Discussion

Some observations are now appropriate about the interactions together as an exercise in control.

### *Being* in *control*

First, there appear to be grounds for arguing that Trigg has used his words to control Bennett. In the corridor he forced Bennett to think and talk about staffing. However, Trigg failed to persuade Bennett to refrain from raising the topic at the staff meeting (as he initially sought to do (1, 49, 107)). Trigg then tried to confine the scope of any discussion (9, 13, 23) by having Bennett commit himself to as few definite grade arrangements as possible. That he failed in this endeavor as well is evident from a comparison of these suggestions with the detailed arrangements given by Bennett in his opening remarks in the staff room (345). While 'the position is still unclear' (345), things are more 'definite,' as Bennett says, than Trigg was prepared to concede.

This leads to the suggestion that Bennett was in control and less passive than he appeared to be. Up to the point at which Bennett begins to reveal the grounds for his position (256), he has allowed Trigg to elaborate his point of view. Darling (1978:84) made a pertinent observation that expresses how Bennett was controlling Trigg. He said, 'Never answer an outburst with argument. Let the protester blow himself out and only when he has finished and can say no more, reply.' Up to utterance 20 Bennett has been caught unprepared, but from then on he tries to draw Trigg out (50, 52, 72, and especially 244, 248, 250, 252 254). While he might appear to be acceding to Trigg's formulation and framing of the topic he is gaining time for his later actions. In other words he is granting Trigg a hearing and trying to listen. Forester (1980: 222) makes the important point that:

> We hear with our ears, but we listen with our eyes and bodies as well, we see gestures, expressions, postures – bodies speak and we listen and understand, but hearing is much more narrow . . . there is more to listening than meets the eardrum, far more than the hearing of words. Listening to what someone says can be as dependent on our knowing *them* as upon our hearing of their *words*. . . . In listening we pay attention not to the sound of the person, but to the person of the sound. . . .

Bennett's action throughout this episode is in keeping with Weick's (1978:52) plea for the docile, protean leader and his statement that 'to control a thing you have to listen to it.' A 'plastic-spined' leader is, in Weick's (1978:58) terminology, loosely coupled to his or her environment; however, being loosely coupled suggests an inner mental attentiveness, a tight coupling to the words of a fellow interactant.

### Talk and control

Words do the work because each participant has a subjective understanding of school life that is made manifest in speech. If some degree of inter-subjectivity is to be attained, they must to some extent share meaning and engage in sense making (Ball, 1972). Talk becomes necessary and is powerful in two senses: first, talk does things for the speaker, making known his or her version of something to others that must be attended to; second, talk gets others to do things, not only to take note or account of what is said, but to be influenced by what is said. Pocock (1973a:79) pointed out that 'in the absence of automatic compliance with norms, words must increasingly be used,' but teachers as professional or semi-professional persons, do not always automatically comply or defer to administrators.

The reasons for this derive from the characteristics of the classroom, the environment of pedagogy, and the characteristics of teaching. While organizationally teachers are subordinates, vis-à-vis pupils they are superordinates. Managing classrooms means controlling people. As Denscombe (1980:290) suggests, 'The closed classroom, indeed, exacerbates a concern with classroom control and, under certain circumstances can lead to a situation where teachers become pre-occupied with issues of control.' To facilitate children's learning, teachers structure tasks. Time is a scarce resource and constrains the tasks (Denscombe, 1980). Classrooms are structurally tight in the structurally loose school (Weick, 1976; Denscombe, 1980). Teacher talk is used to achieve and maintain pupil control. Classrooms are talk-saturated environments in which teachers, as speakers, direct pupils, as hearers or listeners. The typical three-part talk pattern to a lesson is initiation (teacher), reply (pupil), and evaluation (teacher) (Mehan, 1978).

Most school principals are promoted through the ranks of the teaching service before becoming principals. Prospective principals assimilate these techniques of classroom talk and control as part of their administrative socialization. Two points suggest themselves. First, teachers often carry their classroom superordinancy over into their relationships with their administrative superiors. They try to use words to get them to do things, just as they have learned to do with children. Trigg is a good example. Second, as a consequence, teachers who become administrators have to adjust to having teachers attempt to control them. This means listening to staff speaking as authorities before replying authoritatively. They have to listen, like Bennett, and be verbally parsimonious in exercising their control by making their own words count and knowing when to make them count. A principal has to learn, during his or her career, to initially tighten the grip, as a teacher, then to slacken and loosen the grip (or coupling, to use Weick's term) but never to lose one's grip.

## Concluding remarks

Kariel (1981:727) has recently advocated the search for new perspectives on organizations that give status to the features of organized life that have been labeled pathological. Similarly, Weick (1978:60) has urged researchers 'to spend more time watching leaders "on line"' in the belief that 'some of the least important realities about leaders are being accorded some of the largest [amounts of] attention.' He goes on (1978:60): 'We have to put ourselves in a better position to watch leaders make do, let it pass, improvise, make inferences, scramble, and all the other things that leaders do during their *days between* more visible moments of glory.' This case study portrays a leader on line and it is in regard to Weick's recent work on the coupling of human action and intention in organizations that it is significant. Since the mid-1970s, Weick (1974b:357, 426–7) has tried to dereify the language of organizational relationships. In his programmatic paper on schools as loosely coupled systems, Weick (1976:11) wrote that 'it becomes crucial for the organization to have tight control over who does the work and on whom.' He continued by saying (1976:12) that 'members of educational organizations should be most explicit and certain when they are discussing issues related to certification for definition and regulation of teachers, pupils, topics, space, and resources.' The actors in this case study are addressing Weick's (1976:11) very question 'Who does the work?' The issues then become: is this an instance of 'tight' coupling?; how tight is 'tight'?; and what makes for tightness?

The school principal is a visible administrator, and as P. W. Jackson (1977:427–8) indicated, 'Attention was automatically bestowed upon me as a function of my new status. It went with the territory.' Moreover, 'it was there all the time, wherever I went within the school buildings and their environs.' Even as time went on the 'self-conscious feeling of being on stage, as it were, almost all of the time,' never went away. Visibility, in turn, means vulnerability and that means interruptions. Weick (1974a:498) wrote: 'A manager may make the poorest decisions either when he is interrupted early in an act or late in an act. It is not yet clear which way the relationship goes, but either way it has a direct bearing on organizational theory and behavior.' Bennett's case suggests that the flow of events initiated by an interruption is an initial period in which the administrator is caught off guard, followed by an accommodatory interlude in which sense making is facilitated by listening, and finally a phase of progressive retrieval prior to the issuance of a suitably chosen authoritative utterance.

In contrast to teaching, which takes place in a classroom, is organized into lessons, includes a range of standard pedagogical activities and observes set rituals and codes, administration in a school can take place anywhere. It is time-consuming; it observes no set time schedule; and follows no set order or format; for it can arise out of a chance meeting and can include matters that might be routine, spontaneous, trivial, planned, or highly eventful. The school principal is a drifter moving in and out of different locations and areas and in and out of relationships and encounters. The apparent haphazardness and the improvization that the transcripts in this case study reveal show school administration to be antithetical to the obsession with order often put forth in the writings of scientific management theorists.

This extemporaneity and improvision is evident in the two interactions prior to the staff meeting and Bennett's announcement of the position (345). All three speakers display hesitancy and inner uncertainty in their talk. There is a great deal of backtracking and talking the topic round in order to sort out or work out a possible set of arrangements within the constraints faced. Following Goffman's (1976b) dramaturgical frame, these two encounters are like rehearsals, and in learning their scripts, the actors are exploring what their roles entail. A good deal of looseness belies the appearance of tightness.

However, it is words that make for overall tightness. The best way to capture the full impact of this is to make use of Weick's (1979:64) sense-making recipe, made up of the components, knowing, thinking, seeing and saying, that is: 'How can I know what I think till I see what I say?' Weick (1979) suggests shuffling the components. Bennett's case suggests two shuffles and a slight variation of the components. In the first, listening replaces seeing and gives: how can I [the administrator] know what I think till I *listen* to what they [staff] say? In the second, doing replaces thinking and gives: how can I [the administrator] know what I've *done* till I've seen what I've said?

This case study consists of 'strips of everyday, actual doings involving flesh-and-blood individuals in face-to-face dealings with one another' (Goffman, 1975:563). In three sets of interactions it has been shown that talk does the work. No attempt has been made to go beyond each setting because, as Garfinkel (1967:viii) argues, the formal properties of settings 'obtain their guarantees from no other source and in no other way.' If, however, Weick's recipe is to be taken literally, namely that persons can only know and interpret what they have done *a posteriori* (Weick, 1979), then some means of allowing them to inspect their own actions, reflectively and retrospectively, seems called for. Scrutiny of action performed could be facilitated were it possible to later *see* (in written transcript form) and to *listen* (by replaying a tape recording) to what has been *said*. Such a proposal is beyond the confines of the present article, but a preliminary attempt is documented in Gronn (1981b). Nevertheless, an inspection would show that while 'administrative power is the ability of the administrator to have his will and get his way' (Hodgkinson, 1978:81), the power to control must be worked at linguistically and worked at never-endingly as an ongoing everyday activity.

## Notes

1. An earlier version of this paper, under the same title, was presented at the annual conference of the Australian Communication Association, Sydney, 1981. The text that appears below is an extensive revision of the original. I should like to thank the three *ASO* reviewers as well as my friends and colleagues Tom Greenfield, Alec McHoul, John Hunt, Philip Greenway, Alan Rice, Robin Small, Helen Praetz, Ray McCulloch, and Michael Norman for their helpful criticisms and advice during the writing of this article. Thanks are also extended to Cath Henderson and Bev Schneider for typing the manuscript.
2. In Australia, 'head' and 'headmaster' are used in independent schools and follow the English public school usage. 'Principal' is the normal term in government schools.

## References

Austin, John L. (1978). *How to do Things with Words*, 2nd edn J. O. Urmson and M. Sbisà, eds Oxford: Oxford University Press.
Ball, Donald W. (1972). 'The Definition of the Situation': Some theoretical and

methodological consequences of taking W. I. Thomas seriously. *Journal of the Theory of Social Behaviour* 2:61–92.

Blakar, Rolv M. (1979). 'Language as a means of social power: Theoretical-empirical explorations of language and language use embedded in a social matrix. In R. Rommetveit and R. M. Blakar (eds), *Studies of Language, Thought and Verbal Communication*. New York: Academic Press.

Burns, Tom. (1954). The directions of activity and communication in a departmental executive group. *Human Relations* 7:73–97.

Clegg, Stewart (1975). *Power, Rule and Domination*. London: Routledge & Kegan Paul.

Coulthard, Malcolm, and Margaret Ashby (1975). Talking with the doctor. *Journal of Communication* 25:140–7.

Darling, Sir James (1967). On headmastering. In B. W. Hone and P. J. McKeown (eds), *The Independent School: Papers Presented to the Headmasters Conference*. Melbourne: Oxford University Press.

Darling, James R. (1978). *Richly Rewarding*. Melbourne: Hill of Content.

Denscombe, Martyn (1980). The work context of teaching: An analytic framework for the study of teachers in classrooms. *British Journal of the Sociology of Education* 1:279–292.

Duignan, Patrick (1980). Administrative behaviour of school superintendents: A descriptive study. *Journal of Educational Administration* 18:5–26.

Flathman, Richard E. (1980). *The Practice of Political Authority: Authority and the Authoritative*. Chicago: University of Chicago Press.

Fletcher, Frank (1937). *After Many Days: A Schoolmaster's Memories*. London: Robert Hale & Coy.

Forester, John (1980). Listening: The social policy of everyday life (critical theory and hermeneutics in practice). *Social Praxis* 7:219–32.

Friesen, David, and Patrick Duignan (1980). How superintendents spend their working time. *Canadian Administrator* 19(5):1–5.

Garfinkel, Harold (1967). *Studies in Ethnomethodology*. Englewood Cliffs, NJ: Prentice-Hall.

Gibb, Jack R. (1961). Defensive communication. *Journal of Communication* 11:141–8.

Goffman, Erving (1975). *Frame Analysis*. London: Penguin Books.

  (1976a). Replies and responses. *Language in Society* 5:257–313.

  (1976b). *The Presentation of Self in Everyday Life*. Harmondsworth: Penguin.

  (1979). Footing. *Semiotica* 25:1–29.

Gronn, Peter C. (1979). The politics of school management: A comparative study of three school councils. Unpublished PhD thesis, Monash University, Australia.

  (1981a). Accomplishing the doing of school administration: Talk as the work. Paper presented at the annual conference of the Australian Communication Association, Sydney.

  (1981b). A school council at work: The micro-organization of school politics. In A. R. Welch (ed.), *The Politics of Educational Change*. Armidale, Australia: Centre for Social and Cultural Studies in Education, University of New England.

  (1982) Neo-Taylorism in educational administration? *Educational Administration Quarterly* 18(4) (forthcoming).

Halpin, Andrew W. (1960). Muted language. *School Review* 38:85–104.

Healey, Colin (1978). Scotch College, Melbourne, 1964–1975. In S. Murray-Smith (ed.), *Melbourne Studies in Education 1978*. Melbourne: Melbourne University Press.

Hodgkinson, Christopher (1978). *Towards a Philosophy of Administration*. Oxford: Basil Blackwell.

Horne, J. H., and Tom Lupton (1965). The work activities of 'middle managers – An exploratory study.' *Journal of Management Studies* 2:14–33.

Jackson, Philip W. (1977). Lonely at the top: Observations on the 'genesis' of administrative isolation. *School Review* 85:425–32.

Kariel, Henry S. (1981). Perceiving administrative reality. *Journal of Politics* 43:720–36.

Keith, Bertram, R. (1977). *The Lives of Frank Rolland*. Adelaide, Australia: Rigby.

Kress, Gunther (1979). The social values of speech and writing. In R. Fowler, B. Hodge, G. Kress, and T. Trew (eds), *Language and Control*. London: Routledge & Kegan Paul.

Martin, William J., and Donald J. Willower (1981). The managerial behavior of high school principals. *Educational Administration Quarterly* 17:69–90.

Mehan, Hugh (1978). Structuring school structure. *Harvard Educational Review* 48:32–64.

Mintzberg, Henry (1973). *The Nature of Managerial Work*. New York: Harper & Row.

Ochs, Elinor (1979). Transcription as theory. In E. Ochs and B. B. Schieffelin (eds), *Developmental Pragmatics*. New York: Academic Press.

O'Dempsey, Keith (1976). Time analysis of activities, work patterns and roles of high school principals. *Administrator's Bulletin* 7(8):1–4.

Peterson, Kent (1976). The principal's tasks. *Administrator's Notebook* 26(8):1–4.

Pocock, J. G. A. (1973a). *Politics, Language and Time*. London: Methuen.

    (1973b). Verbalizing a political act: Towards a politics of speech. *Political Theory* 1:27–45.

    (1981). The reconstruction of discourse: Towards the historiography of political thought. *Modern Language Notes* 96:959–980.

Pondy, Louis (1978). Leadership is a language game. In M. W. McCall, Jr and M. M. Lombardo (eds), *Leadership: Where Else Can We Go?* Durham, NC: Duke University Press.

Sacks, Harvey, Emmanuel A. Schegloff, and Gail Jefferson (1974). A simplest systematics for the organization of turn-taking for conversation. *Language* 50:696–735.

Soskin, William F., and Vera P. John (1963). The study of spontaneous talk. In R. G. Barker (ed.), *The Stream of Behavior*. New York: Appleton-Century-Crofts.

Spiegelberg, Herbert (1973). On the right to say 'we': A linguistic and phenomenological analysis. In G. Psathas (ed.), *Phenomenological Sociology: Issues and Applications*. New York: Wiley.

Sproull, Lee S. (1981). Managing educational programs: A micro-behavioral analysis. *Human Organization* 40:113–22.

Thomas, A. Ross, Quentin Willis, and David Phillips (1981). Observational studies of Australian school administrators: Methodological issues. *Australian Journal of Education* 25:55–72.

Weber, Max (1970). *From Max Weber: Essays in Sociology*. Translated and edited by H. H. Gerth and C. Wright Mills. London: Routledge & Kegan Paul.

Weick, Karl E. (1974a). Amendments to organizational theorizing. *Academy of Management Journal* 17:487–502.

(1974b). Middle range theories of social systems. *Behavioral Science* 19:357–67, 426–7.

(1976). Educational organizations as loosely coupled systems. *Administrative Science Quarterly* 21:1–19.

(1978). The spines of leaders. In M. W. McCall Jr and M. M. Lombardo (eds), *Leadership: Where Else Can We Go?* Durham, NC: Duke University Press.

(1979). Cognitive processes in organizations. In B. M. Staw (ed.), *Research in Organizational Behavior*. Greenwich, CT: JAI Press.

Willis, Quentin (1980). The work activity of school principals: An observational study. *Journal of Educational Administration* 18:27–54.

Wolcott, Harry (1973). *The Man in the Principal's Office*. New York: Holt, Rinehart & Winston.

Wood, A. Harold (1976). Methodist Ladies College, Melbourne, 1939–66: A personal memoir. In S. Murray-Smith (ed.), *Melbourne Studies in Education 1976*. Melbourne: Melbourne University Press.

Woods, Peter (1979). *The Divided School*. London: Routledge & Kegan Paul.

**Section VI**

# After school

# 18
# Principles and politics: an interpretative framework for university management

**Tony Becher**

*Abstract*

From the standpoint of internal university management, four models – hierarchical, collegial, anarchical and political – can be seen as exemplifying various aspects of academic organizations. These models operate in three arenas – front stage, back stage and under the stage – each with its distinct sets of values and procedures. The resulting analytic framework is illustrated through a brief case study of the responses of a number of UK universities to the major budgetary cuts imposed in 1981–2. A concluding section draws out some implications for managers in higher education, with particular reference to the conflict of interests between the institution and its basic units.

## Introduction

The focus of this article is on the internal management of institutions, rather than on issues at the level of the system as a whole. However, its central theme does not concern the management process as such, but rather the nature of academic organizations and their modes of operation. An issue of particular interest in this context is the interface between the institution and its constituent academic departments. The relationship between the two, as is suggested later, can give rise to the ability to translate even quite substantial outside pressures for change into comparatively minor local changes.

The concern of the paper with institutional and departmental politics is based on the view that academic managers need to take into account the private as well as the public lives of universities, and to understand the interplay between them. An appreciation of this complex set of organizational characteristics makes it possible to recognize the limitations of top–down, rational management approaches, and to accommodate to the inevitable and legitimate differences between departments. The role of the institution, arguably, should be to determine the guiding principles of action, rather than to lay down uniform procedures; the corresponding role of the basic units should be to interpret such principles in terms of their own particular forms of academic practice.

There have been numerous studies, in the last decade or so, of universities as organizations. For the most part, organizational theorists seem to agree that academic institutions, being highly complex, follow not just one but at least four main patterns or models of organizational behaviour. Sometimes, one or other of these patterns will manifest itself in a particular form of activity; at other times, two or more may compete for dominance. Since the details are likely to be familiar to many readers, each of the four models will be reviewed only briefly here.

The first form of organization, the hierarchical, is characterized by a well-defined framework: authority conferred from above; recognizable chains of command: predetermined regulations and procedures: and clearly specified roles. Typical examples of hierarchies include the civil service, the armed forces, and some of the more traditional branches of industry. The universities do not seem to fit easily into this pattern. However, the need for at least some degree of hierarchy emerges in the person of the institution's leading academic (vice-chancellor; rector; president or whatever), who is expected to act as the main channel of communication between his academic colleagues and the outside world. This form of leadership may involve persuasion more often than command, but coherent institutional policies have nevertheless to be forged, by one means or another, out of a diverse set of priorities. There is likely to be a need for a coordination of views at a number of different levels, and hence for a hierarchy of responsibility, if not of power.

At the same time, it remains a fundamental value within the academic community that the trade in ideas should be free, and that every individual must have the right to test his or her own ideas against those of fellow-professionals. The result is a strong sense of collegiality, in which scholars are called upon to respect each others' intellectual independence regardless of age or position. In organizational terms, the collegial tradition is significantly different from the hierarchical one. Authority is in this tradition always subject to ratification from below; members enjoy equal rights in policy-making: decisions have to be exposed to possible dissent; individuals enjoy a high level of discretion to conduct their affairs in their own way, subject only to minimal constraints.

The differences between these two approaches – hierarchical and collegial – have been neatly pinpointed by Charles Handy (Handy, 1977). As a former management consultant who had become an academic, he attempted on one occasion to discuss why his instructions had not been carried out by a more junior colleague. 'You cannot *tell* me to do something', this colleague explained gently, 'you can only *ask* me. On the other hand', he went on. '*I* don't ask *you* if I'm going to do something, I *tell* you.' Even so, the need for managerial responsibility is clearly acknowledged. As Handy remarks:

> the manager is meant to manage . . . no one wants to do anyone else's work for him. It is consultative management, not participative management. . . . The individual may not want to be involved but he does want to be consulted . . . [to have] a right to be heard. Committees and meetings in these organisations will be large but they will not be decision-making forums. They will be rather the testing grounds of decisions, the platforms for dissenters. It is when the management confuses the need to be consulted with the need to participate, or feels that a minority's desire to be heard means a wish to veto, that the organisation of consent becomes a bog of talk and inertia.

The duality within universities of collegium and hierarchy is reflected in the coexistent and not always compatible structures of committees and of executive positions (which would in the UK system include vice-chancellor, pro-vice-chancellor, dean, head of department, and a variety of less senior offices). These structures intertwine in complex ways, making it difficult to analyse what goes on in terms either of a typical community or of a typical bureaucracy (Becher and Kogan, 1980). The strand of collegiality creates, one might say, a babel of demands which the hierarchy has somehow to resolve. (One means of doings so is by casting such demands into high-minded statements of purpose which are so general as to be almost incontestable).

The third model, the anarchical, should perhaps be described as more anti-managerial than managerial, concerned more with disorganization than with organization. Its relevance to universities stems from the high degree of autonomy enjoyed by academics. Because many of them have powerful allegiances and strong professional identities outside their own institutions, they are often well placed to resist internal sanctions and pressures. The plurality of values even within a single department – let alone the university as a whole – makes it difficult for managers to identify unambiguous goals, or to find ways of achieving such few shared purposes as may exist. Professional expertise is another factor which reinforces the atomistic, decentralizing tendency of the anarchical model. It is quite inconceivable that institutional leaders should be knowledgeable enough to make informed policy decisions on key academic issues across the whole range of academic activity. So they are inevitably dependent at times on the advice of disciplinary specialists, rather than on the judgement of professional administrators. It is in the light of these various considerations that universities have been described by some organizational theorists as 'organized anarchies' (Cohen and March, 1974).

The remaining form of organization, the political, identifies universities as collections of loosely structured interest groups. Such groups, like the shifting coalitions familiar in local politics, have a fluid membership and a pattern of participation which varies with the issues involved. Authority, in this model, derives from personal power rather than from the power attached to a particular office. Decisions result from the resolution of conflicting interests, often through a process of negotiation and compromise (Baldridge *et al.* 1978).

The four patterns of organizational behaviour are summarized in Figure 1.

**Figure 1**

| Organizational pattern | Characteristic features |
| --- | --- |
| Hierarchical | Authority conferred from above<br>Recognisable chains of command<br>Predetermined regulations and procedures<br>Specified roles |
| Collegial | Authority ratified from below<br>Equality of rights in policy-making<br>Decisions exposed to dissent<br>High personal discretion |
| Anarchical | Authority eroded by external loyalties<br>Emphasis on individual autonomy<br>Ambiguous goals; pluralistic values<br>Influence based on expertise |
| Political | Authority deriving from personal power<br>Conflict as basis for decisions<br>Policies based on compromise<br>Influence deriving from interest groups |

As noted earlier, it is not often that all four models are in full operation at one and the same time: typically, two or three may be dormant at any given period, though they can be brought rapidly into operation at times of conflict or crisis. However, their coexistence within the framework of a single institution makes life complicated for both management and staff. Davies and Morgan (1982) paint a perhaps overstark picture of the difficulties which beset the latter:

> decisions which are carried through are usually partial, short range and based on compromise . . . the academic finds himself in several concurrent dilemmas: he doesn't like meetings, yet he must generate or attend them to preserve his interests and influence, the direction and substance of his plans; he does not wish to spend too much time himself on planning matters, yet he is reluctant to trust others, including administrators; he wishes to plan in the sense of having a stable framework in which to operate, yet he resents being constrained by a substantive plan;

he wants a power fixer on whom he can rely to sort out difficult issues, yet he resents the growth of power centres which are beyond the effective control of himself and his colleagues.

As far as management is concerned, 'decisions which are carried through are usually partial, short range and based on compromise'. Long-term plans and major reforms are difficult to implement, though the system allows many small, incremental developments to occur at a multiplicity of levels. Even substantial changes imposed from outside tend – as we shall see below – to be translated into relatively minor and localized shifts in the existing forms of academic enterprise.

## Areas of activity

In his study entitled *Morality and Expediency*, the anthropologist F. G. Bailey (Bailey 1977) identifies three main arenas in which the game of academic politics is played out. These arenas can be seen as complementary to the four models already discussed, and as providing useful illustrations of how and when they come into play. Bailey characterizes these arenas by using the metaphor of a stage: the front stage is the public arena; the back stage is where deals are done; under the stage is where gossip is purveyed.

His descriptions of the first two arenas in particular are worth quoting in the context of this present discussion:

> On the front stage parade . . . people who . . . hold resolutely to their principles, believing firmly in the good university as a place of learning, or a collegiate institution, or an instrument to be used in the service of outsiders. Holding on to these principles is non-rational, because they cannot be justified; only asserted. Consequently, when people feel the need to make a deal which sacrifices some of these principles, they get off the front stage and go out of sight where they can behave in an 'unprincipled' fashion by making compromises. The front stage is the home of non-rationality and back stage is where reason takes over, and where adjustments are made to the inescapable demands of an outside world.

Elaborating on the contrast, he writes:

> Up front people are proclaiming the principles by which they are 100 per cent guided; behind the scenes they reveal that in fact they are only 80 per cent guided by these principles, and someone is perhaps going to give them something in return for trading off the other 20 per cent.

Bailey also suggests that different types of academic committee characteristically occupy different arenas. For example, the large, representative committee (such as an academic senate) has little choice but to work front stage; the small, powerful expert committee (such as planning and finance) is in general a back stage enterprise. But Bailey is careful to point out that his arenas represent modes of activity rather than fixed domains: it is possible, within a quite short space of time, for any particular committee to switch from one mode or arena to another and back again. Even though the dissemination of gossip (which takes place under the stage) is an informal rather than formal activity within any institution, it may sometimes occur within the setting of a quite formal committee (though certainly outside its agenda).

Returning now to the four basic organizational models, it can readily be seen that the hierarchical aspects of universities are typically expressed in the formal managerial structure of the institution (underpinned by the interconnected networks of academic officers and professional administrators). Since these are subject to a high degree of institutional scrutiny and public accountability, it would appear that the hierarchical pattern of management operates in a front-stage mode.

As we have noted, the collegial form of organization appears in many respects to be the antithesis of the hierarchical. Nevertheless, it embraces a set of concepts – notably those of open government and collective authority – whose realization closely depends upon operating in the public domain, rather than on bargaining behind the scenes. Its operations are in fact institutionalized in the structure of large public committees. So collegiality, too, may be identified as a front-stage model.

When it comes to the anarchical aspects of university organization – those which emphasize the autonomy of individual academics (derived from professional expertise, and reinforced through external reference groups) – it is clear that the organizational emphasis falls on the domestic politics of the subject department. It is the department which has the prime task of attempting to reconcile a plurality of goals and values into some kind of working consensus. The pattern here is one of personal interaction among close colleagues – the informal gossip of the understage arena, rather than the more stylized backstage mode of negotiation.

The political model, typified by conflict, bargaining and the operation of interest groups, is easy to locate. Its institutional form is the small committee which operates through compromise; it functions more effectively in private than in the open. It is, in short, the embodiment of back stage activity, focusing on issues of institutional concern rather than on the more narrowly domestic issues raised in the anarchical pattern.

To summarize, the four models can now be further classified into two pairs. The first pair, in the public domain, are respectively the hierarchical (embodying the university's public administrative structure) and the collegial (embracing the university's public committee structure). Both these can be located as front-stage forms of operation. The second pair, in the private domain, are the anarchic (as reflected in private departmental politics), occupying an under stage position, and the political (giving a focus to private institutional politics through small 'trading-off' committees), which operates back stage.

## Applying the framework

It may be helpful to illustrate how this set of analytic ideas can be applied in practice. The example I have chosen concerns the major reductions made in the UK higher education budget in 1981–2. The theme has, I would suggest, a more general relevance, in that similar cut-backs have occurred in several OECD member states during the late 1970s and early 1980s.

The overall decline in university funding in the United Kingdom was estimated at the time to be approximately 20 per cent over three years, although its scale has in practice turned out to be somewhat less. The cuts were not distributed evenly across the sector as a whole: a few universities had to face huge reductions, of the order of 40 per cent, while a few others escaped with relatively minor penalties of 10 per cent or less. The case study which follows relates to the institutions between these extremes, where the response was one neither of coping with a crisis of major proportions nor of making comparatively limited adjustments. I have no grounds to claim that the interpretation I offer applies to all UK universities averagely affected by the cuts, but it appears to be relevant to most with whose reactions I am familiar. I would also expect the account to be recognizable to a number of those concerned with the management of universities in other countries facing a similar budgetary decline.

After the initial shock, the first response to the retrenchment was typically a political one. The major power blocks in the university came together to work out a back stage deal which left each other as unscathed as possible, based on careful guesses about how far they could get away with proposing significant reductions to the politically vulnerable elements in the institution. Those departments known to have strong cohesion and unity and a strong sense of confidence were seldom selected; those which were internally divided, those which were small and often relatively new – and especially service units such as those providing teaching media, staff development, student counselling and the like – were most clearly at risk.

The results of this initial backstage bargaining process were not of course made public in their raw state. The next step was to submit them to cosmetic surgery, translating them as far as possible into persuasive arguments about the long-term academic needs of the institutions. Once an ideologically acceptable version of the power-block proposals was available, it was fed into the hierarchical management system to emerge in the front stage arena as a proposed university plan.

In most cases, however, the process did not stop there. The reaction at the grass roots was, typically, antagonistic. Many of those who were adversely affected by the proposals protested vigorously at their unfairness, embracing any allies prepared to share their concern and to put forward counterproposals of their own. The result was a set of fragmented, anarchistic plans which, being developed largely in the under stage arena, were (like the earlier back stage negotiations) not suitable for public discussion in their existing form.

The protesters' arguments had now to be fed into the institution's collegial structure, laundered of their more obvious expressions of self-interest, and translated into claims about the advancement of institutional well-being. In this acceptable front-stage form, they acquired the status of a widely supported collegial response to the official university plan.

At this point in the proceedings, there were two rival sets of proposals being advanced in the front stage arena; the first having emerged hierarchically and the second collegially. Since, in F. G. Bailey's words quoted earlier, neither could 'be justified; only asserted' (the first resting on a power-political bargain and the second on an anarchistic counter-protest), the only way forward lay in compromise. So once again, the action moved back stage, 'where reason takes over, and where adjustments are made to the inescapable demands of the outside world'.

The result of this further set of negotiations, in most institutions, was an agreed programme for the cuts, duly and solemnly ratified in the front stage arena. For the most part, both the senior academic management (whose job it was to implement the cuts) and the university staff at large (who had to suffer their effects) ended up being reasonably satisfied with the compromises which were made. Those in the hierarchy were realistic enough to accept that their initial plan was no more than a first approximation, and that their best political guesses were unlikely to turn out exactly right; those in the collegium were pleased – and possibly a little surprised – that at least a number of their demands had been met.

The typical sequence of events is summarized in Figure 2.

In several institutions (excluding those where the budget reductions were exceptionally high) the end point of the process was characteristic and predictable. Responsibility for implementing the cuts was devolved to the basis units within the institution (departments, faculties, programmes, etc.). This has in practice proved problematic, in that there is a tendency for basic units to be governed by expediency, not principle, and to seek solutions in terms of factors such as eligibility for early retirement, rather than by considering such fundamental issues as academic balance or the cumulative effect on the institution itself. Even so, this 'laissez-faire' strategy may be defended as the most appropriate one in a highly pluralistic organization where common criteria and standards are virtually impossible to establish.

### Conclusion

The analytic framework which has been the subject of this paper has only an indirect bearing on management in higher education. It does not provide a

**Figure 2**

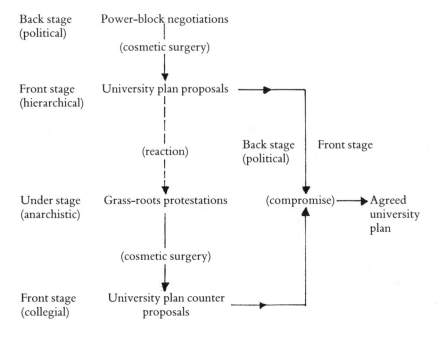

usable technique to improve decision-making, nor a predictive tool to estimate the impact of particular policy choices. It offers no more than one particular way of interpreting the complex ebb and flow of political life in academic institutions.

There are however some implications of this perspective, if it is held to be illuminating rather than misleading. In the first place, it portrays universities, in Burton R. Clark's words, as 'bottom heavy' organizations, in which it is unreasonable to expect that 'large results can be obtained by top–down manipulation' (Clark 1983). In other words, it suggests that the task of academic management is more subtle and more demanding – though perhaps also more frustrating – than that in many other organizations. It may be more fruitful to think in terms of short-range, localized, incremental policies than of large-scale and long-term development plans.

A second, closely related point concerns the depiction of the pluralistic character of academic institutions and the emphasis on their lack of common goals. Although seemingly a disadvantage, this feature of universities does help to ensure that all major issues are widely discussed before decisions are made about how best to deal with them. Despite the anarchical tendencies to reject centrally devised plans, the collegial tradition generally helps in the end to bring about some form of convergence. As a result, the policy that emerges is more likely to reflect the views of those who have to put it into practice than are most hierarchical decisions based upon an imposed consensus.

Thirdly, the importance given in the framework to institutional politics helps to focus attention on the key role of the departments or other basic units within the university and on their wide diversity of needs. Each basic unit has its own particular type of academic challenge, its own style of operation, its own set of professional practices, its own disciplinary culture. In consequence, solutions to management problems have necessarily to be adapted to the needs of the individual unit rather than applied globally and without differentiation. The business of implementation, on this view, is best left to the people who know most about how particular policies could be put into effect, and who have to live with their consequences.

Finally, despite this emphasis on devolution to the basic units, there emerges a strong role for central management. Each institution has at any given time to develop a set of collective policies, and to ensure that they are consistently and fairly applied. Consistency and fairness do, however, call for a rigid uniformity of practice. Universities are the right bodies to formulate the administrative and procedural ground rules which their departments should follow, but (as noted above) the crucial academic choices of how to proceed in complying with those ground rules can most sensibly be made with the departments themselves (Becher, 1983).

To quote F. G. Bailey once again, one might conclude that the manager in higher education has somehow to mediate between

> the open world of principle and the shadowed world of action. To choose one or the other is foolish, and the sensible man can only pilot his way between them. In the end it makes no sense to ask who steers the ship: Is it morality or expediency? Are the men in the smoke-filled rooms really those at the helm? They may be at the helm, but if there are no principles and there is no front arena, they have no course by which to steer.
>
> Scylla is the rock of principle: expediency is Charybdis. Politics being what they are, the ship seldom contrives to steer a straight course between them. Usually, if there is progress, it is achieved by bouncing from one rock to another.

## References

Bailey, F. G. (1977). *Morality and Expediency*. Oxford: Blackwell.
Baldridge, J. V., Curtis, D. V., Becker, G. and Riley, G. L. (1978). *Policy-making and Effective Leadership*. San Francisco: Jossey-Bass.
Becher, T. (1983). 'Managing Basic Units'. *International Journal of Institutional Management in Higher Education* 7:1, 89–95. Paris: OECD/CERI.
Becher, T. and Kogan, M. (1980). *Process and Structure in Higher Education*. London: Heinemann.

Clark, Burton R. (1983). *The Higher Education System*. Berkeley: University of California Press.

Cohen, M. D. and March, J. G. (1974). *Leadership and Ambiguity*. New York: McGraw-Hill.

Davies, J. L. and Morgan, K. W. (1982). 'The Politics of Institutional Change'. In Wagner, L. (ed.), *Agenda for Institutional Change in Higher Education*. London: Society for Research in Higher Education.

Handy, C. B. (1977). 'The Organisations of Consent'. In Warren Piper, D. and Glatter, R. (eds), *The Changing University*. Windsor: National Foundation for Educational Research.

# 19

# Witches and witchfinding in educational organizations

**Frank W. Lutz**

*Abstract*

Modern organizations, particularly loosely coupled education organizations, may exhibit behaviors structurally similar to those of 'simple societies.' This article suggests that behaviors akin to witchfinding in preliterate societies may be used in education organizations to maintain social order and the status quo – to defeat change attempts and defeat change agents. The anthropological literature is reviewed and a generalized model produced. Case data in higher education are provided and analysed using the witchfinding model. Possibilities for restructuring the organization in education are suggested.

## Introduction

Through the experience of serving as an administrator in higher education this author was struck by similarities between education-organizational behavior and anthropological accounts of behavior in so-called 'simple' societies. The basic conceptual constructs of preliterate societies such as ritual, belief, magic, and witchcraft can be seen as important factors in modern complex organizational behavior. In several articles over the last twelve years the author has suggested that a better understanding of complex organizations is to be gained by viewing these organizations using anthropological models.[1] Although theoretically understandable, complex organizations are not often operationally predictable. They are political entities and their futures are best predicted not by a single hypothesis but by a set of scenarios. There are useful theories that may be described as forming the core of an administrative science. But the practice of administration is more like the art of crap shooting than like a science: one had better know something about the probabilities (a science), have a reasonable amount of risk capital (for probability assures you won't always win), and then be endowed with a greater than average amount of luck. Prophesy will fail!

There has been a tendency to explain the lack of 'organizational tidiness' and even the lack of goal accomplishment in universities by contending that, by their natures, education organizations must be loosely coupled and that as loosely coupled organizations they are incapable of the organizational control required for accomplishing certain goals. An alternate assertion can be derived from the description of the Kuikuru's political behavior.[2] This description demonstrates a striking conceptual similarity between the methods used by Kuikuru to maintain social and political stability and those used in higher education to accomplish those same tasks. Researchers in Educational Administration may express disbelief when confronted with this assertion. However, by focusing on the lack of formal leadership and control that may be exhibited in educational organizations one can find that similarities exist between a preliterate society and higher education organizations. The lack of formal leadership and control while not universal in education organizations, is prevalent enough that it cannot easily be dismissed. Finding these similarities points to the possibility that the Kuikuru model could be helpful in examining certain administrative and organizational behavior.

Among the Kuikuru there is a system of social control and informal power based within a normative belief system that not only works but is 'hard to beat' if you are in it:

1. There is a general lack of understanding of empirical causes of the disasters in the society.
2. Given the absence of other explanations, mystical explanations are employed. Witchcraft is responsible and the witch is sought out.
3. The shaman, after obtaining consensus through the informal gossip network, publicly accuses the witch.
   (a) If consensus is not obtained, the shaman can retreat and try again without the risk of having made a public blunder.
   (b) The accused is often a relative outsider, low in tribal esteem and always without strong supporters who could defend the accused or take revenge on the accusers.
4. Once identified, the witch is ostracized, driven out, or killed; and the tribe returns to normal. Tension and anxiety are relieved and the status quo is re-established.

It should be understood that witchcraft is not being proposed as an empirical phenomenon. It seems clear, however, that some individuals in preliterate and modern societies do believe in witchcraft. Such a belief can be a powerful force and the witchfinding accusations that follow are also a powerful social force.

For the purpose of this article witchcraft in modern society may be defined as an extreme and consistent violation of the norms of the informal organization, believed to bring harm to the organization and its members. For instance, some institutions of higher education have historically been 'teaching institutions'. In such institutions even the assertion that research /publication is an important and a required activity may be assumed to be 'cursing teaching' and threatening the life of the organization and its members. Those who pose the threat may be thought of as tantamount to witches and the effort to rid the organization of their threatening presence is similar to witch accusing in preliterate societies.

In the Kuikuru and other societies described below, witchcraft accusations and witchcraft have been found to be useful in maintaining social order. The following statements are relevant to that process:

1. The use of a belief in witchcraft and the accompanying activities of witchcraft and witchfinding generate social solidarity in the face of threat and disaster.
2. The naming of 'witches' as scapegoats for such disasters, real or impending, is useful to powerful insiders in controlling the balance of institutional power.
3. The use of the fear of 'witchcraft' (i.e. the use of subtle informal threat) by the powerful is useful in obtaining conformity among weak and powerless 'internals' in the modern organization.
4. Witch accusations against newly arrived change agents is a useful tool in the hands of powerful insiders who find advantage in the status quo.

These are among the lessons to be learned from a review of the anthropological literature and will be used to explain a case of modern witch accusing in a higher education organization. They should prove helpful in understanding the cross-cultural perspective below.

## A cross-cultural perspective

As a means of social control, people who are unable or unwilling to empirically explain misfortune and disasters that befall their society turn to a witchcraft explanation. They have ritualistic means of witchfinding and accusation and methods of dealing with the witches found guilty of causing the misfortunes they cannot otherwise explain. In her classic work, *Return to Laughter*, Bowen describes her feelings as she observed a preliterate society that had dealt with a smallpox epidemic by blaming the disaster on witchcraft. She says, 'I stood for a while looking at them. They knew how to live at close quarters with tragedy, how to live with their own failures and yet laugh.'[5] She failed to note, however, that lost in their laughter were not only the dead witches but also the opportunity to deal differently with the epidemic: to inoculate the tribe against smallpox and avoid a similar misfortune in the future.

Consistently, preliterate societies tend to deal with otherwise un-explainable misfortune and tragedy and re-establish social order and control by relying on practices associated with witchcraft and witchfinding.[6] Misfortune which 'mankind' is unable to otherwise explain is disruptive to social order and the established social control mechanisms. As Winter explains, 'Everywhere and at all times, men have sought to penetrate behind the façade of the observable world to grasp the meaning of human misfortune. Witchcraft offers one solution . . . People, then, are not paralysed but instead are able to take action which reduces their anxieties.'[7]

In the majority of cases where witchfinding provides the mechanism for social control it is the weak and powerless who are accused and suffer the fate of 'guilty' witches as among the Kuikuru. But among the Tonga tribe, where there is a well-established system of rank and power, it is the powerful who are thought to work witchcraft against the powerless. In this tribe the witches are given the opportunity to repent and again ally themselves with the social structure. Failing to do so results in their loss of power and ostracism, even by their own wives and families.[8] The effect seems to be the same, although among the Tonga it would seem possible (although the idea is not suggested by Colson) for a strong and clever person to submit and later take revenge upon the accuser. Thus, among the Tonga one accusing the witch takes a greater risk than does one among the Kuikuru, who only accuse the marginal and powerless.

In the above societies the antisocial, powerful or powerless, are controlled by accusations of witchcraft. In Southeast Ambrym, the powerful, who can use witchcraft, control the antisocial and less powerful by casting the curse rather than by accusing the witch. Tonkinson[9] notes this as an effective mechanism of social control, for the powerless must conform to the social order (the norms of the society) or flee for fear of the curse cast by the chief. Again, as Tonkinson notes, there is the same effect, 'particularly in relationship to social control and inhibition of anti-social conduct.'[10]

It is not only preliterate societies that have used the belief in witchcraft and the practice of witchfinding to restore social order, remove antisocial and powerless people, and restore the status quo. Harris[11] points out that the witch mania in Europe, when hundreds were killed as convicted witches, shifted the blame for political-social problems from the real culprits who were the powerful rulers to the helpless, thereby re-establishing the status quo. The same phenomenon accounts for the witch hunts in Salem, Massachusetts, in colonial America.[12] In modern society, Leininger[13] notes the socially integrating effect of the witchcraft-witchfinding process: transferring guilt and relieving in-group tension. While asserting that there can be some socially disruptive aspects of witchcraft, Geertz[14] admits to its 'harmonizing, integrating and psychological supportive aspects' and notes that the majority of anthropological literature supports such a conclusion. Middleton,[15] Gray,[16] and Harwood[17] all make similar observations. Even Winter,[18] who suggests the disintegrating aspects of witchcraft, points out that the structure of witchcraft among the Amba is but the inversion of the moral structure, requiring re-examination and re-affirmation of the moral structure and in the end permitting action – which is better than being paralyzed because one can find no *acceptable* reason for one's misfortunes. Witchcraft accusations and witch-finding can also be used as an 'instrumental technique' notes Crawford,[19] contesting the ownership of property or of public office. In such a way witchcraft further serves the purposes of the powerful.

### The process of witchfinding

Both witchcraft and the process of witchfinding are basically in the minds of the 'true believers' of the society. 'There is no evidence which indicates that witches exist anywhere except in the minds of the Amba,' states Winter.[20] Yet Tonkinson notes that, until recently, in Southeast Ambrym, everyone was able to provide countless examples of themselves and their relatives being the victims of witchcraft practices. Such persons had 'evidence' that they were the subject of a curse because 'lele,' persons who had the ability to identify victims of a curse, got 'an itching on the left side of their nose just as they [were] thinking of that particular person.'[21]

Such is the substance and proof in witchfinding. Something is wrong! The 'insiders,' those who are in control of the system and who are rewarded by it, are either unable or unwilling to find an empirical reason. But it is unacceptable to sit paralysed, unabled to do anything about the anxiety produced by the misfortunes. Thus, they 'adopt' phenomenological causes and mystical culprits.

As suggested in the Kuikuru case, the process of witchfinding must begin with the informal group network. Colson notes the same element among the Tonga stating that the people had known for a long time who the witches were and that the local gossip had long affirmed that fact. Given misfortune in society, an accepted diviner or shaman is appointed, not to discover but to proclaim the witches so they can be dealt with.[22]

Levi-Strauss[23] noted that science and magic are but parallel ways of knowing. Perhaps he might have noted that any society or organization probably participates in both ways of knowing. By claiming to be a complex-rational organization, modern organizations attempt to appear empirical. After all, getting an itch on the left side of one's nose is an empirical reality.

Such a process is described by Jules-Rosette who tells us that the process of witchfinding cannot be proven or disproven in the same way a rational declaratory statement is tested. Witchfinders use phenomenological proof. They do not object to other facts but call those other facts into question and assert their solution as 'superseding other interpretations.'[24] Supporting this notion Winter suggests that the process of witchfinding has a logic of its own. He points out that the Azande deliberately use an enigmatic form of speech and the public accuser always uses 'rhetorical' language when accusing witches.[25]

### Escaping the accusation

Not every accused witch is burned at the stake, however. The anthropological literature describes three methods of escaping that fate: (1) the strong and powerful may simply deny it and brow-beat the accuser into backing down; (2) when the accusation is 'improperly' made, the accused may establish another guilty 'witch'; (3) the accused witch may submit and publicly assert intent to refrain from such activity in the future.

Harwood[26] describes the first method, where a powerful person was able to accomplish acquittal and receive damages from the accuser by public and forceful intimidation of the accuser.

Werbner describes the second method. A mother thought her daughter bewitched by a particular woman in the society. Without waiting for proper divination she rushed into the street shouting abuse at the suspected witch and accusing her, a procedure not in accord with accepted witchfinding practice. The accused woman's son hired a 'proper' diviner. That diviner consulted with 'established insiders' and publicly reminded the society of other troubles they were aware of and other antisocial persons they had long suspected of causing their troubles. This alternative accusation was 'properly' made and accepted by their society.[27] The people had their witch!

Finally, the process of public submission is described by Evans-Pritchard.[28] He recounts the advice given by an Azande father to his son who was accused of witchcraft. Among the Azande an accused witch could deny the *intent* of evil doing but admit the possibility of being used for evil purposes and by 'blowing water' from his mouth, ritualistically showing that the evil had left him and he would refrain from such behavior in the future. The father advised his son that the accusation of witchcraft was absurd. Yet it was only polite to 'blow water' when requested to do so, and it was no more than any 'good citizen' would do. (No doubt this was also the safest thing to do.)

### Applying the preliterate model to modern organizations

Colson[29] concludes from his study of witchcraft that societies which have a hierarchically structured social order are more likely to attribute success to attained abilities and hard work, while societies that have little social stratification or mobility are most likely to attribute success to witchcraft. Such a statement allows some speculation about the type of modern organizations that might be most susceptible to witchcraft-witchfinding behaviors: those with little stratification and mobility within the organization. Such organizations modify but do not give up the notion of witchcraft as a means of control.

Tonkinson's description of Southeast Ambrym demonstrates that the advent of modern society and the Christian Church did not put an end to witchcraft. The Church declared witchcraft neither unreal nor powerless. It proclaimed it evil, less powerful, and in 'direct opposition to the Tambu Spirit' – God. The Church did not act against the witches or deny their power. It stated that the Tambu Spirit would turn the witches' own evil back into them, and they would surely die.[30] Of course they would die – don't we all! Thus modern society added a superstructure to the belief in witchcraft, making Christians and the Church the top of that power structure.

### Witchcraft-witchfinding in modern organizations

The following propositions, derived from the studies cited above, provide a model of witchcraft-witchfinding in modern organizations. These propositions will not provide a failsafe formula for administrative survival in education organizations. They may serve as a useful perspective for examining such organizations, particularly universities. Further, the model may provide a means to reassess and perhaps explain some behaviors in modern organizations in general.

(1) Witch-hunting and the accusing of witchcraft-type behavior shifts the blame for organizational failure from the powerful persons responsible to the accused witches; usually marginal or weak persons without strong protectors.

Education organizations often have been described as loosely coupled organizations.[31] As such, they tend to have vaguely defined goals, indeterminate technology, and changing personnel. Elsewhere this author has suggested that it might be that the loosely coupled description often results from organizational behavior that is tightly coupled in some aspects and uncoupled in others.[32] In those uncoupled areas powerful individuals attempt to avoid responsibility for unaccomplished goals and unpopular decisions. Organizational use of loose coupling explanations and witchcraft-like accusations may both be methods of establishing scapegoats, escaping responsibility and surviving.[33]

(2) Decentralized organizations without a hierarchy of rank through which one expects to rise, and those organizations that attribute success to acquired traits (i.e. years of service) as opposed to accomplishments (i.e. published articles) are more likely to use witchfinding to reduce organizational tension.

Institutions of higher education are not very hierarchically structured in the formal organizational sense. While professional ranks exist, they are not usually related to differentiated tasks and only marginally related to salary. The hierarchy that does exist (e.g. department head, dean, vice-president, president) are as often a subject of professional humor or disdain as they are a classification of status and esteem within the 'academic community.'

Progress through those organizational ranks, either the professorship or the institutional role, appears to be at least as much a matter of length of service as a matter of scholarly production. A look at the career histories of administrators in higher education might demonstrate that high scholarly production is negatively related to selection of an administrator. A glance at the scholarly production may suggest that scholarly production is not as important as years of service as a criterion for promotion and tenure in professional rank. These factors suggest that selected institutions of higher education may be prime organizational candidates for witch-hunting-like behaviors.

(3) As witchcraft and its modern organizational equivalents are capable neither of proof nor disproof, the accused are helpless to prove their innocence.

Appeals to whether or not individuals *conform* to the informal norms of organizations are often made based on phenomenological criteria. Selection, retention, and promotion of academic personnel, both professional and administrative, certainly involve such criteria. In such a way the 'antisocial' are 'weeded out.' It is not merely a matter of scholarship, teaching, or service. Those can be objectively measured, but they will not suffice. The accusations of not being a good colleague or failing to support academic freedom (used by some as academic license) is a perception, and difficult to refute. Regardless of scholarly production, the single most important criterion often appears to be 'do you get along,' which means do you conform to the norms of the informal organization.

(4) After an informal rumor has established the witch in the minds of the group, a proper 'shaman' publicly accuses the suspected witch.

Rumor and gossip establish the guilt of the witch in the informal organization prior to formal accusation. The people 'know' who their witches are. Formal accusations only put the formal process into action. It publicly establishes the scapegoat, long disliked as a troublemaker. If the public accusation is done properly, the witch's innocence is difficult, if not impossible, to establish. The people of Salem knew who the witches were. The witch trials were merely the means of putting them to death.

(5) An 'outsider' who becomes change agent of the organization, offending many norms of the informal organization, is perceived as 'antisocial' and likely to be accused by the 'shaman' in the informal organization of some sort of witchcraft.

Education literature has identified the outside successor in administration as the change agent with a mandate.[34] This places such a person in a difficult position between the formal and informal organizations. In order to succeed in the formal mission, such a person must propose modifications likely to be in conflict with certain informal norms. In loosely coupled organizations there is little formal protection and likely strong informal opposition and hostility toward such a person. Using the rumor and gossip network of the informal organization, leaders of that informal organization can propose the existence of maleficent behaviors on the part of the change agent. These accusations and the accompanying behaviors are parallel to those used in witchcraft accusations in preliterate societies.

(6) If one is accused of witchcraft-type behavior, that which is incapable of proof or disproof, the safest action on the part of the accused is to admit to the behavior (or at least that possibility) and proclaim one's lack of malice or intent and one's sincere desire to avoid such behavior in the future.

Like the accused Azande's son, an individual accused in the fashion described is best advised to 'blow water.' What a wonderful concept, to *blow water*; to publicly and ritualistically admit to what you know is not true but are incapable of disproving. In doing so one is reunited with the belief system of the informal organization and escapes the fate of all witches. If the change agent can then fain some change, something that does not impact the informal organization but is perceived by the top management as meeting the mandate in a non-threatening manner, the change agent may be allowed to survive. But, of course, a change agent who changes nothing is hardly a change agent. Is that perhaps what we look for in administrators, after all?

(7) Rumor and gossip are essential aspects of witch accusation; open communication should be helpful in reducing the occurrence of witch-hunting.

But administrators, outsiders, and change agents are seldom in control of (or have much access to) the informal organization where gossip and rumor thrive. Formal communication, no matter how open, is not an acceptable substitute for rumor and gossip in the informal organization. It is almost hopeless for an outside change agent administrator to attempt to use the formal lines of communication to successfully combat witch accusations in the informal network. Such communication is suspect at best and self-serving and rejected at worst.

(8) Allegations against witches usually occur during periods of high organizational conflict and anxiety.

The disliked change agent is the easy scapegoat or the witch responsible for organizational misfortune, such as periodic lack of public support. Eliminating the witches may not solve the problem; but as history teaches, likely the problem will soon go away. Even the smallpox epidemic described by Bowen went away.[35] Eliminating the witch will allow the informal organization to relieve its tension and return to its comfortable status quo.

(9) If one is powerful enough and/or has powerful friends, immediate denial and confrontation of the accuser may prove successful, but the risk of this behavior is great.

Proposition 7 warns change agent administrators against believing they control communication. Add to that the fact that formal rank is not the equivalent of informal influence and power, that threatened formal top administrators cannot always be counted upon in times of trouble (even to support their own mandates), and the impact becomes clear. Confrontation and change is a risk. For the compassionate change agent it is even a greater risk for, in a Machiavellian sense, being unwilling or unable to kill the other person is seen by many as being powerless.

(10) If one is to avoid the consequences of being accused of witchcraft, a 'proper witchfinder' must be sought out who will point out other long-felt and well known troubles and hostilities and effectively lay the blame for these at the doorstep of another who is already suspected by the organization of causing its troubles.

This process is more likely accomplished when the original accusation has been improperly done. Under those circumstances, an outside but informed 'expert' will be more effective in proving the innocence of the accused than will an insider who may already be predisposed to believe the original accusation. Given that one chooses not to 'blow water' but to avoid open confrontation, another option remains. This will be made easier if the original accusers have been socially clumsy or psychologically unstable. Such an accuser is likely to become 'too quickly public' and violate the norms of the informal group. The accused should then seek an informed 'expert,' accepted by the informal group, to disprove the allegation. In doing so the informal norms must be supported, not attacked! Long known troubles confronting the group must be recalled and other antisocial persons need to be suggested as being the cause of these troubles, rather than the person originally accused.

## Method of data collection

As a participant observer in higher education in top administrative roles, the author collected data for three years. These data included a daily participant observer diary, letters, memos, notes of telephone conversations and meetings, official minutes and policy statements, and vita of faculty participants (which provided some measure of professional geneology). The descriptive case presented in this article was developed from these data and verified with two other persons who held roles in the organization during data collection.

### Data: a description of witchfinding in education organizations

The ethnographies cited in the introduction to this article are descriptions of witchcraft and witchfinding in preliterate societies. Modern society labels witchcraft 'evil and primitive,' As exemplified in Southeast Ambra, modern organizations do not always move to eliminate witchcraft, but sometimes use it to promote their own ends. The works of Harris and Hansen[36] describe and attempt to explain more modern witchcraft and witchfinding behaviors.

It is unlikely that modern organizations would willingly label any of their behaviors as witchcraft and witchfinding. It may be possible, however, that some behaviors in modern organizations have elements similar to those called witchcraft and witchfinding when they are observed in preliterate societies. The propositions offered in the previous section were derived from the ethnographies in the introduction and suggest how witchcraft-witchfinding behaviors would manifest themselves in modern educational organizations if they do exist.

What follows is a brief description of organizational behaviors in a higher education organization that appears to closely parallel the elements of preliterate witchcraft as a means of social control.

Southern State University (SSU) had grown over the past forty years from a small state teachers college to a middle-sized university with six separate schools, graduate programs, and over 10,000 students. It was in the process of developing a national image in athletics; it had an excellent library for its size, a well-kept campus, and a reputation among the middle and lower classes of the state as a fine liberal arts, non-urban, rather conservative institution. Several of the liberal arts departments had good reputations, but there were few productive scholars or researchers on the faculty. Several resignations in the natural sciences were reportedly due to perceived broken promises made by the president to individuals regarding the research support they would receive and the importance of research to the university.

Although teacher education gave the institution birth, it became a department in the Liberal Arts School during the first years of university status. With the growth of public education during the 1950s and 1960s, the Lab School was closed. That school's faculty was given tenure positions on the university faculty, and a School of Education was created. At that time the department of education faculty joined the staff of the Lab School to form the faculty of the new School of Education. The principal of Lab School became the first dean, winning the position over the leading candidate from the old department of education. That losing candidate stayed on the faculty as a department head and twenty years later served as acting dean when the first dean resigned and took a position on the faculty. Over 90 per cent of the faculty was tenured and all but two of the untenured faculty were members of a newly created department in the School of Education.

In the late 1970s a new president came to SSU. Although not himself a model of scholarship, he recognized the social-political pressures in higher education in the 1980s: the likelihood of declining enrolment and the shift toward higher academic standards and faculty scholarship and production. Faced with a 'graying' faculty and the heavily tenured status of the faculty in education, he opted to attempt change in the School of Education by hiring an outside change agent as a new dean. He precipitated the resignation of the old dean (who remained on the faculty) and hired a person of some national recognition as a scholar in education. In order to accomplish that, he had to reject one set of candidates recommended and to reorganize the original search committee. Commensurate with his values, and permitted by board policy, he stated that he could not give the new dean tenure but would 'protect retreat rights into the faculty.'

Prior to the new dean's arrival, remodeling and space demands resulted in a presidential decision to take over one section of the old Lab School building occupied by the School of Education, thought by the education faculty as 'their building,' and still referred to as the 'Lab School.' Even before the new dean's arrival on campus the rumor was circulated that the new dean had 'given away our building.'

During the time prior to the new dean's official arrival, he visited the campus on several occasions. During these periods he invited any of the faculty to meet with him to discuss their ideas, hopes and aspirations. He also met with the president on each occasion to get his evaluation and discuss a complete renovation of the school of education facilities.

Most of the faculty discussions centered around their displeasure with the president, and their dislike for him and his low evaluation of their works. As for the president, his comments were the antithesis of that scenario. During one meeting he was looking at the new dean's campus appointments for that visit. 'Don't see that guy – stay away from him,' he ordered 'He's crazy. I've done him a lot of favors. I sent him to China as a university representative. But he's crazy. He has ridden his bicycle around campus with signs suggesting the faculty go on strike.' The new dean explained that the appointment had been made and had to be kept.

By official arrival time it was clear that the president expected emphasis on publication and research and wanted a reorganization of the school. During this time and for the first six months of the new dean's service, an interim vice-president of academic affairs was operating that office, and a search was in progress for a new vice-president.

Immediately upon arrival the new dean initiated a reactivation of the 'Dean's Advisory Committee', which had met only twice in the previous three years according to a faculty informant. The dean began weekly department chair meetings with prepared agenda and published minutes and initiated a series of meetings and programs for local superintendents. His message to the faculty was that many of the excellent things they were doing were going unrecognized. The president expected change and that included doing more research and publication. At the very least some ideas were needed to 'repackage' the present product because no matter how good it was, it wasn't selling with the president. The college budget, always held close to the chest by the former dean, was decentralized to department chairs. A small fund of $5,000 was reserved for research-related travel and faculty members always received full funding when they did such travel. Thus the dean failed to support the notion that no changes should take place.

In October, a group of seventeen long-tenured faculty members, many from the old Lab School faculty, requested a meeting with the dean. They told him, 'We are the people you must get along with to succeed here.' They would tolerate no changes. Attempts to demonstrate to them that the dean wanted to 'get along,' welcomed, and desired their input into the changes mandated by the president were unconvincing to them. An anonymous letter informed the dean, 'You and "old Danny Boy" should both get out of here if you don't like the way we do things.' The reference was to the president, whose first name was Dan.

The dean continued to support the president and seek change ideas from the faculty. He insisted, in the face of the opposition of the vice-president for business, that department committees be involved in and approve renovation changes for their departmental space renovation. In October, the president addressed a school of education faculty meeting and informed the faculty that he was, 'damned tired of their complaining and crap.'

By Christmas vacation the dean had visited and taken part at conferences sponsored by the elementary, psychology, special education and administration departments. He had contributed funds from his budget to those events and just before the holiday had the entire faculty to his home for a Christmas reception. Over one hundred faculty and spouses attended that event, paid for with the dean's personal money. He thought perhaps things were getting better.

Late in the winter the new dean asked the elected 'Faculty Advisory Committee' for options regarding school reorganization. They developed a set of organizational options and, at the request of the dean, submitted them to the faculty for an advisory vote. At that faculty meeting an old time faculty member publicly accused the new dean of outright 'dishonesty' in the matter, of total disregard of the faculty, and capitulation to the president. Instead of quietly submitting or waiting for other opportunities and outside support, the dean angrily responded during the meeting.

Shortly before this time a new vice-president was hired, and the interim vice-president slipped back into relative administrative obscurity. The faculty's informal gossip and rumor system, already in operation, shifted into high gear led by one particular department head who had been at the university for more than twenty-five years and epitomized the faculty norms – he had never written or published. Teaching was touted as the only goal in the view of the majority of the faculty. Research was believed to be done at the expense of teaching, and to promote research was to 'curse teaching.' To disagree with the faculty norms was to oppose academic freedom.

Although resources and enrolment were increasing, most of the faculty actually believed things had never been worse. Research and publication increased slightly, largely due to the untenured faculty in a single department. This was perceived as a harbinger of the evil that would surely befall use of school education if it did not place teaching first. Anonymous letters and phone calls defaming the new dean were made to the president. Accusations of 'not listening to the faculty,' threats of going 'to the board' and even suggestions of alcoholism on the part of the new dean were made in the rumor mill. Then one faculty member did call a board member, who called the president. During spring vacation the president called in the new dean and made it clear that he would not support him. 'How did you ever get the idea that you should reorganize the school?' the president asked.

The president showed the dean an inch thick folder of letters and notes on phone calls he had received, mostly anonymously, from faculty – all reportedly complaining about the dean and asking that the president remove the dean. The president, with the new vice-president present, showed the dean a pre-typed letter of resignation. He asked the dean to sign it immediately and offered the dean the position of school research director without salary reduction and with tenure if he would sign. The dean declined.

During the next few weeks, the vice-president indicated that an evaluation would take place during the next nine months and some decision made by the following December. The dean responded that if it were to be a popularity contest it was of no matter for he had already lost faculty support by his support of the president.

The following June all other deans were evaluated by the standard procedures. The dean requested the same evaluation and was refused, in writing. In October a special form was devised and sent to all faculty members, a process unheard of at SSU before or after. Faculty were asked for *opinions* about the dean. Leaders of the opposition offered 'help' to faculty members in filling out the evaluation. This was reported to the vice-president by supporters of the dean – and subsequently ignored. It was reported to the president that the chair of the search committee was going to write a letter to the president supporting the dean and indicating that he was doing a good job of what he was hired to do. The president met the chair's spouse at a community affair and told her *twice* during the evening, 'Tell your husband I don't think he should write that letter.' The letter was *not* written!

Around the first of December, the dean was offered a deanship at another university. He called the vice-president and asked about the results of the evaluation which had been in for three weeks. He was told the president was in China, not to worry about it, he would be back in two weeks. In those two weeks the other university went to their second choice who accepted the job.

During the third week of December the dean received a long-distance telephone call while at an out-of-state conference. He was to make an appointment with the vice-president immediately upon his return.

At that meeting he was told that the faculty had divided; one-third strongly supporting him and two-thirds strongly opposing him. Again he was given a letter of resignation to sign and twenty-four hours to do so. If he refused, the president would remove him by official action. This time he signed. He stayed in a temporary position the following year at a $10,000 reduction in salary. A long-time insider, who had never published, was appointed new dean and things returned to the original status quo.

*Analysis of the data*

Of course the above is surely not 'thick description.' Space prohibits that, but the pattern and elements are in place. The new dean was an outside change agent. All attempts to interact with the faculty were useless as a means of obtaining general faculty support. The dean was antisocial, offending and not conforming to the informal norms of the faculty. The president disassociated himself from the beginning by not providing tenure for the new dean and was 'uncoupled' from the interactions between the dean and the faculty. The new vice-president had no hand in bringing in the new dean, was uncoupled from the usual strong link between dean and vice-president of academic affairs, and was instead closely coupled with the president.

Although in control of the formal communication system, the dean had no effective input into the informal system. The informal group effectively used rumor and gossip within that system to accuse the dean of phenomenological faults. Empirical data were rejected by the president and vice-president. When accused improperly by the 'old timer,' the dean might have saved himself, either by 'blowing water' or by refraining from like public confrontation by calling in an outside expert. He did neither. He relied on formal rank and logic, completely impotent tools in the witchcraft process. The matter was over almost before it began, and the 'tribe returned to laughter' with a long-time insider who adhered to the norms at the helm as dean.

## Summary

One swallow does not a summer make. A single case does not establish a perspective as a set of laws. However, this illustration may make it possible to raise the question of whether the structure of a modern organization can 'evolve' in a way so as to meet important informal social goals (e.g. preserving order and the status quo) thereby sacrificing the organization's ability to meet formal goals. If so, is it possible to make assumptions about the relative importance of those goals? Might those relationships be changed if they were better understood?

Even if this argument displaying witchcraft in higher education organizations is convincing to some, it certainly does not account for all behavior in such organizations. To the extent, however, that it better accounts for and explains some behavior, this perspective has improved understanding of those organizations. To recognize that 'primitive behaviors' can and do occur in modern organizations, that irrationality often wins even in 'rational' organizations, may make organizational worlds more 'livable.'

It would seem that a witch cannot kill with a curse alone. However, the effects of the belief in witchcraft are believable and organizations sometimes attribute cause to phenomenological factors, including witchcraft-like behaviors. It seems possible, at least there is some scientific argument, that the belief in a witch's curse can kill.[37] In this perspective the argument has been that when, for obvious reasons, the members of a modern organization choose to avoid the responsibility of their own problems, phenomenological (unprovable) reasons for those troubles are likely to be substituted and believed by the organizational faithful. These substitutions in modern organizations often take a form similar to the accusing of witches by appointed witchfinders. The result of this process is real. It relieves tension within the organization, removes marginal persons against whom powerful insiders hold hostile feelings and grudges, and returns the organization to its former status quo, preserving the positions of the powerful insiders who otherwise might be held responsible for the organization's problems.

Perhaps Hansen, writing about *Witchcraft at Salem*,[38] has raised an important point for institutions of higher education. He says:

> Any Community [or organization] so beset [by witchcraft-like behaviors] might well take Salem's experience as a warning and recognize . . . that in matters of malice the devil suits his actions to man's belief about them.

### Notes

1. F. W. Lutz, 'The Ghost Dance of the Elementary Principal,' *Pennsylvania Elementary Principals Journal* 19, 2(1969):7–9; Idem, 'Cultures and Councils in Educational Governance,' *The Generator* 8, 2(1978):13–20; Idem, 'Tightening Up Loose Coupling in Higher Education,' *Administrative Science Quarterly* 24 (1982):653–669; and F. W. Lutz and T. G. Dow, 'National Departmental Recognition in Programs in Educational Administration,' *Planning and Changing* 12, 1 (1981):54–62.
2. G. E. Dole, 'Anarchy Without Chaos: Alternatives to Authority Among the Kuikuru,' in *Political Anthropology*, M. S. Schwartz *et al.*, eds (New York: Aldine, 1966), pp. 73–88.
3. R. F. Spencer, 'Shamanism in Northwest North America,' in *The Anthropology of Power*, R. D. Fogelsen and R. N. Adams, eds (New York: Academic Press, 1981).
4. E. S. Bowen, *Return to Laughter* (New York: Harper & Brothers, 1969).
5. *Ibid.*, p. 297.
6. J. Middleton, 'Witchcraft and Sorcery in Ligabara,' in *Witchcraft and Sorcery in East Africa*, J. Middleton and E. H. Winter, eds (London: Routledge & Kegan, 1963).
7. E. H. Winter, 'The Enemy Within: Amba Witchcraft and Sociological Theory,' in Middleton and Winter, eds *Witchcraft and Sorcery*, p. 291.
8. E. Colson, 'The Alien Diviner and Local Politics Among the Tonga of Zambia,' in Schwartz, ed. *Political Anthropology*, p. 224.
9. R. Tonkinson, 'Church and Kotson in Southwest Ambrym,' in *Vanuatu: Politics, Economics, and Ritual in Islands Melanesia*, R. Allen, ed. (New York: Academic Press 1982), pp. 237–68.
10. *Ibid.*, p. 259.
11. M. Harris, *Cows, Pigs, Wars and Witches: The Riddle of Culture* (New York: Random House, 1974).
12. C. Hansen, *Witchcraft at Salem* (New York: George Braziller, 1969).
13. M. M. Leininger, 'Witchcraft Iratoces and Psychological Therapy with Urban U.S. Families,' *Human Organizations* 32 (1973):73–83.

14. C. Geertz, *The Interpretation of Cultures* (New York: Basic Books, 1973).
15. Middleton, 'Witchcraft and Sorcery.'
16. R. F. Gray, 'The Shetani Cult Among the Segeju,' in *Spirit, Mediumship and Society in Africa*. J. Beattie and J. Middleton, eds (New York: Homes & Meier, 1969), pp. 171–87.
17. A. Harwood, *Witchcraft, Sorcery and Social Categories among the Safwa* (London: Oxford University Press 1970).
18. Winter, 'The Enemy Within,' p. 291.
19. J. R. Crawford, *Witchcraft and Sorcery in Rhodesia* (London: Oxford, 1967), p. 161.
20. Winter, 'The Enemy Within,' p. 28.
21. Tonkinson, 'Church and Kotson,' pp. 256–7.
22. Colson, 'The Alien Diviner,' pp. 221–8.
23. C. Levi-Strauss, *Savage Mind* (Chicago: University of Chicago Press, 1966).
24. B. Jules-Rosette, 'The Veil of Objectivity: Prophecy, Divination and Social Inquiry,' *American Anthropologist* 80 (1978):549–70, pp. 560, 561.
25. Winter, 'The Enemy Within,' pp. 1414, 1415.
26. Harwood, 'Witchcraft, Sorcery and Social Categories,' p. 259.
27. R. P. Werbner, 'The Superabundance of Understanding: Kalanga Rhetoric and Domestic Divination,' *American Anthropologist* 75 (1973):1414–40, p. 1428.
28. E. E. Evans-Pritchard, *Witchcraft Oracles and Magic among the Azande* (London: Oxford University Press, 1937), p. 124.
29. Colson, 'The Alien Diviner,' p. 138.
30. Tonkinson, 'Church and Kotson,' pp. 259, 260.
31. K. E. Weick, 'Educational Organizations as Loosely Coupled Systems,' *Administrative Science Quarterly* 21 (1976): 1–19; and J. F. Padgett, 'Managing Garbage Can Hierarchies,' *Administrative Science Quarterly* 25 (1980): 583–604.
32. Lutz, 'Tightening Up Loose Coupling.'
33. In their excellent book, C. Argyris and D. Schön, *Organizational Learning: A Theory of Action Perspective* (Reading, Mass.: Addison-Wesley, 1978), state that the O-I organization 'is so awe inspiring in its apparent irrationality that one is moved to ask how it can possibly result from apparently rational processes of organizational design. After all, formal organizations are consciously designed; they are calculated to achieve intended objectives. But when we look at what actually goes on in organizations . . . we find much that is counterproductive' (p. 119).

    But as social scientists, Argyris and Schön assume organizational rationality and proceed to instruct their readers on how to 'help organizations move toward Model O-H learning systems' (p. 129). Fine for social scientists/professors. However, administrative practitioners may well be accused of witchcraft for their troubles. The pretense of rationality is a formidable defense used in irrational modern organizations.
34. R. O. Carlson, *Executive Succession and Organizational Change* (Chicago: University of Chicago, Midwest Administration Center, 1962).
35. Smith, *Return to Laughter*.
36. Harris, *Cows, Pigs and Witches*; and Hansen, *Witchcraft at Salem*.
37. B. W. Lex 'Voodoo Death: New Thoughts on an Old Explanation,' *American Anthropologist* 76 (1974):818–23.
38. Hansen, *Witchcraft at Salem*, p. 227.

# 20
# Strategy formation in the university setting

**Cynthia Hardy, Ann Langley, Henry Mintzberg and Janet Rose**

It is well-known that strategies are formulated before they are implemented, that planning is the central process by which they are so formulated, and that structures should be designed to implement given strategies. At least this is well known to those who have read the conventional literature on strategy-making. In the university setting, these imperatives stand almost totally at odds with what really happens, leading to the conclusion either that universities 'have it all wrong' or that the strategy theoreticians do. Several observers of the university scene have been prepared to argue the former point. Some have suggested that few universities have strategies and that they had better develop them following the methods generally accepted in business (e.g. Dube and Brown, 1983; Doyle and Lynch, 1979). Others have noted that when universities do formulate strategies, they consistently fail to implement them satisfactorily because of a deplorable lack of administrative power, leadership skill, or courage in the face of opposition (e.g. Hosmer, 1978; Ladd, 1970; Lutz, 1982).

We, on the other hand, believe that the conventional view of strategy – as a plan, or a set of explicit intentions preceding and controlling actions – is too narrow to permit a satisfactory understanding of strategy formation in the university setting (as well as many others). An alternate view of strategy focuses not on *a priori* articulation of *intention*, but on the existence of consistency in the actions and/or decisions emerging from an organization. Specifically, we define strategies as *realized* as patterns in streams of decisions or actions (Mintzberg, 1972, 1978; Mintzberg and Waters, 1983). This definition allows basic but unarticulated orientations to be viewed as strategies.

Based on this definition, the study of strategy formation in the university setting takes on a new interest. Rather than merely throwing up our hands at the infrequent use or abortive outcomes of explicit strategic planning, or, alternately, going to the other extreme and dismissing universities as 'organized anarchies' with strategy-making processes as mere 'garbage cans' (March and Olsen, 1976), we are able to focus on how decisions and actions order themselves into patterns over time.

We begin by developing in more depth the concept of strategy introduced above. We then focus on the processes by which various kinds of decisions are made in universities. This leads us to suggest a number of propositions about the patterns likely to emerge and the nature of the strategy formation process in the university, which we relate to some preliminary data from an ongoing study of strategy formation during a century and a half at McGill University.

### Strategies as deliberate and emergent

As indicated above, we focus most of our attention on strategies as realized, rather than on strategies as intended. Thus, for example, a university that puts a scientific slant on all of its activities could be described as pursuing a science strategy, just as one that repeatedly puts its resources into undergraduate programs at the expense of research can be said to pursue a strategy of favouring undergraduate teaching.

By our definition, an organization can have a realized strategy without having an intended one (or, more exactly, patterns can be evident even when *a priori* intentions were not). This means that strategies can exist without the efforts of central actors, that the formulation of strategies need not necessarily precede their implementation, and that strategies themselves need not necessarily be explicit (or, for that matter, even consciously recognized) – in other words, they can form rather than having to be formulated. As shown in Figure 1, the limiting case of this can be referred to as *emergent* strategy, to distinguish it from *deliberate* strategy (where *a priori* intentions were realized, more or less).

It may seem unconventional, indeed questionable, to use the word 'strategy' for patterns in behavior, without considering intentions. We have two reasons for doing so. First, there has to be some way to identify strategies actually pursued. Can we call a stated intention that never evoked effort a

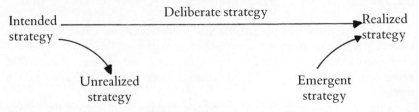

**Figure 1**   Various Types of Strategies

strategy? Indeed, while few people would formally define strategy as we do, many in fact so use the term, for example when an executive infers the 'strategy' of a competitor, or a newspaper does the same thing for a political leader. Second, there is no such thing as a purely deliberate strategy, any more than there is a purely emergent one (by our definition). That is why we believe the same word ('strategy') should be used for patterns realized as well as intentions, so that the two may be compared under the same labels.

The difficulty in distinguishing between relatively deliberate and emergent strategies is to identify the intentions of various actors in a collective context. In a conventional automobile company, it may be sufficient to identify the intentions of the central administrators, who are able to impose their intentions on the rest of the organization. But in the university setting, the intentions of various actors and, more importantly, the extent to which these intentions are shared, must be understood before strategies can be labeled deliberate or emergent. Strategies may in fact be identified with a distinct group (say a department) or even an individual (such as a single professor), or they may form on a consensus basis (becoming collectively intended and then realized by the actions of many actors). A strategy can be partially deliberate and partially emergent, as when the broad outline of it is intended but the details emerge en route or when the process of strategy-making is decided upon in a deliberate way (through the design of committee structures, hiring practices, etc.) while the content of specific strategies (what programs to offer, etc.) is allowed to emerge. Various forms of strategy identified in an ongoing research project of strategy formation in a variety of organizational settings are listed in Table 1, along a rough continuum from deliberate to emergent.

Of course, defining strategy as pattern or consistency in actions says nothing about the actions on which to focus. By this definition, universities can have strategies about everything. But the discovery that all the classrooms of a given university are painted beige would seem to pale in comparison to the discovery of a pattern in actions of favouring the sciences over the humanities. Clearly some patterns deserve more attention than others. One danger, however, is to assume that actions are important simply because they come under the control of central administrators, or, more to the point in the university setting, that they are unimportant because they are controlled by individual professors. Indeed, the key area of strategy-making in most organizations concerns the elaboration of the basic mission (the products or services offered to the public), and in universities, as we shall argue, this is significantly controlled by individual professors (e.g. in their choices of course materials and research projects). We believe other important areas of strategy include the inputs to the system (notably the choice and subsequent tenuring of academic staff, the determination of student enrolment, and the raising of external funds), the means to perform the mission (the construction of buildings and facilities, the purchase of research equipment, etc.), the structure and forms of governance (design of the committee

**Table 1**  Summary description of types of strategies

| Type of strategy | Major features |
|---|---|
| Planned | precise intentions formulated and articulated by central leadership, backed up by formal controls to ensure surprise-free implementation in benign, controllable, or predictable environment; strategies are generally deliberate. |
| Entrepreneurial | intentions exist as the personal, unarticulated vision of a single leader, and so are adaptable to new opportunities; organization is under the personal control of the leader and located in a protected niche in the environment; strategies are relatively deliberate but can emerge inadvertently. |
| Ideological | intentions exist as a collective vision of all actors, in inspirational form and relatively immutable, controlled normatively through indoctrination and/or socialization; organization often proactive *vis-à-vis* environment; strategies rather deliberate. |
| Umbrella | leadership in partial control of organizational actions, defines strategic targets or boundaries within which other actors respond to own forces or to complex, unpredictable environment; strategies partly deliberate, partly emergent (or deliberately emergent). |
| Process | leadership controls process aspects of strategy (hiring, structure, etc.), leaving content aspects to other actors; strategies partly deliberate, partly emergent (and, again, deliberately emergent). |
| Disconnected | actors loosely coupled to rest of organization produce patterns in actions in absence of, or in direct contradiction to, central or common intentions; strategies are 'organizationally' emergent whether or not they are deliberate for individual actors (can be departmental or personal strategies). |
| Consensus | through mutual adjustment, actors converge on patterns that become pervasive in absence of central or common intentions; strategies may emerge through spontaneous convergence but may also be negotiated. |
| Imposed | the environment dictates patterns in actions either through direct imposition or through implicitly pre-empting or bounding organization choice; strategies organizationally emergent, although they may be internalized and made to appear deliberate. |

*Source:* Mintzberg and Waters (1983)

system, the hierarchies, the regulations concerning promotion and tenure, etc.), and the various means of support for the mission (notably the elaboration of the university's support structure, from computers and libraries to alumni offices and printing facilities).

If strategies are taken to be patterns in actions, then to understand strategy formation, we must first consider how actions come about and then consider how these actions converge over time to create patterns. Accordingly, we take up next the issue of how decisions (which are intended to provoke actions or changes in actions) are made in universities, and then consider how they, and the actions that they evoke, form patterns, in order to draw conclusions about the nature of university strategies and the processes by which they are formed.

## Decision-making in the university setting

Were universities to formulate strategies from the conventional perspective, central administrators would develop detailed and integrated plans about the programs to be offered, the courses to be taught, the students to be admitted, the buildings to be built, and so on, much as automobile companies normally work out the design of their product lines and production facilities before they take action. In fact, automobile companies seem to resemble rather closely a model of organization that we call 'machine bureaucracy' (Mintzberg, 1979), in which the overall mission – the mass production of particular products or services – lends itself to extensive rationalization, thereby rendering the operations a sequence of simple routine tasks requiring minimum skills. In this type of organization, the conventional approach to strategy-making seems to make a good deal of sense. The organization needs tight integration of its actions (every part must fit together on the assembly line, marketing must promote the product produced by the factory, and so on), hence its central administrators, who can understand the operating tasks, must exercise tight central control of them. Too much discretion over individual actions (let alone global strategies) in the hands of the final actors would only encourage disintegration.

Universities stand in sharp contrast to this model of organization. For one thing, central administrators cannot possibly understand the wide array of skills and knowledge applied in the operations of their institutions, ranging from the most subtle interpretations of ancient Greek philosophy to the most sophisticated advances in contemporary nuclear physics. For another, and as a consequence of the first, in Weick's (1976) terms universities must be 'loosely coupled' systems, in which the actions of one part need not be tightly integrated with the others (the philosopher and the physicist sharing little more than a faculty club and a system of grade point averages). Universities in fact resemble another model of organization, labelled 'professional bureaucracy' (Mintzberg, 1979).

Because universities require specialized expertise, many of their decisions, and in particular some concerned with the definition of the basic
elements of the mission (teaching and research), can only be made by
individual professors. Others can in fact come under direct control of central
administrators, for example, decisions concerned with the financing of the
university and with the provision of many of its support services. Many
important decisions, however, can be made neither by individual professors
nor by central administrators, but require rather the participation of various
actors with different interests and expertise. Decisions in these cases emerge
from complex collective and interactive processes. It is these interactive
decisions that have engaged most of the interest of the decision-making
theorists who have studied universities. As illustrated in Figure 2, we
examine in turn the decisions controlled by individual professionals, by
central administrators, and by the collectivity, (the latter in terms of four
models of decision-making: collegial, political, garbage can, and rational
analysis).

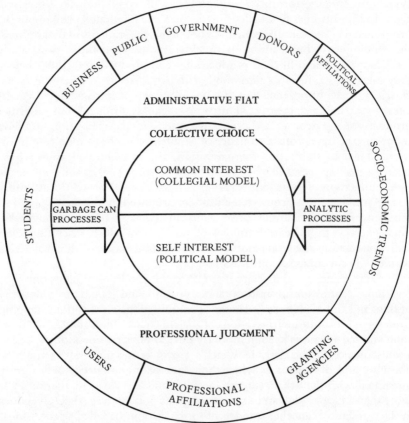

**Figure 2**   Three levels of decision-making in the university.

*Decisions made by professional judgment*

In the university setting, individual professors have a great deal of autonomy over research and teaching because of the difficulties of supervising or formalizing this work. Thus, many of the decisions that, in effect, detail the basic missions of the university come under the control of the individual professor:

> Presidents and their chief academic subordinates concede that much of the structure of academic policy is determined in the individual departments – realistically, often in the individual classroom. . . . Academic 'Policy' is the accretion of hundreds of largely auto-nomous actions taken for different reasons, at different times, under different conditions, by different people. (Cohen and March, 1974, p. 104)

To understand this form of decentralization to the level of the individual professor, two essential concepts about universities (and professional bureaucracies in general) must be understood – pigeonholing and standard-ization of skills and knowledge.

The *pigeonholing* process divides the organization's activities into a series of standard components or programs that are applied to predetermined situations or contingencies, also standardized. As Weick has noted, 'schools are in the business of building and maintaining categories' (1976, p. 8). Clients (i.e. students) entering the organization are categorized according to the set of available contingencies (or categorize themselves) and are then sent to the appropriate professional (or set of them in sequence) to execute the relevant programs. In other words, the object is to force all students into the existing slots. One student exhibits an aptitude for languages and so is directed into a degree in the Spanish or French department, another who wishes to become a manager selects the business school. Once that choice is made, the student is slotted into a series of courses, by which the pigeon-holing process is extended to the level of the individual professor. In other words, each course is itself a standard program of the organization, evoked in response to a standardized stimulus (e.g. the introductory Policy course as a required part of the MBA program).

Note that by partitioning its tasks through pigeonholing, the university buffers or insulates its programs from one another and thereby minimizes the need for coordination across tasks and maximizes the discretion of those who carry out the tasks – in other words, it achieves both its loose coupling and its extensive decentralization concurrently. It also avoids a good deal of uncer-tainty, or at least confines it to the level of the individual program. Once the pigeonholes are defined, whatever variability that does remain is forced into the context of specific programs. Similarly, the domains over which indi-vidual professors retain control are defined by the pigeonholes to which they can be assigned. Simultaneously, it is the very system of pigeonholes that provides that control, for it buffers each professor from activities taking place in other pigeonholes.

Within the domain defined by pigeonholing, what, then, does an individual professor control? Clear examples, at least when courses are not taught in multiple sections, would seem to be teaching method and materials, course content, books, grades, etc.; likewise for research conducted on an individual basis, topic and methodology, etc. But while that control may seem to be absolute from the perspective of the organization, it is not so from the perspective of external influence.

This brings us to the *standardization of skills and knowledge*. The reason why individual professors are trusted to make their own decisions in the areas listed above is that their skills and knowledge have been standardized through long years of training. In a sense they have been programmed through their own doctoral or professional studies to approach their fields of endeavor in generally accepted ways, in terms of what they teach, and perhaps how, as well as in terms of how they carry out research, and perhaps on what. (In referring to this below as *professional* training and affiliation, in no way do we wish to restrict our comments to the formally professional fields, say medicine as opposed to English literature. As should be clear above, professors of English literature are hardly less free of the influence of their implicit profession than are professors of medicine of their official one.)

This may not encourage radical innovation – in Kuhn's (1970) terms, doctoral programs train people to do 'normal science', not to foment 'scientific revolutions' – but it does ensure that professors will act 'responsibly' (given that 'responsibly' means: in generally accepted ways to a community of scholars). Thus professors choose books that tend to be well regarded by their colleagues, they design their courses in ways that reflect their own training, they adopt teaching methods acceptable in their disciplines (and sometimes even sanctioned by professional associations, as in certain practical work in medicine), they research subjects that can be funded by the granting agencies (which in turn are subject to professional influence), and they write articles in styles acceptable to the journals referred by their peers.

Pushed to the limit, then, 'academic freedom' can look like professional control – it may be explicit freedom from administrators, even from peers in other disciplines, but it is not implicit freedom from colleagues in other universities. Of course, tenured professors may feel some release from these pressures to conform, but by the time they receive tenure, most have become socialized into the predominant norms – that is probably how they gained tenure in the first place. It is hardly surprising, therefore, that they tend to become the main defenders of the norms. Thus we have titled this section decision by 'professional judgment', the implication being that while judgment may be the mode of choice – professors being free in these choices from having to bargain with colleagues or to carry out formal analysis – this is informed judgment, mightily influenced by professional training and affiliation.

Other influences, of course, impinge on the choices of individual professors. Student feedback can modify classroom techniques, demographic factors influence class size that in turn may affect course offerings, corporations can influence research in a field such as engineering by virtue of providing sites for conducting enquiry, and so on. Overall, the general environment plays a significant role in the selection of topics of research and teaching, as individual professors respond to the concerns of the day – aerospace issues after Sputnik, women in management issues in the 1980's, and so on. But no force matches that of the implicit and explicit influence of professional affiliation.

Note that it is this standardization of skills and knowledge that enables the organization to achieve much of the coordination that remains to be effected across pigeonholes (indeed, to set up the whole system of pigeonholes in the first place): 'the system works because everyone knows everyone else knows roughly what is going on' (Meyer, quoted in Weick, 1976, p. 14). Thus a professor teaching physics to engineering students need not spend a great deal of time coordinating his or her efforts with another teaching calculus to the same students: the former has been trained to know what to expect in a standard calculus course. The necessary coordination between the two can therefore be effected almost automatically, with hardly any need for personal contact. To use an old expression, universities, as professional bureaucracies, are organizations designed to allow everyone to grind in his or her own mill. The label 'bureaucracy' has been used expressly because of this emphasis on standardization (as well as pigeonholing), which creates a certain stability in procedure. To repeat, these are not organizations designed to innovate so much as to apply and elaborate complex standards. To quote Herbert Simon:

> The pleasure that the good professional experiences in his work is not simply a pleasure in handling difficult matters; it is a pleasure in using skillfully a well-stocked kit of well-designed tools to handle problems that are comprehensible in their deep structure but unfamiliar in their detail. (1977, p. 98)

*Decisions made by administrative fiat*

Expertise, professional autonomy, and coordination through standardized skills and knowledge (largely imported to the organization via professional training and norms), all facilitated by the pigeonholing process, sharply circumscribe the capacity of central administrators to manage the university's professional staff in the ways of conventional bureaucracy – through direct supervision, namely the issuing of direct orders, and through the designation of standards within the organization (e.g. rules, job descriptions, policies).

Even the designation of output or performance standards is discouraged by the intractible problem of operationalizing the goals of universities.

To carry this point further, it is in fact the academics who control much of the administration. This they do by staffing the committees and task forces that make many of the key decisions, or by suspending their academic duties to fill administrative posts for a period of time. In other words, the academic staff controls much of the administration by virtue of being seconded to administrative duties for either a few hours or a few years at a time.

While many of the administrative decisions are subjected to collective choice – involving various academics as well as administrators – there are certain ones that fall into the realm of what we are calling administrative fiat. In other words, they are the exclusive prerogatives of the senior administration, under which term we include the board of regents (or equivalent), the president or principal of the university (i.e. the chief executive officer), as well as the senior echelon of administrators who surround that person. Administrative fiat is meant to describe the situation with respect to other members of the university community; it is not meant to suggest that administrators do not vie or bargain with each other over choices. (Although we refer to senior administrators in relation to the whole university, many of these points would also apply to deans in relation to their schools or faculties.)

The types of decisions that fall into this realm are rather circumscribed. Childers (1981) for example shows that decisions concerning the missions of teaching and research as well as many stages of personnel decisions fall outside this realm. But others do fall within it. Childers (1981) identifies these as 'institutional management' decisions. For example, many financial decisions are made exclusively at this level, although the question of which specific ones varies from one university to another. In general, decisions to invest in stocks (or disinvest in South African ones), buy and sell property, and embark on fund raising campaigns, tend to be taken by central administrators in relative isolation from the remaining members of the organization.

A number of external influencers affect these finance decisions, especially those who supply funds to the university – the government in the case of public universities (Gross, 1968) and individual donors in the case of private ones. For example, government budget cuts stimulate decisions about budget reallocation and cost cutting, many of which tend to focus on the central administrative level. By virtue of their donations, private individuals can, for example, evoke administrative decisions about the location of new buildings, the establishment of chaired professorships, and the eligibility requirements of student scholarships. The very fact that these external influencers interact with the central administrators, whom they view as responsible for the activities of the organization, gives the latter a certain power in these specific spheres of decision-making.

Because many of the support services of the university are organized in a conventional 'top-down' hierarchy – machine bureaucratic in nature – they also tend to fall under the control of the central administration. These include, for example, alumni and public relations, athletics and archives, accounting and payroll, building services and physical plant, and printing and translation services. The specific services may be executed well down in the hierarchy, but decisions concerning their basic orientations – that is, the 'strategic' decisions – tend to be controlled well up in the administration. However, power over certain other support services more critical to academic matters – e.g. libraries or computers – tend to fall into the realm of collective decision-making, where the central administrators join the academics in the making of choices.

Central administrators may have formal authority (power of veto) over administrative appointments, promotions, and tenure decisions. In many cases, however, this formal authority is not exercised (Cohen and March, 1974). Even when it is, such decisions have typically been initiated and filtered by various review committees in the collective process before they reach the administrative level. Central administrators may also play a role in determining the procedures by which the collective process functions – what committees exist, who gets nominated to them, and so on. It is the administrators, after all, who have the time to devote to administration. This role can give skilful administrators considerable influence, however indirect, over the strategies developed by others. We shall return to this point when we discuss collective decision-making.

In addition, in times of crisis, administrators may acquire more extensive powers in order to deal with the pressing problems of the moment. In other words, decisions that were collective can move into the realm of administrative fiat. For example, the 1964 crisis at Berkeley caused the Board to institute new disciplinary regulations, withdraw previously delegated power, and strengthen the hand of the administration (Smelser, 1973). Such centralization is to be expected in the event of a perceived crisis (Hermann, 1963; Smart and Vertinsky, 1977), for two reasons. One is that time pressure requires speedy action, necessitating centralized directive. A second is, when faced with uncertainty, others tend to defer to the central leadership, granting it more authority to come up with the correct response to reduce the uncertainty (Billings, Milburn and Schaalman, 1980). We suspect, however, that once the immediate crisis passes, typically decision-making becomes decentralized once again.

A mixture of judgmental and analytic processes may be used to make decisions at the central administration level. It is interesting to note that Cohen and March (1974), in their study of presidential power, found that universities tended to have detailed, explicit plans in precisely those areas in which central administrations had the most influence: capital physical planning and fiscal planning dealing with income uncertainties, cash-flow problems, and short-term investment. It is notable that these plans generally avoided academic issues. The 'academic plans' in fact compiled were essentially 'the natural consequence of asking each department to prepare a plan and then binding all the documents together without editing' (Cohen &

March, 1976). In other words, the central administration did not participate except to request the plan in the first place. Cohen, writing about the French national planning experience suggests that national 'planning' is either political or decorative (1977, xv). Several authors (e.g., Porter, Zemsky and Oedel, 1979; Richardson and Gardner, 1983) have made a similar point and the Cohen and March (1976) study suggests that much central university planning in the past has, in fact, been 'decorative' – aimed at external public relations rather than internal action.

### Decisions made by collective choice

Many decisions in universities are determined neither by administrators nor by sole academics, but evolve out of a variety of interactive processes that occur both within and between departments, and that involve various mixtures of academics as well as administrators from a variety of levels. In our opinion among the most important of these decisions are ones related to the definition, creation, design, and discontinuation of pigeonholes, that is, programs, departments, research centres, and at a lower level, individual courses. Other important decisions that fall into the realm of collective choice include promotion, tenure, and hiring, in some cases, budgeting, and establishing and designing the interactive procedures themselves.

Interactive processes within a department may involve members of the same discipline, as in the case of content decisions concerning a specific degree program (e.g., Master in Social Work) or even a single course that is team-taught. Other interactive processes cross departments, bringing members of different disciplines together to decide on issues ranging from the selection of computing equipment to the design of tenure regulations (or the granting of tenure in a single case). Formal groups abound in these interactive processes, comprising *ad hoc* task forces as well as standing committees, which typically include academic policy committees (at departmental and university levels) and senate, usually the highest ranking academic body of the university.

The interactive processes can involve both 'vertical' and 'horizontal' relationships. Within a given committee, individuals interact horizontally with one another to produce outcomes by mutual adjustment. But this committee will itself interact vertically with other levels in the hierarchy that may have the direct power to change or veto their outcomes, or which may dictate *a priori* guidelines and boundaries within which the deliberations of the committee must fall. These interactions among individuals and groups can be enormously complex and the distinctions between horizontal and vertical interaction can become blurred. For example, 'A single individual – faculty member or administrator – will frequently find himself involved in a particular decision at three or more points through membership of several overlapping committees' (Ladd, 1970, p. 206).

*Phases of interactive decision-making*

To help understand the roles that various individuals and groups may play in influencing decisions, we can break down the decision-making process into three major phases (after Mintzberg, Raisinghani and Théorêt, 1976) – identification, development, and selection (which themselves need not proceed in sequential order, but rather tend to involve complex cycles and interruptions).

The *identification* phase involves the recognition of the need to make a decision, and diagnosis of the situation. Many decisions, of course, arise on a routine basis (as in the case of promotion decisions), and so need no special impetus for identification. But changes to the organization or to its established procedures (or pigeonholes) do need identification, and this tends to happen more by individual initiative than by collective interaction. Given the complexity of decision-making in universities, and the rigidities that result from the pigeonholing process, change is difficult to imagine without the individual 'champion' or 'sponsor,' who initiates it in the first place and or at least pushes it through the complex interactive process to its completion.

> Strong, serious leadership is virtually mandatory for the success of any serious effort at educational reform . . . to try to counter the pressures favouring the *status quo* by creating or maintaining an atmosphere of receptivity to change. (Ladd, 1970, p. 205–206)

Obviously, different individuals will champion different issues depending on their own particular interests. We believe that professors are most likely to champion the creation of new pigeonholes, since these are closest to their own interests. Administrators, on the other hand, are more likely to champion changes in resource allocation procedures, or perhaps promotion and tenure regulations, although they may sometimes promote program additions when they perceive gaps in the services offered by their institution. Students also act as champions on occasion, but they are most likely to promote issues related to program flexibility or student participation in decision-making.

Issues that lack champions may, in fact, be avoided by the organization. Who, for example, relishes sticking his or her neck out to champion the discontinuation of a pigeonhole (program, faculty, research centre, etc.)? While the resources released by such a decision could be spent elsewhere, no one professional individual or interest group is likely to receive sufficient benefit to justify such championship, except in special circumstances. Financial pressure is likely to be felt more directly by the administrators, but there may be little incentive for them to attempt to initiate the closure of pigeonholes, at least when times are good. Resistance will be violent from those threatened, while support from other groups is likely to be weak.[1]

The second stage in decision-making, the *development* process, involves the search for and design of alternatives and solutions. In some cases, champions perform this function, proposing rather detailed solutions. In others, when only the need for decision has been identified, or when a champion is attempting to solicit ideas or at least generate commitment for his proposal, the issue will tend to be developed by *ad hoc* groups, or task forces. Obviously the members of these groups can have substantial influence on the decisions or recommendations put forward, and, indeed, often become the collective champions of the proposals they produce. Administrators may also have substantial influence at this point, through their ability to decide who gets to participate in the task forces, what the mandates of these tasks forces will be, and what procedures they will use. As noted earlier, the administrators are the ones with time for administration, and that includes in good degree the design of the interactive procedures as well as representation in them.

The *selection* process involves the screening, evaluation, choice, and authorization of alternatives and solutions. In most universities, this involves several layers of standing committees and individuals, with power of veto or the ability to return issues to lower levels for further development. These standing committees will, however, rarely get involved in development or initiation work directly (although their members might, of course).

The structures involved in this stage of decision-making in universities are well known for being cumbersome and slow, especially in large institutions. For example, a proposal for a PhD program in management at McGill University was first worked out by an *ad hoc* committee and then was approved within the Faculty of Management by its Graduate Program Committee, Academic Committee, and Faculty Council; from there it went to the Executive Committee and the Council of the Faculty of Graduate Studies; then it moved on to the Academic Policy Committee of the Senate of the University and then to the full Senate itself; from there it went to the University Programs Committee (composed of academics of various universities) of the Quebec government Ministry of Education and then into the Ministry itself, and then back and forth between these bodies and the university administration a few more times until it was finally approved (as a joint program of four universities).

This complexity provides a strong incentive for individuals and groups to attempt to satisfy their needs locally and informally, without embarking on the time-consuming championship and justification process necessary to obtain formal recognition. In other words, the incentive is to try to work within existing pigeonholes, even to adapt them in a clandestine manner when change is desired.

Thus, to simplify somewhat, in the case of non-routine decisions, we may roughly associate the *identification* of the decision process with individual professors and administrators, the *development* of solutions with *ad hoc* groups (task forces) interacting 'horizontally', and the *selection* of alternatives and solutions with a 'vertical' hierarchy of permanent groups (standing committees) as well as administrators and (in public universities), perhaps, government representatives as well.

It is also, perhaps, important to note that individual professors need not participate in interactive processes to any significant extent. They may leave this to their more active colleagues (at their own risk, of course: the dilemma of the academic who simply wishes to do his or her research is that he or she leaves collective choices, some concerning that research, to those who, by virtue of choosing to do administration, may be less sympathetic to research). Many professors, in fact, champion an issue hardly more than once in their career, in effect working to establish a new research center or degree program (or even a course) and then settling down to practice their own standardized skills within it. The individual professional, as we noted in the Simon passage quoted earlier, gets his or her pleasure from working within pigeonholes, not in designing them (in other words, doing operating rather than administrative work). Nevertheless, almost everyone has to serve on one standing committee or another – for the sake of maintaining professional control if none other – and all occasionally get bludgeoned into participation on a task force or two. Administrators, on the other hand, virtually always participate in collective decisions – especially those that cut across departmental lines; that indeed, is a good part of their jobs.

*Models of interactive decision-making*

How do the individuals participating in these interactive processes in fact perceive and act out their roles. Universities have traditionally been associated with a *collegiality* model, where, in the view of some writers, decisions are made by a 'community of individuals and groups, all of whom may have different roles and specialities, but who share common goals and objectives for the organization' (Taylor, 1983, p. 18). This is reflected in the system of governance that decentralizes decision-making and provides opportunities for individual academics to intervene in the process. Although different interest groups exist, differences between them are considered to be overridden by the fundamental agreement concerning the overall purpose of the institution. *Common interest* is the guiding force in this view of collegiality, and decision-making is therefore by consensus (Taylor, 1983). Obviously, in this extreme form, the model presupposes an unrealistic level of harmony and consensus. As a result, many writers (see, for example, Baldridge, 1971; Baldridge, Curtis, Ecker and Riley, 1978) have dismissed collegiality on the grounds that it is an idealistic norm rather than an accurate description of university processes.

These authors instead propose a *political* model, in which the irreconcilable differences of interest groups cannot be accommodated by consensus around common goals. Participants thus seek to serve their *self interest*, and political factors become instrumental in determining decision outcomes (Bucher 1970; Ladd, 1970; Baldridge, 1971; Baldridge *et al.*, 1978). Clearly, while this model has much to offer, it too seems overstated: common interest can no more be dismissed than can self interest.

Proponents of the political model have appeared to assume that the existence of fragmented interest groups *alone* gives rise to politics. In general, however, organization theorists have argued that a number of other conditions have to be met before political behavior can occur. In addition to the presence of conflicting goals, interest groups must be interdependent, resources scarce, and issues critical (see, for example, Pettigrew, 1973 and Pfeffer, 1981). To take an example: in times of financial constraint, the English Department requests from its dean additional resources to appoint five academics to staff a new area of modern literary criticism. One might expect other departments in the Arts Faculty to use whatever power is at their disposal to ensure that the dean does not accept the proposal. This is not simply because this proposal is different from that of Economics, which wants to expand undergraduate enrolment, or of Political Science, which wants to develop a new program in third world studies. Rather it is because the proposal, if approved, will affect the funding of the other departments, possibly preventing them from realizing their own intentions and possibly even taking resources away from existing activities. Political behavior occurs because *all* the conditions have been met – conflicting goals, interdependence, scarcity, and criticality. If the request had been made when funds were plentiful, it would probably have evoked a collegial response, with interested members of the English Department debating the benefits of including modern literary criticism in their programs, followed by a recommendation to the dean that may well have passed up the hierarchy without incurring political opposition from other departments.

Clearly, neither common interest nor self-interest will dominate decision processes all the time. Some combination is naturally to be expected. There may be commitment to certain common goals, but conflict over how they should be achieved; alternatively, consensus can sometimes exist among individuals who wish to pursue different goals – Democrats do, after all, vote with Republicans on many issues in the US Congress.

Decision-making is more likely to be political when declining resources intensify competition (Hardy, 1982, forthcoming) or when dramatic shifts in the distribution of resources threaten the power positions of particular groups (Pettigrew, 1973; Mumford and Pettigrew, 1975). Collegiality is more likely when there is a commonly accepted ideology or mission, as tends to happen in small, prestigious units, or departments with charismatic leaders, or when there is sufficient slack to accommodate disparate goals. And even when two factions fight politically at one level, other more objective observers may exist at another level who can evaluate cases on their merits. In other words, except in the most polarized situations, politics and some form of collegiality almost inevitably co-exist (Childers, 1981).

Previous writers appear to have dismissed the possibility of collegiality and politics co-existing because they have tended to assume that each produces totally different kinds of behavior.

If we believe the system is political, then we form coalitions and exert pressure on decision-makers accordingly. If we think the situation is collegial then we try to persuade people and appeal to reason.

(Baldridge *et al.*, 1978, p. 28).

This is misleading because the distinction between the two lies not so much in the behavior produced as in the motivation behind the behavior. Thus the very same behavior can be used for the common interest or for self-interest. For example, a professor may by-pass the dean and approach the president in an attempt to set up a robotics centre because he believes this will be the quickest way to set up a much needed institute that will enhance the reputation of the university and so win it research grants, or because he knows the dean will oppose the idea, thereby denying his one chance to become the leader of a prestigious research institute. Likewise, information can be hidden in the common interest (e.g. in tenure decisions to ensure objective choices: see Moynihan, 1980) or in self-interest (e.g., to avoid personal embarrassment).

In other words, judging by behavior alone, it is difficult to distinguish collegiality from politics. Moreover behavior that seems clearly to be the one can sometimes prove to be the other. Thus, successful politics often requires a collegial posture (Pfeffer, 1979). One must cloak self-interest in the mantle of the common good. By the same token, changes that will ultimately benefit the institution at large may sometimes evoke conflict between individuals who have different conceptions of the common good. Furthermore, as we have discussed, universities are bureaucratic in their standardization of skills and knowledge and in their pigeonholing; effecting changes in these requires champions who are able to counter the forces of the status quo (Mintzberg, 1979: pp. 229–230, 446–52). These champions may have to resort to the use of power to effect changes regardless of whether they are promoting the common interest or their own self-interest.

Thus, we distinguish collegiality and politics on the basis of motivation rather than behavior. The former refers to actions which are used to push through decisions that are genuinely considered beneficial for the institution, the latter refers to actions designed to defeat opponents in the pursuit of self-interest (MacMillan, 1978, p. 8). (Note that the definition of politics in terms of self-interest rather than common interest has parallels with other views that associate politics with the illegitimate use of power. See, for example, Mintzberg, 1983, ch. 13.)

A third model that has been used to explain decision-making in universities, described as 'organized anarchies', is the *garbage can*. Here decision-making is characterized by 'collections of choices looking for problems, issues and feelings looking for decision situations in which they may be aired, solutions looking for issues to which they might be an answer, and decision makers looking for work' (Cohen, March, and Olsen, 1972, p. 1; see also Cohen and March, 1974 and March and Olsen, 1976). Behavior, is, in other words, non-purposive and often random, because goals are unclear and the means to achieve them problematic. Furthermore, participation is fluid because of the 'cost' of time and energy. Decisions are not systematically resolved; instead, solutions attach themselves randomly to problems. Even proponents of the political model have pointed out that although involvement in decision-making is sometimes politically motivated, for much of the time it is an uninteresting, unrewarding .process (Baldridge *et al.*, 1978). Thus, in place of the common interest of the collegial model and the self-interest of the political model, the garbage can model offers an active kind of *uninterest*.

The important question is not whether garbage can processes exist – we have all experienced them – but whether they matter. Do they apply to key issues or only incidental ones? And, even if they appear in key issues, do they represent little more than noise in a system of forces that ultimately balance themselves out and proceed on some course determined by other factors?

Where decisions are important, participation may cease to be fluid because the cost of not participating would outweigh the cost of doing so. Some decisions are important only to individuals (their champions), and so, while their colleagues may play in the garbage can, they play seriously. They have their solution, and know exactly to which issue they wish it to apply. Other decisions are important to many people, and so all play seriously. Of course, some decisions are not that significant to anyone, but these are usually intrinsically peripheral, as when the English Department discussed above makes a request for resources to fund one additional graduate teaching assistantship. Such a decision is probably of insufficient importance to provoke a major collegial debate or political resistance but it could well end up in the garbage can. There is always someone with free time ('looking for work') willing to challenge a proposal for the sake of so doing, or perhaps to stimulate some academic debate (to 'air issues or feelings'), or simply to see if valid arguments underlie the proposal. Thus, like common interest and self-interest, uninterest neither dominates decision processes nor is absent from them. In our view, a combination of collegiality and political will most influence decision-making processes that have strategic implications for many actors, while the garbage can model may help describes decision processes that are peripheral, to some actors at least.

Finally, *analysis*, or the 'rational actor' (Allison, 1971), may be considered as a fourth model of decision-making. Here calculation is used to select the best alternative, or at least to distinguish acceptable from unacceptable proposals. Such an approach seems consistent with machine bureaucracy, where central administrators make strategic choices unilaterally, typically in the presence of considerable 'hard' data. Accordingly, conventional wisdom would suggest that we would expect to find the use of this model in universities only in the realm of administrative fiat, and that we should not look for it at the collective level of decision-making.

In fact, we wish to argue that analysis figures prominently in both collegial and political processes, as well as in garbage can ones, stimulated by the existence of ambiguous goals and multiple actors. Under ambiguity, there is more to be discovered by analysis, and there are more ways in which issues can be logically structured. And with multiple actors, there is more reason for each to attempt to structure issues in his or her own way in order to direct the thinking of others through the use of rational argument:

> We predict that almost all disputes in the organization will be defined as problems in analysis, that the initial reaction to conflict will be problem-solving and persuasion, that such reactions will persist even when they appear to be inappropriate, that *there will be a greater explicit emphasis on common goals where they do not exist than where they do*, and that bargaining (when it occurs) will frequently be concealed within an analytic framework.
>
> (March and Simon, 1958, p. 131, emphasis added)

In machine bureaucracy, analysis is likely to be the exclusive tool of top and middle management, supported by an elaborate technostructure of staff experts, and directed at control and coordination or else at strategic decisions made for the organization as a whole. It may not be greatly overstated to describe analysis here as top–down, unitary, and aimed directly at producing coordinated action. In the professional bureaucracy, in contrast, rational analysis is much more likely to be fragmented, harnessed by and subordinated to the interactive processes through which so many decisions are made. There may be relatively few staff experts, but individual professionals and groups will undertake their own analyses of issues that concern them in order to influence decisions.

Rational analysis is necessary in universities for a number of reasons. The interactive process itself forces deliberations to be structured and requires that arguments be made explicit for purposes of communication. Disagreements concerning different intuitions are likely to lead to the collection of more information when issues can be verified empirically. Moreover, the hierarchy of selection (particularly authorization) encourages the development of analytic support for proposals, especially when the champion may be denied representation at higher levels. Everything must be made as explicit and rationally persuasive as possible. Also, senior administrators, who often lack direct knowledge about what is going on in many areas of the organization – i.e. lack the ability to develop intuitive perceptions – may request more 'hard' analytic information on which to support or authorize projects.

Of course, when goals and technology are ambiguous, analytic information inevitably contains logical flaws that can be easily traced by those who are threatened by the information. Detailed responses, also expressed in rationalistic terms (i.e. counter analyses) will therefore often be generated in an attempt to redress the balance. Finally, the democratic nature of universities means that many decisions require the agreement of large numbers of people who are not particularly committed one way or the other *a priori*. These people must be convinced. Of course, the fact that university professors are frequently by nature and experience superb analysts practised in the craft of rational argumentation through their research and teaching also, no doubt, contributes to the tendency to react to issues analytically. Porter *et al*. (1979) provide an interesting case study of this phenomenon. A tenure planning model developed by a planning group reporting to central administration was vigorously 'counter-analyzed' by a threatened faculty – and then counter-counter-analyzed by the planners. Several iterations took place in full view of the Council of Deans and of top administrators before the issue was resolved by a compromise, which at least in this case was largely in favour of the planners, although it incorporated some of the faculty's concerns. The point is, however, that even when analysis is initiated by central administrations, it often becomes inextricably linked with the interactive processes of decision-making.

In the collegial situation, in which people are assumed to be working in a cooperative manner, analysis will be used mainly to develop understanding, to achieve consensus, to aid communication, and to defend the legitimate interests of the entire group. Analysis may also be used within the group to defend different perceptions of organizational interests and to integrate individual projects into these perceptions.

In the political situation, where self-interest dominates, analyses of all kinds are likely to proliferate, directed at persuading the uncommitted. Competition for resources under tight constraints also means that analyses are more likely to be counter-analysed by affected groups. One might, of course, ask what can be the overall value to the organization of analyses that are likely to contain considerable bias. It can be suggested (as Lindblom and Cohen, 1979, do, for example) that the benefit of analysis in political situations stems from the picking of holes in the argument of one side by the other: the truth is more likely to emerge and the issue most likely to be understood when opposing analyses, counter-analyses, counter-counter-analyses, etc., are available for the scrutiny of the uncommitted majority.

However, in extreme cases, politics can preclude the effectiveness of analysis too. When an issue is important enough and concerns them directly, the majority of actors may become committed early, and polarization may prevent analysis from being particularly influential unless its conclusions are so overwhelming as to be difficult to refute. In the ideal situation, concerned but uncommitted participants use opposing analyses to judge the different positions with respect to the common good and that determines the outcome (i.e. a remnant of collegiality remains despite the politics).

Analysis will even be used in a garbage can situation. It will play the role of focusing attention on issues, problems and solutions. The committee member, described earlier, who in 'looking for work' challenges proposals for the joy of academic debate, in fact encourages analysis and may thereby play the functional role of forcing out ill-conceived proposals. However, because participation is haphazard and interest low under this model, analyses may tend to go unopposed and errors and biases may remain undetected. Thus, analysis under the garbage can will tend to be of relatively low quality. But, as we noted earlier, this may tend to apply to relatively unimportant decisions.

To summarize, analysis in universities serves more as a means of exerting influence in interactions rather than of resolving issues of its own. It may be used to aid personal understanding for individuals or groups, but it also serves as a means of communication and attention focusing, as a means of legitimizing decisions, as a means of consensus-building, and perhaps most importantly as a means of persuasion. In this way, analysis helps to ensure that what does get decided in fact has some justification in principle.

To conclude, as we showed in Figure 2, we believe the collective sphere of decision-making is characterized by combined collegial and political processes, with garbage can influences encouraging a kind of haphazardness on one side due to cognitive and cost limitations (at least for some, less important decisions), and competing analytical influences on the other side encouraging a certain logic or formal rationality (serving as an invisible hand to keep the lid on the garbage can, so to speak!).

## Strategies as patterns emerging from decision processes

In the first section of this paper we described strategies as patterns in decisions and actions, while in the second section, we described how decisions (which commit the system to actions) come to be made in the university setting. In this concluding section, we draw our findings from the first two sections together in terms of a number of propositions about strategies and their formation as a result of the decision-making processes in the university setting.

We begin with general propositions about the system at large, and then we focus on the strategies generated at the three levels of decision-making – professional judgment, administrative fiat, and collective choice – before closing with general propositions and some evidence about the stability of strategies in universities.

### General propositions

1. *Many different actors are involved in the strategy formation process in universities.* As soon as we relax the conventional assumptions of strategies as deliberate and determined centrally, it becomes evident, first, that strategies, as patterns, exist in universities, and, second, that many other actors participate in their formation. If strategies are patterns, then strategists are people responsible for creating or even reinforcing patterns. And, given the decentralization and loose coupling of university structures, many different people

become involved in this process, ranging from the professor who sets a precedent (e.g. introduces a new course) to the administrator who reinforces the resulting pattern through the allocation of financial resources.

2. *Some of the university's strategies pertain to the whole, others to particular parts.* Some patterns cut across the entire organization, particularly ones that pertain to facilities, support services, or certain administrative processes (e.g., building campaigns, the provision of library services or athletic facilities, promotion and tenure regulations), while others pertain to particular parts, whether departments (e.g. program design, student selection) or individual professors (e.g. course design, research projects). Thus, it is as reasonable to describe Professor Bess's strategy of studying higher education as it is to talk about NYU's strategy of sustaining its status as a private institution. For while NYU may exhibit that central strategy in that area, in the area of research content, the strategy of NYU is the sum total of the strategies of all the professors who carry out research in that institution. Thus:

3. *We should expect to find a good deal of fragmentation in the strategies pursued by universities.* The leaders of Volkswagenwerk may decide what models they wish to produce and then develop a number of auxiliary strategies concerning sourcing, manufacturing, marketing, servicing, and so on, to support the basic product strategies. No such integration is to be expected in the university setting. Forces do exist to tie activities together (as we shall discuss later), but many of the strategies are relatively unrelated to each other – hardly even loosely coupled – so that individual ones can be changed without upsetting the system. Earlier, in Table 1, we introduced these as *disconnected* strategies. This is most clear in the case of pigeonholing, which allows the strategy of one department or even one professor to develop quite free of the strategies of all the others. As Riesman, Gusfield, and Gamson note:

> Looked at in comparative and historical perspective, American higher education is astonishingly pluralistic. No central Ministry of Culture or Education determines who is to teach what to whom at what level. Neither the Federal Trade Commission nor the regional accrediting agencies police the way in which American colleges advertise themselves (including their use of such terms as 'college' and 'university').
>
> (1975, p. 250)

But the same is true even within given universities. As Riesman alone notes in another publication, 'I think one could argue that the publicized overall reforms in Harvard College are less important for the fate of students than the subtle changes in the microclimates of departments which are themselves sometimes mini-universities with many subclimates' (in Lipset and Riesman, 1975, p. 285).

We have been tracking strategies, as patterns in streams of behaviors, at McGill University across a century and a half of its history. While many of the mission strategies have left little or no systematic traces (teaching methods, specific research projects, course content), at the aggregate levels such traces are available, and revealing. Figure 3, for example, shows the enrolment for the entire university as well as for some of its key faculties over time. (Logarithms of the data are used to emphasize rates of change rather than absolute levels, and to enable us to display the data, which ranges widely over the course of a hundred and fifty years, comprehensively.) At least two distinctly different strategies are indicated by this graph. One is open enrolment, where the faculty sets minimum standards and then accepts all applicants. This can be seen particularly in the Faculty of Arts, where wide swings are evident. The other is limited enrolment, where the faculty sets a limit on how many students it is willing to accept. This is most clear in medicine, which shows stable enrolment in the late 1860s and 1870s and particularly from the 1920s to the 1960s (except for a brief dip during the Second World War). Of course, open enrolment is more compatible with a faculty such as Arts, which itself is an agglomeration of all kinds of disciplines. In contrast, limited enrolment, which would seem to have to be far more deliberate in nature, is compatible with a faculty that focuses on one basic degree program. In this regard, it is interesting that Engineering, composed of a set of majors within a central degree program (B. Eng. in Civil, Mechanical, Electrical, etc.) shifted back and forth between the two strategies, depending largely on student demand.

4. *Control of specific strategies may reside with individual professors, within the administrative structure, or in the collectivity.* In other words, decison-making at each of the levels we have discussed can lead to important patterns of action, namely strategies. While the senior administrators may decide on salary issues, and thereby create patterns, and the individual member of faculty may establish a pattern of researching institutions of higher learning, the collectivity may set a pattern in the making of promotion and tenure decisions. Of course, some areas can fall under the control of more than one level. In the case of funding, for example, central administrators seek support from private donors, as might the members of particular departments, while individual professors seek the financial support of granting agencies. Below, we discuss the patterns that appear out of decision-making in each of three levels.

### Propositions about professional judgment

5. *The mission strategies of the university are largely aggregates of the personal strategies pursued by individual professors, based on professional judgment.* As noted, each professor makes many of his or her own decisions concerning product and market: decisions about course content, teaching method, research topic, and research methodology. These decisions in turn create patterns (courses are repeated year after year, research projects carry on, etc.), leading to what can be called the *personal* strategies of individual professors (see Table 1). From the individual's point of view, such strategies are often

**Figure 3**    Enrolment at McGill University

likely to be deliberate (i.e. the patterns were intended), although from the organization's perspective, they might very well be emergent (i.e. the system at large, whether that means its central administrators or the collectivity, did not necessarily intend that they teach and research in those ways). It is, of course, the pigeonholing process that allows these personal product/market strategies to develop. But these strategies are not chosen at random:

6. *Many of the personal strategies are influenced by, indeed often imported through, professional training and affiliation.* Sometimes professional bodies dictate specific orientations, as when the American Association of Collegiate Schools of Business introduced new criteria for accrediting business schools several years ago that had the effect of introducing new theoretical and quantitative material to specific courses. In the terms introduced earlier, this can be called an *imposed* strategy. More often, the influence is less direct. The fact that a certain Roger Bennett teaches marketing in McGill University's MBA program by the case method is hardly independent of the fact that he was so trained in Harvard's MBA and DBA programs. And as professional norms change, so too do the strategies: if Bennett's notion that the 'marketing concept' has outlived its usefulness catches hold among his marketing colleagues (a process Bennett encourages through his publications in professional journals and his speeches at professional meetings), then the nature of marketing courses all over North America will change. We can say that a new *consensus* strategy will emerge, but across rather than within universities (i.e. in marketing departments in different universities, but not beyond marketing even to accounting). Thus Riesman has 'described American higher education as a snakelike procession in which the bulk of institutions followed what they took to be the models set by the most prestigious leaders' (Riesman, Gusfield, and Gamson, 1975, p. 254). The result of all this is that:

7. *To a great extent, many important strategies associated with mission cut across universities.* Because of the standardization of skills and the sharing of norms, it becomes more accurate to talk of a strategy for teaching marketing than a strategy for teaching at McGill. That is, there is probably far greater consistency among marketing professors all over the world than there is among Bennett's neighbors in the Faculty of Management at McGill University (let alone his colleagues in physics, philosophy, and pathology elsewhere at McGill). This is the result of the fact that the range of professional influences is far greater than the more focused institutional influences, at least in the sphere of the provision of the basic mission.

### Propositions about administrative fiat

8. *In the realm of administrative fiat, central administrators may impose deliberate strategies on the entire organization.* Where the administrators have definitive control – portfolio investment, property management, some of the support services – patterns of strategies are not only likely to exist, but to be rather deliberate in nature. In the terminology of Table 1, they may be formally planned (i.e. articulated) or they may derive from the personal vision of a leader, which we labeled *entrepreneurial*. The latter appears to show up especially in the formative years of a university, or at least when its ideological foundations were established by a strong leader (Clark, 1970, 1972). Thus, in the 1890s, McGill's most influential principal took advantage of the

retirement of the bursar to restructure the university's administrative offices and bring in professionally trained officials for the first time.

9. *In addition, central administrators seek to exert influence in other spheres through the use of umbrella and process strategies.* In the terms of Table 1, where central administrators cannot act deliberately – predetermining patterns in streams of action – they seek to have deliberate influence on emergent patterns. In other words, they try to affect the broad directions such patterns may take.

The *umbrella* strategy reflects an attempt to define broad guidelines within which emergent strategies should fall. For example while administrators may not be able to dictate course content or teaching methods, they might at least be able to control parameters that constrain these choices. Constructing only large classrooms encourages formal lecturing, while small classrooms encourage closer rapport between students and faculty. Similarly, administrators can use their powers of persuasion within the interactive process to encourage or discourage the projects championed by others or, at the limit, they can evoke their powers of veto to block certain projects.

*Process* strategies relate to control of how things get done rather than what gets done. Course content may not be controllable, but control over hiring (at least to the extent of veto) can be tantamount to considerable influence over course content. Indeed, given the influence of the individual professor in the system, staffing must be considered a form of strategy making in the university, perhaps its single most important component. The hiring of a single professor amounts to the introduction of a product-market strategy! Likewise, the ability to design the committee structure, and especially to staff the committees, can have a profound influence on the outcome of committee deliberation. The administrator intent on reform in a certain academic sphere may not be able to dictate to a committee, but his power to staff that committee with reformers may be all he needs.

It is interesting that in Hodgkinson's study of the perceptions of the most significant changes in universities, the presidents reported 'changes of internal authority and the governance structure of the institution' (1977, p. 219) most often by far. (Imagine the presidents of manufacturing firms reporting such changes in preference to ones in products and markets!) The fact is that people focus on what they can change, and in the case of university administrators that centers more on administrative process than on academic content. In the same spirit, a number of the recommendations Cohen and March make to university presidents, such as 'spend time' (on decision-making activities), 'facilitate opposition participation,' 'provide garbage cans' (to deflect attention from more important issues) (1974, pp. 206, 209, 211), encourage them to manage the process.

10. *Crises enhance the power of central administrators over the formation of strategies.* Strategies, as patterns, often emerge from precedent-setting decisions, and these often occur during times of crisis, when radical actions must be taken quickly. A hasty decision to call the city police onto campus to quell

a revolt may encourage the bringing in of the police for minor disturbances later on. Moreover, decisions that would be blocked for years in the interactive process can sometimes be made quickly by administrative fiat in times of crisis. For example, a weak department may hang on for years, developing supporters in return for cooperation on various university committees. But come a severe budget squeeze, all those marginal supporters may be just as happy to see the department eliminated by administrative initiative. In other words, decisions in the realm of collective choice may move into that of administrative fiat in times of crisis, during which shrewd administrators, by establishing important precedents or breaking established patterns, can alter strategies long after the crisis has passed. Clark (1970, 1972) in fact describes how the entire ideology of a college can be established by a strong leader during a major crisis, even though he may not even remain to see it fully implemented.

Deep crisis in the established organization thus creates some of the conditions of a new organization. It suspends past practice, forces some bordering groups to stand back or even turn their backs on failure of the organization, and it tends to catch the attention of the reformer looking for an opportunity . . . Crisis and charisma made possible a radical transformation out of which came a second Antioch, a college soon characterized by a sense of exciting history, unique practice, and exceptional performance.

(1972, p. 180)

11. *Some strategies resulting from administrative activity are in fact imposed by external influencers.* Much as personal strategies may be imposed by professional bodies, so too administrative strategies may be imposed by influential outsiders, such as donors or governmental officials. When endowment income constituted the major part of McGill University's budget, donors had considerable influence. For example, a donation made in 1886 provided the necessary funds to establish McGill's first program for women's instruction. The donor insisted, however, that the women's classes be held separately from those of the men. The principal was prepared to accept this ultimatum and later stated that he probably would have done so even if he had been a committed co-educationist (Frost, 1980). However, given the decentralization of power over many key strategy areas, external influencers have often been reduced to controlling peripheral strategies (what kind of football team the old alma mater will have) or have been limited to what Cyert and March (1963) call 'side payments' (a seat on a weak board, a name on a new building). More recently, the government has provided the lion's share of the operating budget, as can be seen from Figure 4, and it has displaced the donors as the major influence. One example of this has been the government's refusal to allow tuition fees to be increased in recent years, thus further increasing the dependence of the university on the government.

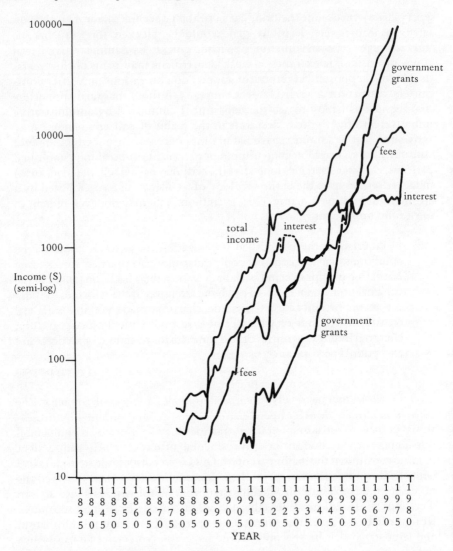

**Figure 4**   Income at McGill University

*Propositions about collective choice*

12. *At one extreme, interactive processes can encourage some loose cohesion in fragmentated activities, leading to negotiated departmental or university-wide strategies.* When interactive processes are no more than political in nature, we might expect the greatest fragmentation of activities, as each actor seeks to

satisfy his own self-interest. But that does not preclude the appearance of consistencies in the actions of the organization over time, which we refer to as *negotiated* strategies (see Table 1). At the very least, the negotiated outcomes of interactive decisions – for example, about hiring and promotion, tenure regulations, program development, or enrolment – can lead to a kind of 'style' of a given department or of the entire university. Essentially, collective choice means that people from a variety of departments or pigeonholes are committed to the outcome, which can produce patterns across these divisions. Moreover, collective choice influences individual professional judgment; for example, who gets hired determines what research gets done.

13. *At the other extreme, interactive processes can produce strong consistent themes, leading to pervasive ideological strategies.* As Clark (1970, 1972) describes the 'distinctive colleges,' academic institutions sometimes develop powerful and pervasive systems of beliefs which produce strong consistency across all kinds of decisions; we characterized such consistency in Table 1 as an *ideological* strategy.

Clark traces the origins of such ideologies to strong leaders in the organization's past, whether at the time of formation, during a later crisis, or just when the time happened to be right for change. By the same token, of course, such leadership can emerge in a department, so that the ideology remains at that level. For years, the Psychology Department at McGill University exhibited a strong physiological orientation in its teaching and research. This could be traced to Donald Hebb, its most distinguished member, who developed his reputation in that sphere and in turn exercised an informal leadership in the interactive processes of the department. Eventually consistency became ideology.

Note that while the origin of the ideology may be individual – a central administrator or even a single academic who, for example, creates a new pigeonhole – its institutionalization can only occur in the collective process, as a variety of individuals interact to reinforce the new beliefs (which Clark refers to as the 'fulfilment' stage, noting that it often happens after the leader has left). Once these beliefs emerge as traditions, the ideology is set; thereafter, it is reinforced through various forms of identification, as individuals preselect themselves to join the group, or are selected to do so, based on their natural identification with it, or else develop such identification after joining through processes of socialization and/or indoctrination (see Mintzberg, 1983, ch. 11).

Thus personnel decisions are critical in the development and perpetuation of ideological strategies, especially in universities where the individual professor has so much autonomy. A powerful academic orientation can dominate a department or university only if those invited to join and remain with the group conform to its beliefs. Thus the McGill Psychology Department could sustain its physiological orientation only so long as it recruited people with that outlook, or at least encouraged people to adopt that outlook once hired. Likewise, a college intent on sustaining a strong Baptist tradition cannot tolerate 'radicals' intent on promoting other religious beliefs. Thus, collegiality reigns supreme in the case of ideological strategy: the emphasis is on unity and the common interest.

14. *Between these two extremes, interactive processes create consistencies through formal procedure and implicit habit, leading to (more or less) planned and consensus strategies.* Sometimes the interactive processes produce consistency in a formal way, as when a senate enacts new tenure regulations to apply to the whole university. These can, for example, be designed to tilt tenure decisions in favor of research, so that, assuming successful implementation, the university may be described as pursuing a deliberate, more or less *planned*, strategy. Assuming broad concurrence, the strategy may also be described as one of explicit consensus.

But *consensus* strategies of an implicit and more emergent nature (as described in Table 1) can also appear out of the interactive process. They develop through precedent and habit, as well as informal mutual adjustment among the different actors in the system. People abide by them, not necessarily out of ideological commitment *per se*, but more from a sense of how 'things are done' in the institution. Thus, formal changes in the tenure regulations enacted by the McGill Senate several years ago have not affected the implicit norms that favor the granting of tenure in a large proportion of cases. This stands in sharp contrast to many equivalent American universities that usually deny it, sometimes even having a quota on tenured slots. McGill perhaps pays more attention to who is hired in the first place (or at least certain departments do, again reflecting the fragmentation of strategies), and then is able to achieve a more collegial, less threatening atmosphere by diminishing the importance of the tenure decision.

To sum up, we have suggested in the last three propositions that the interactive process may produce a range of strategies, from weak negotiated ones to strong ideological ones, with ones of a planned or consensus nature in between.

## Concluding propositions

15. *University strategies tend to exhibit a remarkable degree of stability, discouraging any form of strategic 'revolution'.* Were garbage can processes predominant in university decision-making, one would not expect stability and patterning, but the reverse: unpredictable, random swings in behavior. Our belief, however, is that this randomness is restricted to relatively minor issues, and tends to balance itself out, so that it appears more in the form of random variations around more stable patterns. Thus, two factions in the medical faculty might fight idiosyncratically about whether or not to admit eight more students, while the overall pattern remains rather stable. It may go up or down by a few students as one side occasionally scores points and then the other. But the pattern will not change unless something fundamental does – like the occurrence of a war or of new restrictions imposed by the local college

of physicians and surgeons. In other words, we suspect that garbage can processes create 'noise' in the system, and show up as the short-term variations around long term trend lines.

There are many good reasons not only why patterns should appear in universities, but why they should exhibit considerable stability – why strategic 'revolutions', when many key strategies change suddenly, should be rare in universities.

Perhaps the most fundamental reason is that responsibility for strategy is divided among so many people: many autonomous individuals are unlikely to change their collective mind, at least not simultaneously, radically, and consistently.

At the individual level, professors who have invested time and effort to learn their standardized skills are unlikely to change them frequently or radically. Hence the mission of the university, represented by the aggregation of the personal strategies based on these skills, is likely to be highly stable. Even the change that does take place is likely to be localized to specific pigeonholes, so that the aggregate mission strategies are hardly affected at any one time. Moreover, the rooting of these personal strategies in professional affiliations makes them even more immutable. Many of these strategies are, after all, established by consensus among professionals flung far and wide, and are upheld by the most respected members of the profession. Forces for change from within an academic istitution can, therefore, be countered by the forces of the status quo elsewhere:

> Less commonly commented upon is the increasing degree to which departmental power is abetted by professional accrediting agencies – external to, and largely independent of, the university. In most of the cases, colleges, schools, or other subunits, all with interests to defend, were also involved. All these individuals and groups have overlapping and conflicting interests and jurisdictions which are bound to be affected by changes in educational policies, and consequently the forces toward maintaining the status quo are enormous.   (Ladd, 1970, p. 206)

Collective decision processes also encourage stability of strategies. We have already noted how staffing decisions can perpetuate established ideologies. In addition, the sheer weight of the interactive processes (especially in the selection phase) is likely to discourage all but the most dedicated and determined champions of change. Moreover, power tends to become institutionalized over time: it is a self-perpetuating phenomenon – those who have it use it to get more (Gaventa, 1980; Lukes, 1974; Pfeffer, 1981; Salaman, 1979). Another factor is that new members are often selected to fit in with the existing culture of the organization or of a department, and socialization reinforces that tendency.

The strategies that develop through administrative fiat may be more flexible than those emerging from collective choice. This is partly because they tend to be more deliberate and impersonal and are thus more easily confronted than the more emergent strategies of the collectivity. Moreover, these strategies fall under the control of relatively few people. Thus a new university president can change the strategies of his or her predecessor far more easily than those that have emerged from collective processes. A strategic revolution may, therefore, be conceivable only in the limited spheres of administrative fiat, or only when a severe crisis concentrates more pervasive decision-making power in the hands of a few people for a period of time.

What, in our view, typically characterizes university strategy formation, then, is not revolution, nor the randomness of garbage can processes, but a fundamental stability. To take the case of McGill University, aside from a small Veterinary Science program that was terminated in 1908 and a Common Law program terminated in 1926 (to be reinstated in 1968), no basic degree offering has ever been eliminated. (Even majors within such programs have rarely been dropped.) This absence of change in basic product offerings may not seem terribly surprising to anyone familiar with universities, but when put into a broader perspective, it does have an important message.

IBM has lived through several generations of computers; in the mid-1960s it voluntarily obsoleted its major project lines by developing the new 360 System (Pounds and Wise, 1966). Volkswagenwerk underwent virtual revolution to shift from its basic Beetle model to its newer line of Rabbits, etc. McGill University, probably like many of its sister institutions in Canada, the United States, and Europe, has undergone no such revolution in over a century. It has certainly added programs and elaborated a number of the ones it had, especially in the 1960s and 1970s. But it has faced no major upheaval in its basic orientation, no 'quantum' change in its strategies (Miller and Friesen, 1980). Even the student confrontations of the late 1960s, which it too experienced, produced hardly a ripple in the long-established patterns.

Indeed, a glance back at the curve of total student enrolment in Figure 3 suggests just how stable those patterns can be. Given the different shapes of enrolment curves in the individual faculties, and the plethora of decisions that make up each of these curves, the remarkable thing about the total enrolment curve is its rather linear growth over the very long term, from a level of about 200 students in 1860 to just over 20,000 in 1980. A straight diagonal line on semi-log paper suggests a constant rate of growth; the straight line that could easily be drawn through 120 years of this total enrolment curve indicates a mean annual growth rate of 3.75 per cent. Variations do occur around this mean; what is remarkable is that the university always returned to the trend line. Accelerated growth followed by return to the trend line can be seen especially in the 1870s, again in the 1880s and 1890s, and finally in the 1960s and 1970s. This long-term trend was maintained despite two major shocks to the system, around both world wars, with similar patterns, as the university lost enrolment to military enlistment, then made a special effort to accommodate the returning veterans, and thereafter fell right back to the long-term trend line. The depression of the 1930s, that followed the first of these shocks, imposed a new and slower rate of growth, itself very steady to near the end of the Second World War, as if the lost growth of the depression substituted for the decline expected when war broke out. Finally, there are many brief variations in the curve – almost like vibrations around the longer-term trends. Perhaps it is these that reflect garbage can processes: as noted earlier, professors arguing with each other irregularly about whether to accept a few more students in Medicine, or to lower the standards in Arts by a percentage point or two, while the whole system followed its stable long-term course.

This remarkable stability over the long term might be explained by environmental trends that themselves remained stable – the amount society has been willing to spend on higher education, the growth in population and student demand, etc. Another explanation may be that the university as a system has followed its own internal growth imperatives. Too little growth, as we noted earlier, could generate conflict, putting different groups into competition with each other. But too much growth may have been more than the system could handle, creating a certain chaos which led to its own kind of conflict. Hence, there may have been an incentive to follow the line of least resistance – to grow slowly and steadily, in this case preferably in the 3–4 per cent range. This might be called the 'range of ostensible collegiality,' where the system was best able to maintain what at least appeared to be collegial relationships (in behavior if not intention), and minimize overt conflict. By this argument, every time the system was forced by the environment to speed up, it eventually had to slow down to absorb the expansion; every time it was impeded from growing as it wished, it sought eventually to speed up to recoup its losses. There may be a grain of truth in both environmental and internal imperative explanations; the subject would seem to merit further investigation in any event.

16. *Changes in university strategies do occur, constantly and gradually, in lagged response to environmental forces, driven by professional judgment, administrative fiat, as well as the collective processes of politics, collegiality, and analysis.* While strategic revolution may be rare in universities, we believe gradual, incremental change is endemic. At the broadest level, of mission offerings and ideologies, change may be difficult. But at the narrowest – inside tiny pigeonholes – the 'snakelike' development (described in proposition 7) occurs continuously. Research topics change, new course texts are adopted, course content is updated. Universities change much as the Volkswagen Beetle did for years and years – a larger window here, a new tailpipe there, and so on. Thus, while the Faculty of Medicine at McGill awards in 1983 the same MD degree it did in 1840, the content of that degree has changed completely through countless individual professional decisions, consolidated by occasional collective efforts at program redesign. But the complexity of the collective process encourages change to take place at the individual level, in fact, sometimes in a clandestine manner. Thus, we would expect the university to experience many imperceptible mini-revolutions in place of any

overt pervasive ones. In this respect, some of the collective change that does appear may simply be the formal acknowledgment and consolidation of many small individual changes – after the fact. The emergent patterns are thus made deliberate.

Bolder change does, of course, take place on other levels. In the realm of administrative fiat, as noted earlier, change is easier to achieve since the decision-making process is so much simpler and more centralized. Thus 'revolutions' in support services (say, student residences or the printing service), or in budgeting techniques or fringe benefits, are to be expected occasionally, and these may occur in more academic areas when centralization arises in times of crisis (as when weak departments or programs are terminated).

Despite the difficulties, however, collective processes can also promote strategic change. As power shifts, based on environmental forces – for example, as the sciences gained influence, in the form of greater access to research funding and increased student enrolment, at the expense of the humanities after Sputnik – so too do decisions change, leading to new patterns of behavior. This process is speeded up by individuals who expend energy from political or collegial perspectives to champion new interests. The necessity for them to couch their ideas in analytical terms, and the critical appraisal to which their analyses will be subjected by their opponents, works to produce the rejection of irregular and unjustifiable projects, which in turn enhances stability. But the same forces can also create greater receptivity to those ideas which have a sound underlying rationale.

In all these ways, adaptation to environmental forces can occur gradually and without revolution, although in lagged response to environmental events and trends.

In summary, universities are paradoxically extremely stable at the broadest level and in a state of perpetual change at the narrowest. One may in fact explain the other. Revolutions are perhaps only necessary in organizations that cannot adapt sufficiently at the narrowest level. While Volkswagenwerk could change its Beetle continously, it could not fade that model into the Rabbit in the way McGill was able to fade the 1840 MD into the 1983 version. Hence Volkswagenwerk underwent system-wide revolution while McGill did not.

To conclude:

17. *Strategies abound in universities.* If strategies are patterns in activity over time, then much of the literature on the functioning of universities argues against the occurrence of strategies. Planning is discouraged, decision-making is fragmented, politics encourages conflict, garbage can processes promote idosyncrasy.

But our findings are quite to the contrary. Standardization of knowledge and skills together with pigeonholing certainly encourage order and patterning, as does professional affiliation; and analysis encourages stable responses to external needs, while collegiality promotes consistent behavior within the system; even politics works to stop some change and slow the pace of the rest. As for the garbage can model, it may in large part represent the unexplained variance in the system – that is, whatever is not understood might look like organized anarchy. If true, then the more we come to understand strategy formation in the university setting, the less explanatory the garbage can model should become. Our discussion suggests, in fact, that university behavior is epitomized by order and patterning of all sorts – in actions as well as in processes. As soon as strategies are defined from the perspective of realization instead of intention, universities can be seen to have strategies, indeed, when all of the different patterns are considered, to be inundated with strategies!

To close this discussion, we do not wish to leave the reader with the impression that we are totally complacent about strategy formation in the university setting, that is, that we believe universities 'have it all right.' We too have had our frustrations with the processes described, whether they be fighting to push a PhD program through the collective process, struggling to gain acceptance for unorthodox research, or merely trying to avoid being prematurely pigeonholed! But of one thing we are certain: the problem is not that universities do not have strategies, but that they do – and with a vengeance.

## Note

1. This aspect of retrenchment in universities is currently being studied at McGill by one of the authors. See, for example, Hardy (1983).

## References

Allison, G. T., *Essence of decision*, Boston: Little, Brown & Co., 1971.
Baldridge, J. V., *Power and conflict in the university*, London: Wiley, 1971.
Baldridge, J. V., Curtis, D. V., Ecker G. and Riley, G. L., *Policy making and effective leadership*, San Francisco: Jossey-Bass, 1978.
Billings, R. S., Milburn, T. W., and Schaalman, M. L., A model of crisis perception: A theoretical and empirical analysis, *Administrative Science Quarterly*, 1980, 25, 300–16.
Bucher, R., Social process and power in a medical school, In M. Zald (ed.) *Power in organizations*, Nashville: Vanderbilt University Press, 1970.
Childers, M. E., What is political about bureaucratic-collegial decision making, *Review of Higher Education*, 1981, 5, 25–45.
Clark, B. R., *The distinctive college: Antioch, Reed and Swarthmore*, Chicago: Aldine, 1970.
——. The organizational saga in higher education, *Administrative Science Quarterly*, 1972, 17, 178–184.
Cohen, S., *Modern capitalist planning: The French model*, Berkeley and Los Angeles, California: University of California Press 1977.

Cohen, M. D. and March, J. G., *Leadership and ambiguity: The American college president*, New York: McGraw-Hill, 1974.

Cohen, M. D., March J. G. and Olsen, J. P., A garbage can model of organizational choice. *Administrative Science Quarterly*, 1972, *17*, 1–25.

Cyert, R. M. and March, J. G., *A behavioral theory of the firm*, Englewood Cliffs, NJ: Prentice Hall, 1963.

Doyle, P. and Lynch, J. E., A strategic model for university planning. *Journal of Operational Research*, 1979, *30*, 603–9.

Dube, C. S. and Brown, A. W., Strategic assessment: A rational response to university cutbacks. *Long Range Planning*, 1983, *16,* 105–13.

Frost, S. B., *McGill University for the advancement of learning*, Montreal: McGill-Queen's University Press, 1980.

Gaventa, J., *Power and powerlessness*, London: Oxford University Press, 1980.

Gross, E., Universities as organizations: A research approach, *American Sociological Review*, 1968, *33*, 518–44.

Hardy, C., *Organizational closure: A political perspective*, PhD, Warwick University, 1982.

——. *Managing university cutbacks: Issues and problems*, Paper for the Annual Conference of the Inter-American Organization for Higher Education, 1983.

——. The contribution of political science to organizational behavior, In J. Lorsch (ed.) *Handbook of organizational behavior*, Englewood Cliffs, NJ: Prentice Hall (forthcoming).

Hermann, R., Some consequences of crisis which limit the viability of organizations, *Administrative Science Quarterly*, 1963, *8*, 61–82.

Hodgkinson, H. L., *Institutions in transition: A profile of change in higher education*, New York: McGraw-Hill, 1977.

Hosmer, L. T., *Academic strategy*, Ann Arbor, Michigan: University of Michigan, 1978.

Kuhn, T. S., *The structure of scientific revolutions*, Chicago: University of Chicago, 1970.

Ladd, R., *Change in educational policy*, New York: McGrawl-Hill, 1970.

Lindblom, C. E., and Cohen, D. K.: *Usable Knowledge*, New Haven, Conn.: Yale University Press, 1979.

Lipset, S. M., and Riesman, D., *Education and Politics at Harvard*, New York: McGraw-Hill, 1975.

Lukes, S., *Power: A radical view*, London: Macmillan, 1974.

Lutz, F. W., Tightening up loose coupling in organizations of higher education, *Administrative Science Quarterly*, 1982, *27*, 653–69.

MacMillan, I. C., *Strategy formulation: Political concepts*, New York: West, 1978.

March, G. and Olsen, P., *Ambiguity and choice in organizations*, Bergen, Norway: Universitetsforlaget, 1976.

March, G. and Simon, A., *Organizations*, New York: Wiley, 1958.

Miller, D. and Friesen, P., Archetypes of organizational transition, *Administrative Science Quarterly*, 1980, 268–99.

Mintzberg, H., *Research on strategy-making*, Proceedings of the Academy of Management Conference, 1972.

——. Patterns in strategy formation, *Management Science*, 1978, *24*, 934–48.

——. *The structuring of organizations*, Englewood Cliffs, NJ: Prentice Hall, 1979.

——. *Power in and around organizations*, Englewood Cliffs, NJ: Prentice Hall, 1983.

Mintzberg, H., Raisinghani, D. and Théorêt, A., The structure of 'unstructured' decision processes, *Administrative Science Quarterly*, 1976, *21*, 246, 275.
Mintzberg, H. and Waters, J. A., *Of strategies, deliberate and emergent*, McGill Working Paper, 1983.
Moynihan, D. P., State as academic: Nationalizing the universities, *Harpers*, December, 1980, *261*, 31–40.
Mumford, E. and Pettigrew, A. M., *Implementing Strategic Decisions*, London: Longman, 1975.
Pettigrew, A. M., *The politics of organizational decision-making*, London: Tavistock, 1973.
Pfeffer, J., Power and resource allocation in organizations, in R. H. Miles and W. A. Randolph (eds) *The organization game*, Santa Monica, Calif.: Goodyear, 1979.
———. *Power in organizations*, Marshfield, Mass: Pitman, 1981.
Porter, R. Zemsky, R. and Oedel, P., Adaptive planning: The role of institution specific models, *Journals of Higher Education*, 1979, *50*, 586–601.
Pounds, N. J. G. and Wise, T. A., IBM's $5 billion gamble, *Fortune Magazine*, 1966, *74*, 118–23.
Richardson, R. C. and Gardner, D. E., Avoiding extremes on the planning continuum, *Journal of Higher Education*, 1983, *54*, 181–92.
Riesman, D., Gusfield, J. and Gamson, Z., *Academic values and mass education: The early years of Oakland & Montieth*, New York: McGraw-Hill, 1975.
Salaman, G., *Work organizations: Resistance and control*, London: Longman, 1979.
Simon, H. A., *The new science of management decision*, Englewood Cliffs, NJ: Prentice Hall, 1977.
Smart, C. and Vertinsky, I. Designs for crisis decision units, *Administrative Science Quarterly*, 1977, *22*, 640–57.
Smelser, N. J., Berkeley in crisis and change, in D. Riesman and V. A. Stadtman (eds) *Academic transformation*, New York: McGraw-Hill, 1973.
Taylor, W. H., The Nature of policy making in universities, *The Canadian Journal of Higher Education*, 1983, *13*, 17–32.
Weick, K. E., Educational organizations as loosely coupled systems, *Administrative Science Quarterly*, 1976, *21*, 1–19.

# Index